STUDIES IN DIPLOMACY
AND STATECRAFT

STUDIES IN DIPLOMACY
AND STATECRAFT

By

G. P. GOOCH, D.Litt., F.B.A.

Author of *History of Modern Europe,* 1878–1919, etc.

LONGMANS, GREEN AND CO.
LONDON · NEW YORK · TORONTO

LONGMANS, GREEN AND CO. LTD.
OF PATERNOSTER ROW
43 ALBERT DRIVE, LONDON, S.W.19
17 CHITTARANJAN AVENUE, CALCUTTA
NICOL ROAD, BOMBAY
36A MOUNT ROAD, MADRAS

LONGMANS, GREEN AND CO.
55 FIFTH AVENUE, NEW YORK

LONGMANS, GREEN AND CO.
215 VICTORIA STREET, TORONTO

First published 1942

Reprinted by Photolithographic process, 1942

CODE NUMBER 17710

Printed in Great Britain by
BISHOP & SONS, LTD., Photo-Litho Printers, EDINBURGH.

PREFACE

How rulers and statesmen have used or ought to use their powers, particularly in the sphere of foreign affairs, is the central theme of the studies collected in this volume. With one exception they have been previously published, though not all in their present form. My thanks are due to the editors, publishers and societies who have generously given permission to reprint.

Franco-German Relations, 1870–1914, is a revised and enlarged version of the Creighton Lecture delivered in 1923. Published in the same year and reprinted in 1928, it has been out of print since Paternoster Row went up in flames in December 1940. *The Diplomatic Background of the First World War*, an attempt to summarise the voluminous evidence of recent years on the development of the European situation after 1871, is new, as are the conversations with two German ex-Foreign Ministers, Kühlmann and Jagow, which are appended to it. *British Policy before the War in the Light of the Archives*, an address delivered at Chatham House in October 1938 and published in *International Affairs*, January 1939, was occasioned by the completion of *British Documents on the Origins of the War*, edited by Gooch and Temperley. The appended conversation with Lord Grey took place early in 1929, when the writer was preparing two lectures on his foreign policy for the Hochschule für Politik at Berlin. Portions of *Prince Bülow and his Memoirs* appeared in the *Contemporary Review*, December 1930, and February 1931, and in *History*, July, 1933. *Kiderlen-Wächter, The Man of Agadir*, is expanded from an article in *The Cambridge Historical Journal*, 1936. *British and Foreign Policy*, 1919–1939, is an expansion and continuation of a brochure published by G. Bell and Sons for the Historical Association in 1936 : it appeared in its present form in the *Contemporary Review*, October 1940–May 1941. *Political Autobiography* grew out of an address delivered to the Royal Society of Literature in 1936 and published in its Transactions, Vol. XV. It began to appear in its enlarged form in the *Contemporary Review*, November 1941. *The French Revolution as a World Force* was delivered at the fourth of the Unity History Schools, held at Birmingham in 1920. It was published by the Oxford University Press in the volume of addresses on that occasion entitled *The Evolution of World*

v

vi

PREFACE

Peace, edited by Dr. F. S. Marvin, of which a cheap edition appeared in 1933. *Politics and Morals*, the Merttens Lecture for 1935, a discussion of the problem of *raison d'état* raised by the teaching of Machiavelli and his disciples, was published by the Hogarth Press in the *Day to Day Pamphlets*. The Europe of 1935 has been swept away, but readers can bring the survey up to date for themselves. *Hobbes and the Absolute State*, delivered in 1940 as the annual lecture on a *Master Mind* at the rooms of the British Academy, was published as a brochure by the Oxford University Press and included in Vol. XXV of its Proceedings. Its relevance to an Age of Dictatorships does not need to be pointed out.

G.P.G.

CONTENTS

FRANCO-GERMAN RELATIONS 1871–1914

I

THE war of 1870, though contrived by Bismarck, was begun by Napoleon III, and defeated France had to pay his debts. The military hegemony of Europe passed from Paris to Berlin, but in the moment of victory the Iron Chancellor committed the greatest mistake of his life. After vetoing the annexation of Austrian territory in 1866 and thereby rendering possible a speedy reconciliation, he allowed the soldiers to have their way in 1871. " After this war," he declared on the morrow of Sedan, " we must expect another aggression, not a durable peace, whatever conditions we impose. France will consider any peace a truce, and will try to avenge her defeat directly she feels strong enough, alone or with allies." Outside France the annexation of Alsace and a portion of Lorraine was generally regarded as the natural punishment of the Power which had declared war and had been beaten. Where is the nation which, with bitter memories like those of the invasions of Louis XIV and Napoleon, would have returned empty-handed from a sanguinary struggle, and would have left in the possession of its defeated enemy rich territories which had formed part of its own vanished empire ? If France had won, she would doubtless have annexed part of the Rhineland. It is a crime to transfer masses of human beings from one allegiance to another against their will, but amputation is the common practice of conquerors. The peacemakers of 1919 had no title to cast stones at the peace-makers of 1871 : both alike built for the day, not for the morrow.

Bismarck was dimly aware of the unwisdom of the settlement which he was called upon to sanction. " I did not want too many Frenchmen in my house," he exclaimed. " Personally I was opposed to the annexation of Lorraine," he confessed to a French diplomatist, " but the military influences were too strong." His plan, which received the weighty approval of the Grand Duke of Baden, was to content himself with Alsace, to dismantle Metz, and to exact a larger indemnity; and it was a calamity for France, for Germany and for the world that it was not adopted. Perhaps he could not have got his way, for the Generals even resented leaving Belfort to France. But he never fought for his policy, and he deserves graver condemnation for the neglect of the *imponderabilia* than the soldiers whose horizon was bounded by strategical considerations. It is possible that Alsace, German in blood and language, might gradually have been reconciled by admission to the federal empire on equal terms with Baden and other South German states. Lorraine, on the other hand, was bound to prove as indigestible as Posen, and Germany, efficient, but heavy-handed and unimaginative, never learned how to win the allegiance of racial minorities.

France never accepted the situation.[1] The thirty-six deputies of the lost provinces in the Bordeaux National Assembly unanimously protested against the cession, and 50,000 inhabitants left their homes within the year allowed for option. A far larger number followed later, particularly from Lorraine, until nearly a third had gone. The story of Franco-German relations since 1871 is mainly the record of France's endeavour to regain her lost territories and of Germany's attempt to retain them. The one remembered the aggression of 1870, the other the settlement of 1871, and the writers of school-books in both countries took good care that the children should inherit the passions of their elders. The statue of Strassburg in the Place de la Concorde was draped in black. There was no finality about the settlement, for the provinces which had been won by the sword might be lost in the next encounter. Family and business ties were severed, French propaganda was active, and the excellence of German administration evoked no gratitude. There were pauses between the rounds, but the wrestlers never left the arena. Each of them sought and found allies, until almost the whole of Europe was involved in their vendetta.

While Bismarck kept France in quarantine by alliances or understandings with other Powers, the French rebuilt the fabric of their national life with unexpected rapidity. In no responsible quarter was there a notion of challenging Germany to another conflict for a long time to come. " The *revanche*," writes René Pinon, " was the natural and spontaneous reaction, the appeal to the future, arising from the abuse of force. It lived as a sacred ideal in the soul of the nation, but has never been part of the Government programme." France had to

[1] See Linnebach, *Deutschland als Sieger im besetzten Frankreich*, 1871-3, and Herzfeld, *Deutschland u. das geschlagene Frankreich*, 1871-3.

pay the indemnity, terminate the occupation, frame a constitution, restore her finances, reform her army and find an ally before she could make fresh plans ; but the tradition of *les frontières naturelles*, inherited from the Monarchy, the Revolution and Napoleon, lived on. " Our policy is peace," declared Thiers ; " a reorganized France will always be necessary to Europe." The gospel of work was to restore her strength, her prosperity and her self-respect. One of the chief lessons of history is the resilience of nations. The transition from war to peace was eased by the conciliatory methods of Manteuffel, the Commander-in-Chief of the army of occupation.

The Monarchists possessed a majority in the French Assembly, but they were divided. The future lay with the Republicans, whose leader, in peace and in war, was Gambetta. The first President could be none other than the veteran Thiers, but it was the hero of the National Defence who represented France to herself and to the world. Perhaps in his own good time, it was whispered, in some manner then undreamed of, he might be able to win back the provinces. By tongue and pen he kept courage and hope alive. He founded a journal, *La République Française*, as " a tribune from which the appeal for our rights and our ravished provinces may be made before Europe day by day. France is at the mercy of Germany. We are in a state of latent war ; neither peace nor liberty nor progress is possible." France, he proclaimed in a celebrated speech at St. Quentin, must resume her *rôle* in the world. " Let us not speak of the foreigner, but let him be ever in our thoughts. Alors vous serez sur le chemin de la revanche." " Bismarck," he wrote with piercing foresight, " has transformed a divided and impotent Germany into a great, disciplined and powerful empire, but the annexation of Alsace-Lorraine is the death-germ of his work. In such an advanced civilization moral conquest never follows material conquest. Till they have repaired their error no one will lay down his arms. The peace of the world will remain at the mercy of an incident."

Next to the great tribune Paul Déroulède was the most popular man in France. Enlisting as a private in 1870 he had been wounded, taken prisoner at Sedan, escaped, rejoined the French forces, and fought to the end of the campaign. In 1872 he published a little volume entitled *Chants du Soldat*, which, like the *Nouveaux Chants* three years later, were hummed by young conscripts at their work as Körner's stirring lyrics had

been sung in Germany sixty years earlier. His songs, with
their simple vocabulary and obvious rhymes, printed in pocket
editions for a few sous and in illustrated editions for a few
francs, sold by scores of thousands and fostered the moral
convalescence of France. The opening poem of the first
volume was entitled

VIVE LA FRANCE

Oui, Français, c'est un sang vivace que le vôtre !
Les tombes de vos fils sont pleines de héros.
Mais, sur le sol sanglant où le vainqueur se vautre,
Tous vos fils, O Français, ne sont pas aux tombeaux.

Et la revanche doit venir, lente peut-être,
Mais en tout cas fatale, et terrible à coup sûr ;
La haine est déjà née, et la force va naître :
C'est au faucheur à voir si le champ n'est pas mûr.

Perhaps the most popular of the series was the salute to the
poilu.

Dans la France, que tout divise,
Quel Français a pris pour devise
Chacun pour tous, tous pour l'État ?
    Le Soldat.

Dans nos heures d'indifférence,
Qui garde au cœur une espérance
Que tout heurte et que rien n'abat ?
    Le Soldat.

Qui fait le guet quand tout sommeille ?
Quand tout est en péril, qui veille ?
Qui souffre, qui meurt, qui combat ?
    Le Soldat.

O rôle immense ! O tâche sainte !
Marchant sans cris, tombant sans plainte,
Qui travaille à notre rachat ?
    Le Soldat.

Et sur la tombe obscure et fière,
Pour récompense et pour prière,
Que voudrait-il que l'on gravât ?
    Un Soldat.

The few Frenchmen who accepted the situation were regarded with angry contempt. When the Alsatian Scheurer-
Kestner, then a young man, visited Grévy, the first President

of the Chamber, he received an unwelcome homily.[1] " My children, it is grievous to have lost one's country ; but the régime which weighed so long on France could only leave disaster behind. I know you are for war. I tell you, who voted against the peace—France must not think of war. She must renounce Alsace. The tears rolled down our cheeks. The President took us by the hand and added, Do not believe the madmen who tell you the contrary, and who are the cause of our troubles being increased by a hopeless struggle. Resenting the reference to Gambetta we went away broken-hearted, as if an evil genius had taken from us the remainder of our courage. That day I took Grévy's measure. Since then I have only had official relations with him." Grévy, however, never ventured to say in public what he said in private, and no French Minister of the Third Republic ever dared to accept the Treaty of Frankfurt except under protest.

Bismarck had no illusions. When the French Chargé, in his first interview in August, 1871, expressed his confidence that relations would improve, the Chancellor replied that he was glad to hear such language but could not believe that France sincerely desired peace. " I do not think you wish to break the truce now. You will pay the first two milliards, but in 1874, when the other three are due, you will fight us." " France," added the Chargé in reporting the conversation, " is recovering too quickly. He thought that he had finished with her for twenty years at least, and he is becoming alarmed." When Gontaut-Biron took up his duties at Berlin early in 1872 he received a cordial welcome from the Emperor and Empress ; but the Chancellor, though at first polite, took no pains to hide his suspicion. The despatches of the first Ambassador of the Republic depict a relationship of tension and protests in which each party suspected the other of designs to renew the struggle.

Arnim's despatches from Paris were no less pessimistic. Thiers, he reported on May 6, 1872, desired a long peace, since France was not in a position to wage a new war. Later, when she had recovered her strength, declared the President, she would naturally seek compensation for her losses ; and if Germany were ever in difficulties with other Powers she would find her chance by bartering her aid if not by war. " There can be no doubt," wrote the Ambassador on October 3, 1872, " that of the 38 million Frenchmen not one hundred thousand

[1] *Souvenirs de Jeunesse*, 262–4.

regard the present frontier as permanent. The instinct for revenge, indeed, is so deep that they are insufficiently conscious of the unfavourable diplomatic and military situation to prevent them one day being suddenly carried away by their passions. The German Empire can no more co-exist with the France of to-day than Rome with Carthage." Bismarck replied to these gloomy vaticinations that France was not dangerous without allies, that the Republic was much less likely to find friends than a monarchy, and therefore that the French Royalists should not be supported. "The frankness with which hatred of Germany is proclaimed and encouraged by all parties," he added on February 2, 1873, "leaves us in no doubt that any Government will regard the *Revanche* as its principal task. The only question is how long the French will need to organize their army or their alliances before they think they can resume the struggle. Directly that moment arrives the Government will be compelled to declare war on us." The danger appeared to be increased in 1873 by the fall of Thiers, whom Bismarck liked, respected and trusted, for he had opposed the war of 1870. His successor was Marshal Mac-Mahon, distrusted by Bismarck as an Ultramontane, with the Orleanist Duc de Broglie as Foreign Minister, which the Chancellor interpreted as a step towards a royalist restoration. When Arnim, who favoured the French Royalists and had no love for Thiers, was recalled in 1874, Bismarck gave Hohenlohe, his successor, the maxim for his guidance that France must not obtain sufficient strength at home or consideration abroad to secure allies.

While the payment of the indemnity in two years instead of four and the consequential evacuation was an unwelcome surprise in Germany, the increase of the army and the refusal of public opinion to accept the Treaty of Frankfurt as anything more than a truce angered Bismarck and alarmed the military authorities. In 1873, when some French Bishops indulged in violent comments on the May Laws and the *Kulturkampf*, the Chancellor decided that a sharp warning was needed. It was not enough that the Bishops were ordered by their Government to abstain from attacks, he declared to the French Ambassador : they must be punished. "It is a question of our security. Your Bishops foment revolt in the empire, and that we cannot stand. If you allow these proceedings to continue, you will make war inevitable ; and we shall begin it before the clerical party gains power and declares war. That is why I dislike your projects of restoring the monarchy. I mistrust the influence which your clericals would have on the Comte de Chambord." The threat was repeated in the *Norddeutsche Allgemeine Zeitung*, which declared that from the moment France identified herself with Rome she would become the enemy of Germany, and that peace could not subsist with a France subject to the Vatican. " If France supports the Catholics in Germany," he added ominously, " I shall not wait till she is ready, as she will be in two years, but I shall seize a favourable opportunity." Moltke declared in January, 1874, that another war was inevitable before many years, and Bülow, the Foreign Minister, warned the Ambassador that the repetition of episcopal imprudences might lead to very grave complications. On February 10, 1874, Queen Victoria wrote to the Emperor William urging him to keep the peace despite French provocations, and received the reply, " We shall not make war."

The Bishops were muzzled though not punished, and the rest of 1874 passed without incident, except that in the first general election in Germany fourteen out of fifteen members from the Reichsland protested against the annexation, demanded a plebiscite and left the Reichstag. The Chancellor had no desire to attack France, but he did not intend to allow another attack on Germany. " We wish to keep the peace," he observed in 1874 to Hohenlohe ; " but if the French so order their preparations that in five years they will be ready and determined to strike, then in three years we shall begin war." Since the Treaty of Frankfurt imposed no limit on French armaments he could only proceed by warnings and threats.

Incensed by French intransigence Bismarck lashed out at the Francophils of the Rhine provinces.[1] The purpose of the annexation, he proclaimed in the Reichstag, was not to make them happy but to build a bastion against the everlasting irruptions of the French. " We conquered these lands in a war of self-defence. Our soldiers shed their blood not for Alsace-Lorraine but for the German Reich, for its unity, for the defence of its frontiers. We took the lands in order that the French in their next attack, which God grant may be distant but which they are planning, should not have the Weissenburg salient to start from, but that we should have a

---

[1] There are useful chapters on Alsace-Lorraine in Wahl, *Deutsche Geschichte*, 1871-1914, especially vols. 1 and 4, cp. Schneegans, *Memoiren*.

glacis on which we can defend ourselves before they reach the Rhine." The Glacis speech of 1874 was grist to the mill of the French propagandists, who seized on it as a confession that Berlin had no interest in the happiness or welfare of the populations. Yet at this very moment the provinces were conceded a Diet of thirty members, in which the so-called Autonomists, led by Schneegans, a Strassburg journalist, for some years played an active though unpopular part.

In 1875 the nerves of Europe received a formidable shock.[1] At the end of February the Chancellor was informed that France was ordering a large number of cavalry horses in Germany, and, after forbidding their export, he wrote for explanations to Hohenlohe. The Ambassador replied that France had no present intention of war, but that all parties hoped to reconquer the provinces when she found allies. War was neither near nor distant : nobody could say. A few days later, on March 12, the French Chamber, outstripping the proposals of the Government, increased the battalions in a regiment from three to four. The German Staff calculated that the increase would be 144,000, which would make the French army larger than their own. " This means an attack very shortly," observed Moltke to the Belgian Minister ; " we must not wait till they are ready." Opinion was genuinely alarmed. " Faites vous forts, très forts," remarked Gortcha-koff to the French Ambassador. Bismarck, he added, saw the hand of France in everything. On April 5 the *Kölnische Zeitung* expressed its fear of a Franco-Austrian alliance with the backing of the Pope and a clerical Monarchy in France. On April 8 the *Post* published an article headed " Is War in sight ? " which created the first dangerous crisis since 1871. War, it declared, was in sight, for France was preparing a war of revenge, but it was still possible that the clouds might disperse. It was widely believed that the article was inspired by the Chancellor ; but the supposition was unfounded, for it was written by Rössler on his own responsibility. Bismarck told Hohenlohe that he was surprised by the article, but he welcomed it as calculated to awaken Germany to the danger and to frighten France. On April 11 the *Norddeutsche Allgemeine Zeitung* declared that, though the fears of the *Post* in regard to

[1] J. V. Fuller, " The War-Scare of 1875," *American Historical Review*, January 1919, states the case against Bismarck. K. Herzfeld, *Die Deutsch-französische Kriegsgefahr von 1875*, and Rachfahl, *Deutschland und die Weltpolitik*, i, 45-76, defend him. The most illuminating discussion of a complicated problem is in the *Life of Lord Odo Russell*, ch. 5, by Winifred Taffs.

Austria and Italy were groundless, its anxieties about French armaments were correct. " The burden is too heavy even for the richest country to bear for long," added the semi-official organ ; " they can only be preparations for the object which no clear eye can fail to see." The *Preussische Jahrbücher* declared that arms must decide.

On April 15 Gontaut-Biron, who had been away from Berlin, returned to his post and explained to the Foreign Minister that the horses had not been ordered by the War Office, that the simultaneous reduction of the size of the battalion would reduce the increase of the army to about 30,000, and that there was no thought of attack. Bülow appeared to be satisfied ; and the same evening the Emperor, always since 1871 an influence for peace, meeting the French Military Attaché at a reception, observed, " On a voulu nous brouiller . . . Maintenant tout est terminé, tout à fait terminé." Unfortunately the danger was not over, for Gontaut-Biron learned from friends that Bismarck was not yet pacified. "Von Krieg ist gar keine Rede," he remarked to Lucius von Ballhausen on April 11 ; but on April 21 at a dinner at the British Embassy the French Ambassador heard from the lips of Radowitz, a Foreign Office functionary, words which filled him with terror. When he complained of the German press campaign and spoke of the pacific intentions of France, Radowitz replied, " Can you answer for the future ? France is bent on revenge. Why then should we wait till she is strong and has found allies ? " Radowitz's own official report of this conversation omits these words and suggests that he was merely explaining the ideas which found utterance in the German press.[1] The Ambassador, however, believed that he was expressing the views of the Chancellor, who had used very similar words, and feared that a preventive war might be launched at any moment. His report alarmed Decazes, the Foreign Minister, who forwarded a copy to the representatives of France abroad, with instructions to bring it to the notice of the Governments. At the same time he ordered the French Ambassador at St. Petersburg to appeal for a public promise by Russia to draw the sword in the event of a German attack. The Tsar had already told Le Flô that there was no danger, and that, if there were to be, he would tell France himself. He now replied, " I shall not draw the sword, nor will you." He added that he was shortly to visit Berlin. Meanwhile Decazes explained to Hohenlohe that France did

[1] *Die Grosse Politik*, i, 275–7.

not want war and could not wage it. If Germany invaded French territory, he added, she would withdraw her troops without fighting.

On May 5 the French Foreign Minister received a fresh shock, when Hohenlohe informed him of a despatch just received from the Wilhelmstrasse. The German Government, it declared, was not entirely convinced of the inoffensive character of French armaments, and the General Staff considered war as the ultimate object of recent military measures. Decazes, fearing that the next step might be a demand for the reduction of the army, informed Blowitz of the situation, and on May 6 a despatch from its famous Paris Correspondent entitled " A French Scare " appeared in *The Times*, revealing the threats and arguing that Russia alone could prevent a conflict. The despatch aroused consternation throughout Europe ; but on the previous day Schuvaloff, the Russian Ambassador in London, had passed through Berlin and explained to the Emperor and Bismarck his master's attitude. On May 7 William I expressed a wish in writing that the offending German editors should be reproved for alarming Europe and destroying the gradual growth of confidence that peace would not be disturbed. Lord Derby instructed the British Ambassador at Berlin energetically to support Russian representations, and Andrassy, the Austro-Hungarian Foreign Minister, assured Russia of the approval of Austria. Annoyed at what he called British credulity Bismarck informed the British Ambassador that the project of a German attack was a legend ; and when the Tsar and Gortchakoff reached Berlin on May 11 they were met with peaceful assurances. The six weeks' crisis was over. The French President wrote to thank the Tsar for his timely aid, and Decazes spoke cheerfully of the resurrection of Europe.

That a preventive war was advocated by the army chiefs in Germany, and that cool observers like Lord Derby and Odo Russell believed in the danger, is beyond dispute ; but we cannot be certain what was in Bismarck's mind. The Tsar believed that he invented the danger of a French attack in order to demonstrate the need of keeping him at the helm. The statement in his *Reflections and Recollections* that " the myth of a German attack " was a conspiracy against him engineered by Gontaut-Biron is ridiculous, but there is no ground for the belief that he had resolved to fight and was only restrained by the veto of Russia. If he had really desired to go to war, he would have done so. " Bismarck," observed the Duc Decazes, " wants us to believe that he wishes for war, but he does not wish for it himself." He was however gravely and even neurotically alarmed by the reports from his secret agents abroad. Though he did not share the bellicose views of Moltke, he desired France to know that Germany was watching her very closely, and that she would be wise to abstain from military or diplomatic measures which pointed towards a renewal of the struggle. But a policy of intimidation may easily lead to war without actually intending it. His resentment against Gortchakoff and Derby, and his fruitless request for the recall of Gontaut-Biron, showed that something had gone awry. The spectre of a coalition had appeared, and he was conscious that by playing with fire he had partially forfeited the confidence in him which Europe had begun to entertain. Everyone was asking apprehensively what he would do next. Gortchakoff acidly remarked to Lord Odo Russell that the Chancellor was suffering from nerves as a result of over-eating, over-drinking and over-working. It was certainly not his finest hour.

The conflagration in the Balkans which began soon after the war-scare of 1875 claimed Bismarck's attention for the next three years and thereby diminished the tension in the West. He continued to dread the royalist movement in France, and feared that MacMahon's clerical sympathies might lead him to attempt a *coup*. " If the French Government can permanently free itself from clericalism," he wrote to Hohenlohe in 1876, " good relations would be easy and there would be less chance of the *revanche*." He declined an invitation to take part in the exhibition planned for 1878, despite the desire of the Emperor and the Crown Prince to accept it. His fears seemed to be confirmed by the anti-Republican demonstration of May 16, 1877, when the President dismissed the Ministry of Jules Simon and summoned the Royalist leader the Duc de Broglie; and he observed that the France which stood behind Mac-Mahon would not be able to avoid war. There were two nations in France, he declared. The provinces were pacific and only wanted to work ; Paris, on the other hand, loved noise and conflict, and it was Paris which determined the character of the press.

II

A *détente* began with the triumph of the Republicans in the French elections of December, 1877, which removed the fear of a clerico-monarchical restoration. The recall of Gontaut-Biron, with whom the Chancellor had hardly been on speaking terms since the crisis of 1875, was hailed by him as an olive branch, though his departure brought tears to the eyes of the aged Emperor. The appointment of the Comte de St. Vallier, who had established excellent relations with Manteuffel during the occupation of French territory, confirmed the favourable impression of the Dufaure Ministry and of Waddington, the new Foreign Minister. On February 4, 1878, the Ambassador reported that the members of the Bundesrath saw in his appointment " a new era," and the Chancellor showed himself particularly amiable in their first interview. An invitation to take part in the Congress of Berlin was accepted, and Bismarck went so far as to offer the presidency to Waddington, in whom he expressed the same complete confidence that he had felt for Thiers. Even in Alsace-Lorraine there was a slight temporary *détente*.

When Waddington learned during the Congress of Berlin that Great Britain had secured the occupation of Cyprus from Turkey, he told Beaconsfield that he must withdraw; but Salisbury was ready with a *solatium*. " You cannot leave Carthage in the hands of barbarians. Do what you like there." The advice was supported by Bismarck, and on his return Waddington secured from Salisbury a written assurance of *désintéressement* in Tunis. No action was taken at the moment, but the conversations at Berlin opened a new chapter in Franco-German relations. In January, 1879, Bismarck invited St. Vallier, whom he described as " notre drapeau de paix et d'entente," to Friedrichsruh, where he urged the seizure of Tunis. " I think that the pear is ripe and that it is time for you to gather it. I do not know if it tempts you, but I must repeat what I said last year to M. Waddington. My desire is to give you pledges of goodwill in matters which concern you and where German interests do not collide with yours. It is only fair, for I appreciate the efforts which he and you have made to restore confidence between our two countries. Neither the Emperor nor I want another war on our hands. I believe that the French people need some satisfaction for their *amour-propre*, and I sincerely desire to see them obtain what they want in the Mediterranean, their natural sphere of expansion. The more success they find in that sphere the less will they be moved to assert their grievances against us." When the Ambassador observed that he should report these words textually, the Chancellor replied that he would put them in writing if requested. It has often been argued that the object of his suggestion to take Tunis was to drive a wedge between France and Italy. He may have foreseen such a result, though he could not know in advance that France would seize the country without consulting or compensating her rival. His main object was to diminish the tension which threatened the stability of his work. " M. Waddington in office and you here are a pledge of peace and understanding."

The *détente* bore fruit when the administration of the Rhine provinces was transferred to Strassburg. Field Marshal Manteuffel, the first Statthalter, was an admirable choice. *Le bon vieux*, as he was called, once again showed his conciliatory disposition. He liked the French and respected their intransigence. " Je crains bien que nous avons fait une faute en gardant Metz," he remarked to Gontaut-Biron. " C'est là ce qui blesse les Français." In his heart he despised Schneegans and other Autonomists, who, next to the German immigrants, were the chief bulwark of the Reich. If his native province of Pomerania had been lost, he confessed, he would never have recognized its finality. The Statthalter carried on his pacifying policy so far as he was permitted by Berlin. A Council of State was appointed, the powers of the Diet were enlarged, and Commissioners represented the interests of the provinces in the Bundesrat. It was hoped in some quarters that they might be transformed into a federal unit like Baden or Württemberg, but this had to wait for another thirty years. No gratitude was felt and none could be expected, for the hearts of the majority of the people were still French. At the moment when fresh responsibilities were entrusted to the inhabitants the Autonomist party, which had stood for co-operation with the Reich, collapsed under the burden of popular disfavour ; and Schneegans, its leader, had to leave Alsace and accept employment in the Consular service.

" Thanks to Prince Bismarck and yourself," wrote St. Vallier to Waddington in September 1879, " great progress has been made during the year and a half I have been in Berlin. Our work will be completed when every Frenchman is certain, as I am certain, that Germany meditates neither aggression nor invasion, and when every German is certain, as you are, that France dreams neither of revenge nor demands." When Bismarck went to Vienna in the same month to make the Dual Alliance, he explained to the French Ambassador in that city that there was nothing to excite the apprehensions of France. "The policy of moderation inaugurated by Thiers and henceforth faithfully pursued has gradually dissipated the prejudices arising from your form of government. M. de St. Vallier and I understand each other perfectly. The relations of our countries are excellent and I have no desire except to preserve and consolidate them." In March 1880 the Emperor and Empress dined for the first time at the French Embassy. Despite these reassuring signs the Chancellor was always haunted by the possibility of a *Revanche* Ministry in France and a Franco-Russian alliance.

The sun continued to shine, however feebly, for several years. When the Powers met at Madrid in 1880 to discuss commercial and other problems in Morocco, Bismarck instructed the German representative to follow the lead of his French colleague ; and when in 1881 France proceeded to establish a Protectorate over Tunis by force of arms, he afforded the moral support he had promised and received an expression of gratitude from Jules Ferry. The opening of a new phase of colonial expansion announced that she was prepared to resume her activities as a Great Power, and Bismarck frankly admitted his hopes that it would turn her thoughts from the lost provinces. It was at this moment that Hohenlohe was instructed to convey to the Foreign Minister the Chancellor's hope that France would one day realize that German friendship was of more value than a million inhabitants of Alsace and Lorraine. The message was received by Barthélemy St. Hilaire with a smile but without comment. "We desire the friendship of Germany, not her protection," he wrote to St. Vallier. The statesmen of France naturally preferred smiles to frowns, but they were aware that there were limits to the Chancellor's indulgence. "Russia is inclined to a rapprochement," explained Waddington to Freycinet in handing over the reins in 1879, "but Bismarck has his eye on us. The menace of an alliance might decide him to open hostilities." The velvet glove scarcely concealed the iron hand. "He is guided not by petty ideas of hatred and rancour," explained St. Vallier in 1881, "but by higher and more serious considerations, based on what he believes to be the interest of Germany. To attain his goal, namely the consolidation of his work, he would gladly co-operate with his foe of yesterday or break with a friend." In a word Bismarck was a pure realist and he never pretended to be anything else.

The *détente* which began in 1877 was approved by the greatest of French citizens. Gambetta's longing for the recovery of the provinces remained, but after the crisis of 1875 the possibility of winning them by negotiation occupied his thoughts. He was no longer the *fou furieux* he had seemed to Thiers. We can trace the evolution of his thought in his correspondence with Ranc and in the sparkling memoirs of his friend and hostess, Mme Adam. " If by diplomacy we can avoid or at least postpone the conflict," he wrote in September, 1875, "should we not try it? But how? Our colonies. Which is the best, to keep our distant possessions or our future generations? Let us face this cruel dilemma—the lives of young France or portions of our colonial territory. Ought we not to profit by the taste of Germany for colonies ? We have what they want. Is that not our chance ? " The unfounded rumour that Bismarck was about to visit Paris for political conversations in December, 1875, filled him with excitement. " Must I stand aloof ? Is it really my duty as a Frenchman ? You know the dreams of a colonial future for his people, and his country is strong, perhaps invincible. Should we not avoid the noble but fruitless sacrifice of our young men whose death would enfeeble France for ever ? " When Bismarck announced in 1878 that a Congress would meet at Berlin, Gambetta, after brief hesitation, favoured participation. " We must profit by the rival ambitions to declare our legitimate demand. .d create an agreement." His readiness to meet the monster, as he called him, had now grown into eagerness. At the end of 1877 Count Henckel von Donnersmarck, returning to Paris where he had lived under the Second Empire, wrote to Bismarck, " I guarantee to bring Gambetta to Varzin on a public or a private visit, whichever you prefer. He will propose to you a rapprochement and collaboration with France." The Chancellor evaded a reply ; but when the proposal was renewed in April 1878, he accepted it, and a *rendezvous* was arranged for April 30 at Berlin. At the last moment, however, Gambetta drew back. " Man proposes, Parliament disposes," he wrote to Henckel on April 18. " When I readily accepted yesterday I did not allow for the unexpected. The questions relating to the Ministry of War have become increasingly important. I cannot abandon

my post. So I must postpone the execution of the plan."
The state of business was a pretext, for at the last moment
Gambetta shirked the interview. It could only have led to
disappointment, for, according to Blowitz, Bismarck told
Holstein that he would have made it a condition that the provinces should not be mentioned. The faithful Spuller, who
detested the notion of a rapprochement, warned his beloved
leader to be prudent, and the *pourparlers* were never resumed,
though Gambetta continued his visits to Germany and to the
end Bismarck desired to meet him. The French statesman
persevered in the new path, and a common friend encouraged
him to hope for a change when the Crown Prince should come
to the throne. Some of his friends turned their backs on the lost
leader, among them Mme Adam, who founded *La Nouvelle
Revue* in 1879 to preach the *revanche* and the need of a Russian
alliance. " You follow your sentiments, I my reason," he
remarked to her in 1878 ; " let each of us go his own way."
The *revanche* was merely a means to an end, the recovery of the
provinces, and he had come to believe that it might ultimately
be secured without a war, perhaps by an alliance with England
and Russia.

Gambetta continued to make speeches which suggested that
another conflict was inevitable, and in Germany it was believed
that his accession to power might be the signal for the attack.
" Les grandes réparations," he declared in his celebrated speech
at Cherbourg in 1880, " peuvent sortir du droit. We or our
children can hope for them, for the future is open to us all. It
has been said that we have a passionate cult for the army. It is
not the spirit of war which animates this cult ; it is the necessity, after seeing France fall so low, to raise her up so that she
resumes her place in the world. If our hearts beat, it is for
this goal, not for an ideal of blood ; it is that what is left of
France may remain entire ; it is that we may count on the
future. There is on earth an immanent justice which comes at
its appointed time." Freycinet, to whom some of the Ambassadors complained, assured them that the speech was
pacific in intention ; but the critics cried, *Gambetta, c'est la guerre*,
and Bismarck exclaimed, " Gambetta in power would act on
the nerves like a man beating a drum in a sick-room." A year
later, at Menilmontant, he made his pacific attitude clear beyond
controversy. " France intends to win for herself such power
and such prestige that in the end, by force of patience, she will
receive the reward of wise and good conduct. If she is vigilant

and prudent, taking her share in international affairs but eschewing conspiracy and aggression, I think and hope I shall see the day when, through the majesty of right, truth and justice, we shall regain our lost brothers."

The Republican triumph of 1877 made Gambetta's accession to power a mere matter of time, and when Grévy succeeded MacMahon as President in 1879, it was felt that the hour was nigh. Grévy, however, whether owing to jealousy or to fear of foreign complications, postponed the summons, and it was not till the summer of 1881 that he confessed that the next Ministry must be formed by the Republican leader. The Emperor was a little apprehensive, and St. Vallier attempted to remove his fears by describing a recent conversation with Grévy. " So long as I hold my post," declared the President, " I will never allow France to launch an attack. I shall know how to pursue and make all the Ministers pursue a policy of peace. In home affairs I shall not intervene, but I will never compromise on the maintenance of good relations. Germany can count on me and trust my word." When *Le Grand Minis-tère* was at last formed in December, 1881, Gambetta asked St. Vallier to report the effect. The Ambassador replied that the Emperor was apprehensive and Bismarck suspicious, but official relations remained friendly. The Chancellor informed St. Vallier, and Hohenlohe assured the Quai d'Orsay, that the formation of the Gambetta Cabinet would in no way diminish the friendliness of Berlin. *Le Grand Ministère*, however, only lasted two months, and in less than a year the great patriot died in his forty-fifth year. That he had ceased to think of a war of revenge was known only to his intimate friends.

The diplomatic rapprochement inaugurated by Waddington and approved by Gambetta was confirmed by Freycinet and Jules Ferry, though the deep estrangement of the two peoples remained, the German Government often complained of the utterances of the French press, and no one on either side of the Rhine imagined that the volcano was extinct. At no time since 1870 had the wires between Paris and Berlin worked so smoothly as during the second Ministry of Ferry, which lasted from 1883 to 1885. The chief architect of the new French colonial empire, himself a Lorrainer, lamented the defeat of 1870 as much as other men ; but he believed that Germany would remain the stronger Power, that France needed an outlet for her energies, and that she could only give hostages to fortune in Africa and Asia if assured against attack from beyond

C

the Rhine. The fiery Déroulède founded his Ligue des Patriotes in 1882 with its organ *Le Drapeau*, in which he continued to proclaim that what had been lost by arms must be regained by arms, and denounced the Premier as an atheist of patriotism. " You will end by making me think you prefer Alsace-Lorraine to France," rejoined Ferry; " must we hypnotize ourselves with the lost provinces, and should we not take compensations elsewhere ? " " That is just the point," retorted Déroulède. " I have lost two children, and you offer me twenty domestics." For the moment France was pleasurably excited by the excursions and alarums of colonial adventure, but the type of uncompromising nationalism represented by Déroulède and Clemenceau was soon to change the political landscape.

The year 1884 witnessed the foundation of Germany's oversea empire and a brief estrangement between London and Berlin. Angered by the procrastinating conduct of Lord Derby, our Colonial Minister, Bismarck sought to win France for a new plan. " I wish to establish a sort of equilibrium on the seas," he declared to the French Ambassador on September 23, " and France has a leading *rôle* to play in this connection if she will enter into our views. I do not wish for war against England, but I wish her to understand that if the navies of other nations unite they will compel her to consider the interests of other people. For that purpose she must accustom herself to the idea that a Franco-German alliance is not an impossibility." Throughout the winter the Chancellor continued his efforts. " I hope to reach the point when you will forgive Sedan as you have forgiven Waterloo. Renounce the Rhine, and I will help you to secure everywhere else the satisfactions you desire." He praised the statesmanship of Ferry and expressed the wish to meet him, perhaps in Belgium or Luxemburg or even in the south of France. These flattering advances made no impression on the new Ambassador in Berlin, Baron de Courcel. " At bottom," he reported, " Bismarck wishes to do England a bad turn and to use us for the purpose." On January 20, 1885, the sceptical Ambassador defined the schemes of the Wilhelmstrasse. " To soften our memories, to turn our thoughts from the past to an indeterminate future, and thus to lead us imperceptibly to swallow 1815 and 1871, so that France, accepting the hegemony of Prussia, henceforth gravitates in German orbits—such is Bismarck's policy towards us. We must do him the justice to recognize the frankness and sincerity with which he declares it." In regard to amputations, declared the Ambassador in a private letter to Jules Ferry, a nation should neither forgive nor forget unless it wished to share the fate of Poland. Moreover, *l'amitié de l'Allemagne est une amitié orageuse*.

Though Baron de Courcel had no intention of walking into Bismarck's parlour, some of his countrymen seemed prepared for the great surrender. " You cannot think how much good our rapprochement has done," observed Barrère, the French Minister in Cairo, to Herbert Bismarck. " I cannot say there is no longer enmity, for that needs time, but there is no longer mistrust among us. It will still be a fairly long time till 1870 becomes merely a memory, but only patience is needed for that. The rapprochement is not only the best thing for the two countries but for the world. We must think of future generations and remember that the strongest alliance would be France and Germany." In the same month of September, 1884, General Campenon, Minister of War, entertained the foreign officers at the manoeuvres at dinner, and observed to the chief of the German mission that the Government desired a rapprochement. " A Franco-German alliance," replied his guest, " is only possible if you recognize the Treaty of Frankfurt." " That is what I am always telling my colleagues," replied Campenon. " We should no longer weakly occupy ourselves with the past, but should reckon with the present. With such an alliance France would at one blow regain her standing. France and Germany united would rule the world." A fortnight later Herbert Bismarck visited Ferry, who charged him to tell the Chancellor that he would not take the smallest step in Egypt without consulting the Wilhelmstrasse. " We are on the high road," remarked the Director of the Finance Ministry to Herbert Bismarck ; " first the *détente* and then the *entente*."

III

That Bismarck was satisfied with the German frontiers established by his three wars is beyond doubt. " I know I am accused of wishing to sow dissension between France and England or between England and Russia," he remarked to the French Ambassador on May 10, 1885. " But what have I to gain from such dissensions ? Germany's position is now strong enough, and she is entirely content with her relations to her two Imperial neighbours. She asks nothing more than to live at peace with all her neighbours. She has no interest in taking anything from any of them. On the Russian side we have already too many Poles and we certainly do not want more. On the Austrian side could we desire to annex the Czechs or the Viennese ? They would be a cause of much embarrassment. On the French side you know my opinion that we have taken too much French territory. Could we aspire to conquests at the expense of France, Belgium or Holland ? They would be recalcitrant nations. Looking all round our frontiers every gain would be a loss, every increase a cause for weakness." This was true enough, but the status quo was not good enough for France.

In the opening weeks of 1885 the news from Tonkin, which Ferry had added to the French colonial empire, became more and more alarming ; but on March 29 the Premier assured the Chamber that General Négrier possessed the forces needed to hold Lang-Son and defend the frontier. On the following day a telegram announced that he had been wounded and compelled to evacuate Lang-Son by superior forces. A wave of panic and fury, unknown since *l'année terrible*, swept over France. When the doomed Ministry demanded credits to retrieve the situation, Clemenceau sprang to his feet. " We can enter into no discussion with you. We have no longer Ministers before us but men charged with high treason, on whom the hand of the law will descend, if the principles of justice still exist." Ferry was hurled from power, peace was concluded with China, and the first period of colonial expansion of the Republic came to an abrupt end. The vote of March 30 was the condemnation not only of a French statesman but of the principle which had guided the policy of France since the Congress of Berlin. Gambetta and Ferry, with the encouragement of Bismarck, had sought compensation overseas for the loss of the provinces which, in their opinion, could not be regained within any measurable time; and now the glittering fabric of the young empire seemed to crumble into dust. No more colonial adventures ! No more hazardous expeditions ! Ferry—*le trâitre*, *le Tonkinois*—had forgotten the Vosges. He had danced to Bismarck's piping and wasted blood and money in the far places of the earth. *À bas le Prussien !* Back to the *revanche !* It was the hour of Clemenceau.

The atmospheric change was reflected in the Ministerial declarations of the Brisson Cabinet. " By a watchful and circumspect policy we must guarantee our position amidst the questions which preoccupy Europe. The Republic desires nothing but peace, peace accompanied by the dignity which a nation like ours demands, peace assured by a solid army of defence." The same *Leitmotif* was heard after the general election in the autumn. The first duty of the new Chamber, it was explained, was to strengthen the army. So powerful was the reaction that a demand for the total evacuation of Tonkin was only defeated by four votes. When Freycinet succeeded Brisson at the opening of 1886 his programme was fixed in advance. "If there is one point on which the ballot-boxes have expressed themselves without ambiguity," ran the Ministerial declaration, " it is on the direction to be followed in foreign affairs. It is understood that France is to have a policy of dignity and peace, and that her forces are to be concentrated on the Continent, respected by all and menacing none. France desires no more of these distant expeditions, which are a source of sacrifice without any obvious compensation."

The foreign policy of the Third Republic was dominated by the two ideals of the recovery of the Rhine provinces and the foundation of an empire. For the first two decades it seemed impossible to pursue them simultaneously, and it was equally impossible to secure colonies without the assent of Berlin. The first act ended when Gambetta and Grévy, Waddington and Ferry postponed the *revanche* to the Greek Kalends and acted on the suggestion to take Tunis. The second act ended with the reverse in Indo-China, and the temporary abandonment of colonial expansion carried with it the termination of the *détente*. The obvious tasks before France in her new mood were to strengthen her army and to seek for allies. The history of French policy during the decade following the fall of Ferry is the record of her successful pursuit of these objects.

Freycinet, who belonged to the school of Gambetta and Ferry, desired to continue the friendly relations with Berlin; but he showed less than his usual insight in choosing a Minister of War whose sinister activities were to bring France and Germany to the verge of war and to threaten the existence of the Republic. At this time, however, Boulanger was the *protégé* of Clemenceau and the Radicals, and no one could foresee coming events. He had seen service in Algeria, Italy, Indo-China and the war of 1870, and had served as Director of Infantry at the War Office and commander of the army in

Tunis. He proceeded to justify his selection by a series of reforms in the organization and munitioning of the army, the strengthening of fortifications, and the provision of creature comforts for the *poilu*. Since the mind of France was focussed on national defence, and since no comprehensive reforms had been made for a decade, he became a celebrity and the acclamations of the crowd aroused his political ambitions. Déroulède, who as early as 1883 announced that at last he had found a man, " I might even say our man," offered him the services of the 300,000 members of the Ligue des Patriotes. *La France Militaire, Le Drapeau, La Frontière, l'Anti-Prussien, La Revanche,* and many Chauvinist pamphlets sang his praises, announced that France was ready, and preached the holy war.

" Monsieur le Ministre de la Guerre," observed Freycinet one day in July 1886, " vous faites un peu trop mon métier." The gentle rebuke produced no effect, for the General relished his position on the crest of the wave. People began to whisper and to watch. " The topic of the day," reported Lord Lyons, the British Ambassador, on July 2, " is the conduct of Boulanger. He has by degrees put creatures of his own into the great military commands, and he is said to have used strange language in the Council of Ministers. From the way people talk one would think the question was whether he is aiming at being a Cromwell or a Monk." A fortnight later Lord Newton, of the British Embassy, described his appearance at the *fête* of July 14. " The mountebank had provided himself with a high-actioned black circus horse. As he pranced backwards and forwards and the public yelled their acclamations, President Grévy and the uninteresting crowd of bourgeois Ministers and Deputies seemed visibly to quiver and flinch. From that day Boulanger became a dangerous man." The German Military Attaché sent home long reports on his activities and on the provocations of the press. " The last few days have witnessed several remarkable outbreaks of chauvinism," reported Count Münster, the German Ambassador, on October 14. " The artificially stimulated hatred of Germany is if possible stronger than ever, but the war of revenge is far from being popular. The wish that there may be one day a holy war is common to every Frenchman, but the demand for its speedy fulfilment is met with a shake of the head." Boulanger himself, he added a few weeks later, was believed by some intimate friends to be afraid of war, since he knew too well the weak points of the army ; but he kept his fears to himself.

After a year's absence from Paris Prince Hohenlohe, the late German Ambassador, described in his diary on November 10, 1886, the new and anxious situation. "What strikes me most is the change in Boulanger's position. In the spring of last year he was considered a *farceur*. To-day he has the majority of the Chamber on his side. Freycinet does not dare to get rid of him, and even Ferry would find it difficult to form a Ministry without him. He knows how to win people and to dazzle the masses. If he stays two years longer in office, the conviction will become universal that he is the man to reconquer the provinces, and, as he is utterly unscrupulous and extremely ambitious, he will carry the masses into war. Blowitz agrees, and says that, if he remains, war will come in 1888. His fall is inevitable directly the country sees where he is leading it. Then he will be swept away, for the country is still pacific. But in a year it will be different." "In Boulanger," echoes the Belgian Chargé a month later, "the whole of France personifies her dreams of future greatness." The German Military Attaché sent home a series of alarming reports on the ambitions and popularity of the new leader.

During this orgy of chauvinism the French Government remained unmoved. The new Ambassador to Berlin, Herbette, who as Director of the Foreign Office had co-operated with Freycinet and enjoyed his confidence, arrived in October 1886, and explained the views of his Government in a remarkable conversation with the Foreign Minister, Herbert Bismarck. The good services rendered by Germany in regard to France's colonial policy, he declared, were known only to the few : now was the time to show the French people the real aims of German policy. "What a *détente* there would be, and how all our suspicions and apprehensions would vanish if Prince Bismarck publicly declared that he would use his immense authority for the maintenance of the *status quo* in the Mediterranean ! All eyes would turn from the East, and we could employ all our resources in the Mediterranean, the theatre of our vital interests. It is a question of existence for us as a Great Power that England should evacuate Egypt. I assure you that the Mediterranean is the pivot of our policy and that the English are abominated in France, far more than the Germans have ever been. The idea of the *revanche* is out of date." There was an element of unreality in such language while Boulanger was the darling of the Paris mob, and it evoked no response in Berlin.

The reforms introduced or proposed by Freycinet and Boulanger, reducing the term of service from five years to three and improving the armament, challenged the superiority of the German army, and on November 25, 1886, the German Minister of War presented a seven-year army bill increasing the troops by 41,000. The aged Moltke delivered a few pregnant sentences. "An *entente* with France has been mentioned. But while public opinion in France persists in demanding the restitution of two essentially German provinces, which Germany is firmly resolved not to cede, an *entente* is an impossibility." The bill was fiercely contested, but its backers found their strongest argument in the growing popularity of Boulanger, who retained his portfolio when Goblet succeeded Freycinet in December. Each side believed or pretended to believe that the other was meditating a sudden attack. In the words of the new Premier, the whole of Europe was living "on a footing of armed peace." "An imprudent word," reported Herbette on January 4, 1887, "any suggestion of an *arrière-pensée* might decide Bismarck to try to crush us as a measure of precaution. But I am convinced we can round Cape Wrath if we are wise."

On January 11, Bismarck supported the Army Bill in one of the greatest of his speeches. Germany, he explained, belonged to what Metternich called satiated States, but all the Powers were busy preparing for an uncertain future. "Everyone asks, Is war coming? I do not believe that any statesman will deliberately apply the match to the gunpowder heaped up in every land. But the passions of the mob, the ambition of party leaders, misguided public opinion—these are the elements potentially stronger than the will of the rulers." Germany had declined to thwart Russian ambitions in the Near East and had tried to oblige France everywhere except in Alsace-Lorraine. "We have no intention and no reason to attack her. I would never fight because I thought a war might be inevitable. I cannot see into the cards of Providence. If the French will keep the peace till we attack, peace is assured for ever. Do we want more French soil? I was not anxious to take Metz. I have complete confidence in the present French Government. Goblet and Flourens are not the men to make war. If you could guarantee their continuance in office, I would say, Save your money. But the stirring of the flames by an active minority makes me anxious. We have still to fear an attack—whether in ten days or ten years I cannot say. War is certain if France thinks she is stronger and can win. That is my unalterable conviction. Where is the Ministry who would dare to say, We accept the Treaty of Frankfurt? She is definitely stronger than she was. If she won, she would bleed us white ; and if we won, after being attacked, we would do the same. There is also the possibility, even if France did not expect to win, that she might launch a war as a safety valve, as in 1870. Indeed, why should not Boulanger try it if he came to power?" On January 28 the Chancellor observed to Herbette that Boulanger's promotion to the Premiership or the Presidency would mean war. "C'est un homme qui médite un coup d'état," though he was only a second-rate comedian. On January 31 the *Post*, in an article entitled "On the razor-edge," which recalled the scare of 1875, argued that the retention of Boulanger in the Ministry was an imminent danger to peace.

The Reichstag accepted the proposed increase for three years instead of seven, as demanded by the Bill, and the Government appealed to the country. Boulanger, it was argued, was organizing the *revanche*. Pictures appeared of the Vosges frontier with huge barracks and swarming *poilus* on the one side and not a soldier on the other. To ensure the desired response by emphasizing the danger, the Government announced the calling up of reservists in Alsace-Lorraine. The atmosphere was electric, and war was anticipated by cool observers in other lands. Flourens, the Foreign Minister, was thoroughly alarmed. On February 8 the French Chamber adopted without discussion Boulanger's demand for a special credit of eighty million francs, though the frightened Cabinet vetoed the proposal for calling up reservists. Münster informally urged his dismissal, and the German semi-official journal observed that not a day had passed since his appointment to the Ministry of War without a measure to increase the striking power of the French army. Once more, as in 1875, the Tsar was asked for and gave a promise of moral support. The German elections supplied the Government with the majority it needed, and the Army Bill in the desired shape became law in March.

With the passing of the Septennate there was a lull in its official German campaign against the French peril, but the psychological results remained. "Bismarck's electoral manoeuvre," reported Herbette, " has been so well engineered that all Germany now believes in the fatality of a war with France and is inclined to wish to get it over at once. This state of opinion is a danger which preoccupies me. We must neither furnish a pretext nor go to sleep." Bismarck, he added, was nervy and irritable. People were asking whether France would intervene in the event of a Russo-German war. De Lesseps visited Berlin on a semi-official mission, and assured the Chancellor of the pacific disposition of the President and the Cabinet; but so long as Boulanger remained a national hero, peace hung by a thread.

At the end of April, 1887, a spark seemed likely to set Europe ablaze. A French Police Commissioner named Schnaebele, an Alsatian who had opted for France in 1871, was invited by a German Police Commissioner to meet him for a discussion of administrative business. On reaching the *rendezvous* on the German side of the frontier he was seized, and after a struggle was carried off to Metz. The excuse for this outrage was that he had misused his official position for purposes of espionage, and that his arrest, if ever he crossed the frontier, had been decreed by the High Court at Leipzig—a fact unknown to the French Government. Once again Boulanger urged a military demonstration, and once more Grévy intervened to prevent it. Flourens kept his head and forwarded to Berlin photographs of the letters of invitation from the German official. Bismarck at once admitted that the invitation implied a safe conduct which must be respected despite Schnaebele's grave offence. A week after his arrest he was at liberty, but he had exceeded his functions and was removed from his post. Though the Governments kept cool, for both of them had been disagreeably surprised by the incident, the temperature of public opinion on both sides of the Rhine had risen to boiling point. The fiery Déroulède taxed the Cabinet with cowardice, and argued that the time had come to finish with Bismarck's "provocations." Frenchmen maintained that Germany had tried to pick a quarrel, and Goblet, the Premier, declared that it would perhaps have been better to fight. The Germans continued to believe that Boulanger was master of France and might give the signal for invasion at any moment.

President Grévy, whose devotion to peace was only equalled by his contempt for Boulanger, remarked to Goblet: "I receive many people; no one desires war, neither the Chamber nor the country." Though this was by no means true he had long determined to get rid of the firebrand, who, as he subsequently confided to the German Ambassador, had on two occasions proposed measures involving war. Goblet resigned in May and Rouvier formed a Ministry without the General, who was appointed to the command of an Army Corps in the provinces. Both the President and the Ambassador in Berlin argued that his influence had been exaggerated and that the excitement had only been on the surface, but the danger was by no means at an end. The mountebank remained the darling of the crowd, and every missile aimed from beyond the Rhine served to endear him to the extreme Nationalists. When " le Général de Revanche " was deprived of his command in 1888 for paying visits to the capital without leave, he stood for the Chamber at a by-election in Paris as a champion of the revision of the Constitution and was elected by an overwhelming majority. Fortunately for the peace of the world he was not built in the heroic mould, and he let slip the opportunity of marching on the Élysée to which his hot-blooded followers summoned him. His old sponsor Clemenceau turned against him, and on learning that an order had been signed for his arrest he fled to Brussels. The bubble had burst. He was condemned in his absence for treason, and a discreditable career was terminated by suicide on the grave of his mistress. Boulanger, declares Freycinet in his Memoirs, never really desired war, but he had been playing with fire. His movement revealed the persistent vitality of the *revanche*, rendered impossible a return to the *quasi-entente* of the Waddington-Ferry-Freycinet period, and prepared the ground for the Russian alliance.

The tension was once again reflected in the military changes with which both Governments occupied themselves. In France the last remains of a professional army were swept away, and every Frenchman on reaching the age of twenty became subject to three years' service. In 1888 Freycinet was appointed Minister of War and held the office for five years, carrying through the three years' law, the development of the reserves and the re-arming of the infantry. Germany replied by an Army Bill reorganizing the Landwehr and the Landsturm. On February 6, 1888, in commending the Army Bill to the Reichstag, Bismarck again swept the European horizon with his telescope. In 1887, he declared, the chief danger had been from France ; now it was from Russia. " Since last year one pacific President has succeeded another. We can count on President Carnot to continue the policy of M. Grévy. We have also seen a change of great importance in the Ministry. The Ministers who had a tendency to place their personal projects before the peace of their own country and of Europe are gone, and more peaceful men have taken their place. I gladly recognize that France is more pacific and less explosive than last year. Yet the danger of coalitions is permanent, and we must arrange once for all to meet it. We must make greater exertions than other nations on account of our position. Russia and France can only be attacked on one front, but God has placed us beside the most bellicose and restless of nations, the French, and He has allowed bellicose tendencies to grow up in Russia. I do not expect an early breach of the peace, but I advise other countries to discontinue their menaces. We Germans fear God and nothing else in the world." It was the swan song of the old Chancellor in the sphere of foreign affairs.

IV

The fall of Bismarck in 1890 was hailed with delight in France. He had helped to keep the peace, commented the French Ambassador, but in every situation his first thought was to counterwork French interests. His marvellous skill, his immense authority on all the Cabinets, his influence on the press, enabled him to keep France in isolation. The new Chancellor, whatever his ill will, could not do her so much harm. A slight *détente* began when the French Government accepted the invitation of William II to send a delegate to an International Conference on social reform at Berlin. The veteran statesman and publicist Jules Simon, who was chosen for the task, was captivated by the charm, the frankness and the energy of his host. The Kaiser expressed his ardent desire to enter into cordial relations with France, and when his visitor replied that the question could not be solved at present, he rejoined that it was never too soon to formulate a good idea. " Your army has made great progress and is ready," he added ; " if it were engaged in single combat with the German army no one could forecast the result of the struggle. Therefore I should regard as a madman or a criminal whoever stirred up the two peoples to make war." Jules Simon had no more doubt of the speaker's absolute sincerity than of the purity of his French accent. His accession had been dreaded in Paris, for his admiration for the army and its glorious traditions was notorious, and it was widely held that he was likely to prove the *enfant terrible* of Europe. The diminution of tension was reflected in a slight mitigation of the rigid and deeply resented passport régime in Alsace-Lorraine.

In the milder atmosphere inaugurated by the visit of Jules Simon, the organizers of a picture exhibition in Berlin to be held in May 1891, invited French artists to take part. The French Ambassador replied that his Government, though unable to participate officially in a private enterprise, would view with pleasure an acceptance of the invitation by French artists. This guarded reply was perhaps as much as Berlin expected, and invitations were now sent to individual artists in France. At a dinner at the French Embassy the Kaiser loudly expressed his admiration for French art, and eulogized with fervour the talent of Meissonier, who had recently passed away. Not content with verbal eulogies, he gave instructions for a letter in similar terms to be written to the French Ambassador, with the request to forward it to the Académie des Beaux-Arts. The French Government in return awarded to Helmholtz the medal of Grand Officer of the Legion of Honour, adding that this was the first time since the war that such a high distinction had been conferred on a German. The *détente*, however, was purely superficial. " Tout le temps qui s'écoulera avant la lutte suprême sert à notre préparation," wrote Herbette to his chief in February 1891.

At this moment the French Ambassador was informed that the Empress Frederick was about to visit Paris incognito. The French Government was not consulted before the decision was reached. Her object, it was explained, was to make purchases for her new home at Kronberg, but she also desired to meet French artists and to induce them to exhibit at Berlin. In telegraphing the news Herbette added that the slightest *contretemps* might have disastrous results. The visit aroused the liveliest interest in both countries, for it was widely though falsely believed to cloak far-reaching political designs. Leading German papers described it as a historic event. " Germany has given a fine example of her desire for reconciliation," wrote the *Vossische Zeitung* ; " will France respond ? May we not hope that the chiefs of the French nation, in view of the noble intentions of the Emperor's mother, will abandon the ideas of revenge ? " Such utterances naturally provoked the Nationalists, who spoke of " our holy hatreds." The ex-Empress, who was never celebrated for tact, added fuel to the flame by visiting the park of St. Cloud and lunching at Versailles. " My mother," remarked the Kaiser, " is not easy to control." A protest meeting was addressed by Déroulède, and several artists withdrew their acceptance of the invitation to exhibit at Berlin. The German press resented the protests and criticisms of Paris. " The French have not the right," wrote the *Kölnische Zeitung*, " to insult the august head of the German Empire and his noble mother. Every German who has the slightest sense of the dignity of his nation feels himself mortally outraged in the person of his Emperor." The Kaiser was furious at the protest meeting, the organizers of which were not punished, and the French Government learned that measures preliminary to general mobilization had been ordered. The danger was obvious, and the most careful precautions were taken to avoid an incident when she left the Gare du Nord. Not till long after did the French people learn of the peril thus narrowly averted.

On February 27, the day of her departure, Marschall von Bieberstein, the Foreign Minister, addressed Herbette in a tone which even Bismarck had never adopted. After emphasizing the good intentions of the Empress, and stating that Berlin had expected a courteous welcome and at any rate official protection against insults, he added : " Clearly one must not demand from a Republic what one would from a strong government." Even after making such allowances, he explained, there were limits to tolerance, and he hinted that they had been reached. The Ambassador, unaware that the Empress had already left Paris, telegraphed in alarm that the slightest manifestation of disrespect to her might involve war. " Nothing will be changed between the two Governments," remarked the Foreign Minister to the French Ambassador, " but I cannot say the same of the two countries; for the sensible and peace-loving people who form the great majority in France let themselves be intimidated by a tiny minority of adventurers. That we shall not easily forget." Thus the visit which was designed to foster a *détente* inflicted fresh wounds and revealed once again that the volcanic fires were ready to burst forth at any moment. There had been no real progress between 1871 and 1891. A few days later the passport régime was restored in Alsace-Lorraine in full rigour. The countries had reverted to the relations of 1887, but on this occasion there was no Boulanger to hurl defiance across the Rhine. France, moreover, had an additional reason to avert or at any rate to postpone a conflict ; for the Russian alliance, long advocated by Boulanger, Déroulède and the Nationalists, was in sight:

Its conclusion by a series of agreements between 1891 and 1894 opens a new chapter in the history of the Third Republic. The inferiority complex disappeared. If the balance of power which had been destroyed in 1870 was not fully restored, there was at any rate no longer an unchallenged German hegemony. " The era of monologues has passed," wrote the *Temps*, " and the era of dialogues has begun." The voice of France would be heard once again. A few far-seeing thinkers like Jaurès recognized that the partnership might drag France into a war for Russian ambitions, but to fiery Nationalists it seemed to bring the *revanche* within sight. To France as a whole it symbolized complete recovery from the disasters of 1870, escape from the quarantine in which Bismarck had kept her, a solid guarantee against menaces, humiliations and attack. " Now you are two," remarked Münster, the German Ambassador, to Freycinet, " you will find it difficult to keep quiet. In France you are very thin-skinned, and the slightest spark will set the powder alight." " What makes us sensitive," replied the Minister of War, " is that we are thought to be weak. The stronger we are, the less inclined we shall be to take offence. Our relations will be easier when we stand on a footing of equality. You will see that our *entente* with Russia is a pledge of peace." Unlike the majority of his countrymen, he knew that Russia had not the slightest intention of shedding her blood for the recovery of Alsace-Lorraine or indeed for the realization of any purely French aims.

Feeling her flank secured, France resumed her colonial ambitions after a lull of nearly a decade. In 1894 Hanotaux entered on his memorable term of office at the Quai d'Orsay. Like Gambetta and Ferry, he believed that France would increase rather than dissipate her resources and her strength by becoming a great colonial power. The only extensive field left for expansion was in North and Central Africa, but to push forward in these vast regions involved friction and perhaps even conflict with England. Thus once again colonial expansion brought a truce in the Franco-German conflict. The Kaiser renewed his attentions, and his telegram on the murder of President Carnot was particularly cordial. In 1894 France and Germany amicably arranged their frontiers in West Africa and combined to tear up a newly made Anglo-Congolese Treaty, while in the following year they co-operated with Russia in forcing Japan to disgorge Port Arthur.

In 1895 an invitation arrived from Berlin to send French

ships to the opening of the Kiel Canal. Several members of
the Cabinet desired to decline ; but when the Tsar formally
urged France to join Russia in attending the ceremony, she
consented on the understanding that the ceremony would be
given no political significance. This formula, needless to say,
failed to disarm the hostility of the extreme Nationalists. For
once the Kaiser's speeches were both tactful and eloquent.
" It is not only for our own national interests that we have
worked. We open the gates of the canal to the peaceful intercourse of the nations. I welcome the participation of the
Powers, whose representatives we see amongst us and whose
magnificent ships we have admired, with all the greater satisfaction because I think I am right in inferring from it the
complete appreciation of our endeavours, the very object of
which is to maintain peace." Despite his welcome to the
French ships, however, he never conquered his instinctive
dislike of France and the French Republic. " The Republicans
are revolutionists *de natura*," he wrote to the Tsar soon after
the Kiel festivities. " The blood of Their Majesties is still on
that country. Has it since then ever been happy or quiet
again ? Has it not staggered from bloodshed to bloodshed ?
Nicky, take my word on it, the curse of God has stricken that
people forever. We Christian Kings and Emperors have one
holy duty imposed on us by Heaven, that is to uphold the
principle of By the Grace of God. We can have good relations
with the French but can never be *intime* with her ! "

A few months after the Kiel festivities the Jameson raid
brought Great Britain and Germany to the verge of war.
On January 1, 1896, the German Foreign Secretary visited the
French Ambassador, and inquired whether France would join
in " limiting the insatiable appetite of England." He did not
propose co-operation in matters calculated to endanger peace,
such as the Near East, Egypt or the Mediterranean, and he
explained that there was no risk of an explosion ; but it was
" necessary to show England that she could no longer take
advantage of the Franco-German antagonism to seize whatever
she wished." Herbette coolly replied that the exclusion of
Egypt removed the principal reason which might induce
France to join. " I do not see what advantage such a league to
hold England in check would be to us if we cannot count on
your support in our interests." Undeterred by this rebuff, the
Kaiser despatched his fateful telegram to Kruger, but the
reaction of England was so menacing that he quickly changed

his course. A few weeks later, when France and Russia opposed the allocation of Egyptian money for the advance to Dongola, Germany supported the British request, and continued to flout French sentiment by encouraging the reconquest of the Sudan.

Though Germany took the British side in the Egyptian quarrel, attempts were made at intervals by the Wilhelmstrasse to draw closer to France. In June, 1898, the French Ambassador called Bülow's attention to *pourparlers* between England and Portugal concerning a lease of Delagoa Bay in return for financial aid, and to the danger of leaving London and Lisbon to settle their business without regard to the interests of France and Germany. On the following day the German Ambassador brought a remarkable Memorandum to the Quai d'Orsay suggesting not only economic reprisals against Portugal, but "practical co-operation between Germany and France in current questions of every kind." The Méline Government had just resigned, and Hanotaux explained that he could merely hand it to his successor. " I gathered from a long talk," reported Münster, " that personally he would be much inclined to co-operate with us in matters of common interest like this." To the Ambassador's surprise, the new Foreign Minister Delcassé made no reference to the subject. To ignore such a direct approach was an astonishing *début*, and his excuse that " no proposals were made to me " was unconvincing. " I greatly regret the departure of Hanotaux," wrote Münster. " My relations with him were of the best. Though he was bound to follow the course of Russian policy, he desired to entertain good relations with us and to improve them. The suspicion of this Minister that I noted in Berlin I find on closer acquaintance to be unfounded. On the other hand I fear that Delcassé will deserve our mistrust. I knew him as Colonial Minister and did not like him." The forecast was correct. Delcassé was the greatest of France's Foreign Ministers between 1871 and 1914, and, with the possible exception of Poincaré, the most inveterate foe of Germany. For a brief moment, enraged by the Fashoda surrender, his thoughts turned to Berlin. A rapprochement with Germany, he remarked to a German journalist, was extremely desirable : the *revanche* had lost ground in recent years, for the younger generation was not interested. " Il faut refaire la politique suivie depuis seize ans." It was only a passing mood and it did not recur. Delcassé never loved England, but he

D

knew in his heart that France could only afford one enemy.

It was natural that German statesmen should attempt to turn the Fashoda mood to their own account, for the bitter humiliation temporarily diverted part of the Nationalist fire to England, described by the *Echo de Paris* as the eternal enemy. What particularly rankled was Salisbury's refusal to grant or even to discuss compensation. The Kaiser, wrote the French Ambassador in February, 1899, was disposed to a rapprochement. The Naval Attaché at Berlin reported a conversation in which he expressed his pleasure at the reception of German ships in Algiers and Tunis, and added that a French ship would be very well received at a German port. " His Majesty is happy to see French public opinion better appreciating the real sentiments of Germany towards France, and he hopes that a real *entente* will soon be reached." The Continent, he added, must unite in self-defence especially against the dictation of England and America. A few days after the outbreak of the South African war Bülow spoke to the French Ambassador of the identity of their interests in different parts of the world. " In Africa you see that our interests are absolutely the same. Except the little triangle in regard to which we reached an arrangement with England last year, there is no point where we could not agree." Delcassé replied that Bülow's opinion deserved to be examined in concert with Russia ; " but I note that his conviction has never led the German Government to formulate any proposition." When the French Ambassador asked the German Foreign Minister if he could explain how he conceived the reciprocal interests, he replied that he must have time to reflect. A few days after this curious remark, which would have been more relevant if the invitation to discussion had come from Paris, the Kaiser journeyed to England for the first time since the Kruger telegram, and Chamberlain, after conversations with Bülow, argued in his historic speech at Leicester for an alliance or entente with Germany and the United States. Neither Berlin nor Washington welcomed the approach, and Bülow, caring more for Russian than for British friendship, ignored Chamberlain's advances and proclaimed his favourite doctrine of the free hand.

The Boer War was as heartily detested in France as in Germany, but Delcassé took a more detached view of the conflict than most of his countrymen. He had plans in his head which would require the friendship or at any rate the acquiescence of England, and he had no intention of steering his country into the German camp. The British reverses at the close of 1899 provoked schemes of European mediation, but they never had much substance. On February 28, 1900, Muravieff, the Russian Foreign Minister, visited Paris and informed Delcassé that the Russian Government wished to make the Wilhelmstrasse declare itself by asking whether it did not think the time has come for a joint *démarche* in London in the interests of peace. Delcassé accepted the idea on condition that the Russian Ambassador at Berlin spoke in the name of Russia and France ; and he added that, if representations were to be made to England, it was indispensable to success that Germany should take the initiative. When the Russian Ambassador approached the German Government the Kaiser suggested that Russia should first inquire how a friendly intervention would be received in London, and added that, as it would be a long business, the intervening Powers should first guarantee each other's European territories for a certain time. Even a temporary recognition of the Treaty of Frankfurt was unthinkable, and the plan of joint mediation fell to the ground.

William II continued his advances, though a genuine rapprochement was at all times beyond his grasp. Germany patronized the Exhibition of 1900. In April, 1901, the French Government accepted a pressing invitation to co-operate in the Bagdad railway, on condition that Russia was admitted to the enterprise ; but the consent of Russia, who regarded the railway as an economic and political danger, was withheld. The conception of a Continental *bloc*, consisting of Germany, Russia and France, continued to haunt the Kaiser's restless brain, and the outbreak of the Japanese war found Berlin and Paris in the same pro-Russian camp. What more natural, he argued, than that France should enter a league which would guard Russia's flank during the conflict, and defend Europe against the maritime and commercial domination of the Anglo-Saxons ? Thus the Treaty of Björkö, after being discussed in 1904, was signed by the Kaiser and the Tsar in July, 1905. The invitation to France to join was never officially made, since the treaty involved the mutual guarantee of frontiers. Even had a guarantee formed no part of the agreement, she would have declined to share in an association directed against England, with whom she had by this time made up her quarrel. The European landscape was rapidly changing, for France was winning friends and Germany was losing them.

V

The surrender of Fashoda led Delcassé to seek compensation in Morocco, and to gain from the friendship of England what he could not secure by thwarting her will. The *détente* began with King Edward's visit to Paris in the spring of 1903, and on April 8, 1904, the two countries sponged off the slate the main causes of friction. The attitude of official Germany towards the Anglo-French treaty was at first friendly. At Delcassé's reception on March 23, 1904, Prince Radolin asked if he might put " an indiscreet question." Was it true that an agreement had been or was about to be signed between France and England ? " Neither one nor the other," replied the Foreign Secretary ; " but we have been conversing for some time with the London Cabinet with a view to the friendly settlement of the questions which interest our two countries. An understanding has been recognized to be possible, and will probably be reached." " Newfoundland is said to be in question ? " " We have spoken of it." " And Morocco ? " " Also. But you know our point of view on that subject. We wish to maintain the political and territorial *status quo* ; but if it is to last it must be improved. We have had to reinforce and increase our troops at considerable expense. The Sultan has experienced the value of our aid. It must be continued ; but it will be given in such a way that every one will derive advantage, since security is essential for commerce. Needless to add, commercial liberty will be strictly respected." " And Spain ? " " We shall respect her interests and legitimate aspirations." Prince Radolin, added the Foreign Minister in recording the conversation, " found my declarations very natural and perfectly reasonable." On April 18, ten days after the treaties were signed, Delcassé instructed the French Ambassador to inform the Wilhelmstrasse that Lord Lansdowne and himself had been concerned exclusively with the interests of their countries, without detriment to those of any other Power. He did not think it necessary to present a copy of the treaty, since it was already known to all the world.

Official comment in Germany was favourable. Germany, Bülow had remarked in January, 1903, to the French Ambassador, had really no interests in Morocco, so insignificant were they at present. " German commercial interests in Morocco are in no danger now," wrote the *Norddeutsche Allgemeine Zeitung*, " and greater stability would benefit us all." " We have no cause to imagine that the Treaty has a point against any other Power," declared the Chancellor in the Reichstag on April 12, 1904. " It seems to be an attempt to remove a number of differences by peaceful methods. We have nothing, from the standpoint of German interests, to object to in that. As to Morocco, we are in essence only interested in the economic sphere. It is therefore of importance for us that tranquillity and order exist there. We have commercial interests, which we must and shall protect. We have, however, no ground to fear that they will be overlooked or infringed." The Pan-Germans, grumbling that Germany had been humiliated, demanded the Atlantic coast, but the Kaiser informed King Edward at the Kiel regatta that Morocco had never interested him.

Despite these reassuring words Germany felt that her interests had been contemptuously ignored. Morocco, wrote Holstein, was one of the few countries where German commerce could compete on equal terms. Railway and other schemes were afoot, and the French system of virtual monopoly would be fatal to its hopes. Even more disastrous would be the loss of prestige if the Government looked on with folded arms while national interests were given away. " If we let ourselves be trampled on in Morocco, we invite similar treatment elsewhere." With this reasoning Bülow fully agreed. He had a good legal case and he was determined that it should prevail : the only question was the time and method of putting it forward. Visiting the Wilhelmstrasse on April 26 to express satisfaction at the Chancellor's speech on April 12, the French Ambassador was struck by the glacial attitude of the Foreign Minister. " More and more," he telegraphed to Delcassé, " I believe that Bülow's declarations dissemble his profound dissatisfaction." He had guessed right. Action in Morocco, wrote the Chancellor to his Ambassador at Paris on July 21, involved far-reaching consequences and required careful thought. It was improbable that England would take her obligations of diplomatic support very seriously. France had paid England a good price and completely ignored Germany, whose commercial activities in Morocco had increased so rapidly that it was vital to prevent a monopoly. How ought they to proceed ? They could provoke an offer of compensation by action in Morocco and by stiffening the Sultan's back, replied Radolin, so long as England left them a free hand. Anglo-French opposition on the other hand could compel

them to retreat. The German Ambassador in London, after
an interview with Lansdowne in August, reported that where
treaty rights existed Germany could safely take a strong line ;
but control of a harbour on the Atlantic would probably be
opposed, and a political challenge to France would range
England on her side. Metternich's interpretations of British
policy, though often ignored, were invariably correct.

The Franco-Spanish declaration of October 3, which
accompanied the secret Franco-Spanish treaty, provoked no
official protest but aroused the same angry suspicion at Berlin
as at Fez. It was in vain that Delcassé explained that the new
pact, in securing the adhesion of Madrid to the principle of
commercial liberty, had strengthened the guarantees of international commerce in Morocco. At the same time the victories
of Japan over Russia were visibly sapping the power and
prestige of the Dual Alliance. When Kühlmann took over the
Legation at Tangier as Chargé d'Affaires in October, 1904, the
temperature fell rapidly. The grievances of the German
Colonial Party, he declared, were receiving more attention
in the highest quarters, and the Chancellor was being re-
proached for not securing the commercial advantages obtained
by England and Spain. Taillandier, the French Minister, was
uncertain how far these sentiments were those of the German
Government, but they were ominous enough as the first
indication by a German diplomatist of a coming challenge to
the ambitions of France.

The despatch of a French envoy to Fez at the end of 1904
with a comprehensive programme of reforms was the signal
for a change of front at Berlin. On February 11, 1905, the
French Chargé at Tangier reported an ominous conversation
with his German colleague. "After the Anglo-French
arrangement," observed Kühlmann, " we supposed the French
Government was waiting for the Franco-Spanish agreement
before putting us in possession of the new situation ; but now
that everything is settled we see that we have been systematically kept aloof. The Chancellor tells me that the German
Government was ignorant of all the agreements concerning
Morocco, and does not acknowledge himself to be bound by
them in any way." Delcassé instructed the French Ambassador at Berlin to complain of this language, and to remind the
Government that he had answered Prince Radolin's inquiries
on March 23, 1904 ; that, except Russia, Germany alone was
informed of the Anglo-French treaty before it was signed ;

that no request for explanations had been made ; and that
Berlin had also been informed of the Franco-Spanish treaty
before it was published in September, 1904. The Under-
Secretary, who received the complaint, replied that he knew
nothing of Kühlmann's declarations, but added that Germany
was not bound by the Anglo-French or Franco-Spanish agreements.

After the despatch of the French mission to Fez, Holstein
suggested that William II should visit Tangier. Bülow
approved the plan, and the ruler reluctantly accepted their
advice. The *Norddeutsche Allgemeine Zeitung* proclaimed that
the French negotiations at Fez did not square with the avowed
policy of maintaining the status quo in Morocco. " It is useless
to attribute to the Tangier visit any selfish purposes against
its integrity or independence," declared the Chancellor in the
Reichstag on March 29, 1905. " No one who does not pursue
an aggressive goal can find cause for apprehension. We have
economic interests, and in Morocco, as in China, it is our
interest to keep the open door." Two days later the Kaiser
landed at Tangier and addressed the German colony. " The
Empire has great and growing interests in Morocco. Commerce can only progress if all the Powers are considered to
have equal rights under the sovereignty of the Sultan and
respect the independence of the country. My visit is the
recognition of this independence." The theme was developed
in a speech to the representative of the Sultan. " It is to the
Sultan in his capacity of independent sovereign that I pay my
visit to-day. I hope that under his sovereignty a free Morocco
will remain open to the peaceful competition of all nations,
without monopoly or annexation, on a basis of absolute
equality." France was not mentioned, but these words were
intended for her ears. The Wilhelmstrasse took advantage of
the opportune collapse of Russia on the Manchurian battle-
fields to menace her ally, but this was not the main ground for
its action. A protest would have been made in any case. Since
the French press had begun to speak of making Morocco a
second Tunis, Germany was convinced that, if she did not call
a halt, the country would be swallowed up before her eyes.
She had now to think not only of her commerce but of her
prestige.

The charge against Delcassé of slighting Germany by not
officially communicating the treaty of April 8, 1904, to the
German Government is trivial enough, but to a graver

indictment there is no reply. His fundamental error was in not purchasing Germany's assent to French aims in Morocco. The good will of Italy had been bought by recognition of her claim to Tripoli, that of England by assent to her position in Egypt, that of Spain by the hypothetical reversion of the Mediterranean coast. It has been argued that since Germany was not a Mediterranean Power there was no obligation to consult her. Yet she possessed treaty rights under the Madrid Convention of 1880 and under a separate commercial pact with Fez ; her trade was rapidly increasing and her readiness to take offence was notorious. It was not only socialist critics like Jaurès who pointed out the dangers of his policy. " By incredible blindness," wrote René Millet, an ex-Governor of Tunis, " the Government took precautions with everybody except the only one of its neighbours whom it had serious cause to fear."

Despite the provocation to which it was a reply, the Tangier demonstration proved a blunder, for the limited obligation of diplomatic support involved in the Anglo-French treaty of 1904 was transformed, in fact though not in name, into a general understanding. Germany was no less excited than France, and the Kaiser delivered a series of ominous speeches on the western frontier. " I hope peace will not be broken," he declared at Karlsruhe on April 27. " I hope the events now in progress will keep the attention of our nation awake and strengthen its courage. I hope we shall find ourselves united if it becomes necessary to intervene in world politics." Similar warnings were uttered elsewhere in the Rhineland. For the first time since 1891 the German sword began to rattle loudly in its scabbard.

On April 11 Bülow, in a circular despatch, defined and defended his new policy. The Morocco treaty, he complained, was never communicated to the German Government. Yet Germany had not moved, since the treaty recognized the status quo, and he therefore assumed that France would consult the Powers if she aimed at changes limiting their rights. " It was necessary to act when the Sultan asked us if France was in truth the mandatory of the Powers, when we learned of parts of the programme, and when great papers pointed to Tunis as a model." A conference, he concluded, was the best solution, since Germany sought no privileges by separate agreement, and her interests were identical with those of other Powers. Meanwhile a German envoy had been despatched to

Fez. A few days after his arrival in the Moorish capital the Sultan rejected the French reform proposals, and invited the signatories of the Treaty of 1880 to a conference at Tangier.

The invitation required an immediate reply, and Delcassé urged that it should be declined. The Foreign Minister had reigned at the Quai d'Orsay for seven years, and had been allowed a free hand in foreign affairs while the Dreyfus case was being liquidated and while Waldeck-Rousseau and Combes were wrestling with the Church. The Tangier demonstration, however, had at last compelled Ministers to lift their eyes from domestic controversies, and Rouvier, the Premier, held very definite ideas as to Franco-German relations. A disciple of Gambetta and an expert in international finance, he had no mind to allow France to be dragged into a hopeless struggle over Morocco. Delcassé, it was clear, would have to resign. The air was thick with rumours of an ultimatum. At the decisive Cabinet, held on June 6, Delcassé argued that France could not go to a Conference without humiliation, that Germany was bluffing, and that he had just received the offer of an alliance from Great Britain. Rouvier, who took the German threats very seriously, replied that the Conference must be accepted. He was supported by all his colleagues, and the Foreign Minister, after warning them that their pusillanimity would encourage German insolence, withdrew and resigned. Rouvier's decision was inevitable, for the Ministers of Defence testified that France was totally unprepared for war, and the British offer of armed support was a legend. It is an axiom of statesmanship that diplomacy should never outpace military preparations.[1]

On the fall of Delcassé Rouvier took over the Foreign Office, and explained to the German Government that he could only consent to a Conference if a preliminary understanding on reforms were reached. " If our proposals are accepted, all the Powers will benefit. We think a Conference dangerous without previous agreement and useless with it. But we do not definitely decline." It would indeed have been dangerous to do so, as the French Ambassador in Berlin suggested after an alarming conversation with the Chancellor. " He was very courteous, but he explained the necessity not to let this *question mauvaise, très mauvaise*, drag on, and not to linger on a road *bordé de précipices et même d'abîmes*. His insistence on an

[1] A detailed account of this dramatic Cabinet meeting by Chaumié, the Minister of Public Instruction, is printed in D.D.F., Deuxième Série, VI, 601–4.

immediate decision struck me deeply and should influence your decision. He added, however, that, if France accepted the Conference, German diplomacy would adopt an attitude which would satisfy us."

In part owing to the tactful mediation of President Roosevelt, to whom the Kaiser had appealed, Rouvier and the German Ambassador exchanged a Declaration on July 8 defining the conditions on which France accepted the Conference, and formally declaring that Germany did not contest the Anglo-French agreement of 1904. A more detailed programme was drawn up on September 28. The Conference was to be held at Algeciras, and both the French and German envoys were to leave Fez. At the end of the year Rouvier informed the Chamber of the agreement, adding that he looked forward with confidence to the meeting. At the same moment the Chancellor in the Reichstag defined his Moroccan policy as the preservation of economic equality in an independent state. Germany, he added, had a legal right to be consulted in any change in Morocco. "The charge that we desire to attack France or to compel her to side with us against England is nonsense. I take full responsibility for the journey to Tangier, which Bebel calls the journey of provocation, but which was useful in bringing to general knowledge the international character of the question. *Cet animal est très méchant ; quand on l'attaque il se défend.*" The situation seemed a little easier, but even Rouvier was now full of apprehensions. The closer intimacy between Paris and London, dating from the Tangier demonstration, received a fresh extension in January 1906 by the opening of authorized discussions between French and British military experts on the initiative of France, which, though they did not commit the Governments, pointed to the probability of co-operation in the event of a Franco-German war.

Despite the preliminary agreements the Conference of Algeciras, which opened on January 16, 1906, was a prolonged battle between France and Germany, who received support from Austria alone. Italy, bound to France by secret treaties, gave her ally no aid. The main struggle arose on the control of the police in the ports. After a rupture had seemed in sight Germany, against the advice of Holstein, who was willing to play for the highest stakes, reluctantly accepted a Franco-Spanish mandate under a Swiss Inspector-General. On the other hand Bülow established his contention that Morocco was the concern of all the Powers and that Germany must not be ignored. Rouvier's Cabinet had fallen while the Conference was in session ; but Bourgeois, who followed him at the Quai d'Orsay, declared to the Chamber that the special rights and interests of France had been preserved. The Chancellor expressed no less gratification. Germany, he explained, had not desired to go to war on account of Morocco, where she had no direct political interests and no political aspirations ; but to prevent her treaty rights being disposed of without her consent was a question of prestige. His country-men, however—and not the Pan-Germans alone—failed to share his apparent satisfaction. He had had a good hand, but he played it badly. He had recalled France from her absorption in domestic controversy to the unchanging realities of the Franco-German quarrel, and had revived French patriotic sentiment. The most enduring result of the crisis was to tighten the bonds between England and France, to break down the barriers which separated England and Russia, and thereby to prepare the ground for the Triple Entente. Though Del-cassé had gone and Bulow became a Prince, the balance of power was tilted against Berlin.

VI

It became the fashion after the first Morocco crisis to speak of *la nouvelle France*, and there can be no doubt that the nation emerged from the ordeal with a heightened self-confidence. " Tangier," wrote the Abbé Ernest Dimnet in *France Herself Again*, " was a flash of lightning, after which the clouds lifted. What has been called the regeneration or even the resurrection of France dated from that shock. Garrison towns like Toul, Lunéville, Verdun, and the lonely forts in their vicinity, the very names of which used to sound disagreeably in the ears of the recruits, became in great demand. The yearly manoeuvres, which reservists had formerly been glad to shirk, were ac-cepted as treats." The moral support of Great Britain through-out the crisis strengthened the position of France as a Great Power. " Henceforth," testifies Poincaré, " we remained at least as closely united with her as with Russia. For several years the two Governments consulted one another day by day and hour by hour." There was not a Premier or a Foreign Minister in the years immediately following the fall of Delcassé who thirsted for adventure, yet there were elements in France to which the watchful waiting of official circles was pain and humiliation. The Nationalists damaged their cause at the time of the Dreyfus controversy by joining the enemies of the Republican régime, and in 1900 Déroulède was sentenced to ten years banishment. He was allowed to return in the autumn of 1905, and the Ligue des Patriotes henceforth confined its energies to keeping alive the ideals of the *revanche*.

Militant Nationalism received a powerful impetus from Charles Maurras, an original member of the *Action Française* founded in 1898 and its guiding spirit for the rest of his life. At first the only prominent Royalist in the movement, he quickly transformed it into a spear-head of the new Royalism which he defined in the most famous of his books, *L'Enquête sur la Monarchie*. His domestic programme, which included the overthrow of Parliamentary Government by a *coup d'état*, the establishment of a strong executive in the hands of a King, provincial decentralization, and a campaign against Jews, Protestants and Freemasons, was reinforced by a foaming chauvinism. The Third Republic, he complained in his scathing work *Kiel et Tangier*, was as flabby in foreign policy as it was weak and divided at home. The *revanche* was preached in strident tones in the columns of *L'Action française* founded in 1908 and sold in the streets by the younger members of the party who called themselves Camelots du Roi. Léon Daudet, a master of invective, joined Maurras in 1904, and Jacques Bainville, though not a royalist, linked the movement to the wider world of bellicose nationalism. The Royalist cause made little progress, but the *Action Française* movement ranks among the influences which braced the French people for the struggle of 1914.[1]

The poignant emotions of 1871 were revived by two famous French authors. The immense popularity of René Bazin's novel, *Les Oberlé*, published in 1901 and subsequently dramatized, revealed the undying interest in the fate of the lost provinces. The tragic cleavage of conviction is mirrored in the fortunes of a single family living under the same roof. The grandfather, paralysed and speechless, but with the fires still burning hot within him, broods grimly over the scene like a figure in a Greek play. The son, to whom the family business has been transferred, is guided exclusively by his interests and has made his peace with the new régime. His

[1] The best account of the *Action Française* movement is by R. E. Balfour, *Cambridge Historical Journal*, III, 182-205.

daughter follows him willingly and his wife unwillingly; but his son, Jean Oberlé, the hero of the tale, though he has been educated in Berlin and Munich and has never set foot in France, discovers on reaching manhood that, though he feels no hatred for Germans, his heart is French. He returns home to find the atmosphere poisoned by the feud. His desire to marry into a family of French sympathies is shipwrecked on the refusal of the parents to accept the son of a man who, in their belief, has been disloyal to France. After a few weeks of torment in his distracted home, where scenes are frequent and conversation impossible, Jean resolves to make his career in the fair country which he has never seen. The story ends with his desertion from Strassburg on the second day of his military service and a bold dash for the frontier, which he crosses with a bullet in his shoulder. His flight breaks off the engagement of his sister to a German officer, who declines to marry into the family of a deserter. Less tragic in character but no less popular were the novels in which Maurice Barrès, a Lorrainer and an ex-Boulangist, depicts the cruel conflict of hearts and minds. *Au Service de l'Allemagne* describes the experience of Paul Ehrmann, a medical student at Strassburg, who, though French at heart, believes it his duty to remain in Alsace and hopes during his military service to make his comrades feel the moral superiority of France. *Colette Baudoche* portrays a girl in Metz who is asked in marriage, and asked in vain, by a German soldier whom she would gladly accept but for the impalpable barrier. The German cause could boast of no champions to counterwork the emotional appeal of Bazin and Barrès.

In the lost provinces time had wrought certain changes, but none of a fundamental character. The so-called Dictatorship clause giving the Statthalter power to suspend constitutional rights and forbid publications was abolished in 1905. It had been rarely used but its removal encouraged the irreconcilable antagonists of the Reich, and athletic societies enlisted the Francophil enthusiasm of the young. The rapid development of industry increased the ties of material interest with Germany, while the growth of socialism in the towns introduced a new line of cleavage. Moreover the breach between the French Republic and the Vatican diminished the desire of Catholics to escape from the German frying-pan into the anti-clerical fire. The old electoral struggle between the Autonomists and the *Protestataires* was in a large measure replaced by the rivalry

of Social Democracy and the Centrum. In 1911 the situation
was superficially eased by the granting of the status of a federal
unit, with manhood suffrage for the Lower Chamber ; but no
concessions made any real difference in local sentiment or
Franco-German relations. The Zabern incident, provoked by
an insulting word of a young Lieutenant, who also struck a
lame shoemaker with his sword, showed that the atmosphere
was ,electric and that Germany was still in the grip of the
military machine. Bethmann confesses regretfully in his
apologia that the Reichsland was regarded primarily as a military *glacis*. Forty years of German rule had brought material
prosperity, but neither liberty nor contentment. The pictures
of Zislin and " Hansi " were received with delight, and the
unchanging demands of the intransigents were voiced by
Abbé Wetterle in the Reichstag. Where France had succeeded in winning and keeping the sympathies of the inhabitants, Germany conspicuously failed.

A further obstacle to Franco-German reconciliation was the
Foreign Legion, in which men of different races who had made
shipwreck of their lives sought oblivion or rehabilitation. To
the new Germany, bursting with pride in her unity and
strength, it was maddening that any of her sons should choose
to enter the service of France, even under the pitiless African
sun ; and it was universally believed that some of the rene-
gades were seduced by French propaganda. The number of
Germans serving at any moment was small, but its mere
existence was a perpetual irritant. It was a favourite theme of
Pan-German agitators, and a special League of Defence
against the Foreign Legion was founded at Munich.

VII

France did not allow the Act of Algeciras to thwart her far-
reaching designs in Morocco. In 1907, in consequence of
local disturbances, she occupied Ujda on the Algerian frontier
and Casablanca on the Atlantic coast. From 1906 to 1909,
however, the rudder was in the hands of Clemenceau, whose
dislike for colonial adventures was undiminished. In January,
1908, Jules Cambon, the Ambassador at Berlin, reported that
the German Foreign Minister desired to discuss an economic
understanding. In March the latter informed the Reichstag
that Franco-German relations were normal and even friendly,
and that Germany fully recognized the loyalty of France to the

Act of Algeciras. These advances, however, were rudely interrupted by an incident which, like the Schnaebele crisis twenty years earlier, for some weeks threatened the peace of the world. Some German residents in Casablanca, aided by their Consul, had established an agency for organizing desertions from the Foreign Legion, and in September, 1908, it persuaded two Germans, a German naturalized as a French citizen, a Russian, a Swiss and an Austrian to desert. The Consul provided them with civilian clothing, hid them for some days, and resolved to embark them in a German steamer lying off the port. Early in the morning of September 25 they were accompanied to the harbour by a member of the Consulate, but their boat capsized and they were forced to return. The Commandant of the harbour noticed them and gave orders for their arrest. A brief struggle ensued, and the German Consul vainly demanded the liberation of the three Germans.

Baron von der Lancken, Secretary to the German Embassy, appeared at the Quai d'Orsay and demanded " prompt and complete satisfaction." Pichon, the Foreign Minister, replied by demanding that the German Consul should be disavowed and censured. Neither side wished to fight, but the temperature rose rapidly. After a fortnight Germany proposed arbitration, which Pichon accepted. The Wilhelmstrasse, however, demanded the punishment of the port authorities at Casablanca and the release of the three German deserters, after which the German Consul would be punished. When Pichon rejoined that the matter was now referred to arbitration, the Ambassador again demanded the immediate liberation of the three Germans who had been injured in the scrimmage, and the Chancellor threatened to break off diplomatic relations. Pichon stood firm, and replied that he must await the arbitral award. The Chancellor now asked for an apology for the arrest of the deserters before the arbitration began. At this critical moment encouragements to stand fast arrived from London and St. Petersburg, and Francis Joseph persuaded the Kaiser to settle the question amicably, since the Bosnian crisis had begun. The storm subsided as suddenly as it had arisen. A declaration was signed by the two Governments regretting the events at Casablanca and referring questions of fact as well as of law to arbitration. The verdict of the Hague Tribunal, given some months later, censured " the grave and manifest fault " of the German Consulate in aiding the escape of the non-German legionaries, and added that the French authorities had acted correctly, except that needless violence had been displayed in the arrest of the deserters.

Though the two nations had once again looked war in the face, the discussion of an economic partnership in Morocco was quickly resumed. By the agreement of February 8, 1909, Germany recognized the special political interests of France and promised not to oppose them, while France undertook not to thwart German commercial and industrial interests. Both were to " seek to associate their nationals in the business which they may be able to secure." On the same day letters were exchanged between Jules Cambon and Schoen, the Foreign Minister, declaring that the political *désir-téressement* of Germany did not affect the positions already held by her nationals, but implying that they would not compete for posts in the public services of a political character, and that when their interests were associated it would be recognized that those of France were the most important. The agreement appeared to embody a profound modification of Franco-German relations. Pichon declared that it removed all causes of conflict in Morocco. Prince Radolin, the German Ambassador, observed that a lasting *entente* had been secured, and the Chancellor explained to the Reichstag that it assured France her legitimate political influence without allowing her to appropriate the country.

The pact of 1909 which raised such high hopes was fated to be an apple of discord, for the good-will of the Governments was paralysed by the rivalry of the business men. The spoils to be divided consisted of mines, public works and railways, and in all three so many difficulties arose that at the opening of 1911 no progress had been made. The question of railways was complicated by the French claim to exclude strategic lines from the *condominium* ; but an agreement was within sight when in March, 1911, a change of Ministry removed Pichon, the author of the pact, from the Quai d'Orsay. His place was taken by the inexperienced Cruppi, who was persuaded to re-open the question. " It would be very inconvenient if we do not sign," telegraphed Jules Cambon from Berlin ; " if we make Germany think that we want to circumvent the Convention of 1909, it would create many difficulties." Despite this sensible advice Cruppi refused to sign without further reflection. The unfavourable impression created at Berlin was deepened by the simultaneous refusal of the French Government to sanction a *consortium* arranged between French capital-

ists in the French Congo and German capitalists in the
Cameroons.

The decision of the Monis Cabinet to reconsider the railway
agreement synchronized with rumours of a forward policy in
Morocco, where civil war, tribal revolts and an empty exchequer had reduced the country to anarchy. Every one knew
that the Sultan was incapable of keeping order. On March 13,
1911, Kiderlen-Wächter, who succeeded Schoen as Foreign
Minister in 1910, uttered a warning to Jules Cambon. " German opinion might be excited, and it would be wise if Germany
were informed in good time. By small successive operations
France might be led on to an even more extended operation,
which would end by annulling the Act of Algeciras." The
Ambassador replied that French plans were not fixed, but that
the Act of Algeciras would be respected. On April 4 he
intimated that France would probably be forced to occupy
Rabat, and Kiderlen replied that he was apprehensive of the
effect of the news on German opinion. On April 19 Cruppi
informed Berlin that in view of the danger to Europeans
France had responded to the Sultan's appeal for aid by organizing a force for the relief of Fez, which was surrounded by
rebels, and that a French column would be available if required
to succour the capital. Bethmann now added his warnings to
those of Kiderlen. Germany, he declared, had no reason to
believe that the Europeans in Fez were in danger, though
foreign military operations might provoke it. " You know
German opinion on Morocco, and I must take it into account.
If you go to Fez, you will stay there, and then the whole
Moroccan question will be raised, which I wish at all costs to
avoid. I do not say No, because I cannot assume responsibility
for your compatriots, but I cannot encourage you. I can only
counsel prudence." " The Chancellor," reported Jules
Cambon, " does not seek adventures in Morocco and only
wishes to maintain Germany's economic interests ; not so the
Pan-Germans. We must try to solve the problem without
putting ourselves too much forward. I deplore the articles in
our press on the Tunisification of Morocco, which are brought
up against our official declarations."

William II was always a moderate in regard to Morocco.
He had shrunk from war in 1905-6, and in 1911 he was much
less disturbed by French schemes than his advisers. " It will
suit us quite well," he telegraphed from Corfu, " if the French
get tied up in Morocco with troops and money, and I think it

E

is not in our interests to prevent it. If they break the Algeciras Act we can first leave it to the other Powers, above all Spain, to protest." If the public demanded the despatch of warships the Chancellor was to damp down the cry. These phrases might have been used by Bismarck. The ruler's influence in the shaping of foreign policy, however, was at all times limited, and on this occasion events moved so quickly that his cautious counsels fell on deaf ears. At the end of April Jules Cambon told Kiderlen that bad news had arrived from Fez, and that France must take measures to rescue French and other European residents. This was no breach of the Algeciras Act, he argued. There was no intention of occupying the capital or infringing the sovereignty of the Sultan. Kiderlen rejoined that he had full confidence in the sincerity of the French Government, but events sometimes produced unintended results. If French troops remained in Fez, so that the Sultan only ruled with the aid of French bayonets, Germany would regard the Act as finished and would resume complete liberty of action. He followed up his warning to France with a memorandum which secured the Kaiser's assent. "The occupation of Fez would prepare the way for the swallowing of Morocco by France. We should obtain nothing by protests, and should suffer a moral defeat which it would be hard to bear. . . . If they establish themselves in Fez out of anxiety for their nationals, we too have a right to defend our own. We have large German firms in Mogador and Agadir. German ships could go to these ports for the protection of these firms." Here was the new course—to take pledges and await a French offer. The German press began to peg out counter-claims, and even the *Berliner Tageblatt* clamoured for a port at Agadir. On May 1 the *Norddeutsche Allgemeine Zeitung* announced that a violation of the Act of Algeciras, voluntary or otherwise, would restore to all its signatories their liberty of action.

Despite these reiterated warnings a French force entered Fez on May 21 and rescued the Sultan from danger. The German view that a new situation had been created was shared by Spain, who proceeded to occupy the northern zone assigned to her by the secret treaty of 1904. Cruppi vainly attempted to reopen the railway negotiations at Berlin, and on June 11 Jules Cambon administered some soothing syrup. France, he declared, had no desire to infringe the Algeciras Act, and she intended to recall her troops from the capital as

soon as possible. " I am still very anxious about Morocco,"
rejoined the Chancellor. " German opinion is on the alert.
French influence is growing, whether she wishes it or not. If
you leave Fez, you will be compelled to return within a year.
In Germany people will say that German interests are being
neglected, and I see the possibility of extremely grave difficulties." " Possibly," replied the Ambassador, " but nobody
can prevent Morocco falling one day under our influence.
Why should we not discuss all outstanding matters except
Alsace-Lorraine ? We could try to give German opinion satisfactions which would allow it to watch our influence in
Morocco develop without disquiet." " I will think it over,"
rejoined the Chancellor ; " but go and see Kiderlen at Kissingen." Jules Cambon took his advice.

On June 22 some plain speaking took place. The situation,
began the Foreign Secretary, had been completely transformed,
with forces under French officers throughout the country and a
Sultan at the orders of France. " Have you forgotten the
compact of 1909," retorted the Ambassador, " which recognizes
French political influence ? " " Influence is not Protectorate,"
rejoined Kiderlen, " and you are on the road to organize a
veritable Protectorate." Cambon observed that it was not easy
in dealing with a barbarous country to fix how far influence
could go, and proposed a general discussion like that between
France and England in 1903. " I agree," was the reply; " if we
confine ourselves to Morocco we shall not succeed. It is
useless to plaster over a tottering structure." The Ambassador
explained that French opinion would not allow Germany any
part of Morocco, but " one could look elsewhere." " Yes,"
replied Kiderlen, " but you must tell us what you want. Bring
us back something from Paris." Cambon travelled straight
home, where he reported the conversation to Cruppi. The
same evening the Monis Cabinet fell.

Till this moment the policy of Germany had been irreproachable. She possessed treaty rights and commercial
interests in Morocco. Warnings conveyed in courteous terms
had produced no effect. Kiderlen, like Holstein before him,
was prepared to take risks. As long ago as April " the Swabian
Bismarck," as his admirers called him, told his friend Weizsäcker, the Premier of Württemberg, that he was meditating
the occupation of Agadir. The action of Spain indicated that
the hour had struck. A Foreign Office memorandum drafted
on May 30 argued that north Morocco would soon be French,

that military domination would involve commercial privilege, and that French public opinion would veto a serious offer. A Sultan who could only rule with foreign help was not the sovereign ruler envisaged by the Algeciras Act. Germany should resume full liberty of action, and follow up her declaration by sending cruisers to Mogador and Agadir. France would then offer compensation, and no storm was likely to arise. If she took it quietly, England would not make difficulties, and she might be told that Germany was ready for a deal if compensation in the French Congo were offered. The Chancellor accepted the plan, the Kaiser's assent was secured, and the *Panther* was ordered to Agadir.

Before the French Cabinet had time to consider Cambon's report on the Kissingen conversations the German Ambassador informed the Quai d'Orsay on July 1 that a gunboat had been sent to Agadir to defend German nationals and interests in that region. The *Panther's* spring, like the Tangier speech, ruined a sound legal case. Both countries, curiously enough, had repeated their mistakes of 1905. France pushed forward in Morocco without buying off German hostility, and Germany replied by banging her fist on the table. On July 9 Jules Cambon and Kiderlen began the conversations which were to continue for four months. Germany, it was understood, would give France a free hand in Morocco in return for compensation in the Congo. When, however, the Foreign Minister suggested the cession of the French Congo, the French Government was alarmed, and Mr. Lloyd George intervened with the strident Mansion House threat. Kiderlen modified his demands, but he continued to ask more than France would consent to give. He had no desire for war, but he was not in the least afraid of playing with fire. " He who announces in advance that he will not fight can achieve nothing in politics," he remarked, and he had a stronger will than either the Kaiser or Bethmann. Early in September a financial panic on the Berlin *Bourse* revealed the acute tension. Despite Germany's superior military strength the Morocco-Congo treaties signed on November 4 were a triumph for France, who rounded off her African Empire at the price of an unhealthy slice of the tropics. The French case had been conducted by Caillaux and Jules Cambon with conspicuous firmness and skill. The German Colonial Minister, who had been overruled, resigned in disgust. The Chancellor's statements that the *Panther* was not sent to acquire territory and that South Morocco was not a desirable possession for Germany were greeted with derisive laughter in the Reichstag. Kiderlen's threats of war and the outbursts in the Pan-German press added to the store of ill-will that had been accumulating in France for forty years. In Germany, on the other hand, the wrath of the people was directed far more against Great Britain for what was considered her needless intervention than against France for the stubborn defence of her acknowledged interests.

VIII

The Agadir crisis was followed in England by a slight Anglo-German rapprochement, inaugurated by Haldane's mission to Berlin, and in France by the accession to power of Poincaré with a strong team. The personality of the new Premier made a deep impression on Iswolsky, the Russian Ambassador, whose despatches vividly portray the revival of self-confidence in governing circles in France. During the twelve months of his premiership the bonds between the members of the Triple Entente were further tightened in view of the European war which few experienced statesmen expected to avoid. A Franco-Russian Naval Convention was signed, the French fleet was transferred to the Mediterranean in friendly agreement with England, and the Grey-Cambon letters defined the relations between London and Paris. When an agent of the German Foreign Office visited Paris in March, 1912, with the offer of " wide autonomy in Alsace-Lorraine " in his pocket, he found no response in the official world. " The German Government," commented Poincaré, " seems to pursue with unwearying persistence a rapprochement which only a complete repudiation of the past would render possible. To listen to such propositions would be to quarrel with England and Russia and to lose the benefit of the policy which France has pursued for years. We should only obtain illusory satisfactions for Alsace, and we should find ourselves next day isolated." Bethmann declares in his Memoirs that after the coming of Poincaré to power the French Ambassador in Berlin was a different man. He remained as courteous as ever, but the improvement of relations was no longer the theme of his conversation. The polite telegrams to the Kaiser which Poincaré quotes as evidence of the correctness of his attitude did not disguise the fact that the two nations had at no time since 1871 been further apart; and France no longer stood alone.

The Balkan wars of 1912–1913 once more led Europe to the brink of the abyss. Though neither French nor German interests were directly involved, their respective allies were ready to fly at each other's throats, and the ten months of conflict left a gnawing *malaise*. The German army, already slightly augmented in 1912 in consequence of the Morocco crisis, received in 1913 an increase of 170,000 men, the largest ever known ; while a capital levy of fifty millions was imposed to bring fortifications and artillery up to date. In introducing the Army Bill the Chancellor justified his demands by the displacement of power resulting from the Balkan wars, pointed to the growing menace of Pan-Slavism and French chauvinism, and spoke ominously of a conflict between the Teuton and the Slav. The Bill passed without opposition, for Germany was convinced that her safety could only be guaranteed by the strength of her right arm. Austria was weakened by racial dissension, Italy an uncertain ally, Turkey defeated, Roumania drifting towards St. Petersburg, while the enmity of France was unchanged, the hostility of Russia increasing, and the loyalty of Great Britain to her new friends beyond reproach.

If Germany was aware of her peril, she was also arrogantly conscious of her strength. Russia, it was widely believed, was rotten to the core, France decadent, England occupied with sport. In the middle of the 'nineties Bebel described his fellow-countrymen as still drunk with victory. Public opinion had grown ever more restless and excitable, and loudly insisted on Germany having her place in the sun. The centenary of 1813 raised the national temperature, though the *Festspiel* of Gerhart Hauptmann disappointed the more fiery patriots. "The Kaiser is profoundly pacific," wrote the Belgian Minister from Berlin on March 8, 1913, "but the spirit of the governing classes is very different." Though the Social Democrats emerged from the elections of 1912 the most powerful party in the Reichstag, the ferment among the middle and upper classes struck all observers. Otfried Nippold, returning after several years in the Far East, was shocked by the change, and in his *German Chauvinism*, published in 1913, courageously held the mirror up to his fellow-countrymen. Bernhardi's *Germany and the Next War* proclaimed, like Treitschke during the Bismarckian era, that war was part of the divine order. The Pan-German League, small in numbers but skilful in propaganda and insatiable in its demands, had been reinforced by the Deutscher Wehrverein, founded in 1912 by General Keim, who declared that a war was inevitable. The unwearying activities of Tirpitz and the Navy League found an eager response. "There is a smell of blood in the air," echoed General Liebert. The political Generals had become a national peril, but some of the journalists and professors were nearly as bad.[1] The peace-loving Bethmann regretfully confesses that Germany got on the nerves of the world.

The European situation was reviewed at this moment in calm but grave tones in Prince Bülow's *Imperial Germany*. "The resentment against Germany might well be called the soul of French policy. The other international questions are more of a material nature and only concern the body. It is a peculiarity of the French nation that they place spiritual above material needs. The intransigence of France is a fact that we must reckon with in our political calculations. It seems to me weakness to entertain the hope of a real and sincere reconciliation with France so long as we have no intention of giving up Alsace-Lorraine, and there is no such intention in Germany. So long as France thinks she perceives a possibility of winning back the provinces, either by her own unaided efforts or with the help of others, she will consider the existing arrangement provisional and not final. The aim of French policy for many years to come will be to create the necessary conditions, which are lacking to-day, for a settlement with Germany with good prospect of success. It is a proof of a lively sense of honour if a nation suffers so keenly from a simple injury to its pride that the desire for retribution becomes the ruling passion of the people."

Friends and observers began to detect a change in the Kaiser himself. "He spoke with a note which was new to me," reported Bishop Boyd Carpenter after a visit to Berlin in June, 1913; "I felt that he was under the influence of a great fear." "From the beginning of 1913," testifies Bethmann, "he spoke to me of the coalition which was forming against us and would fall upon us." His anxiety was revealed to King Albert at Potsdam in November, 1913. "Enmity against us is increasing," wrote the French Ambassador after the Belgian visit, "and the Emperor has ceased to be the friend of peace. His personal influence has been exerted on many critical occasions, but he has come to think that war with France is inevitable. As he advances in years, the reactionary tendencies

[1] See Vergnet, *La France en danger*, 1913.

of the Court, and especially the impatience of the soldiers, obtain a greater hold over his mind. Perhaps he feels some slight jealousy of the popularity of his son, who flatters the passions of the Pan-Germans. The Emperor and his Chief of the Staff may have wished to induce the King of the Belgians not to make any opposition in the event of a conflict between us. Whatever the object of the conversation, the revelation is one of extreme gravity. We must keep our powder dry." In the following months Baron Beyens, the Belgian Minister, noticed that William II was becoming less friendly to French visitors. " I have often held out my hand to France," he remarked at a Court ball in February, 1914, " and she has replied with kicks. They had better take care at Paris, for I shall not always be here." Colonel House, visiting Berlin in May, 1914, with a view to an Anglo-German-American Entente, was appalled by the militarism which surrounded the ruler. " The whole of Germany is charged with electricity," he reported. " Everybody's nerves are tense. It only needs a spark to set the whole thing off." Meanwhile a new series of unfortunate incidents fanned the flame. When a Zeppelin descended at Lunéville, Frenchmen believed that it had come to spy ; and when some commercial travellers were molested at Nancy there was an outburst in the Reichstag, only partially appeased by the dismissal of the Prefect. Though the desire for war with France or anybody else was confined to a small section of the German population, which did not include the Kaiser, the Chancellor or the Foreign Secretary, there was no instinctive shrinking from a conflict and very little anxiety as to its result. Since Moltke's victories the invincibility of German arms had been an article of faith.

The atmosphere in France, though less neurotically excited, contained explosive elements. " The British attitude in 1911," reported the Belgian Minister at Paris in October, 1912, " caused a revulsion of feeling. To say that the French nation has become bellicose would be going too far. The agriculturist, the bourgeois, the merchant, the industrialist know what a conflagration would cost them ; yet the country is confident of success. We must count with the turbulent youth and the military. The men at the head of affairs are sincerely pacific, but their action is excessive. It is good to restore to a nation its dignity but dangerous to foster its chauvinism. They began by military parades and marching through Paris. The visit of the Grand Duke Nicholas excited national sentiment. Millerand, the Minister of War, accompanied him to the frontier, whence the Grand Duchess saluted the lost provinces, and the visit concluded with a review at Nancy which became a demonstration against the Treaty of Frankfurt. Opinion forced the hand of Napoleon in 1870, and could again confront the Governments with a situation leaving no issue but war." The most chauvinist tirades in the theatres and the *café chantants*, added the same witness in May, 1913, aroused frenzied applause. Benckendorff, the Russian Ambassador in London, reported his impression that of all the Powers represented in the Ambassadors' Conference during the Balkan conflict France was the one who would see war with the least regret. The election of Poincaré as President of the Republic in January, 1913, proclaimed and increased the new spirit of confidence. He remarked to the German Ambassador that the people were pacific, but would not tolerate a second Agadir. Delcassé was sent as Ambassador to St. Petersburg to hasten the military measures agreed by the General Staffs. The increase of the German army compelled France to restore the three years' service which had been discarded in 1905 ; and though the law was strenuously fought by the Socialists and the Caillaux Radicals, France, like Germany, was ready for sacrifices.

The atmosphere of Paris during the last years of peace is reflected in the thoughtful Memoirs of Schoen, who succeeded Radolin at the Rue de Lille in 1910. The phrase " friendly and neighbourly relations " was used for the first time on his presentation to President Fallières, and the new Ambassador did his utmost to realize the ideal he had expressed ; but, like other peacemakers, he found the path blocked by the impalpable barrier. " In spite of the lapse of forty years, in spite of the country having achieved renewed prosperity, in spite of the acquisition of colonial possessions, in spite of having long since recovered the position of a Great Power, the wound of 1871 would not heal. The majority of the people were naturally less fiercely patriotic as time went on, but an active minority kept up the smouldering fire with a view to its bursting into flames at the given moment. When I suggested to M. Barthou, the Premier, that it was a great pity to exhaust ourselves on armaments and strife, he replied, *Rendez-nous l' Alsace-Lorraine, alors nous serons les meilleurs amis de la terre.*" How could he say anything else? In his lectures on the origins of the war Poincaré declares that France would never have taken the initiative in a war of liberation, and that no French Minister ever pronounced the word *revanche* ; but he adds that they one and all declined to forget the two provinces and to be guilty of a cowardly betrayal. The watchword of successive governments was : Neither war nor renunciation !

The heads of the French army were no longer mortally afraid of their formidable neighbours. In a series of widely-read works, *La France victorieuse dans la Guerre de Demain, L'Offensive contre l'Allemagne,* and *L'Allemagne en Péril,* Colonel Boucher, ex-Chief of the Department of Military Operations of the General Staff, exhorted his countrymen to sleep quiet in their beds. France, it was true, was outstripped in population, and was weakened by pacifism and ministerial instability. " So Germany thinks she could defeat us, and treats us like a conquered country. But she is mistaken. This book proves that if we are attacked we are certain of victory. If war broke out to-morrow, we should certainly be supported by our two allies, Russia and England. We are sure of resisting till Russia invades Germany, and then we shall take the offensive and recover Alsace-Lorraine." Another officer worked out the partition of Germany after the coming war. During the two last years of peace the German Military Attaché in Paris sent home a stream of reports on the visible improvement of the French army.

In a remarkable volume, entitled *Faites un Roi, sinon faites la Paix,* published in 1913, Marcel Sembat, a distinguished Socialist Deputy of the school of Jaurès, implored his countrymen to reflect and to choose. The system of alliances, he argued, was leading Europe towards war. The question of Alsace-Lorraine dominated the life and fortunes of France. It was necessary to decide between those who reluctantly acquiesced in the status quo and those who aspired to overthrow it at the first favourable opportunity. If the latter aim were adopted as the official policy, it was essential to restore the Monarchy and to concentrate every ounce of material and spiritual energy on preparing for the inevitable conflict. If, on the other hand, as the author desired, France was prepared to accept the verdict of Sedan, the quarrel should be brought to an end, all the more since, in his opinion, the population of the Rhine provinces dreaded nothing so much as war and wished for autonomy within the German Empire.

Frenchmen rejected both the proffered alternatives of

monarchy and renunciation. Ever since the first Morocco crisis of 1905 most of the leading statesmen and soldiers of Europe had regarded a general conflict as extremely probable, though opinions differed as to its date and whether it would start in the east or the west. The Continent was racked by three separate but simultaneous antagonisms. The oldest was the quarrel between France and Germany over Alsace and Lorraine. Second in order of time was the competition of Russia and Austria for hegemony in the Near East. The most recent was the rivalry between England and Germany for the command of the seas. Moreover the network of alliances ensured that a serious quarrel between any two of the Great Powers would develop into a general scrimmage. Diplomatic and military preparations for the struggle were pushed forward everywhere. When the call from St. Petersburg came in July 1914 France's unhesitating response was due, not merely to her loyalty to the alliance which she had sought so eagerly, but to her hope that the sword of the Entente would restore the children whom she had lost in 1871, who had never forgotten her, and whom she had never ceased to mourn. The recovery of the Rhine provinces, declares Paléologue, who worked with Delcassé at the Quai d'Orsay, was his darling dream, the unavowed goal of all his efforts. Millions of Frenchmen felt the same. Peacemakers on both sides of the Rhine had done their best for forty years, but their labours were in vain. The problem of Franco-German reconciliation was insoluble. Some wounds are so deep and painful that they never heal, for man does not live by bread alone.

BIBLIOGRAPHICAL NOTE

This survey is based on the two immense official publications, *Documents Diplomatiques Français* and *Die Grosse Politik der Europäischen Kabinette*. In the former the volumes covering the period from September 1891 to the end of 1900, and from January 1906 to November 1911, have not yet appeared.

The French version of the period may be studied in *Histoire Diplomatique de l'Europe*, 1871–1914, ed. Hauser; Hanotaux, *Histoire de la France Contemporaine*; Lavisse, *Histoire de France Contemporaine*, vols. 7 and 8; Bourgeois et Pagès, *Les Origines et les Responsabilités de la Grande Guerre*; Pinon, *France et Allemagne*; Gontaut-Biron, *Mon Ambassade en Allemagne* 1872–3; Dreux, *Les dernières Années de L'Ambassade de Gontaut-Biron*; Deschanel, *Gambetta*; Mme Adam, *Souvenirs*; Freycinet, *Souvenirs*; Rambaud,

Jules Ferry ; Albin, *L'Allemagne et la France en Europe* 1885–1894 ; Recouly, *De Bismarck à Poincaré* ; Mévil, *De la Paix de Francfort à la Conférence d'Algésiras* ; Taillandier, *Les Origines du Maroc Français* ; Paléologue, *Un Grand Tournant de la Politique mondiale* ; René Millet, *Notre politique extérieure de 1895 à 1905* ; Renouvin, *La Crise Européenne et la Grande Guerre* ; Bourgeois, *Manuel historique de Politique Étrangère* ; Tardieu, *France et les Alliances* ; *La Conférence d'Algésiras* ; *Le Mystère d'Agadir* ; Caillaux, *Agadir* ; Poincaré, *Les Origines de la Guerre* ; *Souvenirs* ; Gérin et Poincaré, *Les Responsabilités de la Guerre* 14 *Questions* ; Mme Tabouis, *Life of Jules Cambon.*

For the German version see Bismarck, *Reflections and Recollections; Memoirs of Prince Hohenlohe* ; Bülow, *Memoirs*; *Imperial Germany*; *Reden* ; Von der Lancken, *Meine Dreissig Dienstjahre*, 1888–1918 ; Schoen, *Memoirs of an Ambassador* ; Jaeckh, *Kiderlen-Wächter* ; Wahl, *Deutsche Geschichte*, 1871–1914 ; Brandenburg, *From Bismarck to the World War* ; Oncken, *Das Deutsche Reich und die Vorgeschichte des Weltkrieges* ; Hammann, *The World Policy of Germany*, 1890–1912 ; Reventlow, *Deutschlands Auswärtige Politik*, 1888–1914 ; Rachfahl, *Deutschland und die Weltpolitik* ; Aloys Schulte, *Frankreich und das linke Rheinufer* ; Schneegans, *Memoiren.*

More detached views are found in Lord Newton, *Life of Lord Lyons* ; G. H. Stuart, *French Foreign Policy* 1898–1914 ; Brogan, *The Third Republic* ; Schuman, *War and Diplomacy in the French Republic* ; Carroll, *French Public Opinion and Foreign Affairs*, 1870–1914 ; Mitchell, *The Bismarckian Policy of Conciliation with France*, 1875–1885 ; Wienefeld, *Franco-German Relations*, 1878–1885 ; Anderson, *The First Morocco Crisis* ; Spender, *Fifty Years of Europe* ; Japikse, *Europa und Bismarcks Friedenspolitik*, 1871–1890 ; Gooch, *Before the War : Studies in Diplomacy*. The most impartial study of the problem of the Rhine provinces is in Coleman Phillipson, *Alsace-Lorraine.*

THE DIPLOMATIC BACKGROUND OF
THE FIRST WORLD WAR

THE edifice which collapsed in 1918 was erected in 1871, when military hegemony in Europe passed from Paris to Berlin. For the next twenty years Bismarck bestrode the Continent like a colossus, but the contriver of three wars was transformed into a pillar of peace. " We are satiated," he declared, and he meant what he said. Henceforth his task was to buttress the status quo by alliances and ententes. He never expected France to forgive the loss of Alsace and Lorraine, but she was too weak to reconquer them while she stood alone. His aim accordingly was to keep her in quarantine. Austria became an ally in 1879 ; the Triple Alliance was formed in 1882 by the adhesion of Italy ; Roumania secretly bound herself to the Central Powers in 1883. With Russia and England it was impossible to conclude similar arrangements, but their benevolent neutrality was secured by the simple expedient of not getting in their way. So far as Germany was concerned Russia could have a free hand in the eastern half of the Balkan peninsula ; and England had no quarrel with a statesman who cared nothing for naval power and little for colonial enterprise. Ruthless in premeditated attack but moderate in the hour of victory, he preached and practised the doctrine of limited liability. Though the German Empire was by far the strongest Power in Europe, he neither overestimated nor overtaxed its strength. It was quite enough to be exposed to the incurable hostility of France. He had created the nation-state which his countrymen had longed to possess, and he wanted nothing more. Bismarck, like Cavour, was a great nationalist, never an Imperialist.

With the dropping of the pilot in 1890 the European situation changed rapidly, and the next twenty-four years witnessed the crumbling of the imposing Bismarckian edifice. The first challenge to the status quo was the Franco-Russian alliance, outlined in 1891, concluded in 1893, and announced in 1895. Holy Russia had overcome her instinctive shrinking from Republican France while the Iron Chancellor was still at the helm ; but it was Berlin's non-renewal of his so-called

Secret Treaty of Reinsurance (concluded with Russia in 1887 for three years) on the morrow of his fall which removed the last serious obstacle to a partnership between Paris and St. Petersburg. If Napoleon used to say that he feared nothing but a hungry Paris, it was the "nightmare of coalitions" which had kept Bismarck awake. When he was gone the danger at once began to materialize. After twenty years of impotence France had recovered her self-confidence and escaped from her narrow cage. The Triple Alliance remained stronger than its rival, but it was no longer supreme.

With the wire to St. Petersburg cut and the Dual Alliance in being, it was vital for Berlin to maintain the friendship of England unimpaired. There were six Great Powers in Europe, of which three were now in one camp and two in the other. England stood aloof, though "splendid isolation" was an attitude, not a principle. She had taken part in the Crimean War and she might intervene in Continental struggles again. Her policy rested on the two time-honoured maxims of Naval Supremacy and the Balance of Power. The first she defined in 1889 by the formula of the Two Power Standard (the British Navy to be stronger than the two next Continental fleets combined), with her eye on France and Russia. The second meant that she tended to oppose, by diplomacy or war, any European state at once so strong and so potentially hostile as to threaten her safety. Bismarck had little respect for our institutions or statesmen, but he fully realized the decisive part we could play. In 1879 and again in 1889 he sounded us about an alliance, and when, yielding to a growing demand, he established a Colonial Empire in 1884 he achieved his purpose without forfeiting our good will. Caprivi, his successor in the Chancellorship, equally understood that, so long as England remained friendly, France and Russia would scarcely dare to attack the Central Powers; and William II, erratic and temperamental though he was, knew too much of the British navy to underestimate its strength.

Here was the acid test of the men who succeeded Bismarck— the young Emperor, Caprivi, Marschall, the Foreign Minister, Holstein, the most influential member of the Foreign Office, Hohenlohe, the third Chancellor. Russia was lost: could the confidence and good will of England be retained? The Kaiser's telegram to Kruger, congratulating him on the repulse of the Jameson raid in January, 1896, gave the reply. Anglo-German relations had been friendly enough in the last

two decades of the Bismarck era, but the launching of this high
explosive destroyed much of his work. The Raid was unauthorized and indefensible and it was promptly repudiated
by the British Government; but the sudden revelation of
German interest in South Africa, and still more the provocative
form in which it was expressed, stirred the British people to
the depths. For the first time since the foundation of the
German Empire both countries talked openly of war. The
crisis passed, and the Kaiser was warmly welcomed in England
more than once in the coming years, but the lightning flash
was never forgotten. The significance of the incident was
seized by Italy, who, mindful of our ancient friendship and
trembling for her undefended coasts, informed her allies that
she could not join in the fight if England were on the opposite
side. It was a plain warning to Berlin that, if the wire to
London were to be cut by some unskilful hand, the wire to
Rome would also cease to work. Almost at the same moment,
Japan was estranged by a Three Power summons to disgorge
the mainland fruits of her victory over China in the war of
1894–5. Russia was an acknowledged rival, and France as
her ally dared not lag behind; but why, asked the Japanese,
should Germany join in the game? "We shall remember,"
observed a Japanese statesman with the pregnant brevity of his
race. The wise Bismarckian tradition of limited liability was
breaking down. The Austrian alliance, the core of the system,
remained intact, but the inorganic realm of the Hapsburgs,
with its diverse racial elements, was weaker than it looked.
When Marschall left the Wilhelmstrasse in 1897 to become
Ambassador at Constantinople the international position of
Germany was decidedly weaker than when he entered it in
1890. A fine vessel had been unskilfully steered.

If William II had made a bad start, the Bülow era, which
opened in 1897 and lasted twelve years, brought no relief.
Germany naturally desired to join in the game of Imperialism
which was being played by all the Great Powers except Austria,
but her citizens had the right to demand that its prizes should
be related to the risks. Since *Weltpolitik* was the order of the
day, two tempting courses lay open—the exploitation of
Asiatic Turkey and the creation of a first-class fleet. The
former was bound to alarm Russia, the latter to estrange
England. Though common prudence pointed to a choice, the
fatal error was committed of pursuing both policies at once.
The creation of a High Seas fleet under the inspiration of

Tirpitz, who was appointed to the Admiralty in 1897, began with the Navy Laws of 1898 and 1900; and the vast project of the Bagdad Railway was launched in 1899, carrying with it the political and economic predominance at Constantinople. In the early stages of these enterprises the danger of Germany shouldering a burden beyond even her gigantic strength was so little realized by William II and his advisers that the golden opportunity presented by British embarrassments in South Africa was allowed to slip.

Before the Boer War cast its shadow over the scene, a slight Anglo-German rapprochement had begun. A secret treaty in 1898 mapped out hypothetical spheres of influence in the Portuguese colonial empire, and Germany obtained a foothold in Samoa in 1899. The seizure of an ice-free Port Arthur by Russia in the spring of 1898, and the Fashoda crisis in the autumn of the same year, provoked by the planting of the French flag on the Upper Nile, emphasized our isolation and turned wistful eyes to Berlin. Commercial competition with Germany was becoming very keen, but it never seriously affected either popular sentiment or official diplomacy. While Salisbury saw no reason to abandon the practice of keeping our hands free, Joseph Chamberlain, the Colonial Secretary, was not the only one of his colleagues who felt the need of a powerful friend to balance the hostility of France and Russia. Without committing the Cabinet he discussed the possibilities of a defensive agreement with the German Ambassador. Never before had a British Minister, officially or unofficially, dangled an alliance before the German Empire, but his advances were coldly received. Such a commitment, in Bülow's eyes, would inevitably antagonize Russia, with whom Germany had no quarrel and against whose enormous army England could furnish no military aid. " At the present time Germany, who is confronted with no immediate or prospective danger, has no reason to shoulder the risks of an alliance. . . . The great majority of the German people do not at the present moment believe they are threatened from the East. It would therefore be difficult to justify an alliance which automatically stamps Russia as our foe."

Bülow's attitude never changed, and his official advisers, with Holstein at their head, approved it. He was favourably impressed by his visit to England in the autumn of 1899, when the Kaiser came over for the first time since the Kruger telegram, but Chamberlain's arguments made no more impres-

sion than in the previous year. When the Colonial Secretary
spoke at Leicester of a new triple alliance or understanding
between England, Germany and the United States, the German
Foreign Secretary in his next speech to the Reichstag pointedly
ignored an utterance which had echoed round the world. It
was true enough that in mentioning the word alliance Chamberlain had overshot the mark, and it was equally true that the
Boer War, which had begun on October 9, 1899, was detested
in Germany. Yet it was a costly error not to nurture the
tender plant of Anglo-German understanding sown at Wind-
sor. The attitude of the German Government throughout the
struggle in South Africa was correct enough, but there was no
longer any confidence between the peoples. The holding up
of German steamers outside Delagoa Bay, wrongly suspected
of carrying contraband to the Boers, caused exasperation, while
the so-called Yang-tse treaty of 1900, designed to defend
British and German commerce against Russian encroachments
in China, did more harm than good owing to differences of
interpretation.

An alliance between England and Germany was officially
discussed for the first and last time in 1901. When the Kaiser
hurried to the deathbed of Queen Victoria in January of that
year, Bülow, who succeeded Hohenlohe as Chancellor in
1900, warned him not to commit himself. " English embarrassments will grow in the coming months, and therewith our
price will rise. . . . It would be a masterstroke if Your
Majesty succeeded in leaving the English their hope of future
intimacy without prematurely binding ourselves. The
threatened rapprochement with the Dual Alliance is only a
nightmare invented to frighten us." There was never much
life in the ensuing negotiations. The proposal of an alliance,
according to Lansdowne, who succeeded Salisbury as Foreign
Minister in 1900, came from Eckardstein, who represented
the German Embassy during the illness of Hatzfeldt, his chief;
but Eckardstein's report disingenuously attributes the initiative
to the British statesman. Bülow naturally accepted the version
which reached him, but he was not tempted by the imaginary
bait. The problem at issue seemed to him quite simple.
Germany was on good terms with Russia, and England was
not. An Anglo-Russian war seemed probable, but why should
Germany be dragged in ? If England would enter the Triple
Alliance, that was another matter and her support would be
welcomed ; but nobody desired to take such a risky step.

F

" The liability of having to defend the German and Austrian frontiers against Russia," wrote Salisbury in an impressive Memorandum, " is heavier than that of having to defend the British Isles against France." He saw no cause for alarm : with an unchallengeable navy England could look after herself. Moreover no British Government could foretell the reaction of public opinion before the *casus belli* occurred. Lansdowne, unlike his chief, was ready for a limited regional agreement with Germany, but this possibility was ruled out at Berlin. As Metternich, the new German Ambassador, remarked at the close of 1901, it was a case of " all or nothing."

The failure of the negotiations left no soreness behind, for neither party cared greatly for their success ; yet from this time onwards the two Governments and peoples drifted ever further from one another. A sharp exchange between Chamberlain and Bülow on the conduct of British and German armies in the wars of 1870 and 1899 generated a good deal of heat. Naval co-operation in the winter of 1902–3 in Venezuela, who refused to pay her debts, was intensely unpopular in England. British participation in financing the Bagdad Railway was approved by Balfour, the new Prime Minister, by Lansdowne, by the City, by the British Ambassadors in Constantinople and Berlin ; but the plan was wrecked by unofficial Unionist opposition in Parliament and the press in the spring of 1903. So unpopular had Germany become even before the naval rivalry was acute that co-operation in any form aroused angry antagonism.

In the history of British policy the years 1902 and 1903 stand out in bold relief. The conquest of the Transvaal and the Orange Free State in 1902, following the conquest of the Sudan in 1898, marks the stage where the sentiment of Imperial expansion reached saturation point. There was no craven fear of being great, to use Tennyson's famous phrase, but we had enough. The British Empire—the biggest in the world— merely desired to keep what it had taken centuries to get. Our battleships remained the first line of defence, yet diplomacy might well assist. Germany had not yet become in any real sense an enemy, but she had ceased to be a friend. Since Salisbury's retirement in 1902 men were at the helm who felt the growing danger of isolation in an armed and threatening world. Fruitless though they were, the Anglo-German negotiations of 1901 revealed that more flexible minds were at work. The century of isolation had reached its close. The first concrete sign of the new spirit was the conclusion of an alliance with Japan in January, 1902, the object of which was to oppose Russian domination in the Far East, which threatened our valuable Chinese market.

Far more important was the rapprochement with France, which began to be academically discussed in 1902 between Lansdowne and Paul Cambon, the French Ambassador. For several years each country had grounds of complaint. Englishmen were deeply shocked at the persecution of the innocent Dreyfus. Frenchmen thought with anger of the forced surrender at Fashoda, and their sympathies with the Boers were unconcealed. Nations, however, like individuals, sometimes change their moods with astonishing rapidity. Moreover, Delcassé, who had been Foreign Minister since 1898, realized that France could not afford more than one enemy. It had been his painful duty to climb down in the valley of the Nile, but he knew that more could be gained from co-operation with England than from sulking or dreams of revenge. With the aid of Barrère, his resourceful Ambassador in Rome, he had liquidated Italian hostility by two secret pacts. In 1900 the countries recognized each other's claims in Tripoli and Morocco, while in 1902 Italy promised neutrality in a Franco-German war. She remained a sleeping partner in the Triple Alliance, but henceforth she had one foot in each camp, and in the following years she moved ever closer to Paris and St. Petersburg.

When he had finished with Italy Delcassé turned to London. With the end of the Boer War warmer airs began to blow. The successful visit of King Edward in April, 1903, was returned by President Loubet, who was accompanied by the Foreign Minister. On July 7 Delcassé and Lansdowne inaugurated the negotiations which led to the Anglo-French treaty of April 8, 1904. The governing factor was the eagerness of France to secure preponderance in Morocco. Italy's assent had been cheaply purchased at the expense of Tripoli. England's price was higher, for our strategic and commercial interests in Morocco were great, and the golden opportunity of securing a free hand in Egypt was seized. Lansdowne's maxim was firmness in Egypt and pliability elsewhere. The final settlement, which was facilitated by the wide scope of the negotiations, was satisfactory to both sides. We declared that we had no intention of altering the juridical status quo in Egypt, and France undertook not to obstruct our action by asking for a time limit to the British occupation or in any other way. France similarly declared that she had no intention of altering the status of Morocco, and we promised not to obstruct her activities. In both countries commercial liberty was to prevail for at least thirty years. No fortifications were to be permitted on the coast opposite Gibraltar. France was to reach an understanding with Spain. A Khedivial Decree laid down regulations relating to the Egyptian Debt, and, subject to acceptance by the Powers, gave the Egyptian Government a free hand in the disposal of its resources so long as the punctual payment of interest was assured. Next in importance was the settlement of the Newfoundland fishery dispute, France surrendering certain treaty privileges in return for territorial concessions in West Africa. A third document liquidated disputes in Siam, Madagascar and the New Hebrides. In addition to the published agreement there were secret articles envisaging the eventual partition of Morocco into French and Spanish zones of influence, a plan worked out in detail in the secret articles of the Franco-Spanish treaty of October, 1904.

Even more important than the terms of the Anglo-French settlement was the new relationship which it created. For Lansdowne it was merely a colonial agreement, the clearing up of tiresome disputes. The idea of encircling Germany, of tying ourselves to France, of building up a Triple Entente, never entered his head. For Delcassé, on the other hand, it was far more than a regional transaction. "We are liquidating all our past quarrels," he remarked to Paléologue, his assistant at the Quai d'Orsay, on February 1, 1904; "but I shall not stop there. It should lead to a political alliance with England. What fair horizons would then open to us! If we could lean both on Russia and England, how strong should we be in dealing with Germany!" The recovery of the Rhine provinces, declares Paléologue, was his darling dream, the unavowed goal of all his efforts. A conflict of arms, if it ever came, must be preceded by a contest of wits. In four crowded years he had bought the consent of Italy, England and Spain to his Morocco plans, had loosened the ties of the Triple Alliance, had won the confidence of England without forfeiting that of his Russian ally ; and perhaps the old and the new friends might one day make up their feud.

The agreement of London and Paris to afford each other diplomatic support in Egypt and Morocco was an elastic formula the full implications of which were scarcely realized in England at the time.   When France, emboldened by her agreements, presented Morocco with a programme of reforms at the opening of 1905, Germany, whom Delcassé had most unwisely omitted to consult, sharply asserted her treaty claims. The Kaiser's declaration at Tangier, Hands off Morocco !, inaugurated the first Morocco crisis and filled Lansdowne with alarm.   He expected Germany to ask for a port on the Moorish coast, and on April 22, 1905, he offered to join France in strong opposition thereto.   It was a false alarm, but on May 17 a historic conversation between Lansdowne and Paul Cambon occurred.   " I observed," reported Lansdowne, " that the moral of all these incidents seemed to me that our two Governments should continue to treat one another with the most absolute confidence, should keep one another fully informed of everything which came to their knowledge, and should, so far as possible, discuss in advance any contingencies by which they might in the course of events find themselves confronted."   When this communication was repeated in a letter, Cambon wrote to his chief that it suggested a general entente which would in effect amount to an alliance. Delcassé, who was now fighting for his political life, informed his colleagues at their meeting on June 6 that an alliance had been offered, and he reiterated the unfounded statement to the end of his life.   France, however, was materially and morally unprepared for war ;   Delcassé, finding himself alone in the Cabinet, resigned, and Germany's invitation to a conference on Morocco was accepted on conditions.   His career at the Quai d'Orsay began and ended with humiliation, yet the larger portion of his work endured.   The reconciliation with Italy and England had changed the face of Europe.   In the grouping of the Powers France had been one of two : henceforth she was one of four.   The imposing Bismarckian edifice was crumbling away.

Germany naturally attempted to follow up her success, and as usual there was more of the iron hand than the velvet glove.   Even Rouvier, the French Premier, who had evicted Delcassé and taken over the Foreign Office, came to the conclusion that France could not continue to retreat.   On January 10, 1906, the eve of the Algeciras Conference, the French Ambassador asked the new Liberal Foreign Secretary whether England would help in the event of aggression.   With his colleagues dispersed and before the electors had spoken, replied Grey, he could merely state his personal opinion that, if France were attacked by Germany in consequence of a question arising out of the agreement of 1904, public opinion would be strongly moved in her favour. This was too vague to satisfy Cambon, who remarked that he would repeat his question after the election. Meanwhile he thought it advisable that the informal discussions which had already begun should continue between the Admiralty and the War Office and the French Naval and Military Attachés, without committing the Governments to action in any way. Grey did not dissent, and, after consulting some of his colleagues, he authorized non-committal communications with French and Belgian experts—in the latter case in order to facilitate the discharge of our duty as a guarantor of Belgian neutrality in case of need.

"We were a little surprised," confesses Huguet, the French Military Attaché, "by the readiness with which the authorization was granted. Campbell-Bannerman, Grey and Haldane were too clever not to realize that the studies now to be pursued would—whatever the qualifications—constitute a moral engagement." He was right, for the Prime Minister used much the same language. "I do not like the stress laid upon joint preparations," he wrote. "It comes very close to an honourable understanding, and it will be known on both sides of the Rhine." Despite this inherent difficulty it was virtually impossible for a British statesman to decline the discussions requested by France. How else could effective aid be given if Germany struck a sudden blow? France was still unready for the fray, and Russia, staggering under the blows of Japan, was temporarily out of action.

When Cambon repeated his question on January 31, Grey replied that no unconditional promise could be given and it would be difficult to formulate conditions. Any change would transform the Entente into a defensive alliance, the necessity for which had not yet arisen. Our attitude in the event of a German attack would largely depend on how it occurred. His personal belief was that, if an attack arose from the Morocco agreement, public opinion would compel the Government to intervene. He had informed the German Ambassador of his view, as Lansdowne had done after the fall of Delcassé. Cambon had expected nothing more, and he was consoled by the hope that the military conversations now officially authorized might ultimately expand a regional agreement into a full working partnership. Promises were declined but expectations were created. Whatever the verbal limitations, a momentous change in the orientation of British policy had taken place. The era of unfettered self-determination was over, the era of Continental attachments and entanglements had begun. The *Entente Cordiale* was the half-way house between isolation and an alliance ; and such relationships tend to grow more intimate with the passing years.

The Conference of Algeciras, which sat from January to April 1906, was a contest of wills between France, backed by England, Russia and Spain, and Germany, tepidly supported by Austria. Italy, with the secret Tripoli pact in her pocket, gave no help to her ally. The main struggle turned on the plan of Franco-Spanish control of the police in the Moroccan ports, and after weeks of acute tension Berlin gave way. Neither William II nor Bülow wished to fight about Morocco, and Holstein, who was quite prepared to draw the sword, resigned. Though the independence and integrity of Morocco were recognized in the Act of Algeciras and commercial equality was assured, as Germany demanded, it was generally agreed that France had won the match. She had recovered from her attack of nerves in 1905, the growing isolation of Germany was revealed, and the *Entente Cordiale*, in the words of Tardieu, passed from the static to the dynamic stage. The new situation naturally afforded greater satisfaction to Paris than to London. Never for a moment did Grey question the utility of the historic reconciliation of 1904, but he was now more fully aware of the price we had paid. We had sacrificed part of our independence, and the baffling problem of recovering the friendship of Germany was complicated by involving us in the traditional quarrels of our new friends.

A British agreement with Russia was the natural sequel to the agreement with France. Friendly discussions, begun before the outbreak of the Russo-Japanese war, were resumed after its close in 1905. Memories of the Crimean struggle and of subsequent occasions when war seemed in sight prevented all intimacy, and the Tsarist régime was profoundly repugnant to British ideas. Yet these obstacles were overcome by two other considerations. In the first place both Governments felt the need of removing a dangerous antagonism ; in the second it was highly inconvenient for the old and new friends of France to be on bad terms. Co-operation at Algeciras paved the way for the official discussions between Nicolson, the new Ambassador to St. Petersburg, and the Anglophil

Iswolsky, who succeeded Lamsdorff as Russian Foreign Minister in 1906. After wearisome negotiations lasting more than a year, an Anglo-Russian Convention was signed on August 31, 1907. Unlike the Anglo-French settlement of 1904, the whole slate was not cleaned, neither the Far East nor the Near East being included. This mattered little, for in the former sphere Russia had for the time ceased to count, and in the latter the interests of other states were involved. The chief source of friction was the Middle East, where the security of India had to be kept in view. Three countries lay between Russia and India, namely Persia, Afghanistan and Tibet. Persia was by far the most important, and here Russia's predominant position was ungrudgingly recognized. The country was divided into a large Russian zone in the north, a small British zone on the Indian frontier, and an extensive neutral belt. To balance this substantial sacrifice we secured the elimination of Russian influence from Afghanistan and Tibet. The settlement was denounced as a needless surrender by Curzon and a few other Russophobes, but its main purpose was achieved. The Indian frontier had been safeguarded, and a formidable rival had been turned into a potential friend. A Russo-Japanese agreement negotiated by Iswolsky at the same time eased the situation still further.

With the return of confidence a new spirit began to emerge. Nicholas II had expressed his wish for a visit from King Edward at the end of 1905, and in April 1908 he renewed the invitation. Two months later the King and Queen steamed into Reval, where they were cordially received. Grey's pledge to the House of Commons that there should be no fresh agreements was faithfully observed, yet the visit was scarcely less important than the memorable sojourn in Paris in 1903. The heart of the conversations between Hardinge, the representative of the Foreign Office, and Iswolsky was the plea of the former that, in view of the growth of the German fleet, Russia should increase her armed strength in Europe. Though the German Ambassador in London was assured that nothing particular had happened, the foundations of a working partnership were laid, and the Kaiser's complaint of encirclement in an emotional speech to his officers showed that he sensed the atmospheric change. Henceforth, though sharp disagreements were to arise in Persia, the two Governments harmonized their policy in an increasing degree. The *Entente Cordiale* with France had widened into a Triple Entente, as

Delcassé had planned.   Grey deprecated the use of the phrase, and he never dreamed of the encirclement of Germany.   Yet the reconciliation with Russia, like the reconciliation with France, had its price.   The greatest empire in the world coveted nothing that it did not possess, yet it might easily be dragged into the quarrels of its new friends, neither of whom was satisfied with the status quo.   The one coveted Alsace-Lorraine, the other the control of the Straits.   It was also possible that the moves of the Central Powers might force us into closer relations with France and Russia than we intended or desired, and thus almost imperceptibly transform the association into an alliance in everything but name.

As the Anglo-French treaty had been followed by the first Morocco crisis, so the Anglo-Russian Convention and the Reval visit were followed by a period of acute international strain.   The Young Turk revolution provided Austria with an excuse for the annexation of Bosnia and Herzegovina in October, 1908.   The provinces had been administered by her ever since the Congress of Berlin in 1878, and no one expected or desired the occupation to cease ; yet the sudden repudiation of Turkish sovereignty was a shock to the world.   Iswolsky, it is true, had consented in return for a promise that Aehrenthal would favour the opening of the Straits to Russian warships. This engagement, however, was unknown to the world, and the announcement of the annexation before the Russian Foreign Minister had time to prepare the ground for the attainment of his own aims turned him into a fanatical enemy of the Austrian Foreign Minister.   For five months he held out against recognition, and it was only when Germany intervened in March, 1909, with what he called a diplomatic ultimatum, that he gave way.   The relations between Vienna and St. Petersburg never recovered from the strain.

The crisis which kept Europe on the rack for six months ended with the forced recognition by Servia of a change which filled her people with anger and grief.   She was much too weak to fight alone, and Russia was still crippled by the Japanese war, but the seeds of future conflict were sown.   The Pan-Serb dream of expansion at the expense of Austria, instead of being shattered, took firmer shape, and sooner or later Russia was certain to resume her historic rôle of patron of the Balkan Slavs.   The annexation of Bosnia, so unskilfully carried out by Aehrenthal, though not a crime, was assuredly a blunder, for it exposed the realm of the Hapsburgs to risks and resentments which it was too racially heterogeneous to face with equanimity.   Henceforth the Triple Entente and the Central Powers were openly ranged against one another, Italy drifted ever further away from her nominal allies, and in the autumn of 1909 a secret treaty, signed during the Tsar's visit to Victor Emmanuel at Racconigi, made her almost a junior partner of the Triple Entente.   Roumania, too, angered by Hungary's harsh treatment of her children in Transylvania, could no longer be relied on to fulfil her obligations to the Central Powers in case of war.   Worst of all, from the standpoint of Berlin and Vienna, the gulf between England and Germany was becoming too wide to bridge.

The conclusion of the Algeciras Conference had brought temporary relief to Western Europe, and in the autumn of 1907 William II paid a happy visit to England, in the course of which participation in the Bagdad railway was again discussed, though without result.   No genuine appeasement was possible in a Continent divided into rival camps, and the Second Hague Conference in 1907 had not even discussed the limitation of armaments.   1908 was a year of blunders and crises.   The German fleet aroused growing alarm, which the Kaiser increased by a well-meant but ill-judged private letter to Lord Tweedmouth, First Lord of the Admiralty.   A new German Navy Bill in April decided the British Government to raise the question of naval limitation officially during King Edward's visit to his nephew at Cronberg on the way to Marienbad in the summer ; but Sir Charles Hardinge, the bearer of the message, found the door bolted and barred.   No discussion of a question involving national honour, declared the Kaiser hotly, could be allowed.   It seemed as if there was nothing for England to do except to increase her navy, while drawing ever closer to France and Russia ; and Lord Roberts began his campaign for a conscript army.   When rumours of secret acceleration of German ship-building reached the Admiralty early in 1909, a panic swept the country, and eight battleships of the Dreadnought type, an unprecedented number, were laid down in that year.

In the summer of 1909, when for the first time the probability of an ultimate collision with Germany came home to the British people, the slippery Bülow was succeeded by Bethmann Hollweg.   The former had never desired war, but he had supported the Kaiser's naval plans, which had done even more than Germany's Morocco policy to drive England into the

Franco-Russian camp. The new Chancellor realized as clearly as Metternich, the Ambassador in London, that the challenge to our naval supremacy was poisoning Anglo-German relations, and his first step was to suggest a naval arrangement as part of a general understanding. His sincerity was manifest, but the coupling of a naval agreement with a political formula ruined the scheme. Our proposals for a reduction of the German shipbuilding programme were rejected in Berlin, and the German request for a pledge of neutrality in a European war was declined in London. Bethmann was never master in his own house, for Tirpitz had the ear of his master, and Kiderlen, whom the inexperienced Chancellor had called to the Foreign Office, was a masterful man. The Franco-German agreement of February, 1909, by which Germany recognized the political preponderance of France in Morocco in return for economic co-operation, had been widely welcomed as the liquidation of a dangerous feud ; but the goodwill of the Governments was not shared by the firms which struggled for orders and openings. There were disputes about railways, mines and public works ; and meanwhile anarchy in Morocco steadily increased. In May, 1911, the French, believing the European residents to be in danger, sent a force to Fez at the invitation of the Sultan. To the annoyance of France, Spain followed suit in June by occupying the zone assigned to her by the secret Franco-Spanish treaty of 1904, and on July 1 the *Panther*, a German gunboat, anchored in Agadir, a closed port on the Atlantic coast. France, argued the German and Spanish Governments, had broken the spirit if not the letter of the Act of Algeciras, and Grey privately admitted that she was skating on very thin ice.

Though reiterated warnings had come from Berlin before the French column set out for the Moorish capital, the Agadir *coup* was a shock to London and Paris. German firms in that district, we were informed, had asked for protection, and the vessel would be withdrawn when order in Morocco was restored. The establishment of French and Spanish posts in various parts of the country, it was explained, had created a new situation. Germany was ready to co-operate with France and Spain in the search for a solution of the Morocco question, and the aid of the British Government in this task would be welcomed. Grey replied that Germany's very abrupt action had created a new situation ; that our commercial interests were larger than hers ; that we must consider our treaty obligations to France, and that we could not recognize any new arrangement arrived at without us. These declarations, though they asked no questions, were intended to produce assurances from Berlin, but no response was sent. When the news reached London on July 18 that Kiderlen had presented unacceptable demands to France, including the most valuable portion of the French Congo, Grey confided his anxieties to Metternich, who was unable to give him any information.

On July 21, Mr. Lloyd George, Chancellor of the Exchequer, made a resounding declaration at the Mansion House, the terms of which were approved by the Prime Minister and the Foreign Secretary but were not seen by the Cabinet. If Britain were to be treated, where her interests were vitally affected, as if she were of no account, " then I say emphatically that peace at that price would be a humiliation intolerable for a great country like ours to endure." Neither Germany nor Morocco was mentioned, but the warning was plain enough. It was precisely the same claim to be considered that the Kaiser had voiced at Tangier, and it produced a similar reaction. A contingent declaration of war was flung across the North Sea. In German eyes England seemed as eager to thwart the colonial and commercial ambitions of Germany as to encourage those of France. After a day or two of dangerous tension, during which Grey believed that the fleet might be attacked at any moment, a reassuring message arrived from the Wilhelmstrasse. Wearisome negotiations between France and Germany, in which England took no part, continued throughout the summer and autumn, and on November 4 the Morocco and Congo treaties were signed in Berlin. France secured the assent of Germany to the establishment of a Protectorate in Morocco, while Germany received moderate territorial compensation in the French Congo. Both Governments pretended to be satisfied, but it was generally felt that in the second Morocco crisis, as in the first, the French had scored. Caillaux, the French Premier, and Jules Cambon, the Ambassador in Berlin, had served France well.

Never since the days of the Kruger telegram had Anglo-German relations been so strained as in the summer of 1911, and never since the creation of the *Entente Cordiale* had Anglo-French relations so closely resembled an alliance. Yet neither London nor Berlin desired a break, and in February, 1912, Lord Haldane visited Berlin to explore the ground, each side believing that the initiative had come from the other. He was welcomed warmly by the Chancellor, politely by the Kaiser, and coldly by Tirpitz, and the discussions were continued in London after his return. Once again, however, the difficulties proved insurmountable. So far from being prepared to reduce her naval programme Germany had decided on a substantial increase, and the British Government would only undertake neither to make nor to join in an un-provoked attack. A promise of neutrality would alienate France, and in any case we could not consent to tie our hands ; for Germany might conceivably use Austria to unleash a war and then demand that we should stand aside. Yet the Haldane Mission was not wholly in vain. Though no more was heard of naval limitation or neutrality formulas, amicable and success-ful negotiations concerning the Bagdad railway and spheres of influence in the Portuguese colonies filled the next two years. Grey and Bethmann trusted each other, for they both desired the preservation of peace ; and Lichnowsky, the new German Ambassador in London, laboured gallantly to rebuild the bridges.

The attempt of Germany to extract a promise of neutrality, or indeed any written declaration likely to fetter our action, was watched with deep suspicion by France, who hailed the failure of the discussions with relief. Poincaré, however, who throughout 1912 combined the offices of Premier and Foreign Minister, feared that the temptation might one day be renewed. An alliance, he realized, was impossible, but the near ap-proach of war in 1911 made further advances practicable. The so-called Mediterranean agreement, by which England recalled part of her fleet to home waters and France trans-ferred her battleships from the Channel and Atlantic, was the result of independent Admiralty decisions in both countries, and the consequential technical agreements involved no obligation of armed support. Yet facts spoke louder than formulas. When France left two of her three coasts exposed, and when we no longer depended entirely on our own strength in the Mediterranean, the conclusion seemed inescapable that we were allies in everything but name. At the suggestion of the French the situation was defined in the letters exchanged by Grey and Paul Cambon on November 22 and 23, 1912, which registered the unfettered freedom of both countries to decide their course but bound us to consult one another in case of need. The formula of consultation, in Grey's eyes, merely recognized existing facts : to the more logical French mind, with its craving for the written word, it was a definite and welcome advance. The Russian alliance had sprouted from a similar germ.

In the Balkan Wars, which lasted from October 1912 to August; 1913, it required all Grey's tact and authority as Chairman of the *réunions* of the Ambassadors in London to prevent Austria and Russia flying at each other's throats. Not that either Power had the slightest desire for war. The venerable Francis Joseph, mindful of previous military disasters, was profoundly pacific, and Russia was well aware that she still needed several years to recover her strength. Great Powers, however, have to think of their prestige, and pride sets limits to surrender. The main object of the struggle, namely the destruction of Turkish rule in the Balkans, was accomplished in the first month by the Allies, but the completeness of their victory complicated the division of the spoils. Russia's chief aim was to enlarge the territory of Servia, while Austria, apprehensive of Pan-Serb ambitions, strove to keep her away from the Adriatic. Thus the most difficult problem was the delimitation of the little state of Albania called into existence under the rule of Prince Wilhelm of Wied. For weeks the peace of Europe hung upon the fate of Djakova, a small Albanian market town, which Austria claimed for Albania and Russia for Servia. Austria finally gave way by order of Francis Joseph himself, and indeed throughout the long-drawn Balkan crisis she played an unexpectedly passive part. When the victorious Allies finally quarrelled and Bulgaria was easily crushed by Servia and Greece, Austria's prestige received a fresh blow. Now that European Turkey had been carved up, the familiar talk of the approaching partition of the Hapsburg Empire was openly renewed.

The last year of peace witnessed a series of secondary crises which revealed the alarming fragility of the European structure. An Austrian ultimatum in the autumn of 1913 compelled Servia to withdraw her troops from Albania, but added new fuel to the animosity of Belgrad. The appointment of a German General, Liman von Sanders, to the command of the First Turkish Army Corps at Constantinople provoked fury in Russia, who had plans of her own for the control of the Straits ; and the compromise by which he exchanged his command in the capital for the supervision of the whole army failed to soothe Russian opinion. For the increase of German influence on the Bosphorus was an undeniable fact, and the prospective strengthening of the Turkish army was not at all to its taste. Early in 1914 a violent press feud in Germany and Russia inflamed the growing hostility. *On se croit quelquefois dans une maison de fous*, lamented Sazonoff, the Foreign Minister. In the west Anglo-German relations were easier, but frontier incidents emphasized the undying feud between Paris and Berlin. The armaments race had been accelerated after the Agadir crisis, the increase of the German army being followed by the restoration of three years' service in France. Except for a few soldiers no one in Europe wanted war, yet the Continent was like a powder-magazine which a lighted match would explode.

The murder of the Archduke Franz Ferdinand and his wife at Serajevo, the capital of Bosnia, on June 28, 1914, was generally felt to be a turning point in history. The murderer, a young Austrian Serb, had been aided and encouraged by Servian officers. The Pasitch Government, though it had no part in the plot, got wind of it, yet failed to warn Vienna. The death of the heir to the throne, unpopular though he was, called for some striking retribution, and the world held its breath while the Dual Empire was considering its course. The first task was to make sure of the full support of Berlin, and after receiving an unconditional promise the Ballplatz went straight ahead. An elaborate ultimatum to Servia was presented on July 23. On the expiration of the forty-eight hour limit on July 25, when its unconditional acceptance was declined, the Austrian Minister left Belgrad. Three days later Austria declared war on Servia.

Berchtold and his colleagues knew what they were doing, but they believed they had no choice. The ultimatum was obviously a gamble, for the localization of the conflict, though naturally desired, was hardly expected. If it failed, the realm of the Hapsburgs would break up and disappear. There was no facile optimism at Vienna. The old Emperor observed that they would be fortunate if they got off with a black eye : even Conrad, the fiery Chief of the Staff, admitted that the most favourable opportunities of fighting a defensive war were past. Why then was Austria so intransigent ? " The Serajevo crime," replies Berchtold, " was simply one of the latest examples of the work of destruction organized against us, of the sapping and mining which was to blow up the house in which we dwelt. The Monarchy was faced by an alternative : a free hand for the housebreaker or a demand for security. On the rejection of the latter a fight for life was all that remained." Better death with honour than a lingering decline !

Russia's choice was equally intelligible. Sazonoff, like the Foreign Ministers in the other capitals, was convinced that he had no alternative. He inherited a long tradition from which he had neither the wish nor the power to depart. Russia's inability to take up the challenge in the Bosnian crisis was a bitter memory, and nobody could expect her to submit to such spectacular humiliation again. Since the main purpose of the Triple Entente, as defined by Sazonoff, was to prevent the domination of Europe by Germany, now was the time to make a stand. As Berchtold saw the long arm of Russia in the Serajevo murders, so the Russian Foreign Minister interpreted the ultimatum as a blow not only at King Peter but at the Tsar. Had Russia left her Servian *protégé* for a second time to the tender mercies of the Hapsburgs, she would have forfeited her old claim to be the champion of the Balkan Slavs and have handed over the Near East to the control of the Central Powers. Though not bound by treaty to intervene, she could no more be expected to remain neutral in face of an attack on Belgrad than England in face of a violation of Belgian neutrality. The same instinctive pride of a Great Power which compelled Vienna to throw down the glove compelled St. Petersburg to pick it up.

Russia's intervention in the Austro-Serb quarrel automatically brought Germany into the fray. When Francis Joseph inquired whether he might rely on her support, William II and his Chancellor answered without hesitation that he could. A refusal would have devitalized, if not actually destroyed, the partnership of 1879, which was the basis of German policy. The error was not in promising help but in allowing Austria alone to steer the ship. In entering on such a perilous voyage, the German Government should have insisted on consultation throughout, weighing every article in the ultimatum and discussing every point in the reply. In a memorable passage in his *Reflections and Recollections* Bismarck declared that Germany could fight for the vital interests of Austria as a Great Power with a good conscience, but he would never have consented to allow the fate of his people to be decided by a foreign will. After recklessly throwing the reins on the neck of the Austrian steed, Bethmann strove in vain to hold it back. He was a great gentleman, but his lack of skill in the difficult art of diplomacy was a calamity.

France played a smaller *rôle* in the days of decision than any of the Great Powers of Europe except Italy. Closely tied to her ally as she was, her consent to Russian policy was taken for granted in St. Petersburg, and she was not even consulted about the order for general mobilization which enlarged an Austrian punitive expedition into a world war. Russia had been very lukewarm in the Agadir crisis, and France, whose relations with Austria had always been friendly, had no desire to fight ; yet she had no choice but to follow where her partner led. In addition to her treaty obligations she knew that her neutrality would ensure German domination of the Continent. All she could do was to appeal to England for help. Every Frenchman longed for the recovery of the Rhine provinces, but few dreamed of unleashing a war for that purpose.

The course taken by the British Government was equally clearly marked out by the declarations and decisions of the last ten years. " My God, Mr. Page," exclaimed King George, " what else could we do ? " The violation of Belgian neutrality, which England, like Germany, was pledged to defend, roused the nation to righteous anger and supplied the theme of our ultimatum, but it was the occasion rather than the cause of a declaration of war. Though our only formal allies were Portugal and Japan, and though in theory we retained entire liberty of action, we had now thrown in our lot with France and Russia. Our diplomatic frontier was on the Rhine. Had we stood aside, the Central Powers would have won an easy victory and we should have found ourselves alone. France and Russia would have scorned us as false friends, who, after years of co-operation and expert discussions, deserted them at the crisis of their fate ; and the German menace, intensified by the collapse of the Triple Entente, would have compelled us to arm to the teeth on land and sea. Grey's assurance to the House of Commons on August 3, 1914, that our hands were free was correct in form but inaccurate in substance, for his whole speech breathed the conviction that we should be not only endangered but disgraced if we left France in the lurch. Opinions will continue to differ as to the wisdom of the policy of Continentalism and as to the particular steps taken or omitted by him in the critical days. What is not in doubt is the sincerity of his efforts to avert the catastrophe and the practical impossibility of neutrality when they failed. In 1914, as in the Crimean War, as in the struggles against Louis XIV and Napoleon, as in 1939, we fought for the Balance of Power, in other words for our own survival and security.

I

CONVERSATION WITH KÜHLMANN, FEBRUARY 22, 1929
(IN ENGLISH)

K. Grey was a great gentleman and he sought peace, but he was not a strong man. I doubt if he was always his own master.

I. Of whom are you thinking?

K. Tyrrell. He was the strongest influence in the Foreign Office.

I. But do you consider he was anti-German?

K. No. He saw the danger of being tied too closely to France.

I. May I ask your opinion of Bülow and the Kaiser?

K. I have no respect for Bülow. He was a *Kleber*. He had no system or principles, except that he wanted to stay in office. I have always liked the Kaiser, and I wrote to him a week or two ago on his seventieth birthday.

I. I know that you deplored the Tirpitz policy.

K. Yes. I agreed with Metternich in deploring that policy, but I did not share his belief that failure to reach a naval agreement involved a total failure to improve Anglo-German relations. I preferred the discussion of concrete colonial problems. Lulu Harcourt and I sketched out a satisfactory African settlement. A naval agreement might have been possible after a colonial agreement. I always regarded the German desire for a neutrality formula as hopeless.

I. Grey inherited the commitment to France and therefore could not make real friends with Germany.

K. Not at once. But with time the older French generation would die out and the younger would think less and less about Alsace-Lorraine. I was in close touch with Paris all those pre-war years, and several influential Frenchmen told me privately that they regarded Alsace-Lorraine as a closed question.

I. They never dared to say so publicly.

K. Time would have helped. Bethmann's Constitution of 1911 was a step. The gradual cessation of complaints from Alsace-Lorraine to Paris would have made a rapprochement possible. I was at Tangier in 1905. I wished to get a good price for consenting to France having a free hand in Morocco. I was for hard bargaining but not for threatening. I was asked by French friends to suggest an arrangement. I replied that I thought Germany should yield on Morocco in return for the whole of the French Congo and the pre-emption of the Belgian Congo.

I. You anticipated Kiderlen's idea of concentrating on a Central African Empire?

K. Yes. Holstein prevented such a bargain. He was the real author of the first Morocco crisis and Bülow could not stand up against him.

K. What did Sazonoff say to Grey at Balmoral in 1912 ?

I. I am afraid I must not quote our documents after 1909 before they are published.

K. He must have thoroughly alarmed Grey about a Balkan explosion ; for the Foreign Office then became extremely anxious for Anglo-German co-operation.

K. I was spending a week-end at Polesden Lacey (Mrs. Ronald Greville's country house) about 1913. The visitors' book there would give the date. Iswolsky was there. I shall never forget our conversation. He said Russia would give any terms to Germany if she would desert Austria and allow Russia to smash her. He was not anti-German, but he was passionately anxious for war with Austria.

I. What a curious legend it was that you were mischief-making in Ulster just before the war !

K. Yes. I was recalled from my leave in Germany at the end of July, 1914. On reaching London I went to Haldane's house on the afternoon of Sunday, August 2. I advised England to stand out at first, and then, after the first shock of arms, to dictate peace by a threat of intervention. Only thus could the war be localized and shortened, and the complete exhaustion of one side or the other be prevented. Haldane was interested, seemed to sympathize with the idea, and said he would bring it before the Cabinet for discussion. Grey now appeared, and I restated my view. He replied in effect that he had an honourable obligation to France. I was surprised by the picture of Haldane as warlike in Morley's Memorandum on Resignation. His talk on August 2 with me was quite the reverse.

K. The world war, in my view, was the war of the dissolution of the Austrian Empire. Franco-German relations would probably have improved with time, and Anglo-German relations were over the worst. Both these problems were infinitely simpler than the Austro-Russian antagonism. War was difficult to avert if Vienna, not Berlin, was in control.

I. As she was from the coming of Aehrenthal till 1914.

K. Yes, except when Kiderlen was in command. Had he lived he would not have given Austria a blank cheque on July 5, 1914, and he would probably have prevented war.

I. Lichnowsky also thought that the war was caused by Berlin surrendering the leadership to Vienna.

K. Lichnowsky had family reasons (through his father) as well as political conviction for his hostility to Austria.

I. Jagow denies that Berlin was taken in tow by Vienna.

K. That is because he was in office himself, but it is true.

II

CONVERSATION WITH JAGOW, FEBRUARY 27, 1929
(IN GERMAN)

I. Have you seen Sir Rennell Rodd's very friendly references to you in the third volume of his *Reminiscences* ?

J. Yes. I was always for good relations with England, and so was the Kaiser. He used to talk loudly and wildly, but I could always tell him what I thought when we were alone together. When I pointed out the objections to any policy or proposal, he was very reasonable. Tirpitz had great influence, but Bülow is chiefly to blame for the estrangement with England. He had no political principles, no system, except to stay in power. He did not dare to tell the Kaiser the truth.

I. He had fallen from power before your appointment as Foreign Minister. Did you know him well ?

J. Very well indeed.

I. I fear Bethmann's task was hopeless, and yours too. You were both called in too late. The harm was done. Equally I feel that Grey could not be friends with France and Germany at the same time. The choice had been made before he took office.

J. Yes, the situation was pretty hopeless. War was practically inevitable, not necessarily in 1914 but some time.

I. I regret Germany gave Austria *carte blanche* on July 5, 1914. Of course you had to stand by her, but why did you not insist on her consulting you at every step ?

J. We did not give her *carte blanche*. We expected she would tell us about the ultimatum in good time. I was continually asking Szögenyi for news.

I. I think you ought to have asked not only to be informed but to have been consulted about the ultimatum, for it was obviously a dangerous path. Yet the Kaiser always said that the matter was entirely one for Francis Joseph to decide. And many believe that Tschirschky was a firebrand. What do you think of his *rôle* ?

J. Tschirschky carried out his instructions and did not exceed them, but he was a pessimist. He did not work or wish for war, but he expected it.

I. Szögenyi reported to Vienna that, in telling him of Grey's proposal for a Conference, you said that the German Government was not in favour of it, and only handed it on because you had to do so. You have denied this, but most people in England prefer Szögenyi's report to your subsequent denial.

J. I know that, but I never said anything of the sort. Szögenyi was really past work. Some time before Serajevo one of the Foreign Office officials said to me, " Somebody must always look through Szögenyi's reports before they go to Vienna." I never said more to him than that we would not leave Austria in the lurch.

I. Grey believes that you, Bethmann and the Kaiser desired peace, but he thinks the military element wanted war and pushed you on.

J. Nothing of the sort. Tirpitz was on holiday and was not consulted. Nor was Moltke consulted till the end. The control of our policy was entirely in civilian hands.

I. I regret you only put pressure on Austria so late.

J. That would have been time enough if Russia had not made war inevitable. We had warned Russia of the effects of such a step. We did put pressure on Austria, but Grey never tried to hold Russia back.

I. Grey says he had no *locus standi*. We were not allies, and he could do nothing more after the rejection of his plan for a conference. He says you were the people to hold Austria back, as you were allies. He thinks there was no danger of you losing Austria if you had taken a strong line, for she could not do without you.

J. That is not the case. She could make friends with France, and then reach some agreement with Russia about the Near East.

I. Any such arrangement would have been a triumph for Russia. We think you could and should have pressed Austria more strongly, just as you think we could and should have pressed Russia. Each of us feared the loss of our friend or ally. The European system was the main cause of the war. Germany was dragged in by Austria, England and France by Russia. It was an East European quarrel.

J. That is so.

BRITISH DIPLOMACY BEFORE 1914 IN THE LIGHT OF THE ARCHIVES

AMONG the manifold results of the war of 1914–1918 was the opening of the archives. The Bolshevists led the way by the publication of secret treaties revealing the Imperialist ambitions of the Tsar and his allies. The Germans followed suit with the "Kautsky documents" on the outbreak of the war, and proceeded to unveil the story of German diplomacy from the creation of the Empire in the colossal enterprise known as *Die Grosse Politik*. The German editors' hope that their example might be followed by the victorious Powers was speedily fulfilled. In 1924 Ramsay MacDonald decided to break the seals; and Professor Temperley and I were invited to select documents illustrating British statesmanship from 1898 to 1914. It was well understood that we should have a free hand. Not only did the Foreign Office make no difficulties, but it supported our resistance to attempts by more than one foreign Power to secure the omission of documents. Had these attempts succeeded we should have resigned. In 1926 Poincaré announced the decision to publish the French documents between the wars of 1870 and 1914. The German and British undertakings are complete, but the French is still in progress. In 1930 the Austrians presented us with eleven thousand documents on the last six years of peace. In 1928 the Russians announced a large-scale revelation, beginning with the last three years of Nicholas II, and the first volume of the German translation appeared in 1930. Italy alone of the Great Powers keeps her treasures under lock and key.

Well over a hundred massive volumes of this official material lie before us. So far as diplomacy is concerned, we know the mind and face of Europe during the generation before the World War as we know no other epoch in history. Verdicts on men, policies and events will continue to differ, for there is no absolute standard of political wisdom and virtue, but uncertainty as to what actually occurred is at an end. Bismarck used to say that true history could not be written from official documents, since the historian is not always aware what was in the minds of their authors; but it is equally true that history cannot be written without them. Moreover, the various series I have mentioned contain an overwhelming mass of material never intended for the public eye. With the aid of private correspondence, departmental memoranda and confidential minutes, we are enabled to watch the makers of history at work, to reconstruct the development of situations and ideas. Biographies, autobiographies and diaries cannot be neglected ; public declarations and parliamentary debates must be kept in view. But the only solid foundation for our knowledge of international contacts is the material which records from day to day, and sometimes from hour to hour, the impressions, the anxieties, the plans and the decisions of the men at the helm. I have attempted to reconstruct pre-War Europe in the light of the new evidence in my book, *Before the War*, and have summarized the sources in *Recent Revelations of European Diplomacy*.

Let us first cast our eyes farther back. The two governing urges of the British people for the last four centuries have been the development of ordered liberty at home and expansion overseas. Since geography is the mother of history, our pitch on the north-western fringe of the Continent is the master-key to our diplomacy. To make and to hold an Empire it was essential to secure and maintain supremacy at sea. " What shall we do to be saved in this world ? " asked Halifax the Trimmer. " There is no other answer but this : Look to your moat. The first article of an Englishman's political creed must be that he believeth in the sea." These words were written in 1694. Next to naval supremacy our course has been shaped by the doctrine of the Balance of Power. There are various interpretations of this celebrated formula. To my mind it means the determination, partly conscious and partly instinctive, to resist by diplomacy or arms the growth of any European State at once so formidable and so potentially hostile as to threaten our national liberties, the security of our shores, the safety of our commerce or the integrity of our foreign possessions. Long before the invention of the aeroplane we were too close to the Continent to be indifferent to its concerns. We grappled at different times with Spain, France, Russia and Imperial Germany. Readers of Mr. Churchill's epic will remember Marlborough's conviction that he was fighting; not for territory, but to prevent the domination of Europe by Louis XIV ; and he did not fight in vain.

After the fall of Napoleon we were united in desiring to keep our hands free, to trust to our fleet for the security which other

States sought in alliances and conscript armies, to plunge into the fray only if our vital interests appeared to demand it or treaty obligations were at stake. The policy familiarly known as splendid isolation, or, as I prefer to call it, the free hand, seemed the wisest course till the close of the nineteenth century, and Salisbury stood by it till the end of his career. The face of Europe was continually changing, and he felt no confidence in any Continental Power. He shared Palmerston's conviction that England has no eternal friendships and no eternal enmities, only eternal interests. As the old chess-player bent over the board he congratulated himself on his liberty to choose his moves. In his own unconventional phraseology, " British policy is to float lazily downstream, occasionally putting out a diplomatic boat-hook to avoid collisions."

Salisbury was typically English in disliking large-scale commitments and in his readiness for a deal. The first significant revelation in *British Documents on the Origins of the War 1898–1914* is his proposal to Russia for a delimitation of spheres of influence in China and Turkey, a promising overture terminated by the seizure of Port Arthur in 1898. When, however, we were invited by Germany in 1901 to enter the Triple Alliance, he argued in an impressive memorandum that the liability of having to defend German and Austrian frontiers were heavier than that of having to defend the British Isles against France. The German Ambassador spoke of our isolation as becoming a serious danger for us, but it would hardly be wise to incur novel and most onerous obligations in order to guard against an imaginary danger. Lansdowne was more ready than his chief to consider some limited scheme of Anglo-German association, but he was equally opposed to entanglement in the meshes of the Triple Alliance. There is a direct conflict of testimony between the German and British documents as to which side initiated the alliance discussions. Eckardstein declares it was Lansdowne, Lansdowne attributes it to Eckardstein. I prefer the testimony of the Foreign Secretary, not because he was our own countryman, but because Eckardstein was hampered by the injunctions of Holstein. Whoever started it, the project of an Anglo-German alliance collapsed and was never revived.

The most important revelations in our early volumes enable us to reconstruct in detail the formation of the Entente Cordiale. The years 1902–4 witnessed two epoch-making changes

in our history.   In the first place, with the annexation of the
Transvaal and the Orange Free State, following closely on the
conquest of the Sudan, the greatest Empire in the world became at last territorially satiated.   It makes all the difference
to a nation's policy if it is reasonably contented with its place
in the sun.   Henceforth our chief task was to keep what we
had and to develop our resources.   The second transformation was the swing over to Continental commitments.   Chamberlain was not alone in sensing the perils of isolation at the
turn of the century.   The new course, however, which was a
continuous process, not a single event, was due to foreign
initiatives rather than to a deliberate shift of purpose.   The
Anglo-Japanese alliance of 1902 was an offshoot of Japan's
rivalry with Russia for the mastery of the Far East, and the
protracted negotiations which led to the Anglo-French treaty
of 1904 were the fruit of Delcassé's craving for Morocco.   That
our price was the recognition of our occupation of Egypt was
an unwelcome surprise to him, but he had no means of escape.

   Which side got the best of the bargain ?   Each Government
announced that it had gained its essential demands and
incurred no serious sacrifice.   The kernel of the whole transaction was the Egypt-Morocco deal, on which the verdict of
Lord Cromer, who took a leading part in the discussions,
is of peculiar weight.   When a deadlock occurred in January,
1904, he was terrified at the possibility of losing the glittering
prize that was almost within his grasp, and he intervened with
a telegram urging concessions.   " I have little doubt from
what I hear on the spot that the danger of a breakdown of the
negotiations is serious. . . . It has to be borne in mind that
the French concessions to us in Egypt are in reality far more
valuable than those we are making to them in Morocco.   Moreover they can greatly hamper us here, whereas if they choose
they can carry out their Morocco policy without our help."
The most piquant feature of this episode, as we learn from the
French documents, is that Paul Cambon pulled the strings to
which Cromer danced.   For it was at his suggestion that the
French Chargé in Cairo was instructed to tell Cromer, as if the
warning came from himself, that the Egyptian settlement depended on adequate compensation for the surrender of French
treaty rights in the Newfoundland fisheries.   The ingenious
plan worked without a hitch.

   When the reconciliation had taken place, the *détente* became
an *entente* which the French unceasingly strove to turn into an

alliance. It was an exciting quest for the editors to attempt to trace the origin of the legend of an offer of an alliance, and we discovered that no such offer was ever made by the British Government. Lansdowne merely observed to Paul Cambon, after the Kaiser's visit to Tangier, that the two Governments should keep one another fully informed and should, so far as possible, discuss contingencies in advance. His words were repeated in a letter, interpreted by the French Ambassador as an invitation to a general entente which would in fact amount to an alliance. Delcassé accordingly informed his colleagues at his last Cabinet on June 6, 1905, that an alliance had been offered, and he reiterated the statement to the end of his life. It is a curious instance of an experienced statesman taking the wish for the deed. He was doubtless misled by the fact that the Franco-Russian alliance germinated from the formula of consultation in 1891.

France failed to secure her alliance, but events came to her aid. Her apprehensions on the eve of the Algeciras Conference induced the British Government to sanction non-committal conversations between military and naval experts. A formal promise of military support in the event of an unprovoked German attack was refused ; but the authorization of military conversations was a new departure of the utmost importance, and should have been reported to the Cabinet at the earliest opportunity. " I do not like the stress laid upon joint preparations," wrote Campbell-Bannerman. " It comes very close to an honourable undertaking." The French request, in my opinion, could not have been declined ; but Grey never seemed quite able to realize how far he had gone in transforming the limited treaty obligation of diplomatic support in the Morocco question into a working partnership, which after the Agadir crisis became a defensive alliance in all but name. What was dimly recognized in London was more clearly understood in Paris and Berlin. Rosebery expressed apprehension at our Continental entanglements, but he stood alone. Salisbury was dead, and the policy of splendid isolation was buried in his grave.

In the autumn of 1906, during the lull which followed the anxieties of Algeciras, Eyre Crowe compiled his celebrated " Memorandum on the Present State of British Relations with France and Germany." It is the longest document in our collection, filling twenty-two large pages of small print. Copies were circulated at the time to the members of the

Cabinet, and I had my first sight of it twenty years ago in Lord Morley's library at Wimbledon. The German translator of the *British Documents*, Hermann Lutz, has written a little book called *Crowe, the Evil Spirit of the Foreign Office*, and his influence cannot be ignored by any student of the period. Grey, it is true, while listening to his advisers, kept the final decisions in his own hands. Yet we must not under-estimate the significance in the formation of policy and opinion of a man whose Germanophobe attitude was so pronounced, whose pen was so active, and whose ability was so great. Grey himself described him as anti-German. No one would dream of comparing him with Holstein, whose figure was shrouded in mystery, for British Civil Servants do not play tricks with their chief. Yet it is no exaggeration to say that, as Holstein towers above the officials of the Wilhelmstrasse, so Crewe stands out in sharp relief. His discovery by a larger public at home and abroad is due to the *British Documents on the Origins of the War*.

The Crowe Memorandum begins with a sketch of the making of the Anglo-French entente and of Germany's attempts to destroy the tender plant before it took root. It had begun as a friendly settlement of outstanding disputes, but as a result of the Morocco crisis there had emerged an element of common resistance to dictation and aggression. The Algeciras Act had settled the Morocco problem for the moment, but a far larger question remained. Was the antagonism to Germany into which England had been led on this occasion without her wish or intention a passing incident, or was it a symptom of some deep-seated natural opposition between the policies and interests of the two countries? Crowe adopts the latter alternative, and relates his attitude to the two traditional principles of British policy, namely maritime supremacy and the Balance of Power. Its general character, he reminds us, is determined by our position as an island State, with a vast overseas empire whose existence and survival depend on naval supremacy. Sea-power is more potent than land-power, because it is as pervading as the element in which it moves and has its being. A predominant maritime State which abused its power would be liable to be overthrown by a general combination. In our case the danger has been averted—and can only be averted—by harmonizing our policy with the interests of as many other nations as possible. How is this to be done? By maintaining their independence. England is the natural enemy of any country threatening the independence of others, and the natural protector of the weaker communities. The only check on a powerful and aggressive State is the existence of an equally formidable rival or a league of defence. The equilibrium established by such a grouping of forces is technically known as the Balance of Power, and it has become almost an historical truism to identify England's policy with the maintenance of this balance by throwing her weight now in this scale and now in that, but ever on the side opposed to the dictatorship of the strongest single State or group at a given time. If this view of British policy is correct, our opposition to any country aspiring to such a dictatorship assumes almost the form of a law of nature.

Crowe, needless to say, had Germany in mind, and the larger part of the Memorandum is devoted to her history and ambitions. England, he declares, seeks no quarrels, and will never give her cause for legitimate offence. But can we be equally certain that she will never desire to destroy and supplant the British Empire? In such a matter we could run no risks. There was no thought whatever of hemming her in or clipping her wings. "It cannot be good policy for England to thwart such a process of development where it does not directly conflict either with British interests or with those of other nations to which England is bound by solemn treaty obligations. Nor was it our place to oppose Germany's building as large a fleet as she wished. Any attempt to dictate would stimulate her to fresh efforts. The best method was to show by ocular demonstration that for every German ship we should lay down two. The policy of graceful concessions, either to Germany or to any other Power, was a mistake. The opposition she met at Algeciras would probably make her more careful to avoid fresh disagreements. In this attitude she will be encouraged if she meets on England's part with unvarying courtesy and consideration in all matters of common concern, but also with a prompt and firm refusal to enter into any one-sided bargains or arrangements, and the most unbending determination to uphold British rights and interests in every quarter of the globe. There will be no surer or quicker way to win the respect of the German Government and the German nation."

These are the closing words of this impressive Memorandum. We can imagine German readers complaining that its tone was rather self-righteous, and that in his historical illustrations the author was disinclined to give Germany the benefit of the doubt. Lord Sanderson, who had been Permanent Under-Secretary for many years before his retirement in 1906, found it unduly severe, and challenged some of its details. The history of German policy towards this country, he maintained, was not the unchequered record of black deeds which the Memorandum seemed to portray. We had often co-operated in a friendly way. But the Germans were very tight bargainers, and they had earned the nickname of " les juifs de la diplomatie." Germany was a young Power, and it was inevitable that she should be somewhat arrogant and impatient; but she was not ungrateful for friendly support. " A great and growing nation cannot be repressed. . . . It would be a misfortune that she should be led to believe that in whatever direction she seeks to expand she will find the British lion in her path. There must be places in which German enterprise can find a field without injury to any important British interests, and it would seem wise that in any policy of development which takes due account of these interests she should be allowed to expect our good will." Crowe replied to his veteran critic, but Sanderson's presentation of Anglo-German contacts seems to me the more judicial.

Not long afterwards, when the Casablanca crisis of 1908 seemed to bring Europe within sight of war, Grey asked Crowe for a Memorandum on Belgian neutrality. The document, published in our eighth volume, took a very strict view of British obligations. The neutrality of Belgium, he argues, was guaranteed not merely because it was a Belgian interest, but because it was an interest of the guaranteeing Powers. Why else should so onerous a commitment have been incurred? Even if her neutrality was violated with her connivance, each of the guaranteeing Powers had the right and the duty to call on its partners to join in enforcing the maintenance of neutrality. Still more interesting than this weighty memorandum is the comment on it by Sir Charles Hardinge, the Permanent Under-Secretary: " The liability undoubtedly exists as stated above. But whether we should be called upon to carry out our obligation and to vindicate the neutrality of Belgium in opposing its violation must necessarily depend on our policy and the circumstances of the moment. Supposing that France violated the neutrality of Belgium in a war against Germany, it is, under present circumstances, doubtful whether

England or Russia would move a finger to maintain Belgian neutrality, while if the neutrality of Belgium were violated by Germany it is probable that the converse would be the case." This brief minute, which appeared to suggest a rather cynical opportunism, attracted more attention in the press than any other of our revelations. Grey wrote to *The Times* to explain that the minutes and memoranda of permanent officials were not authoritative documents, since the writers had no responsibility for ultimate decisions and policy. His own attitude to the problem of Belgian neutrality, as he showed by quotations, had never weakened or changed.

An agreement with Russia was the natural, and indeed almost inevitable, sequel to our reconciliation with France. When the Morocco crisis was over, the discussions begun by Lansdowne and Benckendorff were resumed by Grey. Formal negotiations started when the Anglophil Iswolsky succeeded the colourless Lamsdorff as Russian Foreign Minister in 1906, and Nicolson, our new Ambassador, arrived in St. Petersburg with proposals relating to Tibet. Whereas the Anglo-French treaty had sponged the whole slate clean, the Anglo-Russian discussions were confined to the Middle East. The story of sixteen months, culminating in the Convention of August, 1907, fills our fourth volume, which is the historian's only source, since the Russian material is not yet available. British strategy throughout was to make sacrifices in North Persia while inviting them in Tibet and Afghanistan. There was no enthusiasm for the settlement in either country, for the Tsarist system was detested by Englishmen. The depth of the ideological gulf was revealed in the stormy debate on the eve of the King's journey to Reval, which, as a young Member of Parliament, I was privileged to hear. The Convention and the visit, declared Grey, hung together, and if it were vetoed he would resign. He spoke throughout as a *Realpolitiker*. He disliked pogroms and executions as much as the rest of us, and a great deal more than he admitted in despatches and debate ; but he declined to sacrifice a new and valuable friendship to such scruples. While his critics were denouncing Russian misrule, his eyes were fixed on the darkening clouds in the North Sea.

What happened at Reval ? Here is the vital passage in Sir Charles Hardinge's account of what he said to Iswolsky : " Though the attitude of His Majesty's Government was and had been absolutely correct, it was impossible to ignore the fact that, owing to the unnecessarily large increase in the German naval programme, a deep distrust in England of Germany's future intentions had been created. This distrust would be still further accentuated with the progress of time, the realization of the German programme, and the increase of taxation in England entailed by the necessary naval counter-measures. In seven or eight years' time a critical situation might arise in which Russia, if strong in Europe, might be the arbiter of peace, and have much more influence in securing the peace of the world than at any Hague Conference. For this reason it was absolutely necessary that England and Russia should maintain towards each other the same cordial and friendly relations as now exist between England and France, which, in the case of England and Russia, are moreover inspired by an identity of interests of which a solution of the Macedonian problem was not the least."

Here was a direct invitation to turn the *détente* of 1907 into an *entente*, based on our confidence that in the hour of danger Russia would be on our side. Since Germany's strength and ambition seemed likely to threaten our security, Russia would prove a very useful counter in the other scale. It is the familiar story of the Balance of Power.

British policy in the sixteen crowded years illustrated by the *British Documents* falls into two chapters. The first, lasting from Chamberlain's informal conversations on an Anglo-German alliance in 1898 to the Reval visit in 1908, witnessed our entry into the Continental system. The second, covering the last six years of peace, confronted us with the task of maintaining and developing the Triple Entente. There are no more striking items in our fifth volume, on the Bosnian crisis, than the private letters between Nicolson and his chief when in March, 1909, Iswolsky accepted the annexation as the result of what he called a diplomatic ultimatum from Berlin. The Ambassador, whom King Edward regarded as the best horse in our diplomatic stable, wrote angrily about the sudden collapse, and added: "Our entente, I much fear, will languish and possibly die. If it were possible to extend and strengthen it by bringing it nearer to the nature of an alliance, it would then be possible to deter Russia from moving towards Berlin. . . . The ultimate aims of Germany surely are, without doubt, to obtain the preponderance on the Continent of Europe, and when she is strong enough—and apparently she is making very strenuous efforts to become so—she will enter on a contest with us for maritime supremacy. In past times we have had to fight Holland, Spain, and France for this supremacy, and personally I am convinced that sooner or later we shall have to repeat the same struggle with Germany. If we could keep France and Russia on our side, it would be well."

Grey replied that it was impracticable to change our agreements into alliances : " The feeling here about definite commitment to a Continental war on unforeseeable conditions would be too dubious to permit us to make an alliance. Russia too must make her internal government less reactionary. Till she does, liberal sentiment here will remain very cool, and even those who are not sentimental will not believe that she can purge her administration sufficiently to become a strong and reliable Power. Meanwhile let us keep an entente with Russia in the sense of keeping in touch, so that our diplomatic action may be in accord and in mutual support." Grey knew the sentiments of the House of Commons and Nicolson did not.

One of the obvious reasons against turning the Triple Entente into a Triple Alliance was that it would confirm the German fear of encirclement and ruin any chance of reconciliation with Berlin. Grey was never very sanguine about a rapprochement, and the first Morocco crisis had emphasized the tragic impossibility of being real friends with France and Germany at the same time. Moreover he profoundly distrusted Bülow, and, like the rest of us, he had no exalted opinion of the wisdom of William II. Yet he never abandoned hope of a tolerable relationship, and our sixth volume is the record of his attempts to obtain it. In 1908 we made the first and last formal proposal to abate the naval rivalry which was getting on our nerves. Sir Charles Hardinge, who accompanied the King to Cronberg, was instructed to have a frank talk with the Kaiser. " If the German fleet ever becomes superior to ours," ran the Foreign Office memorandum drawn up for his guidance, " the German army can conquer this country. There is no corresponding risk of this kind to Germany ; for however superior our fleet, no naval victory would bring us any nearer Berlin." There was no need for a formal agreement. " If it could be shown that, as a result of the interview between the two sovereigns, a slackening of activity in the building programmes of the two navies had ensued, there is no doubt that the state of unrest prevailing

in Europe due to apprehensions in England and Germany
would be greatly appeased, and this would be of more value
to the peace of the world than any entente based on the
settlement of territorial or commercial questions." In the
decisive conversation with Hardinge on August 11, 1908,
the Kaiser sharply declared that modification of his ship-
building programme was impossible, and that discussion of a
question involving national honour could not be allowed.
This brief interview was a turning-point in the history of
British diplomacy. During his first two years of office,
Grey's main anxiety arose from the strained relations between
Paris and Berlin. From 1908 onwards the storm-centre
shifted from the Eastern frontier of France to the North Sea.
Once again the old cry rang through the land : " Look to
your moat."

The naval scare of the spring of 1909 followed, based on
rumours of stealthy German acceleration, and in the summer
of the same year Bethmann Hollweg succeeded Bülow as
Chancellor. His first step was to declare his readiness for a
naval arrangement as part of a general understanding. His
sincerity was manifest, but the coupling of a naval agreement
with a political formula ruined the scheme. " To do with
Germany what has not been done with Russia and France,"
wrote Grey to Goschen, " would look as if we were intending
to change friends. I want a good understanding with Germany, but it must be one which will not imperil those we have
with France and Russia. I should have thought some formula
could be found to which they might also be parties. That
would be the best and the most reassuring solution, though
I see that the French could not be a party to anything which
looked like confirming the loss of Alsace-Lorraine." From
this standpoint he never moved during the three years of
negotiation which lay ahead. While the Germans asked for a
neutrality formula, we invited them to reduce their ship-
building programme and offered nothing beyond a promise of
non-aggression. Interrupted for several months by the
Agadir crisis in 1911, the discussion was resumed during the
Haldane mission to Berlin in February, 1912, and continued
after his return. The old obstacles proved insurmountable,
for each side asked more than the other was prepared to grant.
Both the British appeal of 1908 and the German approach of
1909 had failed.

Only once did Grey attempt a comprehensive and con-

H

fidential picture of the international situation as he saw it—in a speech, printed in our sixth volume, delivered at a meeting of the Committee of Imperial Defence on May 26, 1911, to which the Dominion delegates to the Imperial Conference were invited. Separate Dominion navies, he began, necessitated a common foreign policy for the Empire, generally understood and approved. What really determined our policy was the question of sea-power. Next to our navy, we had sought safety in terminating our quarrels with France and Russia. Unfortunately our relations with Germany deteriorated as those with France and Russia improved. If, as he hoped, an improvement occurred, it would have to be a friendship into which we could take our friends. There was only one danger—that some Power or group of Powers should pursue what he called the Napoleonic policy, separating other States from each other, crushing them one by one, and forcing them into its orbit. In such an event the weaker Powers would appeal to us to help them. " Our hands are free. . . . But I do feel this very strongly, that if such a situation should arise, and there was a risk of all the Powers or a group of Powers acquiring such a dominating position in Europe that it would be the arbiter, not only of peace or war, but of the diplomacy of all the other Powers of Europe, and if while that process was going on we were appealed to for help and sat by and looked on and did nothing, then people ought to realize that the result would be one great combination in Europe, outside which we should be left without a friend. . . . There will be no aggression on our part. If we are ever involved in trouble, it will not be for the sake of any ideas of aggrandisement or ambition or any other vain empty things of that kind."

After thus proclaiming the orthodox doctrine of naval supremacy and the balance of power, Grey proceeded to survey the map of Europe. We were on the best of terms with France and Russia. With Austria our relations were quite good, though we seldom came in contact with her. With Italy we had always been excellent friends. With Germany there was only one difficulty, the fleet, but it was a very great one. France and Russia were most peacefully disposed, and we were continually explaining that we did not wish them to have a quarrel with Germany : " You need be under no apprehension that our relations with France and Russia will ever be made a cause of provocation in policy. If Germany is content with the great strength she is getting, that strength which will make her so strong that there is no question of any Power or group of Powers in Europe provoking a quarrel with her, then everything will go well. If she was to use that strength, which I do not for the moment suppose she would, to obtain the dominating Napoleonic position in Europe, then I think there would be trouble."

Had Grey been speaking on the morrow instead of on the eve of the Agadir crisis, his picture would have had darker shadows. For the policy of Germany during the summer of 1911 strengthened his suspicions that she was pursuing what he called Napoleonic aims.

While the search for a political and naval agreement was abandoned as hopeless in the spring of 1912, Anglo-German exchanges shifted from battleships and neutrality to regional pacts. The discussions on the Bagdad railway and the Portuguese colonies fill many hundred pages in our tenth volume. Agreement was reached in both cases, but the welcome *détente* changed nothing in the structure of Europe. Since Agadir the Franco-German antagonism was worse than ever. The year which opened with the Haldane Mission closed with the Mediterranean Agreement and the Grey-Cambon letters. The formula of consultation, which France requested and obtained, seemed to Grey, though not to Poincaré, to change nothing. When, moreover, France left her northern coasts exposed, and we no longer depended entirely on our own strength in the Mediterranean, the conclusion seemed inescapable that we were allies in every-thing but name.

In December; 1912, when the Balkan conflagration seemed likely to spread, Prince Henry of Prussia visited King George V at Sandringham and asked him a question point-blank. In the event of Germany and Austria going to war with Russia and France, would England come to the assistance of the two latter Powers? " I answered undoubtedly Yes in certain circumstances," reported the King to Grey. " He professed surprise and regret, but did not ask what the certain circumstances were. He said he would tell the Emperor what I had told him. Of course Germany must know that we would not allow either of our friends to be crippled."

Grey approved the reply and explained his own attitude : " Your Majesty's Government is not committed in the event of war, and the public opinion of this country is, so far as Sir

Edward Grey can judge, very averse to a war arising out of a quarrel about Servia. But if Austria attacked Servia aggressively, and Germany attacked Russia if she came to the assistance of Servia, and if France were then involved, it might become necessary for England to fight; as the German Chancellor said that Germany would fight for the defence of her position and for the protection of her own future and security." Here was the doctrine of the Balance of Power in its purest form, though the phrase was never used.

While Anglo-German relations steadily improved owing to trustful co-operation throughout the Balkan wars, Franco-German relations remained tense and Russia's relations to the Central Powers grew steadily worse. The appointment of Liman von Sanders to the command of the First Turkish Army Corps in Constantinople at the end of 1913 created a storm of anger in St. Petersburg. Though the German Government gave way, Grey's lukewarm sympathy was resented by Sazonoff, who resolved to put a little more backbone into the Triple Entente if he could. Benckendorff explained to his chief, in a striking private letter published in the Russian documents, why Grey had not been able to do more. Public opinion was opposed even to an alliance with France. Nicolson himself, who desired it, confessed that it was impossible. A fortnight later the Ambassador added a few touches to the picture. He shared his chief's desire for an alliance as the natural conclusion of the entente. It was the general wish in British military and naval circles : it was represented on the front benches and in the Foreign Office. " You will be surprised at my conviction that Grey would do it to-morrow if he could. But he belongs to the class of people who rarely speak about things till they are ripe." The difficulty, he added, was immense. A terrible insularity still remained. Englishmen would only wake up on the eve of a tremendous crisis. The situation could not be forced. Sazonoff was wrong to talk of the blindness of Grey. " The menace of German hegemony is always in his thoughts, and he anxiously follows its advance. Do not believe he is blind. Far from it. He seems much more irresolute than he is. . . . He feels very strongly that he is the pillar and the born champion of the entente to which his whole policy and his own future are welded."

The approaching visit of King George V to Paris provided Russia with the desired opportunity for drawing closer to England. On April 3, 1914, the Tsar told Buchanan that he would like a defensive alliance, or at any rate an arrangement like that existing between England and France, agreeing what each country would do in certain eventualities. It would be useful to arrange for the co-operation of the fleets. Nicolson thought that a discussion on the French model between the naval staffs, without in any way binding the Governments, would have great advantages. Grey's reaction was more cautious. " If the French agreed, we might let the Russians know what has passed between military and naval authorities on each side, but we had better postpone discussion of anything as long as we can." There was, however, no escape from our importunate friends. Nicolson was informed that Sazonoff had asked Doumergue, the Premier and Foreign Minister, to speak to Grey about a defensive alliance or a naval convention. " It is a very delicate matter," minuted Grey on Nicolson's report, " and I am glad to be warned, but it is possible that it is the French who have inspired the Russians with the idea. It is curious that the Russians should be suggesting more than the French have got from us."

For the first and last time Grey accompanied the Sovereign on a State visit, and the intimacy of the Anglo-French entente was emphasized in every possible way. His report of the conversations is brief and colourless, but the French documents provide a detailed account by Doumergue himself. Here is a brief summary :

Doumergue : We have confidence in the friendship of England, and I am sure she would not fail us in the hour of peril. I merely remark how abnormal it is that, while France has naval arrangements with England and Russia, there is no co-ordination between the three. Could not England do with Russia what she has done with us ?

Grey : As regards military co-operation we have done all we can with you.

Doumergue : Of course, and therefore I only have naval activity in mind. Your country and mine have envisaged the co-operation of our squadrons in the North Sea. That is no obstacle to co-operation with Russia in the Baltic. Indeed, the latter is the logical consequence of the former.

Grey : Very well, we might begin by telling Russia of the conversations between our General Staffs and then ask : What have you to say ?

Doumergue : I quite approve this procedure.

Grey : I will speak to Asquith and recommend the plan.

As regards France no English Government would refuse military and naval aid if she were unjustly menaced and attacked. But with Russia it is quite different. With her size and her immense reserves of man-power, people believe she could victoriously resist German aggression.

Doumergue : There is a pro-German party in Russia—Witte is a member—which favours an entente at Austria's expense. If you converse with Russia, and if our three Naval General Staffs have joint discussions, Russia, finding herself tied more closely to us, would be better able to resist German approaches. Do you not think there might be an exchange of letters in which we would agree that, if one of the three countries found itself suddenly menaced, or if the general situation made it appear necessary, a conversation *à trois* would immediately take place ?

Grey : I do not reject the idea, but we must proceed methodically. We could examine that after we have communicated to Russia our conversations relating to naval co-operation.

The Russians asked for it, wrote Grey afterwards, the French pressed it, and we saw no reason to refuse provided that the whole transaction was strictly within the limits laid down in the Grey-Cambon letters. It would indeed have been as difficult to decline the Russian suggestion in 1914 as to rebuff the French in 1906. Yet the proviso that expert conversations left the discretion of the Governments unimpaired failed once again to prevent enhanced expectations of support. Grey passes rather too lightly over the incident in his Memoirs. Our partners in the Triple Entente were delighted at the readiness with which we accepted their plan. England saw no need for an alliance, reported Benckendorff to his chief, but she realized that, if the worst occurred, she would none the less have to march. When the ensuing discussions between British and Russian naval experts began, he joyfully reported that the Triple Entente had at last become a reality. Cambon, he added, had helped with hands and feet. The fly in the ointment was the fact that the negotiations were betrayed by a member of the Russian Embassy in London, and were revealed by Theodor Wolff in the *Berliner Tageblatt* at the instance of the Wilhelmstrasse.

The story of our diplomacy in the last years of peace as revealed by the archives is a crescendo of commitments. The alliance with Japan in 1902, the promise of diplomatic support to France in Morocco in the treaty of 1904, Lansdowne's invitation to continuous discussion of contingencies in 1905, the authorization of non-binding discussions between naval and military experts in 1906, Hardinge's conversations with Iswolsky at Reval in 1908, Mr. Lloyd George's Mansion House speech in 1911, the Mediterranean Agreement and the Grey-Cambon letters in 1912, the naval discussions with Russia in the summer of 1914—here were milestones along the road to full co-operation with France and Russia in the event of war. When the hour of decision arrived, Grey had no more doubt where our honour and interests lay than his official advisers, Nicolson and Crowe, though for constitutional reasons his pace was not as quick as they desired.   There is no more arresting document in our eleventh volume than Eyre Crowe's memorandum to his chief on July 31.

" The argument that there is no written bond binding us to France is correct.   There is no contractual obligation.   But the entente has been made, strengthened, put to the test and celebrated in a manner justifying the belief that a moral bond was being forged.   The whole policy of the entente can have no meaning if it does not signify that in a just quarrel England would stand by her friends."

The incisive words of the Civil Servant embodied the thoughts of the Foreign Secretary throughout his anxious years at the helm.   His task was to work a system constructed before he was called to the helm.   There is no reason to suppose that Lansdowne, its author, would have acted differently in any of the major emergencies of the time, and their joint achievements must be envisaged as an indivisible whole. Criticism both of their policy of Continental commitments and of their handling of particular issues, such as the Agadir crisis and the situation after Serajevo, is bound to continue ; but since the publication of the *British Documents* there is no longer the slightest doubt what our policy was.   The whole story is unified and dominated by our reconciliation with France—not a union of hearts but a *mariage de raison.*

How shall we define British aims after the turning-point of 1904 ?   I answer, to stand by France, first in regard to Morocco as by treaty bound, and later over the whole field of international politics so long as she was unaggressive ; to terminate the hostility of Russia which dated from the Crimean War and which seemed to threaten our Indian frontier ; to strive for a naval agreement and neighbourly relations with Germany ; to maintain our traditions of an invincible navy and a small voluntary army ; to be friends with the United States ; to keep the alliance with Japan in repair ; to work for reforms in Macedonia and the Belgian Congo ; to labour for peace without forgetting the dread possibilities of war. Of such a programme there is no need to be ashamed.

That it proved impossible to avert a catastrophe in 1914 was due to the co-existence of three deep-rooted antagonisms—the Franco-German feud about the Rhine provinces, the Anglo-German dispute about the fleet, the Austro-Russian rivalry in the Near East. For none of them were British statesmen responsible. At the opening of the twentieth century Europe was faced with problems too complex to be solved by a single State. The belief that any nation or statesman was an arch criminal is no longer held by serious students of history. It is part of the tragedy of the World War that every belligerent can make out a case entirely convincing to itself. For tragedy, in Hegel's words, is the conflict not of right with wrong, but of right with right. How could the system of armed groups and alliances in an age of rampant Imperialism be expected to inaugurate a co-operative and stabilized world ? The ultimate cause of the explosion was the European anarchy, the absence of international machinery, the doctrine of the unfettered national State, the universal assumption that the graver disputes could only be settled by war.

CONVERSATION WITH LORD GREY, FEBRUARY 14, 1929

PRINCIPLES OF POLICY

I. Your policy, as I understand it, was based on three principles—two old, one new. The first was supremacy at sea.

G. Yes, but leaving the United States out of account. I never regarded the Two Power standard as applying to them.

I. The second was the Balance of Power.

G. I don't like that phrase.

I. I mean by it what you have expressed as follows : " England has always drifted or deliberately gone into opposition to any Power which establishes a hegemony in Europe."

G. Thus interpreted, I accept it.

I. Your third principle was friendship with France.

G. Yes.

I. You also took over from Lansdowne the policy of a rapprochement with Russia. Nearly all foreign and some English writers make you responsible for the great change over from isolation to what I call Continentalism. It seems to me that the new lines were laid down by Lansdowne rather than by you.

G. That is so.

ANGLO-FRENCH RELATIONS

I. You said during the war that you believed there were no records here of Barnardiston's conversations in Brussels.

G. They were purely academic.

I. They have been found in the War Office. The men who may have known about them had all gone to the war.

G. Are you going to publish them?

I. They were published in our third volume last December. Did you read any parts of that volume?

G. No. I can read so little.

I. If you had consulted the Cabinet in January 1906 about your conversations with Cambon, as you now admit would have been wise, would you have met with opposition? In other words, would it have made any real difference to history?

G. I don't think so. Campbell-Bannerman and Ripon, as well as Asquith and Haldane, knew and approved. We should doubtless have had criticism but not, I should say, opposition. It was impossible to refuse the French request for military consultations: that would have been to undo all the work of 1904-5. Besides, we made it clear that we were to remain absolutely uncommitted.

I. General Huguet, in his book, says that you, Haldane and Campbell-Bannerman were too clever not to realize that these conversations and arrangements constituted something like a moral engagement.

G. If that had been the case, Cambon would have said so in 1914, whereas he only appealed to our interests.

I. Cambon spoke very differently to Wickham Steed, when he asked if the word honour was to be blotted out of the English language.

G. We always made it clear that the conversations left the Governments absolutely free, and we stated it in the letters of 1912, which I think reassured some of my colleagues.

I. Cambon thought that the Liberal maximum might have been only a Conservative minimum. Would the Conservatives have gone further to meet French wishes and been ready to make an alliance?

G. Some Conservatives would have liked to do so, but it would have been impossible. Public opinion would have been opposed to it.

I. The more I study the documents the more I feel that our friendship with France, once made, rendered real friendship with

Germany impossible. Bülow admits in his book that the gulf between France and Germany was too wide to be bridged. France was suspicious of all our approaches to Germany; and German policy in Morocco and in regard to the fleet made friendly relations with us difficult. Your task was pretty hopeless.

G. As long as Holstein was there, nothing could be done.

I. Holstein was half cracked.

G. And Bülow was false. Look at his treatment of Chamberlain.

I. I should prefer the word slippery.

G. Yes, slippery is better.

I. There were difficulties on this side also. I am impressed by Eyre Crowe's intense hostility to Germany.

G. Crowe was anti-German. But I don't think the Minutes of officials ought to be published, or they will be afraid to write them.

I. They add greatly to the interest and value of diplomatic publications. Sir Austen Chamberlain has given us a free hand, except as regards obviously hasty and unconsidered Minutes, which we have no desire to publish.

AGADIR

I. I have always regretted that you authorized Lloyd George's Mansion House speech and did not keep the Agadir issue in your own hands.

G. But Germany had sent me no reply; and did it not prevent war?

I. Possibly, though I don't think it was so near as that. The Kaiser and Bethmann were opposed to war over Morocco. But it made very bad blood, played into the hands of Tirpitz and the Militarists, and led to the increase of armaments.

G. That is very interesting. If it is the case, it shows how bad the situation in Europe was. They began it by sending a ship to Agadir.

I. The Germans think that France began it by the occupation of Fez.

1914

I. Foreigners find it difficult to believe that you never enquired about the details of the naval discussions with Russia.

G. I did not, and I believe very little was actually done. In any case there could have been nothing affecting naval strategy, like the Mediterranean agreement of 1912, which was important.

I. In July 1914 the ideal would have been for you to state in good time what we should do. But I know that was impossible, as the Cabinet was divided.

G. Quite impossible.

I. You were widely blamed for not urging Russia to abstain from any irrevocable step which might start hostilities.

G. I resent that criticism. After Germany refused the Conference, I could not put pressure on Russia. She was far less prepared for war than Germany. If I had tried to hold back her military preparations, Sazonoff would at once have said : Then will you help us if war comes ? It was for Germany to hold back Austria, who was her ally, and to whom therefore she had a right to speak. She should have pressed Berchtold to accept the Conference.

I. She dared not do so. The German Government did not want war, but it had given Austria *carte blanche* and could not regain control of the situation. And it was genuinely afraid of losing its only dependable ally. The Austrians did not want a patched up settlement with Servia, and they had such bitter memories of the Ambassadors' Conference during the Balkan wars that they would not look at the idea. This was thoroughly understood at Berlin.

G. I agree that neither the Kaiser nor Bethmann nor Jagow wanted war. But why should they be afraid of losing Austria ? What could she do ?

I. Germany was convinced that the Alliance was at stake if she declined to play up, and she dreaded isolation.

RUSSIA

I. Many writers, here and abroad, while fully recognizing your desire for peace, argue that you allowed our friends to make the pace. We were a satiated Power ; they were not. We had indeed made up our quarrels with them, but in doing so we got mixed up in their quarrels with other people.

G. That is only partially true. We should never have supported France in aggression.

I. Of course not, and she knew it. But she was tied to Russia, who was both ambitious and untrustworthy.

G. Russia was like a big ship without a rudder. There was no real control. Think of Hartwig at Teheran. War was not inevitable in 1914, but it was almost inevitable some time on account of the state of Europe with its balance of power, alliances and armaments. That is why I am so keen on the League, Locarno, and disarmament. It was a very bad mistake to attribute the whole responsibility for the war to the Central Powers in the Treaty of Versailles, as I have said in the Preface to the cheap edition of my book.

PRINCE BÜLOW AND HIS MEMOIRS

IN the vast literature on the origins of the first world war Prince Bülow's Memoirs hold a place apart. Most of the statesmen who occupied themselves with foreign affairs in the last decade of peace have told their tale, but none of them has covered so much ground. Grey's survey of the crowded years before the catastrophe fills a single volume of moderate size. Iswolsky died at the age of sixty-three, when his narrative had only reached his appointment as Minister of Foreign Affairs in 1906. Bethmann's pathetic apologia begins in 1909, that of Sazonoff in 1910, that of Poincaré in 1912. Berchtold's elaborate presentation, though far advanced, is not yet available. Bülow's narrative, on the other hand, composed at leisure during the decade which followed the defeat of the Central Powers, fills four volumes, the first two dealing with the years 1897–1909, when he was mainly responsible for German foreign policy, the third continuing the story till 1919, and a fourth recording the experiences of his early diplomatic career.

The ex-Chancellor resisted all appeals to allow publication during his life, and his readers benefit by a decision which enabled him to write with complete freedom of his master, his friends, and his foes. Like other statesmen who held high office in the last anxious period of peace, he has been as bitterly attacked by his own countrymen as by critics beyond the frontier. In his *Imperial Germany*, published in 1913 and partially rewritten in 1916, he adroitly defended his handiwork; but that remarkable book was written to form part of a vast co-operative glorification of German achievement during the first twenty-five years of the reign of William II, in which there was no place for criticism. Though he had lost his post and his master's favour, he was not wholly free; for Kiderlen had regained his footing after a decade of disgrace, and Bülow would have been more than human if he had burned his boats. But with the Kaiser in exile, Germany a Republic, and the leading figures of the Imperial régime dead or in retirement, there was nothing to prevent him from saying exactly what he thought. Like Poincaré he fights with the gloves off, hitting out sharply and sometimes savagely at men who put obstacles in his path or criticized his character and policy. Germany is poorer in political memoirs than England or France ; but this massive autobiography finds a place in the first class of this category, yielding in interest and importance, so far as Germany is concerned, to the *Reflections and Recollections* of Bismarck alone.

The figure of William II, full of life and colour, is continually on the stage, and every chapter of the first two volumes contains incidents and comments which help us to visualize him as he appeared to the brilliant Minister. The abiding impression which we carry away is that he never grew up. It reads—and is obviously meant to read—like the story of a tactful tutor struggling to educate an exceptionally gifted, high-spirited and impulsive pupil. On his fall the Prince handed back the hundreds of letters which he had received from the last of the Hohenzollerns ; but we hardly seem to miss them, so abundant is the material provided by the author and other intimates of the *enfant terrible*: His complicated nature could only be understood by those who knew him well, and for that reason the picture drawn in such a well-known book as Count Zedlitz's *Twelve Years at the Kaiser's Court* is unconvincing. The best approach is through Johannes Haller's fascinating life of Eulenburg, and the picture drawn in the biography of the Kaiser's best friend is confirmed by the pen of the fallen Chancellor.

When Bülow was summoned in 1897 to succeed Marschall von Bieberstein as Foreign Secretary, the sun was shining brightly in the heavens. He belonged to one of the oldest and most distinguished of Prussian families ; his father had been Foreign Minister in the seventies ; unlike Marschall, he had never quarrelled with the Bismarcks ; during twenty years at Paris and St. Petersburg, Bucharest and Rome, he had learned the arts and crafts of diplomacy ; his ready wit, wide culture, and personal charm were known to all ; his gifted and delightful wife, a superb musician, was connected with Minghetti and other leading Italian families ; he was only forty-eight and in excellent health ; he was the friend of Eulenburg, who at that time possessed the Kaiser's ear and who had helped to secure his appointment ; he was a *persona grata* to Hohenlohe, the veteran Chancellor, to Holstein, the un-crowned King of the Foreign Office, and above all to the Kaiser himself.

The international situation was not without its difficulties, but there were no black clouds directly overhead. Three bad mistakes in the field of foreign policy had been made since Bismarck's guiding hand had been withdrawn. The refusal to renew the secret treaty of reinsurance with Russia when its three-year term ended in 1890 was a costly error, for it accelerated the drift of Russia towards France. Co-operation with the Dual Alliance to rob Japan of some of the fruits of victory over China angered a nation whose full strength was unrealized and who knew how to wait for the day of revenge. Finally the Kruger telegram ended the cordial relations between the British Empire and the new Germany, and taught the man in the street to think of the two countries for the first time as potential foes. All nations, however, make mistakes at times, and the relations of the Great Powers changed so frequently with their momentary needs or interests that there was always a chance for a resourceful diplomatist to counteract or circumscribe the evil that had been wrought. Germany's strength was undeniable, yet common sense suggested that the Bismarckian maxim of limited liability was still the best. At home the wealth of the country was increasing by leaps and bounds, and there seemed to be no limit to its power and prosperity in the years that lay ahead. All that was needed was skilful steering of the ship.

On the way from Rome to Kiel, where the Kaiser was awaiting him, Bülow stopped in Frankfurt to meet Eulenburg, who gave him a brief but pregnant memorandum. William II, he wrote, took everything subjectively. Only personal arguments impressed him. He liked to instruct, not to be instructed. He hated to be bored. He must shine, and he desired to do and determine everything himself, though often with unfortunate results. He was ambitious and jealous, and a proposal had the best chance of acceptance if made to appear that it came from himself. Everything had to be made easy for him. Bülow must never forget that His Majesty needed occasional praise. He was one of those natures which lose their spirits if they do not receive recognition, and when he deserved it he was as grateful as a good and clever child. No one but Eulenburg, most subtle of psychologists and a born writer, could have described the ruler so accurately in a few sentences, and the advice which Bülow received from other quarters tallied with his testimony. Lucanus, the head of the Kaiser's Civil Cabinet, used to say that he often slipped, but that he usually picked himself up if he had the right counsellor at his side. The Grand Duke Friedrich of Baden, the wisest man then sitting on a German throne, knew the strength and weakness of his nephew's character, and, like King Albert of Saxony, prayed ardently that the new Minister, while utilizing the ruler's shining qualities for the good of his people, might keep his dangerous impulses within bounds.

The relation of the Chancellor to the Minister for Foreign Affairs in the Hohenzollern Empire varied widely with the holders of those high offices. Bismarck's Foreign Secretaries, the elder Bülow, Hatzfeldt, Herbert Bismarck, were cyphers. Under Caprivi, a soldier who knew nothing of foreign affairs, Marschall, with Holstein behind him, had a good deal of power, which he retained under Hohenlohe. When Bülow was installed in the Wilhelmstrasse in 1897 Hohenlohe was seventy-eight, and, though still vigorous in mind, was feeling the strain of years. Thus the first professional diplomatist since the fall of Bismarck to hold the rudder became the main director of foreign policy from the outset, and when he succeeded Hohenlohe as Chancellor in 1900 there was no one to say him nay save the Kaiser himself. That the supreme responsibility for the course of the German ship between 1897 and 1909 is shared by these two men was known to us all, and the exact degree of responsibility attaching to each in the great decisions of the time was revealed by the publication of *Die Grosse Politik*. Bülow's Memoirs are a precious though far less trustworthy addition to our knowledge. He naturally makes the best case for himself, and he is entitled to remind the reader of the unusual difficulties of his position. His welcome at Kiel, he tells us, was delightful in its cordiality and frank simplicity. He adds that it was only by degrees that he learned of the reefs that lurked beneath the shining surface of the sea.

In these glittering pages we see a ruler of outstanding gifts, lofty ideals, and not a few attractive qualities. We read of his friendliness, his goodness of heart, his naturalness when alone with a friend, his willingness to listen to " curtain lectures " from a trusted adviser, his brightness and charm. His intellectual powers were considerable, his knowledge wide if not deep, his quickness of apprehension phenomenal, while his eloquence never ceased to impress such an accomplished rival and such a critical judge as Bülow himself. In the latter respect indeed nature had been too lavish in her favours, for William II thirsted to make use of the gift for speech which he knew himself to possess. On accompanying his master to Vienna shortly after his appointment, the new Foreign Secretary urged him to adapt his Toast to the prosaic temperament of Francis Joseph. " My dear Bernhard," replied the Kaiser in the friendliest tone, " you are, of course, much cleverer than I, but I know more about speaking than you. I believe you have never made a public speech. I have made plenty, and I can say without vanity that they were not bad. So let me speak in my own way." He proceeded to deliver a dithyrambic harangue which obviously displeased the old host, to whom over-emphasis and gush were anathema. Worse was to follow, and it was one of Bülow's constant cares to avert, conceal or explain away rhetorical lapses which sometimes echoed round the world.

" Perhaps the most detrimental speech he ever made " is the comment on the " Hunnenrede " of 1900. The Kaiser's equilibrium was always disturbed when his vivid imagination turned to the Far East. His famous picture of the Yellow Peril, with the inscription " Peoples of Europe, preserve your holiest possessions," was a nightmare to his Ministers, and is rightly described by Bülow as grotesque ; yet reproductions were hung by his orders in the ships of the Hamburg-Amerika and the Norddeutscher Lloyd bound for the East, " to the delight of the English who sucked no small advantage from this offence to Japanese feeling." His aversion to the Japanese as a race extended to individuals, and we are assured that he treated their diplomats and officers badly, despite the remonstrances of his advisers.

If the Japanese were not to his taste, how much greater was his horror of the Chinese ! Never did Bülow find him in a state of such excitement as during the opening phases of the Boxer revolt, and the overstrained nerves found expression in the historic words to the departing troops at Bremerhafen on June 27, 1900. " Pardon will not be granted, prisoners will not be made. As a thousand years ago the Huns of Attila made themselves a name which lives in story and legend, so let the German name be impressed on China by you in such a way that no Chinaman ever again dares to look askance at a German." Before the speech was finished the agitated Foreign Secretary issued instructions that it was not to be published till it had been corrected by himself. The journalists loyally obeyed, but the reporter of a local paper, perched on a neighbouring roof, had caught the fatal phrase and given it to a listening world. The Kaiser was delighted to learn that his speech had appeared in its original form, but his mood quickly changed when Bülow pointed out that it would produce a devastating effect on the reputation of a Christian country. The two men sat up talking till midnight, and on parting the Kaiser shook hands, remarking " I know you wish me well, but I am what I am and I cannot change." " You must deal with this in the Reichstag," whispered Hohenlohe to Bülow as he heard the fatal words, " for I cannot." The Foreign Minister did his best with the inevitable interpellations ; but he could not prevent the foes of Germany in two great wars from describing as Huns " the good and noble German people, the most truly humane in the world."

Next in unhappy celebrity among the Imperial utterances was the declaration at Damascus to " the three hundred million Mohammedans throughout the world " that the German Emperor would at all times be their friend. When the meal was over Bülow instructed the official reporter who accompanied the party to Palestine and Syria that the speech must not be published till he had corrected it. The reporter replied that it had already gone, and quoted the orders of the Kaiser himself. A third phrase destined to immortality was the farewell signal " from the Admiral of the Atlantic to the Admiral of the Pacific " after a meeting with the Tsar at Reval. The cool reply was " Good-bye," and the Captain of the *Hohenzollern* promptly gave orders not to divulge the exchange. The Russians had no reason to be discreet, and the story soon appeared in an English paper. The incident was particularly annoying to Bülow who, despite his outspoken criticisms of his master's technique, repeatedly declares that he never indulged in Napoleonic dreams. Such rhetorical extravagances were merely the expression of temperamental irresponsibility ; but foreigners could not be expected to understand that the last of the Hohenzollerns was an actor, not a man of action, an artist in phrases, not a ruthless megalomaniac. Despite reiterated protests and promises of amendment, he never learned to bridle his tongue.

In addition to the above mentioned slips, and others only a little less known, we learn for the first time in these pages of a letter to Theodore Roosevelt filled with strident vituperation against the Japanese and heated exhortations to his American friend to be on his guard against the Yellow Peril. Not till after its despatch did the writer confess what he had done, and, when the Chancellor convinced him that the letter must on no account reach the President's hands, he was permitted to telegraph instructions to New York to return it unopened to Berlin. The Kaiser, he suggests, must have been glad when the war broke out that such a high explosive was not in the possession of the admirer who had turned into his most uncompromising foe. On another occasion Bülow also narrowly succeeded in averting a costly blunder. " I shall, of course, take no notice of the wife of Franz Ferdinand," remarked William II as they journeyed to Vienna in 1903. Wedel, the German Ambassador in Vienna, who was also travelling in the Imperial saloon, protested in vain. The Chancellor motioned to Wedel to leave him along with his master, knowing full well that he would never climb down in the presence of a third party. The impetuous monarch was still protesting when they reached the terminus. " You have now the choice of making the future Emperor of Austria a friend or a foe for ever," whispered Bülow, shooting his final bolt as the train pulled up. A moment later the Kaiser was greeting Franz Ferdinand in the friendliest manner and saying, " When may I have the honour of paying my homage to your wife ? " The Archduke, blushing with delight, bowed and kissed the Kaiser's hand, and the friendship began which lasted unbroken till the shots rang out at Serajevo. We find in these pages more than one discussion whether William II could be described as altogether normal. Hohenlohe had his doubts. His successor in the Chancellorship maintains that he was, though he was excitable and superficial.

Though the portrait of William II is drawn with special care, every prominent actor on the crowded stage comes up for judgment. Of Bismarck, whom he had known from boyhood and whom he visited at Friedrichsruh soon after his appointment as Foreign Minister, he speaks with unbounded admiration, and he performed the difficult feat of keeping on good terms with Herbert Bismarck to the end. The widowed Empress Frederick appears in her usual rôle of Cassandra. " Remember what I tell you to-day, Donna Laura," said she to the mother of Princess Bülow ; " Mon fils sera la ruine de l'Allemagne." We hear much of the Kaiserin's unselfish devotion to husband and children, and not a little of her trials and overstrained nerves. Hohenlohe is invariably mentioned with respect for his independence and ripe judgment. The sinister Holstein is wittily compared to a watch-dog who defends the house against burglars, though one could not be sure that he would not occasionally bite his master in the leg. The energy and ability of Tirpitz are frankly recognized, but we are assured that he had no head for politics. We often meet the fascinating Eulenburg, whose letters are a delight; but there is usually an undercurrent of criticism, which prepares us for the *débâcle* in the second volume. In the Foreign Secretaries, with the exception of Richthofen, he finds little to praise, and he allows himself to describe Jagow as " small in body and mind." The bitterest attacks are reserved for Count Monts, whose incisive letters fill a larger space than those of anyone else. His offence appears to have been that, after extravagant and interested laudations of Bülow in the years of his power, he turned against him after his fall. The only error to which the Prince pleads guilty is in consenting against his better judgment to the appointment of Monts to the Embassy at Rome. The ex-Ambassador lived just long enough to learn of the posthumous revenge of his old patron, but not long enough to reply.

Bülow peppers his pages with caustic comments on the men who, as he sees it, dissipated the opulent heritage he had left. Every mention of the name of Bethmann Hollweg is the signal for expressions of contempt. In his own apologia, Bethmann hinted pretty plainly that the fourth Chancellor had left him a bad pack of cards. Bülow at once retaliated in an open letter to the *Hamburger Fremdenblatt*, and in his Memoirs he throws all reserve to the winds. Bethmann is denounced as the Minister who with the ultimatum to Servia and his blundering diplomacy committed the most terrible error in the history of Germany and one of the greatest errors in the history of the world. Signing a blank cheque to Vienna was crazy, and the unhappy phrase " a scrap of paper " was the equivalent of a lost battle. The war ended as badly as it began, for the Kaiser should have sought and found an honourable death on the battlefield when all was lost. Of the Emperor Karl, Erzberger, and the Weimar Constitution he writes with disdain.

Amid this throng of bunglers and mediocrities stands Germany's fourth Chancellor as drawn by himself, steering the ship of state, so far as his impetuous master allowed, with effortless superiority. The six years covered in the first volume are tranquil enough, compared with the six that were to follow. The most controversial aspect of his activities between 1897 and 1903 was his handling of Anglo-German relations ; and although no irreparable breach occurred, the opening of a new century saw the Governments and peoples drifting steadily away from one another. Here, indeed, was the acid test of his statesmanship. Bülow's direct knowledge of England was confined to brief visits, and he never fully understood our character and outlook. Since France was notoriously irreconcilable and Russia was the rival of Austria in the Near East, it was vital for Germany to keep in with England, all the more because the loss of British friendship was bound to loosen the slender ties which bound Italy to the Central Powers. Two unfortunate decisions were made which were in a large measure to govern the coming years. The first was the creation of a large fleet, which, though its real sponsor was William II, was welcomed by Bülow and is stoutly defended in retrospect. Repeating the arguments adduced in *Imperial Germany*, he maintains that a Great Power with strongly armed neighbours, oversea possessions, and a worldwide trade, required a navy big enough for defence against any attack, though, of course, a " danger-zone " period, while the ships were building, demanded a particularly skilful hand at the helm if a conflict with England was to be avoided. The policy, he believes, was wise and inevitable, and he is confident that only the substitution of Bethmann for himself deprived Germany of the peace with honour which the *Flottenpolitik* was intended to guarantee.

The second important decision in the field of Anglo-German relations in these years was the chilly response to Joseph Chamberlain's suggestions of an alliance. For his attitude in this critical matter Bülow has been sharply attacked by one after another of his countrymen, Johannes Haller, Eckardstein, Eugen Fischer, Willy Becker, who argued that he threw away a priceless opportunity which never recurred. His rejoinder constitues the most valuable contribution to the history of European diplomacy which these pages contain. Every one should now be aware that no offer of an alliance was ever made from Downing Street by the Prime Minister or the Foreign Secretary, and a good deal of the wind has thus been taken out of Eckardstein's sails. But the fact remains that there were influential men in Salisbury's Cabinet who, in view of the threatening attitude of France and Russia, desired a close working association with Berlin. The Prince's argument is that an alliance with England involved the danger of a conflict with Russia, of which Germany would have to bear the brunt ; that such a risk could only be run in return for ample compensations ; and that no British offer, official or semi-official, ever reached the Wilhelmstrasse which contained the elements of an acceptable bargain.   He adds that all the men responsible for Germany's foreign policy agreed that, while an alliance on favourable terms would have been most welcome, a partnership without equality of risk could not be entertained, since Germany, unlike Great Britain, did not stand alone.   What our Empire was to us, he argues, the Triple Alliance was to her.   No German statesman had a right to expose his country to the hazards of a great war without bringing the Austrian partner into the pact, which British statesmen declined to allow.   It is a plausible argument sustained with the usual skill, and in fairness we must remember that the weakness of the Russian colossus was not revealed till 1904.   But most Englishmen and many Germans will continue to believe that it would have been wiser to win and hold the confidence of the British Empire than, in fear of a breach with Russia, to drive us to turn our eyes elsewhere.

The second volume is even more arresting than the first, for it covers a more eventful period.   The impressions derived from the first instalment of this monumental apologia are confirmed by the sequel.   Bülow wrote as well as he talked, and there is scarcely a dull page in the book.   He looks back with abounding satisfaction on his years of office, his services to throne and Fatherland, his skilful diplomacy, his eloquent speeches in the Reichstag.   The whole work breathes the full-blooded conviction that under his guidance Germany enjoyed power and prosperity, that the subsequent shipwreck was due to the dropping of the pilot and the neglect of his warnings. William II, he declares over and over again, required a counsellor of exceptional wisdom and courage to restrain him from his dangerous follies, and when the fourth Chancellor was gone there was none to take his place.   Tirpitz had no political head. Bethmann was a timid mediocrity, ever unable to make up his mind.   Schoen, Jagow, Monts, Schiemann, and other actors on the crowded stage are rarely mentioned without expressions of anger or contempt.   The Prince even stoops to reveal secrets of the private life of two well-known public men, one of whom was still alive.   Few readers will close this volume without a diminished respect for the character of its brilliant author.

In the field of foreign affairs the book is disappointing.

The years which it covers, 1903-9, embrace the first Morocco crisis, the naval rivalry with Great Britain, and the anxious months of the Bosnian crisis. Students of *Die Grosse Politik* find very little which they did not know, and Bülow makes no serious attempt to rebut the charges of his critics. He continues to assert that his Moroccan policy was the only possible reply to the threatened repudiation of treaty rights, and claims that the Conference of Algeciras gave him the substance of his demands. Yet the guarantees which he secured merely retarded the process by which Morocco passed under the influence of France, and its main result was the cementing of the Entente. He depicts himself as urging Tirpitz and their common master during his last year of office not to antagonize England by forcing the pace of the *Flottenpolitik*, and blames them for resisting his advice ; but he does not appear to realize that the estrangement had already taken place before his belated attempts to put on the brakes, and that the forces which he had helped to set in motion were almost certain to pass beyond his control. He dwells with special satisfaction on his handling of the Bosnian crisis, and claims with truth that he combined unflinching support of Germany's only reliable ally with the maintenance of European peace. He presents, however, only one side of the balance sheet, and omits to mention that the humiliation of Russian national sentiment in March, 1909, rankled on till 1914 and made it difficult, if not impossible, to give way when the Servian *protégé* again appealed for help. The impression which the chapters on foreign policy in this volume are designed to leave is that the diplomatic position when the Prince surrendered the helm was relatively satisfactory, and that it was the fault of his successors that the lights went out. For such complacency there is not the slightest excuse. Relations with Russia, France, England and Italy were demonstrably worse. The Triple Entente, which had been unthinkable in 1897, was a stark reality in 1909.

However disappointed we may be at the author's sketchy treatment of foreign affairs, we are compensated by the scintillating record of his partnership with the Kaiser and of the various stages of the breach. No such damning indictment has ever been made, for none of his chief servants enjoyed the same opportunities of intimate and continuous observation. In length of service he was surpassed by Tirpitz, but the Kaiser never made the Admiral his personal friend. In the course of his reign he had two " favourites "—the expression is Bülow's

—Prince Eulenburg and Prince Fürstenberg, though the latter never won the place in his master's heart that the fascinating Phili had possessed. Neither of them, however, was long in his company at any one time, and neither knew very much at first hand of his graver political activities. For twelve years Bülow was the trusted adviser of the monarch, who enjoyed the society of the most brilliant conversationalist in Germany, and heaped upon him public and private marks of favour. Even if we make allowances for the fact that the fallen states-man is paying off old scores, the picture emerges of a man who was tragically unfit to rule a mighty empire.

That Bülow's indictment of William II never extends to the political system which he inherited is a measure of his limita-tions ; for the English reader, reared in the bracing tradition of self-government, is aware in every chapter that the real culprit was rather the constitution than the man. The Prince repeatedly declares himself a royalist, and there is no reason to doubt his assertion that he always strove to maintain the prerogatives of the Crown ; but on his own showing the result was a lamentable failure. The experience of England and other free countries proves that power cannot be permanently divided between Monarch and Parliament : one or the other must win the struggle. The Constitution of the German Empire, as drawn up by Bismarck, worked fairly well so long as he was at the helm, for everyone knew that he alone was in command. With weaker Chancellors and an Emperor deter-mined to assert himself, the unified control which is equally vital to an autocratic and a democratic government came to an end. Bülow's political philosophy repudiated constitutional monarchy, but demanded that the ruler should always possess and give ear to wise Ministers. That these conditions were unlikely to be filled is clear from a narrative which roundly condemns the mistakes of his predecessors and successors. In his well-known work, *Regierung und Volkswille,* published shortly before the war of 1914–1918, Professor Hans Del-brück glorified the German Constitution as the ideal com-promise between autocracy and democracy. On paper it was doubtless well enough, but it could only succeed by a com-bination of factors which hardly ever synchronized. The Kaiser reserved certain subjects, such as the size of the navy, for his exclusive decision, and the Opposition parties in the Reichstag clamoured for further instalments of democracy. In the most perfectly organized of European States, as

Lord Haldane once remarked, there was anarchy at the top.

Though William II did not relish the control which the Chancellor endeavoured to maintain over his actions and speeches, there was no obvious competitor for the highest post. With the important exception of naval policy he had no deep-rooted confidence in his own judgment in the larger problems of diplomacy. His dependence on Bülow is strikingly illustrated in the well-known correspondence, first published in *Die Grosse Politik* and reproduced in these pages, which followed the signature of the Pact of Björkö in 1905. The Chancellor advised his master to content himself with obtaining the Tsar's acceptance in principle of a defensive alliance, leaving the details to be subsequently worked out by Lamsdorff and himself. " A slight cloud passed over the intelligent and mobile countenance of His Majesty, which told me that it was his desire on this occasion, trusting to the magic of his personality, to manage the whole affair himself. When I asked if I was to accompany him, he replied in the most friendly way that my society was always a delight, but that this time he felt that he would achieve more if he confronted the Russian autocrat alone." The signing of the Treaty was described in the most roseate Imperial telegram which Bülow ever received ; but when the text arrived he discovered to his horror that it was confined to Europe, thereby depriving it of its chief value for Germany in the event of war with England. Still worse was the Kaiser's intention to draw Denmark into the alliance, in order that she might in case of need close the Baltic to an English fleet. Finally the Treaty was countersigned by Tschirschky, an official of the Foreign Office in attendance on the Kaiser, and by Admiral Birileff, who did not even read it.

The Chancellor dispatched a long and devastating criticism to his master, and added that he could not accept responsibility for what had occurred. The ruler replied in an emotional letter in which defence of his handiwork melts into passionate appeal. "I thought I had worked for you and achieved something out of the common, and then you send me a few cool lines and your resignation ! ! ! You will not expect me, dear Bülow, to describe my feelings. To be treated thus by my best and most intimate friend, without any adequate reason, has given me such a terrible shock that I am absolutely broken and fear I am in for a nervous breakdown. . . . I have not deserved it. No, my friend, you remain in office and will continue to co-operate with me *ad majorem Germaniae gloriam*."

A postscript added : " I appeal to your friendship for me, and do not let me hear any more of your going. Telegraph to me All right ! Then I shall know that you will stay. For the morning after the arrival of your request to resign would not find the Kaiser alive ! Think of my poor wife and children."

Bülow's feelings on receipt of this letter are described in one of the most arresting pages of the book. He read it, he declares, with deep emotion. There had been many differences of opinion, " but I loved him with all my heart, and not only for all the goodness he had shown me. I loved the highly-gifted man with his noble qualities, who could be so kind and lovable, so simple and natural, so magnanimous. I am not ashamed to say that I was still quite under his spell. Though scarcely ten years older, I was more mature. My feelings for him were like those of a father for his son who sometimes annoys him and more often causes him anguish, but whose brilliant talents, gifts of mind and heart, and many shining qualities continually delight and attract him. Even in later years, when I had no more illusions as to his superficiality and vanity, his untrustworthiness and especially his lack of truthfulness, even when he fled abroad leaving ruin behind him, I could never resolve to hate him." The appeal was brought to the Chancellor by Moltke, who described in vivid language the lamentable condition of his master, and begged him to write at once and as warmly as possible. If not, " a complete collapse " was to be feared. Bülow's reply, which was written " with my heart as well as my head," evoked the joyful telegraphic response : " Hearty thanks ; I am born again." The Björkö problem proved easier of solution than could be anticipated, for Lamsdorff, m᾿ lful of the obligations of the French alliance, liked the agreement as little as Bülow ; and the treaty, of which the world heard nothing at the time, remained a scrap of paper.

The Chancellor triumphed in 1905, but would the relations between master and servant stand a second and similar strain ? The answer was given in 1908, when the complications arising from the *Daily Telegraph* interview brought the partnership to an end. The story of the separation, which fills many chapters, forms the most dramatic portion of the Memoirs. The Parliamentary crisis was already known from the debates in the Reichstag and the chapter in *Die Grosse Politik*, and the Prince repeats the public defence which he made at the time. When the fateful document reached him at Norderney in the late summer, he was overwhelmed with work, telling Müller, the representative of the Foreign Office who helped him in his daily task, to deal with the matter, and giving instructions for the contents to be carefully examined in the Wilhelmstrasse. That the interview appeared in an unexpected form was, we are assured, mainly the fault of Müller, who died long ago, and Klehmet, the departmental official who was punished by the loss of his post. The Chancellor's story was subjected to a detailed analysis in a little book entitled *Kaiser und Kanzler*, the anonymous author of which argued that he had in fact read the interview but lacked courage to confess it. It certainly seems difficult to believe that, after the agitating experiences of eleven years, he should not have put aside his other papers for an hour and satisfied himself, without waiting for anybody's opinion, that the interview contained no blazing indiscretions. If, as he says, he omitted to do so, it was surely a very grave mistake, necessitating, one would have thought, a frank apology to his master.

William II was so crushed by the weight of the world's displeasure that for a moment he toyed with the thought of resignation. When Bülow went to Potsdam on November 17 for the first interview after the crisis the Empress greeted him with the words, " Be very gentle with the Emperor, he is quite broken." He looked pale and evidently anticipated a lecture. " Help me, save me," were his first words. " What is going to happen ? Shall we pull through ? " Bülow replied that he had no doubt about it if His Majesty would be more careful in future, and reminded him of some of his past slips. The penitent ruler nodded agreement, and remarked that he would most certainly be more cautious. At the end of a long conversation he asked whether a proclamation or a Cabinet Order was wanted, and added in a friendly tone : " I am ready for anything." The Chancellor produced a mild *communiqué* for the official *Norddeutsche Allgemeine Zeitung*, which ended with the statement that His Majesty assured the Prince of his continued confidence. The Kaiser appeared surprised that he had got off so easily, and said with emphasis that he agreed with every word. When the painful conversation was over he kissed his visitor on both cheeks, which he had never done except in conferring the Order of the Black Eagle in 1901. As the Chancellor left the room the host called out : " I thank you, I thank you from my heart." On returning home Bülow observed to his wife : " Once again I have pulled the Emperor and the Crown through.   How long we remain in this house is another question."

When the Chancellor had finished his brief but pregnant speech in the Reichstag on the *Daily Telegraph* incident, his friend Bassermann, the National Liberal leader, remarked : " It was a political and oratorical masterpiece.   But what will the Kaiser say to it ? " Bülow replied that he hoped His Majesty would place the welfare of the Empire above petty personal considerations.   " So he would if he were like his father or his grandfather," rejoined Bassermann ; " but he is too vain." His reading of the Imperial character was correct. Already in the spring of 1908 the Kaiser had remarked to the Minister of War, who passed on the ominous words : " Bülow is getting too big for me."   When the November storm blew over he regained his self-confidence, and the Chancellor's enemies at Court began to whisper that he had let his master down.   Here is the declaration to the Reichstag which led to his undoing.   " Gentlemen, I have formed in these days the firm conviction that the publication of His Majesty's conversations in England, which has not produced the result he desired but has caused great excitement and poignant regret in our country, will lead me to counsel the Emperor to maintain in future the reserve in private conversations which is equally indispensable to the unified policy and the authority of the Crown.   Were it otherwise, neither I nor any of my successors could assume responsibility."   In dictating his Memoirs many years later, the fallen Minister observed that he still believed the words to have been absolutely necessary.

During the following months the ruler's demeanour varied between friendliness and reserve, and once or twice it seemed as if the old cordiality was about to be resumed.   No sharp word was ever spoken, and he never hinted to his Minister that he wished for a change.   But the process by which, in the words of Bülow, " he first turned from me and then against me, behind the mask of friendship and goodwill," went steadily forward, as the Chancellor learned to his disgust both from his friends and his foes.   Courts cannot keep secrets, and in the spring of 1909 he was no longer in doubt that his master was looking round for a successor.   The main Parliamentary business of 1908–9 was the reform of taxation, partially necessitated by the growth of the fleet, of which the most controversial item was a tax on inheritance.   The proposal was bitterly opposed by the Conservatives.   The *bloc* which had been formed at the triumphant elections of 1907 was broken, and when the bill was rejected by a majority of eight the Chancellor promptly resigned. Though the world was informed that his retirement was the result of the hostile vote, every one behind the scenes was aware that the defeat of the inheritance tax was the occasion, not the cause, for he was not responsible to the Reichstag. Much as he loved power he had no wish to remain when his master was tired of him. Both men, with the memory of 1890 in their minds, were glad of a pretext which avoided the necessity of a spectacular breach.

The last chapter describes the parting. Bülow had accepted the Foreign Office on board the *Hohenzollern* in the harbour of Kiel in June, 1897, and he surrendered the Chancellorship in the same place in June, 1909. He found the monarch embarrassed and impatient, but not a word was said on either side of the real cause of the separation. Some idea of the final conversation may be gathered from extracts from his report :

W. I have chosen Bethmann. I am sure you will agree. He is true as gold.

B. He is the best man for domestic politics, but he knows absolutely nothing of foreign affairs.

W. (laughing and gay). Leave foreign affairs to me. I have learned something in your school. It will be all right.

B. I have two requests for Your Majesty, very serious and very urgent.

W. (glancing impatiently at his wrist watch). Dear Bernhard, I have really no time.

B. I am sorry. I will be brief. Try to reach a naval agreement with England.

W. (very annoyed). Have I not told you often enough that I allow no one to dictate to me about ship-building ? Every such proposal is a humiliation for me and my navy.

B. How should our honour suffer if we willingly reach an agreement with England which diminishes the danger of war ?

W. (decisively). I do not believe in such a danger. And what is your second request ?

B. Do not repeat the Bosnian action.

W. (suspiciously). But that was a triumph for you.

B. The situation of last winter will not recur.

W. So you think I must be careful in the Balkans ?

B. Yes, there even more than elsewhere. That is the danger-point.

W. (looking at his watch again). I won't forget. You can

be quite happy. But I must not keep Monaco waiting. I'll take you in my boat.

B. Very kind of Your Majesty. One word more. Just because, to my great regret, you reject an agreement with England on the *tempo* of our naval construction, you must be extra careful with the Russians.

In reading the Prince's reports of his conversations with the Kaiser we must remember that we only possess his version, written down, as he assures us, within a few hours of the event. But when such contemporary records and diary entries are utilized for the purposes of an elaborate apologia in later years, their authors do not always find it desirable to reproduce the exact text of the original. Is there any reason to suspect Bülow of occasionally yielding to the temptation of touching up his materials? That is a question which cannot at present be answered with confidence. Only when his papers become accessible to independent historians will it be possible, by comparing the original notes with the published version, to judge whether there is ground for the suspicions entertained in many quarters.

Our dominant feeling as we close the second volume is that Bülow has had his revenge. Whatever secrets may be lying in the archives of Doorn, it is improbable that this comprehensive indictment will be effectively rebutted or forgotten. The maledictions of Tacitus cling to Tiberius through the centuries, and the scars inflicted by Bülow's sharp pen will never fully heal. The last of the Hohenzollerns, however, found some satisfaction in the knowledge that, in girding at his master, Bülow exposed his own feet of clay, and that his complacent survey of his performances in office did not pass unchallenged at home or abroad.

The third volume, which is only half the size of the others, carries us from the summer of 1909 to the Treaty of Versailles. The fallen statesman retired to Rome, where a substantial legacy had enabled him to purchase the Villa Malta. Rigidly excluded from public affairs, he watched with growing anxiety the gathering of the storm. The criticisms of Bethmann and Jagow for their activities in the fatal weeks of July, 1914, are merciless. While completely acquitting the directors of German policy of a will to war, he condemns them for giving Austria a free hand and for the violation of Belgian neutrality. He himself, we are assured, would have known how to avert the fall of the avalanche ; and Bethmann modestly confessed to Theodor Wolff that his predecessor, with his great experience and resource, might perhaps have succeeded where he had failed. Bülow could certainly not have done worse. Not all his readers, however, will be convinced, for he had unhesitatingly followed the Austrian lead in the Bosnian crisis, and he had known of the Schlieffen plan since its birth in 1905.

In the first winter of the conflict Bülow was summoned from his retirement for a task which he alone seemed fitted to perform. No one had expected Italy to fight on the side of her allies, though the full measure of her estrangement was not known till the secrets of the archives were revealed after the war. The utmost that could be hoped was that she might be prevented from stabbing her old friends in the back. For this object it would be necessary to pay her a high territorial price at Austria's expense, for it was Austrian territory that she coveted. Bülow was aware of the delicacy of the situation, particularly in persuading Francis Joseph and his advisers to make the necessary sacrifice, but he did not regard his mission as absolutely hopeless. That he failed was not his fault. Yet he had no justification for laying the main share of the blame on the statesmen of Berlin and Vienna and their diplomatic representatives in Italy, whom he accuses of sabotaging his efforts. His charges have been indignantly rebutted by Macchio, the Austrian Ambassador, in his book *Wahrheit : Fürst Bülow und ich in Rom* 1914–15, and more briefly by Jagow, the German Foreign Minister, and Flotow, the German Ambassador, in the formidable co-operative volume *Front wider Bülow*, edited by Thimme. We are now aware that failure was inevitable, for Salandra, the Italian Premier, has confessed in *La Neutralita Italiana*, the first volume of his Memoirs, that after the battle of the Marne he decided on war, postponing military intervention till the army was ready.

Bülow earned little gratitude for his efforts, and he knew that he had nothing to expect so long as Bethmann was at the helm. Since, however, the Chancellor's inefficiency in time of war was realized by every one from the ruler downwards, there seemed just a chance that the most brilliant and experienced of German statesmen might be recalled to office. William II had swallowed his dislike of Kiderlen, and with his waning prestige he would hardly have dared to veto such an appointment if it had been backed by a widespread demand. Such a demand, unfortunately for Bülow, did not exist. His offer of concessions to Italy at the expense of Austria deeply wounded the pride of the old Emperor and the Ballplatz, though his mission would have been useless if he had not made them ; and when Bethmann fell in 1917 one of the obstacles to Bülow's return was the resentful hostility of Vienna. There were other obstacles nearer home, for the supporters of his candidature were too few to count. There is a revealing if rather cruel picture of the veteran of sixty-eight in the Memoirs of Scheidemann. On the fall of Michaelis, the feeblest Chancellor that Germany ever possessed, after three months in office, Bülow's name was put forward by his few remaining friends. When pressed to meet him Scheidemann at first refused and only yielded to renewed entreaties. The wooing of the Socialist leader took place in the Hotel Adlon, where the Prince always stayed on his visits to Berlin, but all the arts and crafts of the accomplished *charmeur* were exercised in vain. " He said yes to everything and approved everything that I asked." At parting he held the hand of the visitor long in his own and insisted on helping him into his coat. The sole effect of a conversation lasting two and a half hours was to convince Scheidemann that the ex-Chancellor was past his prime. The last hope of employment disappeared with the collapse of the Hohenzollern Empire in November, 1918. The third volume ends with disparaging references to Erzberger, the Socialist leaders, and most of the other actors on the darkened stage of republican Germany.

The bulky volume on Bülow's early life was the last to be written ; for he was over seventy when he began to compile his Memoirs, and he was naturally anxious first to complete the story of his twelve years of power and to vindicate his Italian mission. Finding himself still in good health when this task had been achieved he resolved to describe the decades of apprenticeship. The fourth volume is the longest of the set and, unlike its predecessors, contains a good deal of padding which could well be spared. Yet, though somewhat prolix and disfigured by the unblushing record of his amours, it is the least disagreeable, since he has fewer old scores to pay off. In the other volumes there is a recurring note of bitterness and revenge : in this it is roses, roses all the way. All doors at Court, in society, and in the diplomatic world were open to the good-looking young man who had fought bravely in the war of 1870, and whose father was Foreign Minister. He climbed up the steps of the official ladder in half the capitals of Europe, meeting all the celebrities of the time. Six years at Paris after the Berlin Congress, four at St. Petersburg under Alexander

III, five as Minister at Bucharest, four as Ambassador at Rome—such were the chief stages of an odyssey in which he learned the secrets of the diplomatic art. Such an autobiography could not be dull. In 1897, when the long-expected call to the Wilhelmstrasse arrived, he might well have felt satisfied with his fortune and himself. He had no serious rivals and no dangerous enemies. His qualifications for the post seemed beyond dispute, and the Chancellorship itself lay not far ahead. For Hohenlohe was seventy-eight and the monarch was beginning to look round for a younger man. *Omnium consensu capax imperii nisi imperasset.*

If it is broadly correct to say that Bismarck's apologia enhanced his reputation, it is equally incontestable that Bülow has damaged his own fame beyond repair. From a literary point of view alone are the Memoirs a success. Nowhere else shall we find such a portrait-gallery of Bismarckian and post-Bismarckian Europe. Though a patriotic German he was also something of a cosmopolitan, loving Italy next to his own country, happy in Paris, and mixing with scholars on easy terms. No one can deny the power, the charm, the human interest of the work. Yet from the point of view of the author, one of the vainest of men, it must be pronounced a failure, for it diminished his moral stature in a surprising degree. Many of his portraits, from the Kaiser downwards, have aroused angry protest, but no one has suggested a lack of accuracy in delineating his own features. No friend, no disciple, no biographer could have painted such an intimate portrait, no foe could have revealed to a similar extent his meanness of soul. It is a psychological riddle how so accomplished a man of the world could forget that in discharging his poisoned arrows he was damaging himself more than those he attacked. The terse verdict of Francis Joseph on Conrad—" he is clever but not wise "—is equally true of the most brilliant political figure of his time. Behind the dazzling *façade* we seek in vain for the nobler qualities of mind and heart. Suspicions of his sincerity were not confined to foreigners like Grey, for his character was least admired by some of his closest collaborators. Kiderlen called him " the eel " ; Schoen and Jagow despised him, and Monts cordially reciprocated his dislike. He would have been wiser had he left his vindication to another hand ; and, if he had told his story with less vanity and malice, he would have occupied a higher rank among the public figures of his time and a warmer place in the hearts of his countrymen.

KIDERLEN-WÄCHTER, THE MAN OF AGADIR

AMONG the actors on the political stage of post-Bismarck-ian Germany Kiderlen-Wächter occupies a place apart.[1] His robust and rather gross personality stands out from the surrounding throng of shadowy figures, beloved by few, disliked by many, ignored by none. To this day the question is asked what he would have done had he been at the helm in 1914, and whether perchance he might have averted the rush of the avalanche. The Swabian Bismarck, as Friedrich Naumann called him, impressed his contemporaries as the ablest and most forceful German diplomatist with the possible exception of Marschall von Bieberstein. His admiring biographer and friend, Dr. Jaeckh, laments that he came too late and went too soon. Less indulgent critics, while admitting the exceptional ability of the man of Agadir, may be tempted to exclaim : *Consensu omnium capax imperii nisi imperasset.*

Kiderlen-Wächter was born at Stuttgart in 1852, the son of a high official at the Court of Württemberg. To the end of his life he was devotedly attached to the land of his birth, speaking its dialect, enjoying its peculiar dishes, loving its free and easy ways. A short spell of war as a volunteer in 1870 separated school from University, and in 1879, after an intensive study of law, he entered the Foreign Office. A brief apprenticeship in Copenhagen was followed by four years in St. Petersburg, two in Paris and two in Constantinople. Bismarck, who kept an eye on the promising young diplomatist, called him to the Wilhelmstrasse early in 1888 to deal with questions of the Near East, and in the same summer selected him to accompany the new Emperor as the representative of the Foreign Office on his summer cruise to the northern capitals. The arrangement initiated by the Iron Chancellor

[1] Kiderlen's diplomacy must be studied in the voluminous German, British, French, Austrian and Russian collections of documents. The official biography, Jaeckh's *Kiderlen-Wächter, Der Staatsmann und Mensch,* 2 vols., is too laudatory. The best short sketch is by Willy Andreas, *Kämpfe um Volk und Reich* 153–186. Take Jonescu, *Souvenirs* ; Otto Hammann, *Bilder aus der letzten Kaiserzeit* ; Rosen, *Aus einem diplomatischen Wanderleben* ; Von der Lancken, *Meine dreissig Dienstjahre* ; Mme Tabouis, *Life of Jules Cambon* ; Pick, *Searchlight on German Africa* ; and Class, *Wider den Strom,* supply valuable information. The French side of the second Moroccan crisis is authoritatively presented in Caillaux, *Agadir,* and Tardieu, *Le Mystère d'Agadir.*

K

continued for ten years without a break. William II enjoyed his jokes and risky stories, though he never became in any real sense the Kaiser's friend.

Kiderlen's importance begins with the fall of Bismarck in 1890. Caprivi, the new Chancellor, was ignorant of foreign affairs, and Marschall, the successor of Herbert Bismarck as Foreign Minister, was by training a jurist. The changing of the guard left Holstein in undisputed command. Careers were usually made or marred, not by the Emperor, the Chancellor or the Foreign Minister, but by the *Éminence Grise*, the mystery man of the Wilhelmstrasse who had lent a hand in the overthrow of the Iron Chancellor himself. Next in the official hierarchy, though far below him in authority, were Kiderlen and Eulenburg. Despite their diverse character and tastes the three men worked harmoniously together till the juniors left for diplomatic posts. Kiderlen, unlike Eulenburg, retained till the end the friendship of the most cantankerous and suspicious old man in the world. Nobody was less of the routine official type. His Bohemian ways were not to everybody's taste, and his domestic life was not beyond reproach. Like many men of superabundant vitality, he frankly enjoyed what are called the pleasures of life. "The Swabian," writes his colleague Hammann, Chief of the Press Department, "was a man of moods. It was often difficult to deal with his obstinacy. In extreme cases one had to approach him from the sentimental side—then he gave way. If he liked people, he was a faithful friend." In a word, a rough diamond.

That the triumvirate in the Wilhelmstresse abused their power was plainly hinted in 1894, first under cover of transparent nicknames, then without concealment, in the *Kladderadatsch*, a Bismarckian organ. Kiderlen challenged the editor to a duel and wounded him at the third shot. Duels in the army were recognized and approved, but civil servants were not supposed to take the law into their own hands. The offender was sentenced to four months, but was freed after a fortnight in the fortress of Ehrenbreitstein. The incident had no damaging effect on his career, for he had been sorely provoked. He had just been appointed Prussian Minister at Hamburg, where he passed a year, and in 1895 he was promoted to Copenhagen. If there was little to be done in the quiet Danish capital there was much to be heard, for the periodical gatherings of the relatives of the venerable Christian IX made it the whispering gallery of Europe. His star was rising when in 1898 a thunderbolt fell out of a clear sky. His summer cruises with the Kaiser proved his undoing. Indiscreet letters to Marschall were found in the Wilhelmstrasse when Bülow was appointed Foreign Minister in 1897. Through whose carelessness or by whose instructions the Kaiser was informed is uncertain. Kiderlen himself believed Bülow to be one of the culprits and despised him to the end of his days. Whether these letters were the sole or the principal cause of his fall we cannot be sure. Sharp words at table are said to have played a part. He drank heavily and had many enemies.

In 1900 the offender was transferred to Bucharest at the age of forty-eight. The Roumanian capital was acceptable enough as a stepping stone to higher things, as in the case of Bülow, but for Kiderlen it proved a *cul-de-sac*. Nobody doubted that he was one of the most forceful and experienced men in the service, but the Imperial frown was an insuperable bar. In the ordinary course of events he might have expected an Embassy after a year or two in the Balkans, and perhaps the succession to Richthofen when that rather colourless Foreign Minister died in 1906. When Tschirschky, who had been a failure in the Wilhelmstrasse, was transferred to Vienna in 1907 Bülow urged the claims of Kiderlen, whom he described to his master as the best head in the diplomatic service. He pleaded in vain, for Schoen, an even smaller man than Tschirschky, was summoned from St. Petersburg.

Though the sense of wasted powers became increasingly poignant, and though he had no liking for the Roumanians, Kiderlen's prolonged residence at Bucharest was not without alleviations. Next to Constantinople there was no better outlook tower in the Balkans. Holstein's letters kept him in touch with home, and there was little going on in the Chancelleries of Europe of which King Carol was unaware. Kiderlen was no great admirer of the Queen or the Crown Princess. Next to the ruler his chief friend among Roumanian statesmen was Take Jonescu, who has left us a vivid sketch. " For more than ten years I was on terms of the closest intimacy with Kiderlen-Wächter. That is to say I had the opportunity of knowing him exactly as he was, with his fine qualities and his failings. First and foremost he had a big brain. Nobody can have had dealings with him without realizing that one was in contact with one of those intelligences which are the ornament of the race. And in Kiderlen the brain was almost everything.

Not that he lacked heart, for he gave indisputable proofs of his deep and unchanging attachment to certain people. Yet, broadly speaking and without doing him injustice, one may say that he was neither a sentimentalist nor an idealist, but above all a practical intelligence."

On two occasions during his long exile Kiderlen was called to play a part on a larger stage. When Marschall represented Germany at the second Hague Conference in 1907, and again when his health necessitated a long holiday in the following year, the Minister at Bucharest took his place at Constantinople for seven and four months respectively. The Kaiser made no objection to such temporary promotion, and the excellent use Kiderlen made of his opportunity helped to soften his heart. " The Foreign Office is full of praise of your achievements," wrote a friend from Berlin, " and His Majesty joins in the applause." Marschall himself, the greatest Ambassador seen on the Bosphorus since Stratford de Redcliffe, was surprised and perhaps not altogether pleased at the success of his junior. Henceforth Kiderlen counted on the succession to the coveted Embassy on the Bosphorus. A series of economic concessions testified to his energy and skill, but his principal achievement was to keep the German flag flying when power passed from the Sultan to the Young Turks in the summer of 1908. Though cries of " A bas l'Allemagne " were heard in the streets, the new leaders were soon seeking his advice, assuring him that the Committee of Union and Progress was not anti-German and that they knew how much Germany had done for their country. When everybody else was in despair, reported the Austrian Ambassador, Kiderlen remained calm. The whole merit of the recovery of German influence under the new régime is usually attributed to Marschall, but the Ambassador only returned to his post in September. Kiderlen had borne the brunt of the revolution, and Marschall reaped where his understudy had sown. Though he liked the Turks he had no illusion about the permanence of their sprawling empire. Turkey, he believed, would only revive when she had shed her racial minorities and become a nation-state.

The road from Bucharest to Berlin ran through Constantinople. Two months after his second sojourn in the Turkish capital Kiderlen was summoned to take charge of the Foreign Office during the illness of Schoen. The amiable Baron knew that he was only a stop-gap, and he modestly remarked that Kiderlen was the man for the job. " I am to pull the cart out

of the mud," grunted the latter, "and then I can go." The
Kaiser shook hands without saying a word. Once again the
experienced diplomat confirmed the lofty expectations of his
friends. Though his commission only lasted four months,
there was time to make history. His first appearance in the
Reichstag was such a failure that it would have thrown a
younger and less confident performer out of his stride. Bülow
had borne the brunt of the debates on the *Daily Telegraph*
interview, but in attempting to exculpate himself he had
reflected on the officials of the Foreign Office. It was Kiderlen's task to defend the working of the department. His
bright yellow waistcoat combined with his Swabian accent to
evoke contemptuous merriment. His argument that the
officials were overworked was unconvincing and his rather
nonchalant attitude irritated his hearers. He took the fiasco
calmly, not merely because he was never in awe of Parliament
or ruler, but also because he rejected the notion of democratic
control of foreign affairs as scornfully as the Kaiser himself.

The chief problems with which the interim Minister had to
deal during his four months in the Wilhelmstrasse were
Morocco and the Bosnian crisis. The Act of Algeciras was
generally regarded as a mere truce in the Morocco struggle,
but after the excitement of the Conference there had been a
welcome *détente*. In September, 1908, however, the smouldering embers burst into flame when deserters from the Foreign
Legion were helped to escape by German officials at Casablanca, who in turn were roughly handled by French officials.
Nothing so alarming had happened since the Schnaebele
frontier incident twenty years earlier, and for a week or two
war was in the air. The crisis passed, partly because it was
clear that both sides had erred, partly because the Bosnian
crisis made it desirable for Germany to keep her hands free.
When the dispute was referred to the Hague Court the danger
was over. In both countries there was a desire to avert the
recurrence of such nerve-racking alarms and both were eager
to trade. The strength of France lay in her position as a land
neighbour of Morocco, the strength of Germany in her treaty
rights.

In January, 1908, Jules Cambon, the French Ambassador at
Berlin, reported that Schoen wished to discuss an economic
entente. Exactly a year later, when the Casablanca crisis was
over, both sides were ready for a deal. "Kiderlen visited me
to-day on behalf of Baron Schoen," he reported on January

26, 1909. " He renewed the assurance that Germany had only economic aims in Morocco. I said that France would emphasize her interest in the integrity of Morocco, and Germany her will not to thwart the political interests of France. Both would express their desire, while keeping in view the special and recognized position of France, to see their nationals associated in economic enterprises." The negotiations, conducted on these sensible lines between Kiderlen and the Ambassador, proceeded with unusual smoothness and rapidity to a happy issue.

The declaration, signed on February 8, 1909, was as follows. " The Governments, animated by an equal desire to facilitate the execution of the Act of Algeciras, have agreed to define the meaning they attach to its clauses in order to avoid all cause of future misunderstanding. Consequently France, entirely attached to the maintenance of the integrity and independence of Morocco, resolved to safeguard economic equality and therefore not to thwart German commercial and industrial interests ; and Germany, pursuing merely economic interests, and recognizing that the special political interests of France are closely bound up with the consolidation of order and internal peace and resolved not to thwart those interests, declare that they will not pursue or encourage any measure of a kind to create in their favour or the favour of any Power an economic privilege, and that they will seek to associate their nationals in the affairs which they may be able to secure." On the same day letters were exchanged between Cambon and Schoen declaring that the political *désintéressement* of Germany did not affect the position already held by her nationals, but implied that they would not compete for posts in the public services of a political character, and that, when their interests were associated, it would recognize that those of France were the most important.

After the tempests of Tangier, Algeciras and Casablanca, it seemed almost too good to be true. Kiderlen was rewarded with a Sèvres dinner service, and never again did he receive such plaudits at home and abroad. Pichon, Clemenceau's conciliatory Foreign Minister, declared that it removed all causes of conflict in Morocco. " Now we can cash the Act of Algeciras," declared the *Journal des Débats*. Radolin, the German Ambassador, added cheerfully that a lasting entente had been secured. Bülow assured the Reichstag that it assured France her legitimate political influence in Morocco without allowing her to appropriate the country. " I rejoice," declared Aehrenthal to the French Ambassador, " and so do all my countrymen, whose cordial sympathy with you grows daily stronger." The Austrian Minister was relieved to know that the Central Powers could now devote their undivided attention to the Bosnian incident. Similar felicitations came from Tittoni at Rome. " Politically it is a great advantage that France and Germany should agree not to quarrel about Morocco," commented Grey ; " commercially I fear other people will lose by an entente between them, though the open door must be preserved on paper." Only Russia was dissatisfied, for she saw in the *détente* fresh evidence of French reluctance to back up her ally in the Bosnian feud. While a duel is in progress the seconds are not expected to fraternize. Had Russian statesmen possessed the gift of prophecy they would not have been alarmed, for the Moroccan honeymoon was destined to be brief.

The second and larger issue was the Bosnian crisis. The decision of Germany to stand by her ally, despite the resentment of her precipitate action privately expressed by the Kaiser and Marschall, had been reached before Kiderlen was summoned from Bucharest. There was really no choice, for Austria-Hungary was her only dependable partner, and Aehrenthal was on strong ground in claiming a reward for services at Algeciras. Moreover the estrangement of England by the *Flottenpolitik* and the consequential tightening of the bonds of the Triple Entente strengthened the pull of Vienna. Bismarck had made the Dual Alliance with Andrassy in 1879 on the tacit assumption that Germany would be the first violin. With the recent shift in the balance of power, the *rôles* began to be reversed, Austria calling the tune and Germany following obediently in her train. Kiderlen resented the change, but he was in full agreement with the policy of standing by Francis Joseph in the Bosnian controversy to the end.

In the opening weeks of 1909 the juridical damage inflicted on Turkey by the action of Austria and Bulgaria was compensated by a small financial *solatium*. These settlements were welcomed throughout Europe, where no responsible statesman desired a conflict. On the other hand they strengthened the position of Aehrenthal, for, now that Turkey was out of the ring, Servia faced Austria alone. That Russia was not in a position to fight the Central Powers was as well known in Belgrad as elsewhere, but the outraged feelings of the Serbs made surrender very difficult. On February 27, terrified by the prospect of a struggle in which Russia would have to choose between humiliating neutrality and military defeat, Iswolsky advised Servia to inform the Powers that she withdrew her territorial claims. Servia, however, was in no yielding mood, and Austria was generally expected to issue an ultimatum. Iswolsky was in a fever of anxiety, not only in regard to the outbreak of war, but owing to Aehrenthal's threat to reveal the negotiations of the previous summer. He implored Bülow to avert the exposure, though he still declined formal recognition of the annexation.

At this moment, in the middle of March, 1909, Germany came forward at the wish of her ally and cut the knot. If Iswolsky had to yield, it was slightly less painful for him to surrender to Berlin than to his hated rival at Vienna, for he had never been and never became a Germanophobe. When the first attempt at mediation by the Wilhelmstrasse produced an evasive reply, a thundering telegram brought the dragging dispute to a head. "Tell Iswolsky," ran the instructions to the German Ambassador at St. Petersburg, "that we are ready to propose to Austria to invite the Powers to accept the abrogation of Article 25 of the Treaty of Berlin. Before, however, we approach Austria we must know definitely that Russia will unconditionally accept. You will inform him that we expect a precise answer—yes or no. We should regard an evasive, conditional or ambiguous reply as a refusal. We should then withdraw and let things take their course. The responsibility for further events would be his alone, after we had made a final sincere attempt to be helpful to him and to clear up the situation in a way he could accept."

This historic communication was approved and signed by Bülow, but it was drafted by Kiderlen. The Chancellor had climbed down at Algeciras, and it was Kiderlen's belief that his courage would have failed again in 1909. In principle he was ready to act, but in such a delicate matter, involving the issues of peace and war, the phraseology is of the essence of the matter. To do Austria a good turn without deeply wounding Russia was like trying to square the circle. Never before or after did Kiderlen take so much trouble over the wording of a document. His object was to produce an immediate surrender while avoiding the harshness of an obviously unacceptable ultimatum. The despatch should be read as a whole, for the celebrated Yes or No passage, taken alone, conveys a slightly misleading notion of its character. Pourtalès, the German Ambassador at St. Petersburg, always contended that it was a friendly *démarche* in the interest of all parties concerned. Iswolsky, on the other hand, described it at the time to Nicolson as a diplomatic ultimatum. It was assuredly a bitter humiliation for such a vain man to drink the cup of failure to the dregs, yet it was a secret relief when the menace of war and exposure was removed. Six months later, when the smart had begun to heal, he confessed to Cartwright, the British Ambassador at Vienna, that Germany had acted in a friendly spirit, and had merely declared that if war broke out between Austria and Russia she would have to stand by her ally.

Kiderlen always spoke with satisfaction of his share in bringing the Bosnian crisis to an end without a breach of the peace. " I knew the Russians were not ready for war," he confided to Take Jonescu, " and I wished to profit by their disability. I wanted to show that the time of German tutelage, which dated from 1815, was gone for ever. Schoen and Co. would never have dared what I undertook on my sole responsibility." He exaggerated his share in the transaction, for without Bülow's approval the high explosive would not have left Berlin. His old friend Holstein, with one foot in the grave, sent him congratulations on his " cheek." Bülow, whose days were numbered, was glad to have had assistance on the bridge during a perilous voyage, and even Marschall, who never liked him, declared that he was Schoen's only possible successor in the Wilhelmstrasse. Despite these compliments Germany was to learn that such forced surrenders leave ugly scars.

The Foreign Minister returned to work at the close of the Bosnian crisis and Kiderlen resumed his task at Bucharest. Yet this time there were laurels on his brow. He had played an active part on a big and brilliantly lighted stage to the accompaniment of general applause. After the nerveless sway of Schoen the Wilhelmstrasse had been glad to feel a strong hand at the helm. Bülow's star was sinking below the horizon, for his handling of the *Daily Telegraph* incident had determined the Kaiser to get rid of him at the first favourable opportunity. Perhaps the next Chancellor might be able to remove the veto which alone stood between Kiderlen and the seat of power.

When Bethmann Hollweg succeeded Bülow in June, 1909, an urgent message was despatched from the Wilhelmstrasse to Bucharest. " The new Chief is extremely anxious to meet you as soon as possible for an exchange of views." The meeting could hardly take place in Berlin, for Schoen was still in office and stood high in the Imperial favour. The Chancellor's first official visit to Vienna in September provided the opportunity for unobserved talk. The impression made by Kiderlen was so deep that he was at once begged to draw up a memorandum on the burning question of Anglo-German relations, which Bethmann, despite his ignorance of foreign affairs, realized from the outset was the key to the European situation. He had already initiated discussions with the British Ambassador, and Kiderlen whole-heartedly approved the attempt to undo the mischief of the Bülow régime.

A week after the interview he forwarded an elaborate memorandum to Berlin. Good relations with England, he began, were undoubtedly one of the principal aims of German policy. Austria would welcome them, Italy would draw nearer to her allies, and Russia would realize the value of German friendship. England was unlikely to attack Germany or to form an offensive alliance against her. On the other hand, Germany might find the British fleet opposed to her in a conflict originating elsewhere, though this danger was not actual so long as no continental war occurred. The greatest peril was that England, without taking an overtly hostile step, could make things uncomfortable for Germany outside Europe in matters of secondary importance, and perhaps confront her with a new Fashoda in which she must either yield or fight. To avoid such a catastrophe a naval agreement would not suffice, for doubts would exist as to its fulfilment. Germany should declare her readiness to recognize England's naval supremacy as a means to bring the discussion on to the political field. If relations of confidence could be restored Germany could be accommodating in regard to her fleet, and should make it clear that she had no desire to weaken England's existing friendships. She would be gently informed that for some time her policy had been, if not exactly hostile, at any rate lacking in friendliness, even when her interests were not directly involved. The removal of this obstacle was essential if a naval agreement was to be approved by the Reichstag and public opinion. British statesmen should not be frightened away by too far-reaching proposals at first. Better a small success than the failure of a larger project. Each should promise not to join a hostile coalition against the other. The reception of this proposal would decide how far the English really desired to improve relations. Premature naval discussions might ruin the whole plan of a rapprochement. " The political factor is more elastic than the military. . . . Our chief aim must be to reach a political agreement, however unimportant. For the mere fact of a minor understanding combined with some naval pact would greatly simplify our policy as a whole."

Kiderlen's advice to decline a naval agreement unaccompanied by a political understanding was in accord with Bethmann's views, and the Chancellor continued to seek his advice. A report of the first detailed conversation with the British Ambassador on October 14, 1909, was forwarded with a draft agreement to Bucharest. Kiderlen wrote to express his satisfaction with the start, but thought the draft too ambitious for England to accept. The difficulty, he added, would be to avoid the suspicion that Germany wished to separate her from her friends. The letter ended with an appeal not to flinch from a fairly far-reaching naval agreement as soon as a visible *détente* appeared. So long as the defence of German shores was assured, a few ships more or less should not stand in the way. The second conversation between Bethmann and Goschen on November 4 was likewise reported, with a grateful letter from the Chancellor. Kiderlen replied that if the thread was not cut, he believed in success. It would be a great gain if Germany's open or secret antagonists could no longer count on Anglo-German antagonism. The negotiations for a naval and neutrality agreement were interrupted in November by the General Election in England, resumed early in 1910 and finally dropped in 1912. The attempt of Bethmann and Kiderlen to mend the wires to London was made in all sincerity, but it came too late for success. Bülow had gone, but Tirpitz, a much stronger man, remained and he possessed the ear of the Kaiser.

At the age of fifty-eight Kiderlen was still a Minister in a minor capital, while younger and lesser men became Ambassadors. The situation was too paradoxical to last, particularly after his notable achievements during the winter of 1908-9. He contemplated resignation from the diplomatic service in order to become the German representative on the Commission of the Ottoman Debt. The rumour that his services might be lost to the State filled his friends in Berlin with dismay. The modest Schoen was no obstacle, for he rightly regarded himself as best fitted for an Embassy. " Bethmann is a soft nature," he remarked, " and I am also rather flabby. With us two a strong policy is impossible, only with Kiderlen." " For heaven's sake," wrote the Under-Secretary, " do not think of resignation. Everybody who knows the circumstances would regard it as an immeasurable misfortune." His champions were to be found not only in the Wilhelmstrasse but on the steps of the throne. Valentini, the chief of the Civil Cabinet, Müller, the chief of the Naval Cabinet, and August Eulenburg, the Court Chamberlain, agreed that he was the man the country needed. The Crown Prince joined in the appeal, and when the Chancellor added his weight the Kaiser had to yield. Even now he warned Bethmann with the inelegant words : *Sie setzen sich eine Laus in den Pelz*. When once his decision was made he treated the new Foreign Minister with courtesy and confidence, but the *camaraderie* of earlier years was not resumed, and the brief reference in his Memoirs is cool enough. Kiderlen never flattered anybody and was well aware of his master's failings, but he admired him more than Bülow, whom in his intimate circle he always called the eel. Like everybody else he respected Bethmann for his high character, but in the realm of diplomacy he regarded him as a mere amateur.

Schoen was packed off to Paris, and Kiderlen's appointment was welcomed on every hand. " Political leadership at last ! " exclaimed old Schlieffen, the famous ex-chief of the General Staff. In the Foreign Office itself, reported the Under-Secretary, there was general delight. " Everybody longs for a strong and a firm hand." The new Minister was resolved to be master in his own house. " With us the post of Foreign Minister is most unenviable," he had once remarked to a friend. " All the successes are put down to the Chancellor, all the failures to the Secretary of State." The relationship, which was never easy, varied with the personalities concerned. Kiderlen's authority rested not only on his own prestige but on his chief's ignorance of foreign affairs. Yet the Chancellor bore the ultimate responsibility, and as Bethmann's self-confidence grew with time his influence in the shaping of policy increased. The Anglo-German naval and neutrality negotiations, for instance, he kept in his own hands.

A few days before leaving Bucharest Kiderlen explained his programme to Take Jonescu. While he was at the helm there would be no war with England. Friendship with France was not to be had. She desired peace and would never attack Germany, but if the latter were attacked from some other quarter, she would join in. He had advised the Emperor to wash his hands of Morocco. While that question was unsolved, Germany could find England at the side of France in all other matters. England could not leave her in the lurch in regard to Morocco, for she had a debt of honour to pay. Moreover, it would be no sacrifice, for Germany could never take Morocco if England objected. " Why then should a useless tension continue ? If we can secure something for ourselves, all the better, but that should not be made a condition." " And you believe this policy will be adopted ? " asked Take Jonescu. " Of course, since I am summoned to the post. You know perfectly well that I am not the man to pursue any policy but my own." Germany, he continued, had nothing to gain from victory, and only too much to lose from defeat. Time was on her side. Every decade increased her lead. Her economic development was astonishing. Moreover, a victorious war would bring a Parliamentary regime. The German people had been rewarded by the plague of universal suffrage for the triumphs of 1870, and a fresh victory would bring a further democratic descent. War would not occur. France was essentially pacific, England would not start a conflict, and Russia knew that Germany was too strong to defeat. It was an optimistic forecast. So far as words went the appointment seemed to herald an era of peace.

The new Foreign Minister was only destined to reign at the Wilhelmstrasse from the summer of 1910 till the close of 1912. In this brief space he played a leading part in four important transactions : the rapprochement with Russia, the Agadir crisis, the Tripoli conflict, and the first Balkan war.

Though the Bosnian crisis had been ended by the peremptory summons from Berlin, the wrath of Iswolsky and the Tsar was directed against Austria rather than her ally. Three months after the surrender Nicholas and William II had a friendly meeting in Finnish waters. Russia's dislike of the Bagdad railway had been unconcealed ; but, though negotiations had slumbered since 1907, she had never been entirely intransigent. If the two countries were to gravitate towards one another, here was the road to follow. It was German ambitions in Turkey and Persia, not the German fleet, which caused anxiety in St. Petersburg.

The visit to Potsdam in November 1910 of the Tsar and Sazonoff, his new Foreign Minister, inaugurated discussions which resulted in the agreement of August 1911. The essence of the deal was the withdrawal of Russia's opposition to the Bagdad railway in return for German recognition of her predominance in North Persia. The material symbol of reconciliation was to be a branch from Bagdad to Khanikin, where it was to meet a line from Teheran constructed under Russian auspices. Though the railway connection was never made, the Potsdam discussions rendered Russo-German relations more friendly than at any time since the Björkö honeymoon.

Family relations still counted for something, and the old argument that the Emperors must stand together against the revolutionary flood had not lost all effect. The *détente* lasted till the Balkan wars revived antagonism between Russia and Austria, and consequently between the Central Powers and the Triple Entente. So far as Persia and the Bagdad railway were concerned, the Potsdam negotiations were successful enough to arouse suspicions of Sazonoff in Paris and London ; but in the larger issue of the grouping of the Powers there was no essential change. In drawing nearer to St. Petersburg Germany did not move an inch away from Vienna. Neither Germany nor Russia expected to be attacked by the other, but nobody could tell what Austria might attempt in the Balkans. Austria, as the Russians were often reminded by Berlin, was an independent state. Here was the snag in Russo-German relations, for Austro-Russian rivalry in the Near East was too old and too acute to be removed by Kiderlen or anyone else.

Before the Potsdam agreement was signed the Foreign Minister's attention was once more called to Morocco, which confronted him with the most difficult task of his life. The treaty of 1909, it was hoped, in addition to producing a political *détente*, would substantially benefit both French and German trade. Everything depended on the spirit in which it was worked, for in the absence of goodwill on both sides the occasions of friction were infinite. While the two Governments were conciliatory enough, greedy commercial firms in both countries played for their own hand. The opportunities of exploitation were to be found in mines, public works and railways, yet in all three directions unexpected difficulties arose. In the first the claims of the Mannesmann brothers were particularly exorbitant. In the second the projected monopoly by French and German interests was challenged by the British Government in the name of the Act of Algeciras. In the third sphere, that of railways, strategic and therefore political considerations were involved, and it was above all the railway dispute which destroyed the economic condominium. The whole story of attempted co-operation has been told with inside information in Tardieu's masterly work *Le Mystère d'Agadir*.

The French military authorities had long demanded lines from Casablanca into the Shawia district and from the Algerian frontier to Ujda, both in French occupation. In January 1911 Germany announced that she did not object to railways in the military zones of occupation if they were open to trade on equal terms for all. But she argued that a special agreement was necessary if the line was built beyond Ujda towards Fez, and suggested the employment of the Société Marocaine des Travaux Publics, an association of French and German capitalists, and the prior construction of a line from Tangier to Fez. When Pichon accepted these conditions an agreement was in sight, and on March 2 Jules Cambon advised his chief to sign the German draft. At this moment Pichon disappeared with the fall of the Briand Cabinet, and his successor Cruppi, ignoring Cambon's warnings, declared that the draft needed further study. At the same moment the new Monis Ministry vetoed an arrangement for Franco-German co-operation in the French Congo. Such a sudden change of attitude at Paris produced the exasperation in Berlin which the experienced Ambassador had foretold.

While the economic *condominium* was breaking down, the political situation went from bad to worse. French loans failed to buttress the Sultan's waning authority, and when the tribes round Fez rose in March, 1911, he had no reliable troops to defend the capital. On March 13 Kiderlen spoke gravely to the Ambassador of rumours of French action. "German opinion might be excited, and it would be wise if Germany were informed in good time. By small successive military operations France could be led on to an even more extended operation, which would end by annulling the Algeciras Act." Here was Kiderlen's first warning. The Ambassador replied that France's plans were not fixed, but she would respect the Act as hitherto. On April 4, after a visit to Paris, he informed Kiderlen that the Europeans in Fez were in danger, and that France would probably occupy Rabat with a view to sending a column to the capital to facilitate their departure. "Your Excellency knows my desire to avoid all public excitement about Morocco," replied the Foreign Minister. "I hope the

Government will only proceed to military occupation in the event of extreme necessity. In that case the German Government would be quite ready to exchange views on the steps to be taken." Here was the second warning. A third came from the Chancellor a few days later. On April 28 Cambon announced that bad news had arrived from Fez, and that France must take measures to rescue the Europeans. There was no intention of occupying the capital or infringing the sovereignty of the Sultan. Kiderlen rejoined that he had full confidence in the sincerity of the French Government, but events sometimes produced unintended results. " If the French troops remained in Fez, so that the Sultan only ruled with the aid of French bayonets, Germany would regard the Algeciras Act as finished and would resume complete liberty of action." Here was the fourth warning.

How seriously Kiderlen took the matter was shown in his elaborate Memorandum dated May 3. " The occupation of Fez would prepare the way for the absorption of Morocco by France. We should obtain nothing by protests, and should suffer a moral defeat which it would be hard to bear. We must therefore decide on an object in the coming negotiations which would incline the French to compensations. If they establish themselves in Fez out of anxiety for their nationals, we too have the right to defend our own. We have large German firms in Mogador and Agadir. German ships could go to these ports for the protection of these firms. They could be stationed there quite peacefully, just to prevent other Powers occupying these most important ports in south Morocco first. In view of their remoteness from the Mediterranean England would scarcely make difficulties." Here was the new course—to take pledges and await a French offer. There was no thought, or at any rate no mention, of occupation of territory. The Memorandum was approved by the Kaiser, who, during a visit to England, assured the King that Germany would never fight for Morocco. He desired the open door and hoped for colonial compensation.

On May 21, undeterred by reiterated warnings, French troops entered Fez where they found the Europeans safe and well. Grey confessed that the French were skating on very thin ice in maintaining that the Act of Algeciras remained intact, and on June 8 Spain manifested her interpretation of French policy by occupying the zone in northern Morocco hypothetically allotted to her by the secret treaty of 1904.

That a new chapter had opened was admitted for the first time by Cambon on June 11. " I foresee extremely grave difficulties," remarked the Chancellor. " Perhaps," rejoined the Ambassador, "but no one can prevent Morocco falling under our influence some day. It seems to me that we could examine the questions which interest us and seek to afford German opinion the satisfactions which would allow it to watch developments without anxiety." " Go and see Kiderlen at Kissingen," replied Bethmann. Here was the first hint of compensation, which it would have been wiser to offer before instead of after the expedition to Fez.

The situation in Morocco, began Kiderlen in the historic conversation of June 21, had been completely transformed, with forces under French officers throughout the country and the Sultan at the orders of France. " Have you forgotten the pact of 1909, which recognizes French political influence ? " interjected the Ambassador. " Influence is not Protectorate," rejoined the Foreign Minister. " You are on the road to a veritable Protectorate. That is not in the pacts of 1906 and 1909, any more than your occupation of the Shawia and the East." Cambon remarked that it was not easy in dealing with an uncivilized Government to fix how far influence could go, and he proposed a general discussion like that of England and France in 1903–4. " I agree," replied Kiderlen. " If we keep to Morocco we shall not succeed. It is useless to prop up a tottering structure." Here the Ambassador uttered a *caveat*. " If you want part of Morocco, French opinion would not stand it. One could look elsewhere." " Yes," replied Kiderlen, " but you must tell us what you wish." At parting he exclaimed : " Bring us back something from Paris."

Up to this point the policy of Germany had been irreproachable. She possessed treaty rights and commercial interests in Morocco. Courteous warnings had produced no effect. French troops had entered Fez, but no offer of compensation was forthcoming till June 11, and then only in the vaguest form. Now it was too late, for the Foreign Minister had made up his mind. In April he had told Weizsäcker, the Premier of his native Württemberg, that he was meditating the occupation of Agadir. A Foreign Office Memorandum, dated May 30, argued that north Morocco would soon be French, that military domination would involve commercial privilege, and that French public opinion would

L

veto a serious offer. A Sultan who could only rule with foreign help was not the sovereign ruler envisaged by the Algeciras Act. Germany should resume liberty of action, and follow up her declaration by sending cruisers to Mogador and Agadir. France would then offer compensation, and no storm was likely to arise. If she took it quietly, England would not make difficulties, and she might be told that Germany was ready for a deal if compensation in the French Congo were offered. The Chancellor accepted the plan, though he admits in his apologia that it was sensational and disquieting.

The Kaiser's assent was secured by the Chancellor and the Foreign Minister on a visit to Kiel on June 26. " Ships approved," wired the latter to the Wilhelmstrasse, and the' gunboat *Panther* was ordered to Agadir. On June 19 Dr. Regendanz, Managing Director of the Hamburg-Marokko Gesellschaft, was summoned to the Foreign Office and instructed to collect signatures from firms interested in Morocco to a petition to the Government which was needed as a pretext for the action about to be taken. The address was quickly drafted, signed and sent to Berlin, though when the *Panther* reached Agadir there was not a German nor any other European at the port.

On July 1 a brief Memorandum was presented at the Foreign Offices in London, Paris and Madrid. " Des maisons allemandes, établies au sud du Maroc et notamment à Agadir et dans ses environs, se sont alarmées d'une certaine fermentation parmi les tribus de ces contrées que semblent avoir produite les derniers événements dans d'autres parties du pays. Ces maisons se sont adressées au Gouvernement Impérial pour lui demander protection pour leur vie et leurs biens. Sur leur demande le Gouvernement a decidé d'envoyer au port d'Agadir un bâtiment de guerre pour prêter, en cas de besoin, aide et secours à ses sujets et protégés ainsi qu'aux considérables intérets allemands engagés dans les dites contrées. Dès que l'état de choses au Maroc sera rentré dans son calme antérieur, le bateau chargé de cette mission protectrice aura à quitter le port d'Agadir."

In presenting this document the German Ambassadors made explanatory statements. The advance to Fez, declared Metternich to Nicolson, the necessity of which was not established by the German reports, and the creation of French and Spanish military posts in various parts of Morocco, had destroyed the Algeciras Act and created a new situation. That Act merely authorized the organization of a police force in certain open ports. It was the duty of the German Government to protect the lives and properties of their subjects in the south where no police forces existed. They were ready to co-operate with the French and Spanish Governments in the difficult search for a definite solution of the Morocco question. The assistance of the British Government would be gladly welcomed. Schoen's words in Paris were slightly different. The situation in Morocco, he declared, necessitated a prompt conversation. It was useless to appeal to the Algeciras Act, which had been too often infringed to possess authority. German opinion was very sensitive about Morocco, and one of the main objects of the despatch of the vessel was to calm it. This precautionary measure should not be allowed to affect the relations of the two Governments, and the Press should not be allowed to misrepresent it. A *communiqué* in the *Norddeutsche Allgemeine Zeitung* completed the official statement of the German case. After announcing the despatch of the *Panther* to Agadir in response to the request of German firms interested in south Morocco it added : " The Moroccan notables in the district have been informed that the appearance of a German warship does not convey any unfriendly intention either towards Morocco or its inhabitants."

Kiderlen explained his attitude to Baron Beyens, the Belgian Minister at Berlin. " If France had continued to advance with calculated slowness, we should have had to submit to her usurpations. One day she would have invoked the hostility of a village which constituted a strategic point to occupy it militarily ; another time she would have made a pretext of the uncertainty of the boundaries to cross them. It would have been the invasion of the drop of oil. I thanked heaven," he added with his malicious little laugh, " when I learned of the march on Fez, for it restored our liberty of action. Yet we did not wish to act without making a last attempt at an understanding. At Kissingen I spoke of a compensation due to Germany. We consented to abandon Morocco in return for territory in Africa. This friendly discussion remaining without result we sent the *Panther*." The concluding sentence was thoroughly dishonest, for he gave the French Government no time to frame a reply.

The arrival of a German gunboat at a closed port electrified Paris and London. De Selves, Foreign Minister in the newly-

formed Caillaux Cabinet, expressed to the German Ambassador
his keen regret at the decision. He desired a conversation
about Morocco, but the despatch of a ship would modify the
situation, and public opinion would find it difficult to accept
the motive alleged. In asking Grey's views and advice he
added that France might be compelled to send a ship to
Mogador. The British Government, replied Grey, had
decided not to send a ship to Agadir. The treaty obligations
to France in the forthcoming discussions would be fulfilled,
and England would share in the negotiations. France should
say whether she wished to return to the Algeciras system or
to purchase German consent to a change.

On July 3 Grey told Metternich that the situation must be
considered by the Cabinet, but the German Government
should be informed at once that we regarded it as new and
important. It was also very delicate, and public opinion in
England and elsewhere should not be inflamed. The German
action was very abrupt. British commercial interests in
Morocco were considerably larger than theirs. We could not
remain passive spectators of a new settlement made between
Germany, France and Spain to replace the Algeciras Act, but
must share in the discussion. The Foreign Secretary's tone,
reported the Ambassador, though not sharp, was serious.

Next day, July 4, after a Cabinet meeting, Grey made a still
more weighty communication. " We must take into consideration our treaty obligations to France and our own interests
in Morocco. We were of opinion that a new situation had
been created by the despatch of a German ship to Agadir.
Future developments might affect British interests more
directly than they had hitherto been affected, and therefore we
could not recognize any new arrangement which was come to
without us." Metternich observed that the new situation had
been created by French and Spanish action, but he added that
the German Government would understand that it was
natural for England to take an interest in the question. Two
days later the Prime Minister announced that a new situation
had arisen in Morocco. " I am confident that diplomatic discussion will find a solution, and in the part that we shall take
in it we shall have due regard to the protection of those
interests and to the fulfilment of our treaty obligations to
France, which are well known to the House."

The official British pronouncements of July 4 and 6, though
they asked no questions, appeared to their authors to invite a

formal response. Unfortunately they were not so interpreted by the German Government, which believed itself to have made the position clear in the communications of July 1. Nothing was heard from Berlin till July 11, when the British Ambassador called at the Wilhelmstrasse on some minor matters. After a general reference by Kiderlen to the Morocco question, Goschen remarked that the attitude of the British Government had been made absolutely clear. A conversation between Germany, France and Spain would be inacceptable. There had never been any idea of such a conversation *à trois*, rejoined the Foreign Minister. He added that he had had very friendly conversations with the French Ambassador, and had strong hopes that they would find a *modus vivendi*. It seemed a hopeful sign that on July 14 Kiderlen suggested to Goschen that a meeting between the German and British fleets arranged to take place at Molde should be cancelled, since the Kaiser was likely to make an injudicious speech.

The first conversation between Kiderlen and Cambon after the Agadir coup took place on July 9, when, after an embarrassing silence on both sides, the Foreign Minister proposed to continue the Kissingen discussions and outlined the settlement which he had long had in mind. The hitch in the railway agreement had opened their eyes and a change would be made. Germany would renounce territorial and political aims in Morocco in return for compensation elsewhere, for instance in the French Congo. The negotiations, he added, must be confined to Germany and France. If any other Power joined in, all the signatories of the Algeciras Treaty would claim to take part. The Ambassador approved both project and method, though he added that the British Government would be kept informed.

Kiderlen's demands went further than France expected. On July 15 the Chancellor informed his master that the Foreign Minister was claiming the whole French Congo as compensation for leaving Morocco to France, and that a favourable result could only be obtained by a very firm stand. To secure the French Congo, he added, would involve the cession of some German territory, perhaps in Togoland. The Emperor complained that Kiderlen seemed to wish to go beyond the limits hitherto agreed. " If your Excellency and the Foreign Secretary think a menacing attitude necessary, His Majesty must at once return. In his absence it cannot be done. His Majesty begs for a prompt explanation." Kiderlen's reply to this implied rebuke was a letter of resignation. The French, he argued, would only make an acceptable offer if they were convinced that Germany meant business. " We must have the whole French Congo ; it is the last chance of getting something substantial in Africa without a fight. We must go up to the Belgian Congo in order to have a say if it is ever partitioned, and, so long as it remains a state, to secure communication through it with German East Africa. Any other solution means a reverse for us, which we can only avert by unflinching resolution." If France declined, Germany should insist on the strict execution of the Algeciras Act. The French should be told that Germany would no longer look on while they broke a solemn treaty and did what they liked in Morocco. " I do not believe that they would take up the challenge, but they must feel that we are ready for everything. If a man says in advance that he will not fight, he will achieve nothing in politics." Since he no longer enjoyed the confidence of the ruler he would resign. Bethmann was also alarmed, but he declared that Kiderlen's resignation would involve his own, and the Kaiser gave way.

As the days passed without any communication from Berlin Grey's anxieties increased, and on July 21 he spoke to the German Ambassador. He had no formal communication to make, but our silence did not mean that we were indifferent. Hoping that France and Germany might reach a settlement on the basis of a rectification of the frontier on the French Congo, we had stood aside ; but the news that Berlin was demanding virtually a cession of the French Congo, which it was obviously impossible for France to grant, made him anxious. If the negotiations failed, a very embarrassing situation might arise. Agadir was the most suitable port for a naval base. What was taking place there we did not know ; perhaps the German flag might already have been hoisted. The longer the Germans remained, the more difficult it became to withdraw and the more necessary to protect British interests. Metternich defended the action of his Government and complained that Grey had two scales, one for Germany, another for France ; but he was not in a position to give any information. The Foreign Minister, he reported to Berlin, feared a breakdown of the negotiations and desired to take part in them. It was clear that he would support the French and would grudge Germany a footing in Agadir, but outside Morocco he was full of good will.

On the same afternoon the Chancellor of the Exchequer visited the Foreign Secretary and asked if a reply had been received to the communication of July 4. On hearing that there was none, he produced a statement which he proposed to read that evening at an official dinner at the Mansion House. Both the project and the text were approved by Grey and Asquith. Neither Germany nor Morocco were mentioned, but the warning was clear enough. " If a situation were to be forced upon us in which peace could only be preserved by the surrender of the great and beneficent position Britain had won by centuries of effort and achievement, by allowing Britain to be treated where her interests are vitally affected as if she were of no account in the Cabinet of Nations, then I say emphatically that peace at that price would be a humiliation, intolerable for a great country like ours to endure."

Three days later, on July 24, Metternich brought the response to Grey's communication of July 21. The *Panther* had been sent to Agadir to protect German interests and for no other cause. Not a man had been or would be landed unless German lives were menaced. Germany had never thought of a naval port on the Moroccan coast and had no design on Moroccan territory. If France wanted a free hand in Morocco she must offer compensation. Visibly relieved by this conciliatory message, Grey asked if he might announce that no landing had taken place. The Ambassador replied that he must consult his Government, and on the following day a less agreeable conversation took place. After the provocative words of Mr. Lloyd George, declared Metternich, the assurance must not be revealed. Nobody must think that the German Government had made a declaration of intentions in consequence of that speech. If France refused an agreement, he continued, Germany must demand that the Treaty of Algeciras should be observed and that the *status quo ante* should be restored. A Conference would be needless. If no other signatory was prepared to join in vindicating the Treaty, Germany unaided would secure by all means full respect for her rights. The Ambassador proceeded to read a vigorous protest against the Mansion House speech. The German proposals seemed to his Government quite acceptable, and they concerned territories in which English interests were not involved. If, however, England had desires, they should surely have been transmitted through the usual channel, instead of by a public declaration which had been interpreted by the British and French press as a warning bordering on menace. That was not the way to foster a friendly understanding between Germany and France. No better means of embroiling the situation and leading to a violent explosion could have been found.

Grey defended the speech on the ground that it merely claimed the consideration due to a great nation; but the conversation, which the Ambassador described as extremely lively, ended on a softer note. It was not intended by anything that had been or would be said, declared the Foreign Secretary, to embroil the Franco-German negotiations, which we sincerely desired to succeed. Grey was profoundly disturbed by the interview. " I have just received a communication from the German Ambassador," he remarked to the Chancellor of the Exchequer, " so stiff that the fleet might be attacked at any moment. I have sent for McKenna to warn him." He trusted the Chancellor, but Kiderlen, who was now at the helm, inspired no confidence. " We are dealing with people who recognize no law except that of force between nations," he complained. After this sharp exchange the situation improved. On July 27 a communication arrived from Berlin couched in the friendliest terms. Adverse criticism from the English side, it stated, must obviously render the negotiations more difficult, while a public statement that England would welcome a successful conclusion of the Franco-German pourparlers would have a most beneficial effect. The desired declaration was made in the House of Commons by the Prime Minister the same afternoon.

The Mansion House pronouncement, while infuriating German opinion, slightly modified German claims. Yesterday's conversation was very different from the last two, reported the French Ambassador on July 24. " Reserving the free export of iron, Germany will let you found this North African Empire which is your great objective." Kiderlen renewed the demand from the Congo to the sea, but offered Togoland, North Camerun and the absolute abandonment of Morocco. Once again the French Ambassador replied that it was impossible to cede the French Congo. On July 28 Kiderlen declared the proposed offer of portions of the French Congo quite insufficient, and added that the French Government seemed disinclined to come to an arrangement. Public opinion in France, rejoined the Ambassador, would be severely critical of the offers already made. There was public opinion in Germany as well, retorted Kiderlen. The pact of 1909, to which appeal was made, depended on the Algeciras Act, which had been infringed. Germany's hands could not be bound by agreements which France had not observed. An understanding should have been sought before the expedition to Fez. He had no other suggestions to make. Since the pourparlers, which ought to have been kept secret, had been revealed he did not consider it consistent with the dignity of Germany to abate her requirements. He would, however, consult the Chancellor and the Emperor on the subject of further discussions and would see the Ambassador again on July 31. It was an alarming conversation, but at the next meeting both parties made an advance. Kiderlen, after seeing the Emperor, declared that the essential demand was for access to the Congo river, while he would not complain of a French Protectorate in Morocco. The principle was accepted in Paris and on August 4 he withdrew his claim to the coast.

Though a certain approach had been made, the bargainers were still far apart, and on August 14 the offer of Togoland was withdrawn on the ground that public opinion would disapprove and that French offers were insufficient to justify the sacrifice. France replied that in that case her offers must also be diminished. By the middle of the month seven German proposals for territorial cessions in the Congo had been rejected by France, and six French offers by Germany. Both sides angrily complained of the frequent changes of front. On August 18 Kiderlen left Berlin to consult the Emperor. "Opinion is excited," reported Cambon on August 20. "If the negotiations fail, Germany will probably refuse a conference. The internal situation affects the external. The elections approach and the parties compete in patriotism. I hope our apprehensions may be groundless, but it would be levity not to see the possibility of a conflict." While Caillaux was still on holiday, he heard that Kiderlen had told certain Ambassadors that the attitude of France made war almost inevitable, and that the situation could not remain as it was. Rumours also reached him of German agents in the hinterland of Agadir and Mogador telling the chiefs that Germany would soon control that territory. Pamphlets appeared in Germany, among them the widely read *West Marokko Deutsch*, by the Pan-German leader Class, which argued that compensation outside Morocco was unacceptable. Caillaux believed that Germany still coveted part of Morocco, and to prevent it he was willing to fight. The situation was as tense as it had been in July.

Returning to Paris on August 17, the French Premier took the rudder from the hands of his feeble Foreign Minister, and on August 22 a special conference was summoned in Paris to decide the course of French policy. The Ambassadors at London and Berlin were present. The Emperor and Kiderlen, reported Cambon, seemed disinclined for war. If, however, the latter failed to secure what German opinion would regard as a success his personal position would be seriously affected, and it was therefore doubtful if he really desired the territorial negotiations to succeed. It was decided to offer territory in the French Congo which, in view of the fact that Germany was only prepared to cede the Bec du Canard, appeared large and adequate.

After a brief holiday Kiderlen returned on August 29 to Berlin, where Jules Cambon arrived on the following day, bringing two sets of instructions, one for Morocco, the other for the Congo. The decisive stage of the encounter had now been reached. Though the Governments desired agreement, public opinion in both countries was dangerously inflamed. On September 4 the draft convention agreed on after the conference with the Ambassadors at Paris was presented. Cambon thought it an inadequate offer for the enormous advantage of a free hand in Morocco, but Kiderlen accepted the main outlines. On September 8, however, a German counterdraft outlined a widely different scheme. The Foreign Minister defended his handiwork as merely designed to prevent the eviction of German industry, but it was described by de Selves as an attempt to secure a right of constant intervention. The hitch became known and a financial panic ensued. German shares fell rapidly, there was a run on the banks, and the bankers declared that Germany was financially unprepared for war. After this revelation of economic weakness Kiderlen again showed himself more accommodating, and a new French draft, dated September 13, met with a friendly reception. Cambon confided to Goschen that, unless something totally unexpected should occur, grave complications were now improbable. A reassuring *communiqué* appeared in the *Lokalanzeiger*, and Bethmann reported to his master on September 16 that the latest French proposals went far to meet German claims. Three more French drafts narrowed the differences still further.

The Morocco agreement was initialled on October 11, the

covering letters on October 14. The settlement, however, was conditional on the success of the Congo discussions. " You will have observed," wrote de Selves to Jules Cambon on October 10, " that French public opinion, despite the paramount importance of the Morocco question, is becoming increasingly hostile to the idea of territorial concessions which would cut our colony in half." Without diminishing the territorial extent of the offer already made, the Ambassador was instructed to offer an alternative leaving the junction between the north and south of the colony intact. When the discussions began on October 15 Kiderlen immediately declared the new proposals impossible. " If you wish for agreement you must give us access to the Congo river. I would rather have less territory, but on that point I cannot yield."

On October 2 Kiderlen introduced a new difficulty by raising the question of French pre-emption of the Congo Free State. " If the matter arises, France must confer with Germany whose interests must not be ignored." His tone suggested a break, reported the Ambassador. The disquieting news was forwarded to London and St. Peterburg with a request for advice. A Russian suggestion that any change of sovereignty in the Conventional basin must be discussed by all the signatories of the Berlin Act was approved in London and accepted in Paris and Berlin. The Congo Treaty was initialled on November 3, and the joint treaty was signed on November 4. Kiderlen and Jules Cambon had had over a hundred interviews. They had grown to like each other and they were well matched. They exchanged signed photographs with the inscriptions "A mon terrible ami" and "A mon aimable ennemi."

The first article of the Morocco treaty declared that Germany, merely pursuing economic interests, would not obstruct the administrative, judicial, economic, financial and military reforms needed for the good government of the empire. The second consented to military occupation and police control by France. The third accepted the diplomatic and consular representation of Moroccan interests by French authorities. The fourth bound France to equality of treatment in regard to tariffs, taxation and transport charges. The following articles dealt with mines, public works, fisheries and the status of foreign protégés. The Congo treaty defined the new frontiers and dealt with questions of railways, navigation and the passage of troops. An exchange of letters by Kiderlen and Jules Cambon of the same date pledged the signatories of the treaty to refer disputed questions of interpretation to arbitration as provided by the Hague Convention of 1907.

The reception of the treaties in Germany was far more hostile than in France, and Lindequist, the Colonial Minister, resigned in disgust. The Pan-Germans were furious at the abandonment of territorial ambitions in Morocco, all the more since they believed Kiderlen to have shared their views. The Chancellor discussed the settlement with his usual moderation. "After the dust of the conflict has settled," he observed to the French Ambassador, " we shall both see the importance of the results obtained, and Europe will find peace therein. The situation has been cleared up. Doubtless Morocco was destined to pass more and more into your sphere of influence ; but we differentiated between political influence (as recognized by us in 1909) and direct authority. Perhaps at Paris they confused these things, and hence arose friction, which will now disappear. You are the masters in Morocco." When Cambon complained of the sending of the *Panther*, Bethmann recalled his grave warnings. " If you could go to Fez, we could go to Agadir." In the ensuing debates in the Reichstag he spoke to a highly critical audience. His statements were supplemented by an address by Kiderlen to the Budget Committee, in which, without consulting the British Government, he gave a detailed account of the critical interviews between Grey and Metternich.

Kiderlen's prestige stood lower at the end than at the beginning of the Agadir crisis, for it was generally felt that Caillaux had won the game. Morocco was French. If it be pleaded that in 1911, as in 1906, the officers on the bridge were in disagreement, he should have taken that factor into consideration before he set the ship on its perilous course. In 1906 Holstein was prepared to fight, while Bülow and the Kaiser were not. Though he possessed an authority such as no Foreign Minister had exercised since the foundation of the German Empire, he was not a dictator. He was blamed by the moderates for leading the country to the verge of the abyss, and by the Pan-Germans for letting them down. His technique was at fault. Russia had yielded to threats in 1909, but in 1911 France, backed by England, stood firm. Moreover, there is a suspicion of ambiguity about his attitude. In public he always disclaimed territorial ambitions in Morocco. In private, according to Class, the Pan-German leader, he expressed sympathy with their demands and encouraged them to pursue their annexationist campaign. On July 1, Zimmermann.

the Under-Secretary, told Class that it was intended to take and keep the Agadir district. Whether or not he agreed with them, Kiderlen believed that the beating of the Pan-German drum would be a useful factor in putting pressure on the French. How little South Morocco was a land flowing with milk and honey he only realized from the report of Dr. Regendanz, who was sent on a mission of discovery in August. That he deliberately deceived the Pan-Germans is less likely than that he changed his mind on the value of the country in the light of fuller information, and reached the conclusion that it was not worth a war. Moreover, his heart was set on Central Africa. He had visions of a broad belt stretching from sea to sea with a portion of the Belgian Congo as the connecting link.

Soon after the storm had abated, Take Jonescu visited his old friend in Berlin. Recalling their conversation at Bucharest, he expressed intense surprise at his Moroccan policy, which had challenged France on the ground where she was strongest, and had still further antagonized England whose friendship he had desired to win. The Foreign Minister put up a very lame defence. He had never wished for war and had merely tried to liquidate the Morocco question once for all. France, he argued, had not desired to carry out the agreement of 1909, and a blow of the fist had been required to make her take things seriously. The blow had succeeded, for agreement had been reached. Henceforth relations with Paris would be normal and those with London could become amicable. If he really believed this nonsense he was living in a fool's paradise. How could either England or France forget the emotions of Agadir? He suffered indeed from a strange dualism. In the words of Caillaux, he combined the intelligence of a statesman with the temperament of a Bismarckian Junker. National psychology, as Hammann, Chief of the Press Department of the Foreign Office, confessed, was not his strong point. Never again did the Chancellor relax control, and his exclusion from the conversations during the Haldane Mission filled him with rage.

Throughout the long Morocco crisis Kiderlen wrote with astonishing freedom to a Russian Baroness of Montenegrin descent living in France. His blazing indiscretions, which revealed divergences between the Foreign Minister and " the two old women " (the Kaiser and the Chancellor), came into the hands of Caillaux, who published selections after the war in the second edition of his *Agadir*. Such intimate outpourings can scarcely have been intended for foreign eyes, though the contrary opinion has sometimes been maintained. Whatever their object, they reflect discredit on the writer. Even more extraordinary was it that in the middle of August, during a short break in the negotiations, he undertook a journey to Chamonix in the company of the Baroness. When the Prefect of the Department of Upper Savoy, by order of the French Premier, greeted him at the station, he promptly recrossed the frontier, leaving Caillaux wondering what object he had had in view. It remains a mystery.

Kiderlen's activities during the last year of his life may be briefly summarized. From the standpoint of Berlin, the Tripoli war, like the annexation of Bosnia, was an unmitigated nuisance. In both cases allies of Germany struck a sudden blow at her Turkish friends, and, though not suspected of being an accomplice, she inevitably lost ground in Constantinople. Italy's flirtations with France and Russia, though not known in detail to her allies, were notorious, and pressure might drive her into the arms of the Triple Entente. Thus in 1911, as in 1908, Germany had no choice but to stand by her ally, trusting to her skill to mend the wires to Turkey when the crisis was past. Yet she displayed far less zeal than Russia for the Italian cause. On both occasions Marschall, the chief architect of the German-Turkish rapprochement, sharply condemned the policies of Vienna and Rome. He was particularly incensed by Kiderlen's passive attitude during the Tcharykov negotiations at Constantinople for the opening of the Straits to Russian ships of war, and despatched his resignation in angry protest. When Tcharykov was repudiated by Sazonoff the resignation was withdrawn, but his resentment at Kiderlen's policy remained. His Turcophilism was well known to Italy, whose desire for a more sympathetic representative of her German ally in the Turkish capital was among the causes of his transfer to London.

Despite the friction with Austria involved in the Tripoli conflict, the Italian Government desired the Triple Alliance to continue. Since Francis Joseph was over eighty and his heir's hostility to Italy was unconcealed, Giolitti and San Giuliano decided to make sure that the treaty, which was to expire in July, 1914, should be prolonged beyond that date. In July, 1911, Kiderlen was confidentially informed of their desire for immediate renewal of the alliance, and passed on the information to Aehrenthal. The plan was approved in principle both in Berlin and Vienna. But it required eighteen months of discussion and a visit to Rome by the German Foreign Minister in January, 1912, before the fifth treaty of the Triple Alliance was signed on December 5, 1912. Italy's new position, with a foot in each of the rival European camps, suited her very well.

Soon after the final abandonment of the Anglo-German naval and neutrality negotiations in the spring of 1912, following the unsuccessful Haldane Mission to Berlin, the centre of political interest shifted to Eastern Europe. Here Kiderlen's knowledge and authority were unrivalled, and with the outbreak of the Balkan war in October, 1912, he came into his own again. In this last phase of his career he, like Aehrenthal after the Bosnian escapade, won back a substantial portion of the influence he had forfeited at Agadir. His determination to localize the conflict was beyond all doubt. The firebrand of 1911 had developed into a pillar of European peace. In co-operating with Grey for this supreme purpose he contributed to an Anglo-German *détente*, and in one of his last letters he wrote that the English were so tame that they fed out of his hand.

In the Balkan wars, as in the Tripoli conflict, Germany left initiatives to other Powers. It was a matter of indifference to him, remarked Kiderlen to the British Ambassador, which side won. Victory for Turkey, which he expected, would be easier to deal with, for she knew that she would not be allowed an extension of territory. If, on the other hand, her enemies triumphed, the status quo could not be maintained. In any case, he hoped that the Great Powers, especially England, Germany and France as the least interested parties, would keep in close touch. When the Allies carried everything before them, he, like the Kaiser, realized that they must have their reward. He was relieved to find Austria peacefully inclined and quite ready for a larger Servia, so long as she did not attempt to secure a port on the Adriatic. On this latter point he supported his allies, and informed the Serbs of his attitude. He warmly welcomed the plan of an informal conference of Ambassadors, and expressed a hope that it might be held in London. Wanting nothing for herself in the Balkans, Germany, like England, worked honestly for conciliation and compromise. The most dangerous phases of the Balkan conflict occurred after his death.

Kiderlen died of a stroke on December 30, 1912, in his

beloved Württemberg, where he was spending Christmas. Like Bülow, whose coming to power had also been hopefully acclaimed, he left the European situation worse than he found it. The edifice indeed was so fragile that every fresh shock left it debilitated, just as an ailing body is devitalized by successive operations, however successful they may seem at the time. No one imagined that Germany had wanted war ; but the Agadir *coup* set the nerves of the Chancelleries on edge again just when they were beginning to recover from the Bosnian alarm. There is no reason to doubt the sincerity of Kiderlen's desire for good relations with the Western Powers of which he had spoken to Take Jonescu, but he went the wrong way to work. He lacked both the imagination and the self-control needed for the highest tasks of diplomacy. In commenting on his death, Jules Cambon emphasized his outbursts of anger, his sarcasms and the bad condition of his nerves. Dr. Rosen, who subsequently held the same high office, goes so far as to say that a careful analysis of him both as man and politician would reveal a strong percentage of alcohol. Though French policy in the spring of 1911 was exasperating, the German reaction was inexcusably inept. Its result was registered in the following year in the Mediterranean agreement and the Grey-Cambon letters. The gulf between the Central Powers and the Triple Entente was widened. The diplomatic ground lost by Germany in 1911 was never fully regained, though Kiderlen did his best to repair the mischief he had caused. The cardinal error of post-Bismarckian statesmen in Germany was the simultaneous estrangement of England and Russia. That they deliberately worked for war is a legend, but their clumsy methods increased the stresses from which it arose.

How Kiderlen would have handled the Serajevo crisis had he lived a little longer it is useless to speculate. "We must not be Austria's satellite in the Near East," he remarked to the Chancellor in September, 1912, when the latter was about to visit Berchtold. Kühlmann has expressed his belief that he would not have given Austria a blank cheque on July 5, 1914, and that he would have prevented the war. That he might have managed better than Bethmann and Jagow is quite possible, for no one could have done worse. Perhaps he might have helped to round one more awkward corner before the old Europe plunged headlong into the abyss. If the opening of the archives teaches one lesson more than another, it is that the sword of Damocles was suspended over our heads, and that no European statesman of the opening years of the twentieth century was of the stature to prevent its ultimate fall. Despite his powerful intellect, Kiderlen was no wiser than the rest.

BRITISH FOREIGN POLICY, 1919-39

I. The Peace Settlement and the League

IN the opening years of the twentieth century British policy was shaped by three major principles. All were designed to ensure the security of our possessions and communications, for the era of expansion was over. Two of them, naval supremacy in home waters and the Balance of Power in Europe, were centuries old. The third, our partnership with France, was new but none the less significant, for she was bound to be either an enemy or a friend. The resolve of William II and Tirpitz to add a mighty fleet to the strongest army in the world drove Great Britain almost automatically into the arms of France and Russia. If the violation of Belgian neutrality was the immediate cause of our declaration of war in 1914 and gave a certain moral consecration to our effort, the deeper motive of intervention was to save France from catastrophic defeat. Lord Haldane used to say that the much discussed question of our commitments was largely irrelevant, since our action was dictated by our plainest interests. If we had stood aside the Continent would inevitably have been dominated by Germany, and the Balance of Power would have been overthrown. Victory was only achieved with the aid of the United States, and was registered in six treaties—with Germany (Versailles) June 28, 1919; with Austria (St. Germain) September 10, 1919; with Bulgaria (Neuilly) November 27, 1919; with Hungary (Trianon) June 4th, 1920; with Turkey (Sèvres) August 1920, and (Lausanne) July 23, 1923. Their disintegration is the main theme of European history during the last two decades.

The disappearance of four empires (Germany, Austria, Russia, Turkey) confronted our statesmen with formidable problems. The immediate task of the Allies was to divide the spoils in Europe and elsewhere. It was not easy, for secret treaties had in some measure tied our hands, and certain parts of Europe were too mixed for effective self-determination; but it was less difficult than the problem of rebuilding a shattered world. For this urgent enterprise there were two alternative schemes. The first, championed with eloquent conviction by President Wilson, called for a new co-operative system embodied in a League of Nations. " What we seek is the reign of law, based upon the consent of the governed and sustained by the organized opinion of mankind." The second sponsored by Clemenceau, was based upon the argument that the war had changed nothing except the distribution of power ; that force would rule the future as it had ruled the past ; that the Germans were incorrigible ; and that the security of France could only be found in perpetuating the weakness of her terrible foe.

The British Delegation stood far closer to the American than to the French programme, though it identified itself with neither school. After four years of desperate strife and un-imaginable suffering it was doubtless impossible to make a more statesmanlike settlement than the Treaty of Versailles, for victory is a heady drink. It was not a " Carthaginian " peace, as Mr. Lloyd George has demonstrated in his impressive apologia ; yet far-seeing men like General Smuts and Colonel House confessed how imperfect it was, not least in its lack of large-scale economic planning. Its unexpected severity struck the frail Weimar Republic a blow from which it never recovered, for democracy was identified in many German minds with humiliation and defeat. On the other hand, France was angered by the Anglo-American veto on the separation of the left bank of the Rhine from Germany and on the annexation of the Saar. Thus, while the bells of victory were still pealing, two grave anxieties loomed up on the horizon— the exasperation of a proud people at the harshness of the victors, and the resentment of the French at the frustration of a settlement which in their belief would have guaranteed lasting security. " If we have not the Rhine and the bridge-heads over the Rhine," declared Foch, in a memorable aphor-ism, " we have nothing." Millions of his countrymen shared his attachment to " les frontières naturelles."

While heading France off the middle Rhine, the British and American Governments attempted to sweeten the pill by a promise of military support against German aggression ; and a Tripartite agreement was signed on June 28, 1919, the same day as the Treaty of Versailles. The obligation, however, was joint, so that, if either guarantor failed to ratify, the treaty would be void. When the Senate repudiated the President, Great Britain was absolved from her promise, and she made no attempt to fill the vacuum. We cannot wonder that France sought compensation in treaties with Belgium and Poland and by co-operation with the Little Entente, hoping thus to obtain the security which she had been forbidden to procure for herself. Nor can we be surprised that she endeavoured to hold Germany down. The League of Nations was an Anglo-American creation, and she placed little confidence in its practical utility in time of need. Europe was sharply divided between the satiated and the hungry, between the Haves and the Have-nots. To the logical French mind it seemed clear that the *status quo* emerging from a hundred per cent. victory could only be preserved by her armed strength and that of her new allies. I have heard " Pertinax " contemptuously dismiss both the Covenant and the Kellogg Pact as scraps of paper. Few people expected the League to take military action, at any rate against a strong Power.

To Great Britain, on the other hand, the signing of the Covenant was more than a formality. Though nobody could tell whether the League would be a fleeting experiment like the Holy Alliance, it corresponded to a keen desire throughout the British Empire for a new departure. Our period of expansion, which had lasted for three centuries, was at an end. As a fully satisfied Power, possessing a quarter of the earth's surface and population, it was natural that we should welcome what appeared to be a stabilizing influence in the life of the world. We had made a mighty effort and we longed for a rest. A return to the isolationist policy of the nineteenth century was impossible, so close and so numerous were the ties which bound us to the Continent. It seemed equally dangerous to continue the policy of partnership with a particular Power or group of Powers, which, in the opinion of many people, had dragged us into the whirlpool. For the essence of the system of Continental commitments is that the enmities of any member of a group are implicitly shared by its associates, and that a limited conflict' is ruled out in advance. In any case, both the Triple Alliance and the Triple Entente had disappeared. The only remaining alternative was the method of collective security, each Power pledging itself to certain obligations for the preservation of peace. This was not enough for France, with her numerical inferiority to Germany and her exposed eastern frontier, but at the moment it seemed enough for us. The German fleet was at the bottom of the sea, the air arm was in its infancy. A League policy appeared to avoid the disadvantages alike of isolation and of competing groups. Though comradeship with France remained an axiom, there was no thought of an alliance, written or implied. It was well understood that changes were inevitable, but it was hoped that they could be peacefully made in the spirit of Article XIX of the Covenant. " We have, as I read the lesson of the time," declared Curzon in 1921, " to keep what we have obtained, sometimes against our will ; not to seize anything else ; to reconcile, not defy ; to pacify, not to conquer." It is always easy for satiated states to play the part of the good boy till the acid test of their readiness to make territorial sacrifices is applied.

II. THE WASHINGTON TREATIES

If our entry into the League, with all that it implied, was the first major decision of British policy on the return of peace, the second was the termination of our alliance with Japan. Formed in 1902 as a barrier against Russian domination in the Far East, and expanded in 1905, it was renewed for ten years in 1911. Japan's debt to us for keeping the ring in her triumphant struggle with Russia was repaid when she drove the Germans out of Kiao-Chau and helped us to clear the Pacific of German ships. Having fulfilled her obligations, she naturally expected the alliance to be renewed. Influential British voices argued that we should be guilty of gross ingratitude in dropping our partner when we no longer required her services, and that the wounded pride of a Great Power might ultimately prove a danger in the Far East. Others pointed to the fact that the disapproval of the alliance by the United States was unconcealed, fearing as they did the possibility of England being dragged into a Japanese-American war. Only a little less pronounced was the antagonism of Canada and New Zealand. It was a formidable dilemma for the Lloyd George Ministry, which desired to combine honourable dealing with a regard for trans-atlantic sentiment.

Fortunately it proved unnecessary for us to show our old friends the door. In the summer of 1921 President Harding invited the Powers to meet in Washington in November for a discussion of naval competition and the problems of the Far East. The aim of the Anglo-Japanese treaty, after the formal annexation of Korea by Japan in 1910, had been to maintain the *status quo* in the north western Pacific. This object was now to be attained in a different way. The signa-

tories of the Four-Power Pact of December 13th, 1921 (the
United States, the British Empire, France and Japan), agreed
to respect each other's rights in the Pacific and to discuss any
controversy between them in a joint conference. The parallel
Nine-Power Treaty of February 6th, 1922 (England, the
United States, France, Italy, Belgium, Holland, Portugal,
China, Japan), pledged the signatories to respect the independence of China, and to afford unfettered opportunity to
the young Republic to work out its own salvation. At the
same time Japan restored Shantung and England Wei-hai-hei.
It was a statesmanlike scheme, placing the peace of the Far
East on broader foundations by attempting to help China
through her growing pains, and to soothe the *amour-propre* of
a powerful nation by merging the Anglo-Japanese alliance in
a larger association. "At any rate you gave it a splendid
funeral," remarked a Japanese diplomatist to a British colleague. A difficult corner had been turned at the cost of
weakening our position in the Far East ; for Japanese sentiment could hardly be expected to remain as Anglophil as it
had been for twenty years. The temperature fell still further
with the decision to create a naval base at Singapore, which
was rightly regarded in Tokio as a token of mistrust. Henceforth she showed scanty consideration to the interests of her
old ally.

Of greater interest to the ordinary British citizen was a
second achievement of the Washington Conference. The
faint-hearted attempt to secure a limitation of armaments at
The Hague in 1899 had failed ; and the Tsar, smarting under
his defeat in the Far East, made no similar effort at the second
Hague Conference in 1907. Four years of a world war, however, wrought an atmospheric change. When the American
Government opened the proceedings with a bold plan for
limiting the tonnage of capital ships of the Great Powers, the
British Delegation headed by Lord Balfour promptly fell into
line. The Five-Power Treaty of February 6th, 1922, declared
that Great Britain and the United States should not exceed
525,000 tons ; Japan accepted a limit of 315,000, while France
and Italy paired at 175,000. The consent of Japan was secured
be a veto on fortification of naval bases within striking distance
of her shores. Four English battleships about to be built were
cancelled, and many ships were scrapped. The agreement,
which was to run till the end of 1936, was memorable for two
reasons. For the first time a limitation of armaments had been

reached by free discussion between the Great Powers, and it was hoped that similar agreements would be made for the land and air.   In the second place it was a public admission by Great Britain that she would be passed by the United States if there were a ship-building race, owing to the superiority of the latter in wealth and population.   It was clearly wiser ungrudgingly to accept parity in capital ships with a nation against which war was unthinkable.   Though Britannia could no longer claim with the old assurance to rule the waves, she still remained the strongest naval Power.   The attempt to secure agreed limitation in the lesser categories unfortunately failed.   Our proposal for the abolition of submarines found no support, but their illegitimate use was condemned.   Our prompt acceptance of the Washington scheme increased the goodwill of the American people, which was further enhanced by the Irish settlement of 1921, and by the debt agreement (more satisfactory to the United States than to England) signed by Mr. Baldwin, Chancellor of the Exchequer in the Bonar Law Ministry, at Washington in 1923.   We undertook to pay about 33 millions for sixty-two years.   Never had there been a more genuine desire on both sides of the Atlantic for understanding and co-operation for the maintenance of peace.   The Washington treaties were proudly described by Balfour as an unmixed benefit to mankind.   No one could foresee that Japan would before long abandon her conciliatory mood, resume her expansionist drive, and tear her treaty obligations to pieces.

III. The Problem of Russia

No problem of post-war policy caused successive British Governments more searchings of heart than the new Russia. Her withdrawal from the conflict in the winter of 1917 facilitated the German offensive of March, 1918, and the butchering of the Imperial family sent a shudder through the world. Having signed the treaty of Brest-Litovsk the Bolshevists were not needed at Paris, where the overthrow of the new régime by the combined forces of the Allies was academically discussed.   Since the task was too formidable for exhausted armies to carry through with success, it would have been wise to leave the Moscow Government alone.   A feeble compromise was found in supplying counter-revolutionary Russian commanders with stores and moral support.   The attacks were beaten off without much difficulty, but their effects remained. A fresh army had been called into existence by the energy of

Trotsky, and Moscow felt angry contempt for the " Capitalist "
Powers, " willing to wound and yet afraid to strike."

A deep gulf yawned between Eastern and Western Europe,
and it was argued in some quarters that, so long as the hated
and irreligious Bolshevists were in control, it ought never to
be bridged. The dislike for the cruelties and fanaticism of
the Russian Government was shared to the full by the manual
workers of Great Britain, who detested the Third International.
But trade was bad, the nation was sick of war, and it was
gradually realized that the Marxist régime had come to stay.
A trade delegation under Krassin visited London in 1920, an
Anglo-Russian Trade agreement was signed in 1921, and
Russia promised to cease hostile propaganda. At the Genoa
Conference in 1922 Mr. Lloyd George made an unsuccessful
effort to bring Russia back to the comity of nations. In
February, 1924, the first Labour Government restored the
diplomatic relations which had been severed in 1917. The
decision was received without enthusiasm and without loud
protest, for we had maintained official relations with Abdul
Hamid and other malefactors in the past. Recognition in no
way implies approval, and our example, preceded by Italy,
was followed by France. The ensuing attempt to settle the
problem of debts was complicated by Russian counter-claims,
and by the request for a substantial loan. A loan, declared
Rakovsky, the Trade Representative in London who had now
become *Chargé d'Affaires*, was the only way to solve the question of pre-war debts. A further complication arose from the
virulent attacks by the Russian press, not only against the
British bourgeoisie, but against the Labour Government
which was assumed to be its obedient tool.

The Conference opened in April and the discussions continued throughout the summer. Both parties desired an
agreement, but there was a long agenda and between their
respective standpoints there was a yawning gulf. The Russians
stood by their principle of the repudiation of public debts and
the nationalization of private property, though they were prepared for certain concessions in order to secure their immediate
aims. The British Government and the bankers, on the other
hand, upheld the sanctity of property and the validity of debts.
When on August 5th the Foreign Office announced the breakdown of the negotiations, a group of Labour Members of
Parliament secured their resumption, and on August 6th Arthur
Ponsonby, the Under-Secretary who had been in charge

throughout, declared that agreement had been reached. A
general and a commercial treaty were signed on August 8th. A
loan was to be guaranteed if and when a second treaty satisfactory to British creditors had been reached. Parliament
adjourned on August 7th, after a short debate in which criticism outweighed approval. Opinion in commercial circles was
almost unanimously hostile, and the Liberal leaders announced
their opposition as loudly as the Conservatives. Since Labour
was in a minority in the House of Commons and the country,
the scheme had no chance of success. Before it could be submitted to Parliament, the MacDonald Government was defeated on a minor issue and swept away. The mystery of the
Zinovieff letter to the British Communist Party, published by
the Foreign Office on October 24th, was never cleared up.
Rakovski declared it a clumsy forgery, but the conviction that
Russian communists were still intriguing against the security
of the British Empire stampeded armies of voters into the
Conservative camp.

Recognition was not formally annulled, but the treaties
signed on August 8 were dropped and the brief *rapprochement* was at an end. In 1926 Russia, through the Comintern,
supported the General Strike. In 1927 the Commercial Delegation in London was raided by the police and expelled,
together with the Embassy staff, on the ground that a confidential document had been stolen. The Trade Agreement of
1921 was cancelled, but *de jure* recognition remained. On the
return of the Labour Party to power in 1929, official relations
were resumed and a new trade agreement was signed in 1930.
The trial of British engineers in 1933 on charges of sabotage
and espionage revived bitter feelings. Not till 1934, when
Russia entered the League, did the thaw begin. In March,
1935, Mr. Eden's visit to Moscow set the seal on official
reconciliation, but the two peoples remained far apart.

IV. THE SETTLEMENT WITH TURKEY

A final settlement with the new Turkey was reached with
less difficulty. The Treaty of Sèvres was dictated by the Allies
to a prostrate foe ; but while the Government at Constantinople was signing the surrender, Mustapha Kemal raised the
banner of independence in Asia Minor. France lost interest
in the Greek cause when Constantine regained his throne in
1920, and in 1921 a Franco-Turkish agreement ended Anglo-
French co-operation in the Near East. Mustapha's significance

was only appreciated in 1922 when the Greek army, light-heartedly pressing far beyond the Smyrna zone, marched towards Angora and was hurled back by the Turks. The Greeks received moral support from the Lloyd George Ministry which, in concert with the French, had approved their occupation of Smyrna in 1919. But moral support alone was of no avail. After chasing the Greeks out of Smyrna, the Turkish army, flushed with victory, moved northwards, where a small allied force was stationed in the neutral zone which protected the Straits. France and Italy promptly withdrew their forces, leaving the British troops alone. Mustapha's demand for their withdrawal from Asia Minor created the most anxious situation for Great Britain since the war, for it seemed equally dangerous to surrender and to resist. Mr. Lloyd George, who had eloquently championed the Greek cause, stood firm and asked for the support of the Dominions in case of need. Happily the moderation of Mustapha and the coolness of General Harington avoided a clash; but the dramatic resurrection of Turkey tore up the Treaty of Sèvres.

Curzon had disapproved the Grecophil policy of his chief, and after the fall of the Coalition it was his task to negotiate a new treaty with the Turks. The Lausanne negotiations in 1922-3, brilliantly described by Mr. Harold Nicolson in *Curzon : The Last Phase*, were conducted between equals. Though months of discussion proved necessary, for Izzet was a hard bargainer, no irreconcilable differences emerged. The Turks were aware that their future was in Asia Minor, their historic home, and that Angora was easier to defend than the city of Constantine. Their new outlook diminished the significance of the Straits, and the consent of Turkey to their demilitarization was the principal advantage from the British point of view of the Treaty of Lausanne, signed on July 23rd, 1923. Henceforth Anglo-Turk relations were undisturbed. A difference of opinion as to the ownership of the vilayet of Mosul was settled in favour of Irak by the Court of International Justice at The Hague, to which it had been submitted by both parties. Turkey at last renounced her old rights in Egypt. After generations of alternating amity and enmity the Turkish question, so far as we were concerned, was at last sponged off the slate. Joining the League in 1930 and signing a pact in 1934 with Jugoslavia, Roumania and Greece guaranteeing each other's Balkan frontiers, Turkey became and remained a stabilizing influence. When, in 1936, she announced her desire and intention to remilitarize the Straits in view of the worsening of the European situation, we supported her claim.

V. FRANCE PROPOSES AN ALLIANCE

The divergence of outlook between London and Paris, which complicated the making of the Treaty of Versailles, increased in the early years of peace. The vital connection between economic recovery and political stabilization was more clearly envisaged in England than in France, who had lost in the struggle a larger proportion of a smaller population. Half-blinded by their terrible sufferings, the memory of ancient feuds and their passionate longing for security, the French resolved to keep Germany down as long as they could. It was obvious that an impoverished nation could not pay vast reparations, and the dread of a formidable neighbour recovering his strength outweighed even the desire to collect the expenses of the war. In pursuance of their purpose of keeping Germany weak, the French encouraged separatist movements in Rhenish Prussia and the Bavarian Palatinate, and installed a representative in Munich, despite the fact that the Weimar Constitution abolished the diplomatic privileges of the federal units of the Reich. These attempts to interfere in German domestic politics were rightly condemned by British opinion, and Curzon ordered the British Consul in Munich to investigate French proceedings in the occupied zone. The publication of the Clive report, though hotly resented in France, where the Government pretended to know nothing of the movement, served its purpose by bringing a crazy experiment to an end. We displayed our willingness to insist on the execution of the Treaty by joining in the temporary occupation of three towns in the Ruhr in 1921 in consequence of default, but we had no desire to go beyond its terms.

The collapse of the Tripartite treaty of June 28th, 1918, left a vacuum which France naturally hungered to fill. With subsequent experience to guide us, it is arguable that we should have offered to renew the pledge which ceased to bind us when the United States withdrew ; but at that time the danger of German aggression seemed remote. Left to her own devices, France concluded agreements with Belgium in 1920, Poland in 1921, and Czechoslovakia in 1924—better than nothing, but a very inadequate substitution for an Anglo-American guarantee. Since the repudiation of Wilson and the return of the Republicans to power, it was useless for her to look across the Atlantic. Why should she not knock again at England's door?

On December 5, 1921, the French Ambassador put before Curzon, " in a purely private capacity," certain views which he had been turning over in his mind. The Tripartite Treaty, he began, was dead, and in any case France now wanted something else. Such a unilateral guarantee by two Powers or one was humiliating, and it turned on the definition of the word " unprovoked." What he had in mind was something much more precise, a defensive alliance against aggression, direct or indirect. The latter was the more likely. For instance, a resuscitated Germany, perhaps in combination with a resuscitated Russia, might launch an attack upon Poland, which France would regard as almost equivalent to an attack on herself. England, of course, viewed the Poles in a different light, yet such an event would involve a menace to her as well. When Curzon inquired what advantages such a treaty would bring us, the Ambassador replied that France would be able to reduce her armaments as we desired, Germany could be admitted to the League and would be dissuaded from a fresh attack, and the three Powers could co-operate in the reconstructions of Russia. Curzon was not impressed. England, he pointed out, disliked military alliances and written engagements. In the first wave of enthusiasm she had joined in the Anglo-American guarantee, but now she was asked to give a pledge alone and in a much more comprehensive form. Moreover, British opinion had not approved certain aspects of French policy. Was the consideration of the treaty of alliance to be accompanied by a liquidation of all outstanding disagreements, for instance, in Morocco and Egypt?

A fortnight later Briand visited London, but failed to move the Government from its standpoint of limited liability. The two Powers, he proposed, should guarantee and defend each other's interests all over the world. British opinion, replied Mr. Lloyd George, was not prepared for such a spacious commitment. We were ready to guarantee France's eastern frontier, but not to be mixed up in Germany's quarrels with Poland. France, replied Briand, wanted more than such a regional assurance. Other nations, including Germany, might perhaps enter a partnership corresponding to the recent Four Power Pacific treaty. Strict military obligations were not essential, but the partners would consult if their interests or the *status quo* were threatened. His main object was to build up a general organization to keep peace in Europe around an Anglo-French nucleus. Germany would see her interest in joining the group, and thereby checkmate reactionary and chauvinist forces in that country. Mr. Lloyd George rejoined that at the moment Parliament was only ready for a guarantee against invasion, but he would consult his colleagues.

When the two Prime Ministers shortly afterwards attended a meeting of the Supreme Council at Cannes, Mr. Lloyd George communicated an elaborate memorandum dated January 4, 1922, offering aid in the event of unprovoked German aggression against French soil. Obligations elsewhere would be contrary to our traditions. A complete entente would have to accompany the treaty, providing for the avoidance of naval competition and for whole-hearted co-operation in the economic and financial reconstruction of Europe to be initiated at a conference attended by Russia. Agreement concerning the Near East was also essential. The Memorandum exhaled an unmistakable resentment, particularly in regard to the French attitude on submarines at the Washington Conference. The French reply on January 8 argued that a guarantee of aid against aggression should be bilateral, for England's island position might one day be threatened by new inventions. Any attempt to remilitarize the Rhineland should be regarded as a case of aggression, and any violation of the military, naval and air clauses of the Treaty of Versailles should involve joint action. The strength of the respective forces should be regulated by agreement ; there should be an understanding between the General Staffs, and the Governments should consult on any threat to the general peace.

A draft treaty dated January 12 merely promised British support in the event of unprovoked German aggression against the soil of France for ten years, and consultation if Germany took military, naval, or air measures inconsistent with the Treaty of Versailles. At this stage Briand was succeeded by Poincaré, who introduced a stiffer tone. His draft proposed a bilateral guarantee for thirty years, continuous contact between the General Staffs, and consultation on threats to peace or to the treaty settlement. An elaborate Memorandum in February explained the French views. A unilateral promise, remarked the French Ambassador, would be contrary to the self-respect of France. Curzon pointed out various objections to the draft, including the term of thirty years ;

Parliament might perhaps accept fifteen. When he suggested that the pact should follow the removal of outstanding differences, the Ambassador replied that Poincaré desired it to be signed before the Genoa Conference. The more the project was discussed, the wider appeared the gulf.

A despatch from Balfour, Acting Foreign Secretary, on June 13, virtually ended the negotiations. " H.M.G. are still of opinion that no such defensive alliance should be concluded unless and until outstanding matters, more particularly the economic reconstruction of Europe, peace with Turkey, and the internationalization of Tangier, have been satisfactorily settled. The prospect of an early settlement of such questions is, I regret to say, far from hopeful, largely owing to the attitude of the French Government ; and in these circumstances no useful purpose would be served by pursuing further at present the conversations on the subject of the treaty of alliance." Poincaré coldly rejoined that France was absolutely indifferent as to whether there was a pact or not. As far as he could judge, it was better to leave things as they were, and to seek friendly agreement on the questions at issue. France knew that Great Britain would be found at her side if she or Belgium were again attacked.

VI. Invasion of the Ruhr

In January, 1923, French and Belgian troops marched into the Ruhr on the plea that German reparations, which were paid in kind, were slightly in arrears. Italy sent a few engineers, but no troops. On the fall of the Lloyd George Coalition in November, 1922, Bonar Law formed a Conservative Ministry, retaining Curzon at the Foreign Office, but the change made no difference in British policy. It was the desire of all parties that Germany should recover her economic prosperity, not only for the sake of our trade, but as a factor in the stabilization of Europe. The industrial boom caused by the voracious demands of war quickly collapsed, leaving us with high taxation and an army of unemployed. An eager desire for a return to normality was combined with a growing conviction that France was pressing Germany too hard. Owing to the withdrawal of the United States, England found herself in a minority on the Reparations Commission, where France could count on the support of Italy and Belgium. The epic conflict waged across the table by Sir John Bradbury, hitherto only known to those behind the scenes, became public property when Poincaré ordered the occupation of the Ruhr. The Bonar Law Ministry declined to co-operate, and the Law Officers pronounced the invasion unauthorized by the Treaty of Versailles, though it was thought best to conceal their report. At no time since the reconciliation of 1903 had the sentiments of the average Englishman towards France been so chilly as during the Poincaré-Curzon era. Neither the French lawyer nor the British aristocrat wore kid gloves. We spoke of a *rupture cordiale*, but there was not much cordiality left.

The old instinct for the Balance of Power may have suggested to experts that French predominance in Europe was becoming excessive, but the reaction of John Bull was less sophisticated. He disliked the notion of trampling on a man when he is down, a process little calculated to increase the flow of reparations, and certain to arouse passionate resentment in a proud nation which was bound to recover its strength. British apprehensions were confirmed by the event. The workers of the Ruhr met the invaders with passive resistance, and the heavy task of feeding the population was assumed by the Reich. The mark, which had lost half its value at the end of the war and had since fallen rapidly, collapsed under the strain. The savings and investments of a thrifty people melted away in a few months, and in September Stresemann, who had been summoned to the helm at a moment of confusion and despair, called off the resistance. The avowed aim of the occupation had been to stimulate the willingness of the German people to pay. That object was not attained. It is astonishing that so able a publicist as Wladimir D'Ormesson should argue, in his brilliant volume on French policy, that the invasion was a success both in the material and the psychological field. The results of an ill-advised adventure were the ruin of the German middle and lower middle classes, the further identification of the struggling Weimar régime with humiliation and suffering, and the clearing of the path for a Dictator. In the words of Mr. Lloyd George, the dead hand of Poincaré lay heavy on Europe, and we were glad to see him go.

The defeat of the *Bloc National* in May, 1924, brought more flexible minds to the Quai d'Orsay. While Poincaré, with his lawyer's mind, regarded the Treaty of Versailles as a legal contract which must be enforced regardless of consequences, Herriot and Briand, the new pilots, held that the security of France would benefit by a *détente* with Berlin. Frenchmen, declared the latter in a famous phrase, must learn to talk European. The thorny problem of reparations, hitherto treated as a political issue, had been handed over to a committee of financial experts under the chairmanship of General Dawes, an American business man, and the elaborate Dawes Report was accepted by the German Government. The Treaty of Versailles merely defined the basis of the victors' claims, for in 1919 it was impossible to forecast Germany's ability to pay. The amount per year was now fixed, a new German currency was created, an Allied loan of 40 millions was raised to start the machinery, and an American Agent-General was installed at Berlin to keep an eye on German finances. The weak point of the scheme was that no time limit was set, so that there was no inducement for the German people to exert themselves. When Marx, Stresemann and Luther met Herriot and MacDonald in London in August, 1924, the bitterness of past years had largely disappeared. For the first time German statesmen were treated as honoured guests, and the agreements of August 16 were described by the Prime Minister as the first Peace Treaty since the war.

VII. The Protocol

England believed in the League, but many Englishmen felt that it was only a beginning. In particular the reduction of armaments, prescribed by Article VIII of the Covenant and urgently desired for financial reasons, was clearly impracticable without guaranteed security, and various projects combining the two purposes were hammered out by ingenious brains. The first, entitled the Draft Treaty of Mutual Assistance, prepared by Lord Cecil with French help, was presented to the Assembly in 1923 by the Temporary Mixed Commission which had been appointed to explore disarmament, and thereafter forwarded to members of the League. It laid down the duty of the signatories to reduce their armaments and to support each other against aggression in ways to be decided by the Council. The general obligation might be supplemented by regional agreements to supply military aid. France, the leading champion of the *status quo*, was its chief patron. Belgium and Czechoslovakia gave it their blessing. The other states were critical or definitely hostile. The Labour Government, which took office shortly after the presentation of the scheme, rejected it on the ground that it was likely to revive the old system of alliances, and was therefore contrary to the spirit of the Covenant, which was based on community of interest, not on geographical position. It was also rejected by the Dominions and the project was dropped.

A more elaborate attempt to find security by combining disarmament with arbitration was made in the Protocol drafted by the Assembly of the League in 1924, and sponsored by MacDonald and Herriot. " Our purpose," declared Beneš, one of its authors, " was to make war impossible." This represented a considerable departure from the letter, if not the spirit, of the Covenant, which permitted war under certain circumstances. Compulsory arbitration in all disputes, juridical or otherwise, was the essence of the Protocol. Issues of legal interpretation were to be settled by the Permanent Court of International Justice ; others, where the Council was not unanimous, by a Committee of Arbitrators appointed by it. A Conference for the reduction of armaments was to be held at Geneva in June, 1925, if enough states had ratified the Protocol, which was only to become operative if the Conference proved a success. The signatories were to work for the introduction of its provisions into the Covenant. The resolution recommending the Protocol to the Governments of the states belonging to the League was passed unanimously by the Delegations present at the Assembly. Ten countries, including France, signed on the spot, and Briand described the adhesion of his country as the most memorable event in his career. The British Delegation, with a world-wide empire to consider, was instructed not to sign ; but Lord Parmoor, its leader, an ardent supporter of the scheme, announced that he would recommend acceptance. Had the Labour Party remained in office, this would doubtless have occurred. The MacDonald Government was defeated before this elaborate and formidable instrument could be discussed by the Cabinet or Parliament, and the Baldwin Government was called on to determine its fate. In an interview with his successor at the Foreign Office, MacDonald argued that it imposed no new obligations and merely rendered previous commitments more precise. Austen Chamberlain, however, like most spokesmen of his party as well as of the Services, disliked the principle of compulsory arbitration and the extended recourse to sanctions which it involved ; and the Cabinet, after mature consideration, decided to reject it. The Dominions were particularly opposed to a plan which appeared to threaten their unfettered control of immigration.

N

On March 12, 1925, in a funeral oration drafted by Balfour, the new Foreign Secretary, Austen Chamberlain, stated the reasons to the Council of the League. The chief objection was the increase of the liabilities already incurred under the Covenant, despite the fact that some of the Great Powers were outside the League. " The fresh emphasis laid upon Sanctions, the new occasions discovered for their employment, the elaboration of military procedure insensibly suggest the idea that the vital business of the League is not so much to promote friendly co-operation and reasoned harmony in the management of international affairs as to preserve peace by organizing war, and (it may be) war on the largest scale." Moreover, disarmament would be brought no nearer, for the fear of aggression would remain. " Either some faithless member of the League will break its pledges, or some predatory nation outside the League will brush the Covenant and Protocol ruthlessly aside, defying all the sanctions by which they are protected." The Protocol multiplied offences without strengthening remedies. It would be wiser to supplement the Covenant by making special arrangements, purely defensive in character and framed in its spirit, in order to meet special needs. Regional pacts, carefully limited and defined, were more likely to be carried out than a scheme of universal insurance. The declaration ended with the announcement that the Dominions were equally unable to accept the Protocol. When the Foreign Secretary sat down the scheme was dead, for no comprehensive system could hope to work without British support. A few days later, in defending the decision in Parliament, Chamberlain revealed the opinion of the experts that its obligations would involve the increase of our armaments. The collapse of the project was deeply deplored not only in League of Nations Union circles at home, but in Paris and Geneva, where he was described by a critic as The Everlasting No. The blow was softened in some degree by the fact that a rival plan, more limited in scope and more congenial to our empirical temperament, was under consideration by the British Government.

VIII. The Sunshine of Locarno

During the early years of the Weimar Republic German statesmen were divided into Easterners and Westerners. That Germany could not dwell for ever in impotent isolation was an axiom, but should she turn towards Moscow or the

Western capitals ? Stresemann, who steered the ship from 1923 till his death in 1929, had no hesitation about the reply. By her cultural traditions Germany belonged to the West, and most of her people looked down on the Slavs as their inferiors. During the war he had been a crude expansionist ready for every step thought likely to lead to victory. The collapse of his hopes taught him that the youthful Republic required different methods from the Hohenzollern Empire in the days of its strength. Co-operation with the Western Powers and the League seemed the wisest course. He was aware that a real *rapprochement* was impossible without freely accepting the loss of Alsace and Lorraine, and he was prepared to pay the price.

On January 20, 1925, Lord D'Abernon, our Ambassador at Berlin, forwarded a German Memorandum proposing a guarantee of existing frontiers in the West. Austen Chamberlain replied that the overture was premature, and suggested that Germany should allay France's fears by entering the League. On February 9 a more detailed German Memorandum was sent to Paris, proposing a pact of peace for a long term between England, France, Germany and Italy; a guarantee by the states interested in the Rhineland of the existing frontier and the continuance of the demilitarization zone; and treaties of arbitration between Germany and her co-signatories. While unable to guarantee her eastern frontiers, which she desired to change, she was ready for arbitration treaties with Poland and Czechoslovakia. Here were the outlines of the future Locarno treaties, little modified by months of discussion. The principle was not a novelty, for in 1922 the German Government had proposed a pact with France, England and Belgium, not to go to war with one another for a generation; but the plan was promptly rejected by Poincaré, at that moment about to march into the Ruhr.

With the defeat of the Bloc National the mood of France changed, and Chamberlain realized that if the Protocol was rejected we should have to put something in its place. He was ready to promise support to France, but knew that such a pledge would be vigorously opposed. Public opinion was intensely suspicious of any particular undertaking, he wrote to Lord Crewe, our Ambassador at Paris, on February 16, 1925; both the Liberal and Labour Parties were ready for a fight at the first indication that he was contemplating a regional pact, and the League of Nations Union disapproved partial arrangements. " Yet I am firmly convinced that the true line of progress is to proceed from the particular to the general, and not, as has hitherto been embodied in Covenant and Protocol, to reverse the process and attempt to eliminate the particular by the general. A form of guarantee which is so general that we undertake exactly the same obligations in defence, shall I say, of the Polish Corridor (for which no British Government ever will or ever can risk the bones of a British Grenadier) as we extend to those international arrangements or conditions on which, as our history shows, our national existence depends, is a guarantee so wide and general that it carries no conviction whatever and gives no sense of security to those who are concerned in our action. If we are to relieve the tension of Europe in the only way in which it can be done, namely by relieving French fear, a more particular and specific guarantee is in my opinion necessary." A guarantee of the eastern frontiers of France and Belgium, he continued, would be much more practical if Germany joined in it.

In the same speech of March 24 in which the Foreign Secretary explained to Parliament the rejection of the Protocol he outlined the proposals which were to lead to the Locarno Pact. Of the sincerity of the German approach he had no doubt. A bilateral guarantee of the *status quo* in the West and a renunciation of war in the East might banish the threatening atmosphere which had endured ever since the Treaty of Versailles. It was essential to such an agreement that Germany should enter the League and the Council on a footing of equality both of obligations and rights. At Birmingham he spoke even more warmly of the German approach. Europe was racked by fear. Alliances among the friends of yesterday against the enemies of yesterday would merely perpetuate the division. We could not give such a guarantee regarding every threatened frontier. Isolation, he further explained in the House on June 24, was impossible, and general commitments extending the Covenant were undesirable. Here was a new opportunity, perhaps the last, to free Europe from the domination of fear. The German initiative had received a most friendly response from France. The plan caused no one anxiety, and even the preliminary exchange of views had eased the situation. Only if England co-operated could the plan on which the peace of the world depended be brought to success.

A good deal of discussion was necessary to settle details,

for suspicions lingered both in France and Germany. The election of Hindenburg as President produced a tremor of anxiety, and an unsuccessful demand from Berlin that the question of war guilt must first be settled provoked annoyance. Without the tact and perseverance of Chamberlain and D'Abernon the project might have been wrecked. The final arrangements for the conference were made when the British, French, Italian and Belgian Ministers met at Geneva in September, and Locarno was chosen to suit Mussolini's convenience. The meeting opened on October 5 and the agreements were initialled on October 16. A German attempt to raise the question of evacuation and reparations endangered the negotiations till it was abandoned by Stresemann. The treaty was signed in London on December 1, 1925, in what was henceforth known as the Locarno room.

A long letter from Chamberlain to Sir William Tyrrell, Permanent Under-Secretary of the Foreign Office, vividly describes the closing phase of the negotiations. " The wonderful week is over. I have lived such days and celebrated such a birthday as it is given to no man to experience twice. . . . Beyond and above all else is my sense of profound thankfulness for the success attained and the way in which it was attained, and my deep gratitude that I was allowed to take part in it. Next comes my wonder at the simplicity of it all. . . . Once the policy was accepted, each step followed the other as of course." Briand took Mrs. Chamberlain's hands in his and, with tears in his eyes, repeated again and again, "*Ah, sans lui je ne l'aurais jamais tenté.*" Next moment Mussolini caught her hand and covered it with kisses. It was the supreme moment of Austen Chamberlain's career. To-day the sunshine of Locarno seems merely a dim memory, but at the time we welcomed its rays with gratitude and relief. The treaty, declared the Foreign Secretary in Parliament on November 18, was not the end of appeasement but the beginning. It marked a turning point in the history of Europe, perhaps in the history of the world.

The work of the Conference was enshrined in eight treaties. We participated only in the guarantee of the Franco-German and Belgo-German frontiers against aggression, popularly known as the Locarno Pact, between England, France, Germany, Belgium and Italy. Germany, France, Belgium, Poland and Czechoslovakia undertook to settle all disputes by arbitration. England and Italy undertook no responsibilities in Eastern Europe, but France concluded treaties of mutual guarantee with Poland and Czechoslovakia. The Council of the League was to decide whether the *casus fœderis* arose, except when unprovoked aggression rendered immediate action necessary. In defending his handiwork Chamberlain claimed that the treaty threatened nobody and was based on the principle of equality, England and Italy undertaking the same obligations to Germany as to France and Belgium. All the agreements harmonized with the spirit and reinforced the authority of the League. The British Government avoided automatic belligerence as it retained the right to decide whether immediate danger had arisen.

The essence of the transaction was the unforced recognition by Germany that Alsace and Lorraine had passed into the permanent keeping of France. The existing frontiers between France and Germany, and Belgium and Germany, were accepted by all three states, and were guaranteed by Great Britain and Italy. We bound ourselves to assist either France or Germany against the unprovoked aggression of the other : what constituted aggression was to be decided by the guarantors. The treaty had no time limit, but it contemplated the ultimate transfer of the responsibility for the *status quo* to the League. On paper it was the most onerous burden we ever assumed, for t hypothetically pledged us to intervene in another terrible struggle. Moreover, it contained no reference to the reduction of armaments. France gave us no reciprocal guarantee against German aggression, and the Dominions declined to share the burden. Yet the pact was acclaimed by British opinion, which realized that it rendered another Franco-German conflict more improbable. It had often been argued that the world war would have been avoided had Vienna and Berlin felt certain that we should intervene if France were attacked. This uncertainty was now removed. Thus the treaty obligation seemed to most Englishmen to diminish rather than to augment our risks, for the absence of such a commitment in no way ensured our neutrality. It was indeed almost an axiom that we should once again stand by France if she were attacked, in accordance with the principle that her overthrow would endanger our safety.

If the acceptance of definite obligations in Western Europe was applauded by British opinion as a whole, the refusal to extend our responsibilities was equally approved. It was natural that Poles and Frenchmen, united by a fear of what

Germany might do when she recovered her strength, should urge us to guarantee the western frontier of Poland as we guaranteed the eastern frontiers of France and Belgium. It was equally natural that we should decline. Poland was farther away, and she meant far less to the man in the street— the ultimate arbiter of British policy—than France and Belgium. Secondly Germany seemed resigned to her losses in the west but not in the east. It is true that she signed arbitration treaties with Poland and Czechoslovakia and pledged herself not to attempt to change the Polish frontier by force ; but there was no renunciation of claims in the treaty, and no thought of it in German hearts. Thirdly our armaments were too small to cover extended liabilities. Our policy may be summarized in a sentence : we underwrote an accepted frontier, and refused to uphold one which was not agreed. Even with this important limitation the stabilizing influence of the treaty was generally recognized. It was widely believed that the hatchet was buried at last. Painlevé, the eminent French statesman, once declared that the reconciliation of France and Germany was the corner-stone of European civilization. He was right, and it seemed as if the miracle had been achieved. Our apprehensions had been removed by the surrender of the German fleet. French anxieties were relieved by the renunciation of Alsace-Lorraine, though Briand's enthusiasm was never shared by the majority of his countrymen. What was left to trouble the peace of Western Europe when Great Britain, France and Germany marched in step ?

It was a fair prospect, all the more reassuring since the treaty was only to become operative when Germany entered the League. This she desired to do, and France was at last willing to welcome her approach. She would have come in when the League was founded, as large sections of British and American opinion desired, had she been allowed ; but French sentiment had been too embittered. In the closing months of his rule Mr. Lloyd George privately tried to open the door, but the French replied that it was premature. During the occupation of the Ruhr no German would have dreamed of joining a body largely dominated by France. Now, after the fall of Poincaré, after the withdrawal from the Ruhr, after the acceptance of the Dawes plan, it was possible to enter without loss of dignity.

Before the outward process of reconciliation was completed a deplorable hitch occurred. Germany, it was well understood, would join on the same terms as other Great Powers, namely as a permanent member of the Council; and she naturally took it for granted that she would enter that select circle alone. When, however, at a special meeting of the Assembly called for the entry of Germany the question came up in the spring of 1926, Brazil audaciously announced that if she were refused she would veto Germany's election. Her claim was rejected, and she withdrew from the League. Briand favoured the addition of Poland and Chamberlain leaned to Spain. To cheapen membership of the Council at the moment of Germany's entry by adding, as permanent members, states not recognized as Great Powers was hardly playing the game, and France's patronage of Poland looked as if she desired a makeweight against the new German element. The difficulty, which ought never to have arisen, was momentarily overcome by the appointment of a committee to consider the whole question. British public opinion had shown sounder judgment than the Foreign Secretary. Germany postponed the final step till the Assembly in September, when she alone became a permanent member of the Council, the claims of her rivals being partially satisfied by the creation of a new class of semi-permanent members. The most memorable day in the life of the League was that on which Stresemann mounted the platform and Briand welcomed Germany to Geneva, proclaiming with incomparable eloquence that both countries had had enough of military glory and could now co-operate in the tasks of peace. During a pleasant informal lunch at Thoiry on September 17 the two statesmen discussed further possibilities, including the evacuation of the Rhineland and the Saar in return for a quicker flow of reparations. Had the Thoiry programme been carried out or the Thoiry spirit preserved, perhaps Weimar Germany might have survived.

IX. THE PACT OF PARIS

With Germany at Geneva and the sunshine of Locarno overhead Chamberlain's ambitions for the organization of peace were fulfilled. " My policy in regard to the League," he wrote in January, 1927, "is to let it develop slowly and naturally, to avoid radical changes and ambitious attempts to recast its constitution, to pray that it may not have to face a great crisis until it is much more firmly established, but meanwhile to try to keep the four Great Powers of Europe together, for if they are in agreement no great trouble is to be expected."

While the Foreign Secretary was thoroughly English in his cautious empiricism more adventurous minds were thinking out lines of advance. How could the breathing space following the world war be used to construct new barriers against another catastrophe ? The idea of Locarno had come from Germany. The next scene was laid in America.

Two years after the entrance of Germany into the League, the signing of the Pact of Paris afforded fresh evidence of the desire to banish the spectre of war. The schemes of 1923 and 1924 had been scrapped, and the vacuum they attempted to fill remained. On April 6, 1927, the tenth anniversary of the entry of the United States into the struggle, Briand proposed to the American people a mutual engagement to outlaw war for a hundred years. Since the renunciation of war as an instrument of national policy was already familiar from the Covenant and the Locarno Pact it attracted little notice, and indeed such a declaration of confidence and goodwill on the part of two old friends would have been scarcely more than a *beau geste*. Professor Murray Butler urged acceptance in a letter in the *New York Times* of April 25, and Professor Shotwell of Columbia drafted an unofficial treaty to which any country could adhere. Why should not all states renounce war, not only for a century but for ever ? The Quai d'Orsay was not enamoured of the proposed extension, and on June 3 it formally suggested a treaty of peace between France and the United States. After a long delay, during which American opinion was being tested, Kellogg replied on December 28, proposing that all states should renounce war as an instrument of national policy. Briand accepted the invitation to join the United States in presenting a draft treaty after sig... g it themselves. The American project, however, so different from Briand's original offer, aroused no enthusiasm among the French, who feared the weakening of existing obligations and deplored the absence of sanctions.

Apprehensions were diminished by Kellogg's formal declaration in an address to the American Society of International Law on April 28 that the signatories were not debarred from the right to defend themselves against unprovoked attack. Any violation of the pact, he added, would automatically release the other parties from their obligations to the treaty-breaking state. This merely stated what everyone took for granted, and since it is the practice of belligerents to assert that they are fighting in self-defence, the reservation reduced the renunciation of war to the level of a copy-book maxim. Its scope was further limited by the British reply. Chamberlain, who felt no enthusiasm for the plan, explained that he could accept no treaty which would weaken the Covenant and the Locarno pact. The request was made that the Kellogg speech, reserving the right of self-defence, should have the same authority as the treaty. Finally, freedom of action was reserved " in certain regions the welfare and integrity of which constitute a special and vital interest for our peace and safety. H.M.G. have been at pains to make it clear in the past that interference with these regions cannot be suffered. Their protection against attack is to the British Empire a measure of self-defence." No details of what was popularly described as the British Monroe Doctrine were given, but the reference to Egypt was clear enough.

The Pact signed on August 27, 1928, aroused more interest in America than in Europe, where the absence of teeth was felt to destroy its value as a practical deterrent from war. If a signatory broke his pledge, was he to be restrained and his victim assisted ? To this vital question it offered no reply. England, like nearly all her co-signatories, had assumed obligations under the Covenant. The United States had not, and they displayed no desire to mix themselves up in a quarrel of the old world. The feeling that the pact was like an outline map prompted Mr. Stimson, Kellogg's successor as Secretary of State, to declare in 1932, with his eye on Japan, that it involved consultation between the signatories if a state ran amok. This, however, was merely a personal opinion, and the pact was contemptuously ignored by Japan, Italy, Germany and Russia during the next few years. If ever an international agreement deserved the name of a scrap of paper, it was the Pact of Paris. The British Delegation at the Assembly of 1929 proposed that its principle should be worked into the Covenant ; but the discussion of the proposed amendments was postponed till 1930, when opposition from several countries led to the dropping of the plan.

The Pact was followed a year later by the decision of the second Labour Government to sign the Optional Clause of the statute creating the Permanent Court of International Justice at the Hague. A few countries, including France, had already signed, but France had not ratified. Though important cases had been referred to the Court with satisfactory results, there was no obligation to employ its services except for states

which voluntarily accepted them in advance. When Mac-
Donald announced the decision to sign the Optional Clause
in the Assembly of 1929, other states, large and small, came
trooping in. In our own case the burden of obligation was
diminished by the reservation of domestic and inter-Imperial
questions. Moreover, signatories of the Optional Clause
pledged themselves only to the submission of legal or treaty
disputes. Since many of the most inflammable problems are
not matters of legal interpretation, the British Government
also acceded in 1931 to the General Act for the Pacific Settlement of International Disputes, providing machinery for
conciliation in cases not of a juridical character, approved by
the League Assembly in 1928. Briand's scheme for a European
federation, outlined at the Assembly of 1929, provoked a good
deal of discussion but was tacitly dropped ; for the states
and peoples had too little confidence in one another to co-
operate systematically in great affairs.

X. THE END OF RECOVERY

The history of post-war Europe falls into three chapters.
The first, extending from 1918 to the defeat of the *Bloc
National* in 1924, was a period of confusion and anxiety. The
second, also covering six years, beginning with the withdrawal
from the Ruhr and the framing of the Dawes Report, was a
time of convalescence. The three Foreign Ministers—Austen
Chamberlain, Briand and Stresemann—liked and trusted one
another, convinced as they were that friendly relations between
their nations were essential to the recovery of Europe ; and
Arthur Henderson carried on the tradition of intimate co-
operation. Further welcome signs of a *détente* were apparent
when the Dawes Plan was superseded by the Young Plan in
1929, slightly reducing the annual burden of reparations and
creating a Bank of International Settlement at Basel. The
armies of occupation, it was agreed, were to evacuate the
Rhineland by the summer of 1930. The territory had been
divided into three zones, which, subject to the fulfilment of
her obligations by Germany, were to be successively evacuated
at intervals of five years, dating from the coming into operation of the treaty in January, 1920. The Cologne zone was
handed back in 1926, one year after the scheduled time. The
Coblenz zone was due for evacuation in June, 1930, but when
the date arrived the Mainz zone was also returned. When
Hitler declares that Germany was trampled underfoot till he

came to power, it should be remembered that the army of
occupation marched away while Brüning was at the helm and
that reparations were dropped in 1932. Yet opportunities of
further appeasement were lost. The vision of a lasting reconciliation between France and Germany symbolized by the
name of Thoiry had failed to materialize.

The third chapter opened with the Reichstag elections of
September, 1930, when the total of the Nazi representatives
jumped from 12 to 107. The march of Hitler towards his goal
was a portent, and the last gleams of the sunshine of Locarno
were swept away. In *Mein Kampf* he had described France as
the deadly enemy who must be struck down before the conquest of the east could begin. In the Nazi gospel of national
resurrection there was no place for the League. The structure
of security so laboriously erected at Locarno and Geneva
seemed tottering to its fall. Brüning remained in the Wilhelmstrasse with his small and precarious majority, but how long
would he last ? Everyone realized that the Nazi triumph was
partly due to the renewed distress generated by the bursting
of the American bubble in October, 1929. But its main cause
was a new spirit of self-confidence and self-assertion. Though
France was the party chiefly concerned, Great Britain, as the
friend of France, could not look on unmoved. It was obvious
that stormy weather was ahead. Two of the pilots had gone
—Stresemann by death in 1929, Austen Chamberlain as the
victim of the General Election of the same year. Only the
ailing Briand remained, the mere ghost of his former self ;
and by this time the average Frenchman had ceased to believe
in the policy of appeasement.

XI. Aggression in the Far East

A year after the emergence of Hitler a resounding blow was
struck at the League and the principles of friendly co-operation
for which it stood. On September 18, 1931, Japanese troops
in Manchuria occupied Mukden on the pretext that the railway
had been cut : probably they had done it themselves. In any
case it was the occasion, not the cause, of the seizure of
Manchuria, for which elaborate preparations had been made.
The Nankin Government was too weak to defend its distant
possession, and none of the Powers was inclined to intervene.
The League appointed a Commission of five, with Lord Lytton
as Chairman, to investigate ; but its members only reached
the Far East in January, 1932, and by the time it reported in

the following September the whole of Manchuria was in the hands of the aggressor. The measured condemnation by the Lytton Report was confirmed by a unanimous vote of the Assembly, and the breaker of the Covenant resigned. No state, however, proposed either military or economic sanctions, and the League merely refused to recognize changes effected in violation of treaty obligations.

Though British opinion was shocked at the action of a Power which was not only an original member of the League but a permanent member of the Council, the Coalition Government formed in the autumn of 1931 played for safety. Japan had broken the Covenant, the Washington Nine-Power Treaty, and the Pact of Paris; yet it was generally agreed that nothing could be done without the co-operation of the United States, whose commercial relations with Japan were more important than ours. Nowhere was greater sympathy felt for the reforming efforts of Young China than in America. Mr. Stimson took the lead in the policy of non-recognition of illegal conquests which was followed at Geneva, but even he felt unable to do more. Everyone knew that a world-wide boycott of Japan's exports would have crippled her power and perhaps rescued Manchuria from her grip; but it might also have led her to hit back, and no Power was willing to run the risk of war against a nation so inaccessible and so strong. Sir John Simon was sharply criticized in various quarters for his cool acceptance of a gross breach of the Covenant and Mr. Stimson was disappointed at his attitude; yet most Englishmen agreed that we could do nothing effective if America declined to move. Inaction, however, while avoiding danger at the moment, was bound to increase the perils of the future by encouraging aggression elsewhere. The alternative to collective security is anarchy. The unopposed seizure of Manchuria opened a new and sinister chapter in the history of Asia, Africa and Europe. The lull which followed the Great War was over. The League was powerless, for its members declined to play up. The world was becoming safe for aggressors provided that the victim was weak; and neutrals, greedy for orders, were only too ready to supply the munitions and materials needed for the success of a criminal enterprise.

XII. DISARMAMENT AND REPARATIONS

A third blow to recovery was struck by the fiasco of the Disarmament Conference. Years of preliminary discussion in the Preparatory Commission appointed by the Council of the League in 1925 had done little more than reveal the difficulties in the path ; and the meeting had been postponed again and again in the hope of securing some measure of agreement. Meanwhile progress was registered in one portion of the vast field. A second naval conference, initiated like that of 1922 by the United States, met at Geneva in 1927 for the purpose of filling the gap left in the Washington treaty, which dealt with capital ships and aircraft carriers. The problem of cruisers, destroyers and submarines remained and proved insoluble. The prospects of the meeting were darkened by the refusal of France and Italy to attend on the ground that naval disarmament could not be discussed alone. To the general astonishment England and the United States found themselves divided by an unbridgeable gulf. Parity in tonnage, which was accepted by both parties, was not necessarily parity in fighting strength. Our world wide empire and commerce, we argued, required a large number of medium and small cruisers. American interests, declared her spokesmen, needed a relatively small number of large and heavily armed cruisers. To this demand we refused to consent. The Conference, in which Japan had played a helpful part, broke down, and Lord Cecil, the second British delegate, resigned from the Cabinet in protest against the stiff attitude of his colleagues in regard to American claims.

The return of the Labour Party to office in 1929 and a visit to Washington by Ramsay MacDonald facilitated the partial success of the third Naval Conference which met in London in January, 1930. This time France and Italy took part, but the former refused to accept the parity with Italy in smaller vessels which she had admitted in 1922 in regard to capital ships. Japanese claims were also less modest than at Washington and Geneva, and her ratio, so far as cruisers were concerned, was raised. England and the United States bridged the gulf which had sundered them in 1927 by the reduction of our cruiser demands from seventy to fifty. The treaty, which was to run till the last day of 1936, was signed on April 27. A naval holiday for five years in the construction of capital ships was accepted by all the five Powers, and submarines were limited in size and armament. Part III, limiting the global tonnage of cruisers, destroyers and submarines, was not signed by France and Italy, who proposed to continue their discussions. Agreement between them was almost in sight in March 1931, but at the last moment new difficulties arose and negotiations broke down.

On February 2, 1932, the Disarmament Conference, attended by sixty-one states, opened at Geneva, with Henderson in the chair. Looking back on its failure we may regret that none of the Great Powers took a strong line at the start. The success of the Washington Naval Conference had been largely due to the leadership of Mr. Hughes, who produced his scheme on the opening day and identified it with the prestige of the United States. He was, of course, the host, and at Geneva there could be no host. It is none the less deplorable that the British Delegation failed to give a firmer lead, and that some of its concessions were held back till enthusiasm had waned and the broad principle of reduction had been smothered beneath the arguments of experts. During the first six months the two Great Powers who appeared most anxious for results were Italy, who announced her readiness to accept any limitation acceptable to the rest, and the United States, whose President unsuccessfully proposed a clean cut of a third over the whole field.

When the Conference adjourned in the summer of 1932 the psychological moment had passed. Germany was rapidly recovering her strength, and could no longer be controlled or ignored. Exasperated by the fruitless talk at Geneva she withdrew her Delegation, but was wooed back at the end of the year by a formula recognizing her equality of status in the matter of armaments in a system of general security. The session of 1933 was as barren as that of 1932, and in the autumn Hitler, who had become Chancellor on January 30, flung out of the Conference and resigned from the League. Failure had been partially due to the undeniable technical difficulties arising out of the claims of states with different problems to face. The deeper reason was the terror (felt not only by the expert but by the man in the street) of embarking on uncharted seas, the fear of each that others might not keep their word, the traditional conviction that safety could only be found in superior strength. " Of a real desire to achieve disarmament for its own sake," declares General Temperley, the British Military Adviser, " I could see no sign anywhere, because they were afraid." It was natural enough, though none the less fatal to success, that the victorious Powers, with France and Great Britain at their head, should desire to retain their superiority. It was equally natural that the defeated

Powers should yearn to escape from the servitudes imposed upon them in the peace treaties. Hitler, for instance, insisted on a short-term army of 300,000. Here was the fundamental cause of the collapse of the efforts for the reduction of armaments and the stabilization of Europe—the sleepless antagonism between the beneficiaries and the victims of the *status quo*. When Barthou, distrusting Hitler's sincerity and alarmed by his armament estimates, broke off discussions with Germany in April, 1934, the Conference was dead.

While the attempt at disarmament was in progress, reparations were virtually wiped off the slate. The American blizzard had interrupted the economic recovery of Germany, whose inability to pay the sums due under the Young Plan was proclaimed by Brüning in 1931 and confirmed by the newly instituted Bank of International Settlement at Basel at the end of the year. When the parties concerned met at Lausanne in June 1932 under the chairmanship of MacDonald, reparation payments were cancelled, except that Germany made herself responsible for interest and sinking fund on 150 millions, to be raised in certain circumstances after three years by the Basel Bank. Ratification of this paper sacrifice by the creditor Powers was made conditional on a settlement between them and their own creditors in the United States. Such an arrangement, however, proved unattainable. Congress declined to cancel or reduce the vast sums due from Europe, and the debtor states were unable to provide or at any rate to transfer their payments in full. England was ready for a deal, and Mac-Donald visited Washington to discuss the problem, but there was no response. We made one more half-yearly payment, followed by one or two token payments. The rest was silence. The whole crazy structure of reparations and inter-allied debts, the existence of which had impeded recovery, had collapsed. By this time, however, the world was too sick to be cured or even sensibly relieved by the removal of these burdens; and the Monetary and Economic Conference held in London in June 1933, attended by sixty-four countries, broke down on the refusal of the United States to consider currency stabilization.

The same summer witnessed a fresh attempt to stabilize Europe by a political pact. Mussolini had realized earlier than most statesmen of the victorious Powers that Germany could no longer be dictated to or ignored, and that the peace treaties, like other settlements, were not sacrosanct. He had also ambitions of his own, and he disapproved the claims of the smaller Powers in the League to share in the control of affairs. Since the end of the war the Continent had been guided mainly by Great Britain, France and Italy. Why should not Germany now be added to the firm ? And why should not the four Great Powers consider in a friendly way the claims for revision which inevitably arise after a dictated peace ? It was impossible for Great Britain and France to decline, for the latter feared a *rapprochement* between Rome and Berlin if she stood aloof. The Italian draft handed to MacDonald and Sir John Simon during a visit to Rome in March in connection with the dying Disarmament Conference envisaged co-operation of the four Powers who should impose their policy on other States ; revision of treaties ; equality of military rights for Germany if the Disarmament Conference broke down ; and colonial readjustments in favour of Italy and Germany. The Foreign Secretary told his host that some amendments were desirable, among them a recognition of the sanctity of treaties, and indeed the scheme was full of explosive matter. The spectre of revision alarmed not merely France, who pressed for modifications, but Poland, who angrily resented her exclusion from the negotiations, and the Little Entente. So shrill were the protests of Beneš and Titulescu that revision dropped out of the programme. The anæmic Four Power Pact for ten years was initialled in Rome on June 7, 1933. In a covering despatch Sir John Simon explained that it was not to be regarded as a substitute for or as set in opposition to the Covenant, nor as an attempt to impose the will of the four signatories on other states. The new machinery was to operate within the ambit of the Covenant and did not imply any extension of our obligations. The pact was never ratified and was forgotten as quickly as made. Two of its signatories were shortly to show how little they were inclined to consult their partners when far-reaching decisions were to be framed. Yet it was not without importance. It marked a further step towards Germany's recovery of status, loosened the ties between Paris and Warsaw, emphasized afresh the difficulty of territorial revision, and wounded its author's pride. Small concessions, it was clear, would be useless, and substantial sacrifices nobody was prepared to make. The problem of peaceful change seemed insoluble.

O

XIII. England and Germany Rearm

The year 1935 opened under relatively favourable auspices. Russia had entered the League with the approval of England and France ; the tension between Jugoslavia and Hungary arising out of the murder of King Alexander at Marseilles had been allayed by its good offices ; and the dangers involved in the Saar plebiscite, after fifteen years of separation from Germany, were averted by the timely despatch of British and other disinterested troops to the district with the approval of all parties concerned. In the first week of the new year Laval visited Rome, and the ill-will between the Latin sisters which had existed since the close of the war was partially dispelled. The reconciliation embodied in the colonial agreements of January 8, implementing the promise to Italy made in 1915, was welcomed by Great Britain, the friend of both, for its relation to the Abyssinian problem was still obscure.

At the beginning of February Laval visited London, and the results of the discussions were embodied in the Anglo-French Declaration of February 3. The two Powers sketched out a plan for the further stabilization of Europe on the basis of three regional pacts. A West European Air Pact of mutual assistance was to be made by the Locarno Powers—Great Britain, France, Germany, Italy and Belgium. The Locarno Treaty pledged us to join France or Germany in resisting unprovoked aggression, but neither Power gave a corresponding pledge to us. The proposal was thus a reiteration and extension of the Locarno policy, equalizing obligations in the particular field where the danger had rapidly grown. The second plan, originally suggested by Barthou in June 1934 and popularly known as an Eastern Locarno, contemplated a mutual guarantee of the existing frontiers between Russia, Poland, Germany, Czechoslovakia, Finland and the Baltic States (Estonia, Latvia, Lithuania). A third project was designed to secure the independence and integrity of Austria, which on two occasions in 1934 the British Government had formally declared a principle of British policy. To spare her pride, and to facilitate acceptance of the obligation in certain quarters, the Pact generalized the promise of non-interference to include other Danubian lands which were not on the danger list. Here was a bold and comprehensive scheme sponsored by the Western democracies with the approval of Italy and Russia. Great Britain only contemplated signature of the first, since she was neither an East European nor a Central

European Power, but they were intended to be taken as a whole. The fate of the project depended on Germany, whose signature was desired for all three. All roads now led to Berlin. Hitler indicated that he would gladly sign the Western Air Pact; that he was ready for pacts of non-aggression in Eastern Europe (except in regard to Lithuania, the owner of Memel), though not for a military guarantee; and that in regard to Austria the meaning of non-intervention must be defined. Thus the Anglo-French scheme vanished almost as soon as it was born. Its essence, but also its weakness, was its comprehensive character; and it came too late.

Hitler's ready acceptance of an Air Pact tempered disappointment at his attitude to the other items, and an invitation to Sir John Simon to visit Berlin for discussion was promptly accepted; but before it was paid two events occurred which revived the suspicion of both sides. On March 4 an argumentative White Paper, initialled by MacDonald and dated March 1, called attention to Germany's illegal rearmament, deplored the failure of what was described as our policy of unilateral disarmament, and announced the decision, in the name of national and Imperial security, to increase expenditure on the three Defence Services. In a passage angrily resented in Germany, attention was called to the systematic militarization of youth practised by the Nazi party as an element in the general feeling of insecurity. The White Paper was not without its critics at home, and the moment chosen for publication was unfortunate. It was asserted by Liberal and Labour spokesmen that opportunities for agreed limitation had been lost at Geneva, and that our participation in the renewed armament race was more likely to intensify than to diminish the peril. Whatever may be thought of its tone and wording, it reflected a widespread conviction that the prospect of the maintenance of peace had diminished. The first note of alarm had already been struck in the previous year when a large increase in our air force was announced, and Mr. Baldwin declared in memorable words on July 30, 1934, that our frontier was no longer on the chalk cliffs of Dover but on the Rhine. Our rearmament had begun at last, though its *tempo* was slow, and the Opposition continued to resist it till the summer of 1938. It was a serious error not to utilize the dynamic energy of Mr. Churchill in preparing for the worst.

It was now Hitler's turn to contribute to the general *malaise*. On March 16, 1935, the German Government announced the restoration of conscription involving an increase of the Reichswehr to thirty-six divisions and about 550,000 men. It had passed the treaty limit of 100,000 before the Nazi revolution, but no one had expected such a colossal jump. That Germany would sooner or later recover her strength, as France had renewed herself after Sedan, was an axiom. Great Powers cannot be kept down for very long, and the more they are trampled on the more vigorous will be their rebound. Since it was also revealed by Göring on March 10 that Germany had within the last year created a formidable air force, and the intention was announced to build submarines and enlarge the navy, it was realized that she was on her legs again. Sir John Simon returned from his visit to Berlin on March 24-25 with increased apprehension, and confessed to Parliament that " considerable divergence of opinion " was revealed. In addition to a conscript army Hitler contemplated a navy 35 per cent. of our own, and air parity between Germany, England and France.

The three Western Powers drew closer together in alarm, and on April 9th it was announced that France and Russia were about to sign a mutual assistance pact. France demanded a special meeting of the League Council. Germany had recovered her strength : what use would she make of it ? She had broken the military clauses of the Treaty of Versailles : which would she break next ? The purpose of the Stresa meeting, April 11-14, attended by England, France and Italy, was to prepare the ground for the Council. The breach of the treaty was condemned and it was resolved to register a formal rebuke at Geneva. The second main topic was the independence of Austria, which had been so nearly overthrown on July 25, 1934, when Dollfuss was murdered by Austrian Nazis. No military guarantee was undertaken, but the three Powers reiterated their attachment to the principle of Austrian independence. " The three Powers," ran the Final Declaration, " the object of whose policy is the collective maintenance of peace within the framework of the League of Nations, find themselves in complete agreement in opposing by all practicable means any unilateral repudiation of treaties which may endanger the peace of Europe, and will act in close and cordial collaboration for this purpose." Here was the charter of the Stresa front. A few days later the Council of the League solemnly censured the German Government, Denmark alone abstaining ; but no further action was taken, and Germany contested the right of her accusers to act as judges. The strength of the Western Powers was enhanced by the conclusion of mutual assistance pacts by Russia with France on May 2 and with Czechoslovakia on May 16. Looking around Europe in the early summer of 1935 it seemed that, whatever danger the new Germany might present, there were ample means to cope with it. For the first time since 1917 Great Britain, France, Italy and Russia appeared to be marching in step, and the sympathies of the Little Entente were not in doubt. Germany stood alone, though, since the Ten Year Pact of Peace and non-aggression of January 1934, Poland was no longer reckoned with certainty among her potential foes. Yet this appearance of solidarity was an illusion, and in a few months the whole landscape was transformed.

The Stresa front was quickly dented by a thrust from an unexpected quarter. Germany had passed the stage of weakness in which her policy could be controlled by her conquerors, and British statesmen no longer made the attempt. Her equality of status within a system of general security had been recognized in 1932 ; and though in 1935 security for all seemed further away than ever, her new position had come to be tacitly accepted by the average Englishman without waiting for the fulfilment of the qualifying condition. When the naval clauses of the Treaty of Versailles went the way of the military and air limitations, we felt a tremor of apprehension and joined in the Geneva protest, but it was clear that we had to make the best of a bad job. Accordingly, when the German Government proposed to adopt a naval strength of a little more than a third of our own, we promptly concurred. Refusal would have renewed the rivalry and revived the alarms of the pre-war era. It was generally agreed that the British Government had no choice ; for the totals—35 per cent. of British strength, with the right to equality in submarines, though Germany promised not to exceed 45 per cent. without notice— were as favourable as we could expect. Moreover, since the size of the German fleet depended on that of our own, we could keep it at a low level if our partner in the pact kept her word.

Though the practical advantages of the agreement were obvious in Whitehall, it aroused surprise and resentment abroad. France was informed of what was taking place, but there was no question of effective consultation or sharing in the pact. To the logical French mind it was a paradox that in

April the British Government joined in the Geneva censure of the treaty-breaker, and that in June it signed a pact condoning a formidable breach. It was in vain that the First Lord of the Admiralty pointed out that we had merely tried to circumscribe the effects of a unilateral decision which we had not been able to prevent. To accept German rearmament as inevitable was one thing, to recognize it in a treaty was another. Still more alarming in French and Italian eyes was our apparent readiness to take independent action in a matter of first-class importance, as if the Stresa pact or the Anglo-French programme of February 3 did not exist. Germany's potential naval strength, which appeared so modest to the British Government, assumed a different aspect when viewed from a Continental angle. Anglo-French relations were of too long standing to suffer permanent injury ; but the pact was a shock, and such Anglophobe circles as survived in France were stirred to fresh activity. The agreement, in a word, was probably the right thing done in the wrong way. A second and mortal blow at the Stresa front from another quarter was soon to follow.

XIV. THE ABYSSINIAN WAR

The Versailles era ended in 1935, when Hitler struck off Germany's military fetters and Mussolini attacked Abyssinia. Henceforth the main problem confronting British statesmanship was that of how to deal with German and Italian ambitions. Broadly speaking, Europe had been controlled since 1918 by the victorious allies, England, France and Italy. Germany was too weak to play an active part, and Russia turned her back on the European game. Such a static simplification could not be expected to last. France had recovered in twenty years from the disasters of 1871, and Germany might well be on her legs again in a shorter time. Russia was certain to resume her place as a Great Power before long. Italy's dissatisfaction with her share of the earth's surface was notorious, and at any moment she might join in the clamour for territorial revision. Her population was increasing and emigration to America was rigidly limited. " Fascist Italy must expand or suffocate," remarked the Duce to an American journalist in 1926. Though he disclaimed war-like intentions, he was bursting with personal as well as national ambition. The barometer pointed to stormy weather. After assuring himself during Laval's visit to Rome in

January 1935, that France would not stand in his way, Musso⁻lini turned to England, a signatory of the treaties of 1906 and 1925 by which England, France and Italy defined their economic interests and aspirations in Abyssinia. On January 29 the Italian Chargé suggested an exchange of views, but the proposal was neither accepted nor declined. A word of warning at this stage might possibly have turned the Duce's mind towards a compromise. An Inter-departmental Committee under Sir John Maffey, Permanent Under-Secretary for the Colonies, reported in June that we had no important interests except the waters of the Blue Nile and that no vital interests necessitated resistance to an Italian conquest. Without waiting for an official indication of our attitude, Mussolini began to despatch troops to Eritrea in February. Here was a second opportunity to inquire as to Italian aims and if necessary to protest ; but the Foreign Secretary merely communicated to Parliament the Italian falsehood that the mobilization of two divisions in no way implied war-like intentions. A third occasion for a warning was neglected at the Stresa Conference in April. The Duce's consent to refer the clash at Walwal to arbitration provided a formal excuse for silence, but the real reason was our fear that opposition would drive him into Hitler's arms. The same motive operated in the Anglo-French refusal to support Abyssinia's requests that the League should deal with the Italian threat. At this point Austen Chamberlain, who was called in unofficially as a *persona grata*, warned the Italian Ambassador that an attack on Abyssinia would have a deplorable effect on Anglo-Italian relations and encourage Germany to aggress. Grandi appeared to agree, but held out no hope that Mussolini would draw back. Our studied silence at a time when the coming campaign was the talk of the world was more eloquent than words. That British public opinion might assert itself never occurred to the Duce, and indeed the widespread support for the principle of economic sanctions revealed in the Peace Ballot, organized by the League of Nations Union, came as a surprise to the Cabinet. By this time, however, Mussolini had gone too far to retreat.

So far from our coveting Abyssinia, as Italians were taught to believe, the Government despatched Mr. Eden with an olive branch to Rome. The Emperor, it was suggested, might present Italy with part of the Ogaden province and receive in compensation a strip of British Somaliland with access to the sea at Zeila. England would also urge Abyssinia to sanction a railway or road connecting Eritrea with Italian Somaliland. The intention was excellent, but it was like offering crumbs to a hungry wolf, and the last thing that the Duce desired was to see Abyssinia in control of a port. A more serious attempt to keep the peace was made in August, when the British and French Governments worked out a plan with the consent of the Emperor, who was prepared for some sort of League control, an exchange of territories, and economic concessions including a railway connecting Italy's two colonies. It was, however, promptly rejected by Mussolini, who was only waiting for the end of the summer rains. When the threat to Abyssinia was at last considered by the League at its annual meeting in September, the time for preventive action had passed. The ingenious attempt of a Commission of five, envisaging international assistance and enlarging the Paris scheme of territorial cessions, was accepted by the Emperor as a basis of discussion but rejected by the Duce.

The British Government and people could no longer evade a decision on the most dangerous issue that had arisen since 1918. On the one hand they desired to honour their obligations under the Covenant : on the other they longed to avoid war. If they resisted aggression the conflict might involve the greater part of Europe : if they stood aside the League would be discredited and the habit of aggression would grow. A Cabinet meeting on August 22 attempted to find a middle path. The closing of the Suez Canal, which might have saved Abyssinia, was ruled out as involving the certainty of war and going beyond the wishes of France. Economic sanctions were to be applied, but not of a kind to goad Mussolini into war. This resolve to limit our liability remained a secret, and it was widely believed that we should stand firm. The Mediterranean fleet was reinforced and France, with other Mediterranean states, was asked for a promise of support if it were attacked by Italy. While Turkey, Greece and Jugoslavia responded, France, determined to avoid a collision with Italy, merely agreed to allow our ships the use of her arsenals.

The speech of Sir Samuel Hoare to the Assembly on September 11 proclaimed that England meant business. " The League stands, and my country stands with it, for the collective maintenance of the Covenant in its entirety, and particularly for steady and collective resistance to all acts of unprovoked aggression. . . . No selfish or Imperialist motives enter into our minds at all." The impression produced both

by the novelty and the precision of this utterance was profound.
When Japan attacked China in 1931 we stood aside. When
we signed the Locarno pact we merely committed ourselves to
a regional obligation. But here was a declaration without
limitations of time or place. The Foreign Secretary was careful
to add that we had no intention to act alone. " If the burden
is to be borne, it must be borne collectively. If risks for peace
are to be run, they must be run by all. The security of the
many cannot be ensured solely by the efforts of a few, however
powerful they may be." After his return he repeated his
Geneva pledge in a written communication to Paris. These
resonant declarations won us a fleeting moral leadership of
Europe, and suggested the vitality of the League. It had
always been realized that its testing-time would come when a
European Great Power aggressed. There had been cogent
geographical reasons for ignoring the challenge of Japan.
Now at last it seemed as if the League was going to act, with
England setting the pace.

It was a false dawn, for the British Government was much
less valorous than it seemed. On the eve of his declaration at
Geneva, Sir Samuel Hoare had a conversation with Laval,
who afterwards revealed its character to the French Chamber.
" We found ourselves instantly in agreement upon ruling
out military sanctions, not adopting any measure of naval
blockade, never contemplating the closure of the Suez Canal,
in a word ruling out everything that might lead to war."
This decision, of course, had not been communicated to
Mussolini, but it would have caused him no surprise ; for he
was sure of France, and England's notorious desire for peace
convinced him that our bark was worse than our bite.

Ignoring threats and appeals he calmly completed his
preparations, and his troops crossed the Abyssinian frontier
on October 3 according to plan. Italy's aggression was
promptly condemned by every other member of the Council,
and the application of sanctions was voted by an overwhelming
majority in the Assembly for the first time. The Committee
appointed to work out details proposed the prohibition of
loans and credits, an embargo on exports of war material to
Italy, and an embargo on all Italian imports. Sir Samuel Hoare
explained that on October 22 military sanctions formed no
part of British policy and that only a boycott was envisaged.
" Nobody in this House can believe that anybody in Europe
desires a war." This ruled out not only military measures,

but any economic action which the aggressor might decide to regard as an act of war. The Duce, seizing his opportunity, announced that if oil were added to the list he would fight. The threat sufficed, and the one article vital to his success in a land of mountains and deserts continued to be freely supplied. Among the vendors, it is sad to relate, was the Anglo-Persian Oil Company, in which the British Government held the majority of shares. The postponement of the date of the operation of sanctions till November 18 enabled the aggressor to accumulate large stocks, and some of Italy's timid neighbours declined to co-operate in the boycott.

The half-hearted attempt merely wounded Italy's pride. Materially she suffered some inconvenience, which might have become serious if the campaign had lasted into a second or third year. Psychologically it was a godsend to the Duce, who now stood forth as the defender of the national dignity against foreign interference. Whether it was worth while incurring the angry resentment of a Great Power by pin-pricks which offered no real prospect of success may be doubted. " If you are going to adopt a sanction," declared Mr. Baldwin, " you must be prepared for war." England was not prepared for war, and Mussolini knew it. It would have been wiser either to follow the 1931 precedent of inaction on the ground that Abyssinia was not worth a conflict, or to cut off the supply of oil and face the consequences. As it was, we fell between two stools.

If England took the lead in the sanctionist campaign, France was the pioneer of mediation, for Laval cared little for the League and was determined not to break with Mussolini. The suggestion that the two countries should explore the possibilities of peace was made in the Assembly by Van Zeeland, the Belgian Premier, and approved by both Governments. Since Abyssinia had no prospect of defeating her powerful enemy, the only way to stop the war, it seemed, was to yield a portion of her territory. At the end of October a Foreign Office expert visited Paris, where a plan was drawn up which became the basis of the Hoare-Laval scheme. The British Minister at Addis Ababa advised the Emperor to open negotiations, and the two Foreign Ministers appealed for peace at Geneva on November 2. When at this point Mr. Baldwin dissolved Parliament, support of the League was as much the declared programme of the Government as of the Opposition ; but when the victory was won the confidential discussions at Paris were resumed.

The finishing touches were put when Sir Samuel Hoare visited Paris on December 7-8. In return for Abyssinia's access to the Red Sea in the south of Eritrea, Italy was to obtain a large slice of her territory in the north-east in full sovereignty, with a sphere of settlement and economic penetration in the south which would remain under the suzerainty of the Emperor and the administrative supervision of the League. Taken together the cuts represented about half the country, the conquest of which had hardly begun. In view of the subsequent collapse of resistance, so much more rapid than the military experts anticipated, it might perhaps be regarded retrospectively as the best solution ; but two vital considerations were left out of account. The Emperor was in no mood to compromise with the aggressor, and British opinion, which had applauded the declaration of September 11, could hardly approve a *volte-face* so rapid and so complete. When the secret was prematurely revealed in the French press on December 9, the Baldwin Cabinet stood by the Foreign Minister till the outburst of popular indignation, led by Austen Chamberlain in Parliament and by *The Times* in the press, induced the Prime Minister to drop the scheme and its author. " These proposals," declared the Emperor, " are the negation and abandonment of the principles on which the League of Nations is founded. For Ethiopia they would consecrate the amputation of her territory and the disappearance of her independence for the benefit of the State which had attacked her. " To this measured condemnation nothing need be added by the historian or the moralist.

The Government's defence was of the most perfunctory character. Mr. Baldwin, visibly ill at ease, confessed that the protest had come from the heart of the people and he recognized it as decisive. Lord Halifax, Leader in the Upper House, explained that Sir Samuel Hoare carried no instructions from his colleagues, and that on reaching Paris he found the French Government anxious to accelerate conciliation. The Government, he added, did not like the terms when they saw them, though they were not so bad as public opinion believed, and the Italian Government was not particularly enamoured of them. It had been impossible to repudiate the Foreign Secretary, absent and unheard. Yet they had made the mistake of failing to appreciate the damage which, rightly or wrongly, the terms would be held by public opinion to inflict on the cause we were pledged to serve.

That Mr. Eden succeeded Sir Samuel Hoare at the Foreign Office made no practical difference, for it was too late to save Abyssinia. We continued to profess our readiness to apply the oil embargo if other states would do the same, but the veto of France blocked the way. Laval fell, but Flandin continued his policy of sabotaging the League. The remilitarization of the Rhineland in March 1936 emphasized the desirability of avoiding a break with Italy. On May 5 Italian troops marched into the Abyssinian capital. In June Neville Chamberlain, Chancellor of the Exchequer, described the continuation of sanctions as midsummer madness, and in July they were dropped. A collision had been averted at the cost of the desertion of Abyssinia, the weakening of the League, the humiliation of England, and the creation of the Rome-Berlin axis. The vacillating treatment of the Abyssinian problem confirmed the growing opinion, not only in Germany and Italy but throughout the world, that the muscles of the post-war Englishman were becoming soft, or at any rate that post-war British statesmen had lost their nerve.

XV. THE RAPPROCHEMENT WITH ITALY, 1937-9

Italian hostility remained one of our chief preoccupations during the following years. Both parties looked round for friends. Mussolini sacrificed the independence of Austria to his need for a partner, and the Axis began to take shape when the dictators supported Franco's revolt. Our first *riposte* was the settlement of the Egyptian question. When the Protectorate proclaimed in 1914 gave way in 1922 to the recognition of Egyptian independence, we reserved four points for discussion, of which the retention of the British garrison and the continued occupation of the Sudan were the most controversial. Four fruitless attempts at agreement were made before the conquest of Abyssinia, which involved greater danger to Egypt than to England, removed the difficulties. In August 1936 England consented to the conditional removal of British troops to the Canal zone and a *condominium* in the Sudan, and undertook to support the abolition of the Capitulations and Egypt's entry into the League. In return we secured the right to station 10,000 men on the Canal till the Egyptian army was strong enough to defend it, and a military alliance was concluded for twenty years. For the first time since the occupation began in 1882 British troops and officials functioned with the formal consent of the Egyptian Government. A year later the Powers cancelled the Capitulations and Egypt entered the League as an independent state.

Our second reaction to Italian hostility was an attempt to end the quarrel, not only for the sake of an historic friendship, but because our abiding interest was peace. Though Abyssinia was a big morsel, the Italian Empire still made a poor show beside the vast possessions of England and France, and the Duce's longing to dominate the Mediterranean was unconcealed. As an advocate of revision his thoughts turned to the other great revisionist Power beyond the Alps, but he realized that exclusive reliance on Berlin would limit the freedom of manœuvre which was the tradition of Italian policy. A speech at Milan in November 1936 held out a diminutive olive branch to England, who responded by removing the British Legation from Addis Ababa. It was not formal recognition, but it looked like the first step.

Before the Abyssinian dispute was liquidated a new apple of discord ripened with General Franco's rebellion in July 1936. A French proposal for a non-intervention agreement was accepted by the British Government, with the dual object of allowing Spain to settle her own problems and of preventing the extension of the war. The latter aim was achieved, but the former completely failed. British policy was neutral in intention but not in effect, for other Powers failed to play the game. Franco was officially recognized by the two Dictators, who loudly denounced the Bolshevist menace in the Mediterranean and declared that their *protégé* must win. Troops were poured into Spain, and at one time Mussolini confessed to having 40,000 Italian soldiers on the spot. In the first autumn of the war Madrid was saved by the arrival of the volunteers from many countries known as the International Brigade, and Russia began to supply munitions and food ; but the Madrid-Valencia Government received only a small fraction of the foreign help which rendered possible the victory of the rebels. Though we continued to recognize the Republican Government till its final surrender, we forbade the sale of munitions to either side, contrary to the usual practice of allowing a recognized Government to buy them wherever it can. Any such support, it was explained, would be followed by increased support to Franco from the other side, and would be incompatible with non-intervention. This decision was passionately denounced by the Opposition as an unneutral act, inspired by an unavowed desire that Franco should win. The Non-Intervention Committee, appointed to supervise the non-intervention agreement and sitting in London under the chairmanship of Lord Plymouth, was a farce ; for the Dictators unblushingly continued their armed intervention, despite the prohibition by the Committee in February 1937 of enlistment or dispatch of volunteers. The only occasion on which we asserted ourselves was at the Nyon Conference in September 1937, called to deal with the destruction of British and other merchantmen in the Mediterranean by unidentified submarines. Neither Germany nor Italy attended, but the latter accepted the scheme of zones of patrol by British, French and Italian ships, and the nuisance was speedily brought to an end.

British opinion, which had been almost unanimous in regard to the rights and wrongs of the Abyssinian conflict, was deeply divided by the issues in Spain. Right wing opinion generally sympathized with Franco, Left wing with the Republican Government, while many Englishmen were disgusted by the savagery of both sides. A further source of disagreement concerned the strategic issues involved in the triumph of one or other of the combatants. Champions of the Republic argued that its overthrow would weaken our position in the Mediterranean and endanger French communications with North Africa by tying Spain to our potential enemies. In other words, a victory for Franco would mean a victory for Mussolini and Hitler. Franco's champions retorted that the Spaniards, a proud and independent race, would decline to alienate territory and would stubbornly resist foreign control. The spokesmen of the Government inclined to the latter view, though they abstained from expressing sympathy with either side. " We wish Spain to emerge with possessions and independence intact," declared Mr. Eden, who quoted Wellington's dictum : " There is no country in Europe in the affairs of which foreigners can interfere with as little profit as in Spain." The value of these conflicting forecasts was soon to be decided by the winner's pro-Axis attitude in a new European war. Whatever might be said for the intentions of the British Government, its Spanish policy suggested a mood of peace at almost any price. It certainly presented a striking contrast to the ruthless vigour of the Axis Powers, determined to secure the triumph of their *protégé* and unafraid of the gravest risks.

In the so-called Gentleman's Agreement between England and Italy concluded on January 2, 1937, the signatories recognized free entry into the Mediterranean, transit and exit, to be a vital interest of both parties and their interests as in no way inconsistent. Both disclaimed any desire to modify the *status quo*, and Italy promised not to retain the Balearic Isles, which she had occupied for the purpose of the Spanish war. It was merely a scrap of paper, for the Italian press and wireless soon resumed their attacks on England, and the increasing support of Franco made nonsense of the pretence of neutrality. The substitution of Neville Chamberlain for Mr. Baldwin in June 1937 was followed by a more vigorous drive for peace. Filled with anxiety by the drift towards war, and undeterred by his inexperience of diplomacy, he took over control of foreign affairs. On June 25 he uttered an earnest appeal to those who held responsible positions at home and abroad to weigh their words. " I have read that in the high mountains there are sometimes conditions to be found when an incautious move or even a sudden exclamation may start an avalanche. That is just the condition in which we find ourselves to-day."

Believing that little could be done at Berlin, at any rate for the moment, the new Prime Minister strove earnestly for appeasement in Rome. A friendly message from Mussolini through Count Grandi evoked by a speech of Mr. Eden on July 19 led Chamberlain to write a personal letter in cordial terms, regretting that relations were still far from the old feeling of confidence and affection, but expressing the belief that they could be restored if misunderstandings and unfounded suspicions were removed. We were ready for conversations at any time. The Duce replied that he too wished to restore good relations and was ready for discussions. We replied that we hoped they might begin in September, but the sky darkened once again. Italian intervention in Spain was naked and unashamed. Italy boycotted the conference at Nyon. Difficulties in the Non-Intervention Committee concerning the withdrawal of volunteers postponed the opening of discussions. Italy's withdrawal from the League, her adherence to the German-Japanese anti-Comintern pact, and the Duce's visit to Berlin in September illustrated the new orientation. The situation, declared Chamberlain, had seriously and steadily deteriorated since the exchange of letters in July. The Italian wireless and press revelled in vituperation, and the garrison in Libya was reinforced. It was clear that no progress could be made so long as recognition of the new Italian Empire was withheld. The Prime Minister was prepared to pay the price, for the danger from Germany was growing from day to day.

A fresh opportunity presented itself from the Italian side early in 1938, when Mr. Eden and Count Grandi had some amicable conversations. On February 10, the Ambassador announced that they had been sincerely welcomed in Rome, and that the Duce was ready for discussion at any time, as wide as possible, including the recognition of Abyssinia. Mr. Eden replied that we were bound to act as loyal members of the League, and that the attitude of the League and the Mediterranean Powers would be affected by an Anglo-Italian agreement. A week later Grandi was instructed to urge an early start. Chamberlain suggested to Mr. Eden that they should see him together, and the Foreign Secretary begged his chief not to commit the Government to anything specific. The advice was accepted, but after the talk the two men disagreed. The Prime Minister argued that a rebuff would confirm the suspicion that we did not want conversations to start and might make war inevitable. Moreover they would probably improve the atmosphere in Spain and elsewhere. The Foreign Secretary, on the other hand, wished to defer the official opening till volunteers in substantial numbers were withdrawn from Spain. The Cabinet sided with the Prime Minister and Mr. Eden resigned. He had no objection to negotiations, he explained to Parliament, for they were implicit in the Chamberlain-Mussolini letters of the preceding summer : the only question was the time and the conditions. Unfriendly propaganda continued, and no progress concerning intervention in Spain had been made. The Gentleman's Agreement of January 1937 had been followed by the first large despatch of troops to Spain—a breach of its spirit if not of the letter. The momentary improvement after the letters in the summer of 1937 had been followed by sinkings in the Mediterranean. We could not risk a repetition of these experiences. " The withdrawal must have begun in earnest before those conversations in Rome can be held on a really solid basis of goodwill which is essential to success." In view of the increasing violation of international agreements this was a moment to stand firm. " There has been too keen a desire on our part to make terms with others rather than that others should make terms with us. . . . I do not believe that we can make progress in European appeasement if we allow the impression to gain ground abroad that we yield to constant pressure." The whole speech breathed a robust and well-grounded suspicion of Mussolini's good faith.

Lord Halifax was appointed to the Foreign Office, but the Prime Minister conducted the negotiations which issued in an elaborate agreement embracing the Mediterranean, North-East Africa and the Middle East, signed on April 16, 1938. Our chief advantage was Italy's acceptance of the *status quo* in the Mediterranean and the Red Sea, in particular the declaration that she had no territorial or political designs in Spain and would withdraw all troops after the war. Italy's principal gain was our conditional promise to recognize the conquest of Abyssinia. The treaty was not to come into operation till " a settlement of the Spanish question " was reached—a condition understood to imply a " substantial " but undefined reduction of the Italian forces in Spain. The agreement was welcomed in France, who desired to find a similar solution of her difficulties with Italy, and it was commended by the new Foreign Secretary as a contribution to general peace.

Chamberlain defended his handiwork in Parliament on May 2. " The situation was as bad as ever it had been, and it seemed to me that unless some further effort could be made it was in danger of rapidly becoming acute." His policy was peace and the restoration of confidence by removing danger-spots, grievances, differences and suspicions one by one. " The signing of this agreement has already effected a radical change in the relations between our two countries : the clouds of mistrust and suspicion have been cleared away." It was only to become operative when a settlement in Spain was reached, and we should then recognize the conquest of Abyssinia. " I believe that for Italy and ourselves this agreement marks the beginning of a new era. In former days we had a close friendship with the old Italy. To-day there is a new Italy, an Italy which, under the stimulus of the personality of Signor Mussolini, is showing new vigour, in which there is apparent new vision and new efficiency in administration and in the measures they are taking to improve the conditions of their people. With the laying aside of temporary differences which this agreement brought about, I believe that we may look forward to a friendship with the new Italy as firmly based as that by which we were bound to the old." Such were the illusions of 1938. Chamberlain seemed incapable of understanding what sort of men the Dictators were.

P

A few days later, on May 12, Lord Halifax journeyed to Geneva and invited the Council of the League to declare that the recognition of the conquest of Abyssinia should be decided by each state for itself. The Government, he explained, had not modified its views of Italy's action, but it was forced to accept the facts. Many states had already taken the step, and nobody suggested that independence could be restored. " When, as here, two ideals are in conflict—on the one hand the ideal of devotion, unflinching but unpractical, to some high purpose ; on the other, the ideal of a practical victory for peace—I cannot doubt that the stronger claim is that of peace." This declaration, which was painful for such a high-minded moralist and such a champion of the League to make, did not constitute recognition, but it indicated that the time was not far off.

The September crisis, which brought us to the verge of war with Germany, fortified the Prime Minister's resolve to keep on good terms with Rome. On November 2 he moved that the treaty should come into force, since the Spanish Government had decided to disband the International Brigade and Italy withdrew 10,000 soldiers. Mussolini promised to withdraw the rest when the non-intervention plan became operative, and to send no more troops nor air forces to replace them. These assurances, added to the withdrawal of 10,000 men, proved his good intentions. Hitler and Mussolini informed him at Munich that they had no territorial ambitions in Spain. " The Spanish question is no longer a menace to the peace of Europe." Mussolini, he added, had helped to keep the peace. " I could not have appealed to him unless our relations had been changed." This optimism was challenged by Mr. Eden, who reiterated his conviction that it was impossible to make a satisfactory agreement with Italy while she was breaking her word in Spain. She had continued intervention on a large scale after signing the treaty, and no settlement was in sight. The Prime Minister had waived his condition and recognized the conquest of Abyssinia without Italy paying the price. Our policy of appeasement had not been reciprocated.

Chamberlain and Lord Halifax visited Rome in January 1939, at the invitation of the Duce. " The impressions which remain uppermost in my mind," declared the Foreign Secretary, " are the cordiality with which we were received by Signor Mussolini and the Italian Government ; the absolutely spontaneous character of the enthusiasm with which the Prime Minister was greeted by the people wherever he went ; and the very definite assurance which we received from Signor Mussolini that the policy of Italy was one of peace. Speaking of the Mediterranean in particular, he assured us that he was well satisfied with the Anglo-Italian Agreement, by which both parties undertook to respect the *status quo*." If the British statesmen really took these assurances of a dissatisfied Dictator at their face value they ought to have known better, and they were quickly undeceived. The Italian people was peaceful enough, but their ruler cherished ambitions which could only be realized by war. Nominally unofficial demands for a share in France's colonial empire had begun at the end of 1938, and the Italian press, which used the soft pedal during the British visit, renewed its bellowings the next moment. An alliance was signed between Italy and Germany in April 1939, promising military support if either was at war : there was not even the customary pretence that it was only to operate in case of defence against aggression. Mr. Eden's suspicions were confirmed when the Anglo-Italian treaty was broken by the rape of Albania on Good Friday, April 7. Once again the promise to respect the *status quo* proved to be a scrap of paper. We contented ourselves with a protest. A year later, without a shadow of provocation, Mussolini declared war on the two Powers who had helped to make Italy a nation and to save her from defeat in 1917.

XVI. The Remilitarization of the Rhineland.

The restoration of the armed might of Germany, inaugurated by the Weimar régime and accelerated by the Nazis, presented an even greater problem than that of Italy's colonial ambitions. Should we continue to content ourselves with verbal protests when treaties were infringed, or should we wait till a smashing blow was struck at the edifice of security and then make a stand ? The practical question arose when on March 7, 1936, German armies marched into the demilitarized Rhineland zone, trampling not only the dictated Treaty of Versailles but the freely negotiated Locarno pact underfoot. Hitler's contention that the Franco-Russian defensive agreement, signed in 1935 and ratified in 1936, had broken the spirit if not the letter of Locarno was a mere pretext, for he declined to submit it to The Hague Court. He would in any case have taken the step as soon as he felt strong enough to do so with impunity. The inequality of status enshrined in the Maginot line on one side of the frontier and the unwalled territory on the other naturally wounded German pride, but there was much more in Hitler's *coup* than the removal of a humiliating disability. It was the turning point in post-war history, since a stout wall in the west would enable him to pursue the forward policy in central and eastern Europe on which he had set his heart.

The French Cabinet, like the French people, was divided on the question whether this glaring breach of treaty obligations should be resisted by force. Clemenceau or Poincaré would doubtless have reacted as Hitler's military and civil advisers anticipated, though not the Dictator himself; but no action was taken. Encouragement from London might have tipped the scale, but England, official and unofficial, was disinclined to move. With our usual sense of fair play we felt instinctively that such an unequal arrangement as the de-militarized Rhineland was bound to collapse directly Germany recovered her strength, but the deeper implications of the event were hidden from our unsuspecting eyes. Warnings had come from our Ambassadors at Berlin directly Hitler had gained control, but they were unheeded. " The spirit of the moment," reported Sir Horace Rumbold in his last despatch on April 26, 1933, " and the Government of this country, for the first time since the war, are giving State sanction and encouragement to an attitude of mind, as well as to various forms of military training, which can only end in one way. I therefore feel that Germany's neighbours have reason to be vigilant." His successor, Sir Eric Phipps, was even more critical. " The conditions here," he wrote in November 1933, " are not those of a normal civilized country, and the German Government is not a normal civilized Government and cannot be dealt with as if it were." What superficial observers took to be a movement of national revival was in reality an armed doctrine, as Burke said of Jacobinism, a revolution which threatened not only peace but the whole stately edifice of western civilization.

The German Memorandum presented on March 7 contended that the Franco-Soviet agreement was incompatible with the Locarno pact, which Germany therefore regarded as annulled. " In accordance with the fundamental right of a nation to secure its frontiers and ensure its possibilities of defence, the German Government have to-day restored the full and unrestricted sovereignty of Germany in the demilitarized zone of the Rhineland." She was ready to conclude new agreements for European security, including a demilitarized zone on both sides of the French and Belgian frontiers on the basis of full parity ; a non-aggression treaty for twenty-five years between Germany, France and Belgium, to be guaranteed by England and Italy ; an air pact for the west ; non-aggression pacts with Germany's eastern neighbours on the Polish model ; and the return of Germany to the League. The Colonial question and the separation of the Covenant from its Versailles setting were matters for friendly negotiation. Mr. Eden deplored the unilateral repudiation of a settlement freely negotiated and freely signed. That the Franco-Russian treaty violated the Locarno settlement, he reminded the Ambassador, was not held by any other signatory, and the matter could have been referred to arbitration. The change of attitude in regard to the League, on the other hand, was most important.

The immediate task was to save as much as possible from the wreck of the Locarno system. The event had profoundly shaken confidence in any future German engagement, declared the Foreign Secretary in Parliament. There was no reason to suppose that it implied a threat of war, but hostilities had to be taken into account. " Should there take place, during the period which will be necessary for the consideration of the new situation, any actual attack on France and Belgium which would constitute a violation of Article II of the Treaty of Locarno, H.M.G., notwithstanding the German repudiation of the treaty, would regard itself as in honour bound to come in the manner provided in the treaty to the assistance of the country attacked." The General Staffs of England, France and Belgium proceeded to concert measures in case of aggression. On March 19, after meetings of the Locarno Powers with the exception of Germany, a special session of the Council of the League condemned Germany's action, invited her to accept certain provisional arrangements for the interim period, and proposed to discuss the status of the Rhineland and pacts for mutual assistance. Mr. Eden suggested that, pending negotiations, she should reduce the occupation to " symbolic " proportions, and that the Hague Court should decide whether the Franco-Russian pact infringed the Locarno settlement. It was also proposed that troops from the Locarno and other Powers should be stationed on the German side of the French and Belgian frontier, and that Germany should neither increase her troops nor build fortifications. The wider programme envisaged a discussion, by the five members of the defunct Locarno system, of the status of the Rhineland and mutual assistance pacts, followed by a world conference, under the auspices of the League, to consider questions of security, armaments and economics.

It was an ambitious project, which travelled far beyond the purposes of Hitler. His counter-proposals of March 31 promised not to increase his troops in the Rhineland for four months, offered a twenty-five years non-aggression pact for France and Belgium, and reiterated his readiness to return to the League. The proposals of the Locarno Powers for an international police force and for keeping the Rhineland zone unfortified were ignored. A British note of May 6 in the form of a *questionnaire* invited him to supply explanations on certain points and to give an assurance that he would respect the *status quo* till it was modified by free negotiation, but no reply was received to a document breathing distrust of his sincerity. The attempt to create a new system of security with German aid was abandoned, and each party went his way. Hitler's declaration that the era of surprises was over brought little comfort, for the choice between guns and butter had already been made. He proceeded to construct the Siegfried line, while England and France drew ever closer together. On December 4, 1936, Delbos, the French Foreign Minister, announced that France would help England and Belgium if they were attacked. England had promised France assistance at Locarno and again in March 1936 without reciprocity. This anomaly was at length removed. A further difference between the Locarno system and its successor was the announcement on October 4, 1936, by King Leopold that Belgium would defend herself if attacked, but would not fight for England or France. The desire of a sorely-tried country to keep out of future conflicts was fully understood by the Western Powers, who promised to aid her in case of unprovoked aggression without asking her aid in return. The Locarno period was over, and an Anglo-French defensive alliance took its place.

In a carefully considered declaration at Leamington on November 20, 1936, Mr. Eden defined our obligations and attitude after the agitations and confusion of recent months. Our arms would never be used for aggression or for any purpose inconsistent with the Covenant or the Pact of Paris. They would be used in the defence of our Empire, in defence of France and Belgium against unprovoked aggression, in defence of Germany, if a new West European settlement could be reached, against unprovoked aggression by any other party to such a settlement. " These, together with our treaty of alliance with Irak and our projected treaty with Egypt, are our definite obligations. In addition, our armaments may be used in bringing help to a victim of aggression in any case where, in our judgment, it would be proper under the provisions of the Covenant to do so. I use the word ' may ' deliberately, since in such an instance there is no automatic obligation to take military action. It is moreover right that this should be so, for nations cannot be expected to incur automatic military obligations save for areas where their vital interests are concerned." Our oldest ally, Portugal, seems to have slipped his memory, but his definition of British policy was generally approved. That treaty obligations, old and new, had to be kept was an axiom. To pledge our support in advance to victims of aggression in every part of the world was ruled out, not only by the limitations of our material strength, but by our geographical position.

XVII. Austria and Czechoslovakia

That Austria had been able to live in an economic sense was largely due to British friendship and financial support, and when Hitler began campaigning against her independence we declared her preservation a British interest. The first declaration was made by England and France in August 1933, when Neurath, the German Foreign Minister, curtly bade us mind our own business. It was repeated in Parliament on several occasions, and nowhere was the murder of Dollfuss in 1934 more sincerely deplored. Since, however, it was well understood that we should not go to war to save the little Republic, our protests produced no effect in Berlin. Its life hung on the slender thread of Mussolini's pledge in 1934 : " I will stand by Austria to the end." The Austro-German agreement of 1936, calling off the Nazi campaign in return for a promise to pursue a German policy, was interpreted as an attempt to procure Italy's friendship by leaving her *protégé* alone. The *détente*, however, was purely superficial, for the feeble dictatorship of Schuschnigg, who refused to accept the Socialists as allies in the defence of the national cause, encouraged the Nazis to work for his overthrow. The last chance of survival disappeared when the Duce's need for German support in his Mediterranean and colonial ambitions outweighed his interest in an independent Austria. At the opening of 1938 Hitler decided to act. Summoning Schuschnigg to Berchtesgaden in February, he compelled him to take the Nazi Seyss-Inquart into the Cabinet, and on March 11 German troops crossed the frontier in order to forestall a plebiscite which was expected to reveal a substantial anti-Nazi majority. Our Ambassador at Berlin was instructed to protest against the seizure of Austria, and to say that it would produce the gravest reactions. When Neurath replied that it was not our business, Chamberlain retorted that we were interested as members of the League and as signatories of treaties providing that her independence was inalienable without the Council's consent. Explanations and protests, however, were of no avail. After more than a thousand years Austria had ceased to exist.

Czechoslovakia, with her southern frontier now open to attack, seemed likely to be the next victim. She was the ally of France, and it was an axiom that we could not allow France to be crushed. Some voices, chiefly in the Labour and Liberal camps, argued that only a public assurance of military support could save the Czechs. Others maintained that our pledges to France and Belgium were as much as we ought to undertake, and that Hitler should be allowed a free hand in central and eastern Europe. The Government chose a middle path, and on March 24 the Prime Minister addressed a warning to Berlin. If Czechoslovakia were attacked we should fulfil our duty under the Covenant. Should we go further if France helped her ally, or should we promise to fight and invite other nations to join in such a declaration ? These suggestions were negatived on the ground that they would automatically destroy our freedom of decision in relation to an area where our vital interests were not concerned in the same degree as in France and Belgium. " But while plainly stating this decision, I would add this. Where peace and war are concerned, legal obligations are not alone involved, and, if war broke out, it would be unlikely to be confined to those who have assumed such obligations. It would be quite impossible to say where it would end and what Governments might become involved. The inexorable pressure of facts might well prove more formidable than formal pronouncements, and in that event it would be well within the bounds of probability that other States, besides those which were parties to the original dispute, would almost immediately become involved. This is especially true in the case of two countries like Great Britain and France, with long association of friendship, with interests closely interwoven, devoted to the same ideals of democratic liberty and determined to uphold them."

This memorable declaration was received with lively satisfaction at Prague, for it seemed to go as near to a promise as the tradition of British policy allowed. In view of the confusion of opinion as to the objects for which we ought to fight, it would indeed have been difficult to go further. Moreover, the backwardness of our armaments suggested caution in the assumption of fresh liabilities, particularly in the case of a country inaccessible by sea. If Chamberlain is to be blamed it is rather for the failure to make known his views in fuller measure in Prague before the breaking of the storm. The declaration pointed to action in the event of an unprovoked attack on Czechoslovakia and of France's assistance to her ally. But what if the demand was merely for the German districts on the fringe? The Prime Minister had his own answer to this question, but he kept it to himself.

That the warning of March 24 was meant to be taken seriously was shown on May 21, when the Czech Government believed a German attack to be imminent and took prompt steps to defend the frontiers. Sir Nevile Henderson was instructed to repeat the declaration, and, though the movement of troops was angrily denied at Berlin, our action emphasized our interest in Czechoslovakia's independence. On the other hand, the encouragement to Prague was partially counteracted by a mysterious episode. At a lunch party given by Lady Astor to Canadian journalists the Prime Minister privately expressed his opinion that the Sudeten districts might have to be ceded to Germany. Unauthorized reports of his table talk in Canadian papers doubtless confirmed Hitler's belief that England would not fight to prevent the German fringe joining the Reich. They produced no weakening at Prague, which offered four successive plans of autonomy, but refused to consider the cession of territories which had formed part of the state for many centuries.

The massing of German troops round Czechoslovakia during the summer and the feverish efforts to strengthen the Siegfried line indicated Hitler's resolve to reach his goal. The September crisis began with his announcement on September 12 at the annual Nuremburg rally that the Sudeten Germans must determine their own fate. Lord Runciman, who had been sent out in August as an unofficial investigator and mediator, reached the same conclusion. In his report, dated September 21, he approved the fourth Czech plan, which ran on cantonal lines, but believed that it had no chance of acceptance, for decisions were now made at Berlin and Henlein had at length thrown off the mask. Still more significant was a sentence in the *Times* leader of September 7 admitting that the cession of the fringe of alien populations might be necessary. A Foreign Office statement the same evening that this was not the policy of the Government failed to remove the impression that the *Times* had been inspired, and that England would not fight for the existing frontiers in Central Europe.

The Prime Minister's dramatic flight to Berchtesgaden revealed his passionate devotion to peace, but played straight into Hitler's unscrupulous hands. His determination to secure the Sudeten districts, even at the cost of a world war, was a profound shock to the visitor. Impressed by the factor of racial unity and convinced that there was no other way to keep the peace, he decided to recommend this solution to his colleagues and the Czechs, subject to it being carried through without war. At a second meeting at Godesberg on the Rhine a week later, after consulting the French Government, he had a further shock, for more drastic demands were presented which he undertook to forward to Prague, though not to recommend. When they were unhesitatingly rejected and mobilization was ordered by the Czechoslovakia Government war was within sight, for Hitler announced that the occupation would take place on October 1. Unwearying in his efforts for peace, Chamberlain sent urgent appeals to Hitler and Mussolini. The former consented to a four-Power Conference (England, France, Germany, Italy) at Munich, where in the course of a few hours a time-table for the successive occupation of the Sudeten districts was drawn up. The Munich terms were a trifle less severe in form than those of Godesberg, but in substance the sacrifice was the same. The country chiefly concerned was informed of the decisions, and peremptorily bidden by her French allies and her English friends to accept. Deprived of the armed support on which she counted, though Russia declared her readiness to fulfil her treaty obligations, she had no option but to yield. The coveted territories, with a quarter of the whole population of the State, and the elaborate mountain defences, passed into German hands without a shot. England attempted to soften the blow by a loan of ten millions, and by a worthless promise to join in an international guarantee of the new frontiers.

The Prime Minister was rapturously acclaimed on his return from Munich, bringing, he declared, " peace with honour." Lord Halifax came nearer to the truth in confessing that the Government had been confronted by a hideous choice of evils. Peace was indeed a boon to a people detesting war, divided in feeling and militarily unprepared. Yet there was another side to the picture. It had been purchased at the expense of a highly civilized democracy, which had fulfilled many of the hopes of its friends and treated its racial minorities better than almost any Continental State. " We have been disgracefully betrayed," cried Beneš in the bitterness of his heart, as he contrasted the promises with the performances of his friends. Many Englishmen and Frenchmen agreed with him. His resignation symbolized the collapse of his country. The rump of the State was incapable of defending itself, was stripped of most of its industrial resources, and was compelled to feed out of Hitler's hand. The best result of the Munich policy was that we gained time for strengthening our defences, the worst that the obvious disinclination of the western democracies to fight encouraged Hitler to fresh aggressions. British policy from 1931 onwards struck even friendly observers as revealing a certain weariness, exhaustion, lack of will, lack of nerve, as of premature old age. Such a series of failures and humiliations, wrote the American historian Professor Bernadotte Schmidt in his critical sketch, *From Versailles to Munich*, was without precedent in British history since the loss of the American colonies.

XVIII. After Munich

The Prime Minister announced his opinion that the Munich agreement on the Sudeten problem meant " peace in our time." Among the grounds of his belief was the document signed by Hitler and himself on September 30, 1938, recording their resolve to deal with other questions concerning their countries by the method of consultation and expressing the desire of the two peoples never to go to war with one another again. A second cause of optimism was the Dictator's assurance that he had no more territorial demands in Europe and that his colonial claims were not a matter for war. Lord Halifax seemed rather less confident than his chief. Speaking at

Edinburgh on October 24 he expressed the hope that the rectification of frontiers on racial lines taking place in Central and South-Eastern Europe would contribute to stability and peace, but he added some prophetic words. " What we are now witnessing is the revision of the Treaty of Versailles, for which provision was made in the Covenant, but which has never till now been made effective." The *détente* did not last long. Hitler's speeches revealed a curious irritability, which Sir Nevile Henderson interpreted as resentment at the interference which prevented him from enjoying a spectacular military success. Moreover he misinterpreted the continuation of British rearmament as a determination to attack. The tidal wave of enthusiasm for the Munich settlement ebbed rapidly, and at the end of the year two Ministerial declarations indicated that the wind had shifted. The Colonial Secretary announced that the return of the German colonies was not now an issue in practical politics, and the Prime Minister assured his critics in Parliament that if the policy of appeasement failed he would change his course.

The rape of what was left of Bohemia and Moravia on March 15, 1939, ended the Munich truce and the policy of appeasement. Surrender, it was clear, had merely stimulated Hitler's appetite and strengthened the resolve to get his way. In breaking his word to the Prime Minister and in seizing a state alien in blood, language and tradition, he revealed Napoleonic ambitions which instantly restored our old principle of the Balance of Power to favour. Many, perhaps most, Englishmen had been unwilling to fight for the retention of the German minority in a Slav state, but the plausible doctrine of German racial consolidation was now thrown to the winds. The larger problem of our own security could no longer be shirked. Hitler's action was rebuked by the disillusioned Prime Minister on March 17 at Birmingham, and protests were presented by the British and French Ambassadors at Berlin ; but Dictators are never impressed by words. If the Western democracies were once again to resist the domination of Europe by Germany, now was the time to build a peace front. There was indeed not a moment to lose. The Nazi press proceeded to turn its guns against Poland, who had declined to hand over Danzig and to allow an ex-territorial road through the Corridor on the ground that the demands threatened her political and economic independence. She had reached her decision before the thunderbolt of March 15 illustrated the danger of admitting the enemy into your house by the back door.

In view of Hitler's habit of striking hammer blows at brief intervals, Chamberlain announced on March 31 that the British and French Governments would give Poland all support in their power " in the event of any action which clearly threatened Polish independence and which the Polish Government accordingly considered it vital to resist with their national forces." A week later, after a visit of Colonel Beck to London, he added that the two Governments were ready to transform the unilateral assurance of support into a permanent treaty of mutual assistance. The agreement was concluded for five years on August 25. It was a momentous commitment which might at any moment automatically involve us in a war for which neither our army nor our air force was adequately prepared. Our obligations were further extended by a promise to Roumania, where a German economic ultimatum was feared, and to Greece, who felt herself threatened by Italy's rape of Albania. On May 12 England and Turkey declared their intention to co-operate if an act of aggression led to war in the Mediterranean, and followed up. the declaration by a treaty of mutual aid. Before March 15 we were pledged to render military support to five countries in case of attack— Portugal, France, Belgium, Egypt (for twenty years) and Irak (for twenty-five years after our mandate ended in 1932). Four more had now been added to the list. To meet our mounting liabilities, the Territorial Force was doubled and compulsory training for six months was introduced for men between 20 and 21, our first taste of conscription in time of peace.

Negotiations with Russia for mutual assistance, if either country were involved in war through support to an aggressed state, began with an inquiry what she would do if Germany attacked Roumania. Instead of answering the question, she proposed an international conference at Bucharest, which, perhaps unwisely, we declined on the ground that the need for action was immediate. The problem of securing her assistance against the domination of Europe by Germany proved more formidable than was expected, for, as Lord Halifax explained, we had to deal with the new German technique of indirect aggression. The chief difficulty, he pointed out on June 8, was the position of the Baltic states, to whose feelings we paid more consideration than Russia. " We should not think it right to attempt to thrust assurances on countries which did not want them, or to take any step which might compromise in other quarters the relations of those countries which only desire to maintain their own neutrality inviolate." He hoped and believed that Russia's legitimate interest in maintaining the independence of her neighbours could be adjusted to the desire of England and France for a united front against aggression.

This analysis of the situation proved too optimistic. Mr. Strang, a Foreign Office expert, was despatched to Moscow on June 12, but the negotiations continued to drag. Russia claimed to protect herself by guaranteeing the Baltic states, who feared Moscow far more than Berlin; and Poland, haunted by bitter memories, declared that she would never allow a Russian soldier to set foot on her soil. The unexplained dismissal on May 3 of Litvinoff, the champion of co-operation with the Western democracies and the League, was ominous. The despatch of British and French Military Missions to Moscow at the beginning of August was taken to mean that agreement was in sight; but while political and military discussions were in progress a Russo-German treaty of non-aggression, of which the secret had been well kept, was signed on August 23. Poland's doom was sealed, for with the removal of the nightmare of war on two fronts Hitler and his army chiefs were ready to strike. Since he was as firmly resolved to possess Danzig as were the Poles to keep it, our final efforts in Berlin to avert the fall of the avalanche were in vain.

The British Government was rightly determined that no such uncertainty concerning our action as prevailed in 1914 should occur. The clearest statement of our intentions was made by Lord Halifax at the annual Chatham House dinner on June 29. We had assumed obligations and were preparing to assume more with full understanding of their consequences. "We know that if the security and independence of other countries are to disappear, our own security and our own independence will be gravely threatened. We know that, if international law and order is to be preserved, we must be prepared to fight for its defence. In the past we have always stood out against the attempt by any single Power to dominate Europe at the expense of the liberties of other nations, and British policy is therefore only following the inevitable line of its own history if such an attempt were to be made again. . . . In the event of further aggression we are resolved to use at once the whole of our strength in fulfilment of our pledges to resist it." There was no thought of isolating or encircling Germany and Italy. Here was the pure milk of the doctrine of the Balance of Power. On August 15 the Foreign Secretary advised the Polish Government to make it plain that, provided essentials could be secured, they were at all times ready to examine the possibility of negotiations over Danzig if there was a prospect of success. But we made no attempt to persuade Poland to surrender the city.

A Russo-German pact, explained the Prime Minister in a letter to Hitler dated August 22, could not alter our obligation to Poland. " It has been alleged that if H.M.G. had made their position more clear in 1914 the great catastrophe would have been avoided. Whether or not there is any force in that allegation, H.M.G. are resolved that on this occasion there shall be no tragic misunderstanding. If the case should arise they are resolved and prepared to employ without delay all the forces at their command." Hitler replied that this statement could not affect his determination to safeguard the interests of the Reich. This was his way of saying that Dictators cannot climb down. Further exchanges during the following days were equally fruitless, and in the early hours of September 1 Germany invaded Poland. Two days later our treaty pledge was implemented by a declaration of war. " No man," declared the Prime Minister, " can say that the Government could have done more to try to keep open the way for an honourable and equitable settlement of the dispute between Germany and Poland. Nor have we neglected any means of making it clear to the German Government that, if they insisted on using force again in the manner in which they had used it in the past, we were resolved to oppose them by force." In September, 1938, there were deep divisions in Parliament and the country : in September, 1939, there were none. There had been grave doubts in some quarters as to the wisdom of our promise to Poland in view of the extreme difficulty of rendering effective aid and in the absence of an understanding with Russia, but there could be no hesitation about keeping our word. In 1938 the question was often heard : Why should we fight for Czechoslovakia ? In 1939 very few voices inquired why we should fight for Danzig. Trusting that we should continue to yield, Hitler had struck again and again till the brutal attack on Poland caused the cup to overflow. For Poland, like Belgium in 1914, was the symbol of a conflict in which not only the right of weak nations to live unthreatened lives but the security of the British Empire was at stake. Security means more than the defence of our possessions against direct attack. It denotes also effective resistance to a state which clearly threatens our lives and liberties before it becomes too powerful for us to effectively resist.

XIX. CONCLUDING REFLECTIONS

The twenty years between the two great wars form one of the most depressing chapters in the history of British diplomacy. If our victory had been used with reasonable intelligence, the whole story would have been different. The Allies, after winning the war, lost the peace. The main problem throughout was Germany, the most formidable, industrious and highly organized nation in Europe, who was certain to recover her strength. It was the task of British and French statesmen to avert another catastrophe in one of the only two possible ways. The first was the path of reconciliation, implicit in the Fourteen Points and eloquently outlined in Mr. Lloyd George's Memorandum of March 25, 1919. It was in this direction that the average easy-going Englishman, when the passions of war began to cool, instinctively desired to travel. It would have involved such steps as the admission of Germany to the League at its foundation or soon after, the fixing of reparation demands at an amount capable of being paid within a generation, the implementation of Article VIII of the Covenant concerning disarmament, and the return of some colonial territory under a mandate. Such a policy would doubtless have been interpreted in some German quarters as evidence of weakness of will, yet many millions of Germans, including the majority of the manual workers and war-weary veterans, were ready for a new deal. Was it beyond the resources of statesmanship to guide our old foe along the road of democracy and international co-operation, to make the growing generation feel that life was not intolerable for the citizens of a defeated country?

The rival policy, favoured by the majority of Frenchmen and based on the assumption that Germany under any régime is an incorrigible offender, consisted in depriving her of the means to aggress, not merely during the first years of peace when she was weak from loss of blood, but for the time further ahead when she had recovered her spirits and her industrial strength. The tragic events of 1940 have helped us to understand the French demand in 1919 for the permanent control of the Rhineland and its bridge-heads. The yearning for this solid pledge of security was frustrated by the Anglo-American veto, and the compensating Anglo-American guarantee collapsed with the repudiation of Wilson's signature by his fellow countrymen. The vacuum, for which France was not responsible, was never filled. During the Locarno *quinquennium* it seemed as if she was converted to the gospel of reconciliation, but the change was only skin deep. Clemenceau spoke of the comedy of Locarno and denounced Briand as the leading light of French defeatism. Beyond the Rhine the political position of Stresemann was equally weak. The League was widely regarded in Germany as a " Committee of Conquerors," and the smart of defeat was still very keen. Locarno was a failure, not necessarily because it was based on wrong principles but because it was not implemented by larger measures of conciliation.

If there was too little conciliation during the Weimar era to win the average German to the new order, there was too little firmness when Hitler came to the helm. Despite his first pacific assertions there was no valid reason to suppose that he had renounced the ambitions enshrined in *Mein Kampf*, or that he would fail in due course to use the armaments he was piling up. The Führer was young Germany's answer to Versailles, his name a symbol of revolt against foreign dictation. Austen Chamberlain and Winston Churchill called attention to the danger. That the British public was sick of war and opposed to expensive rearmament during the early years of the Nazi régime was realized and confessed by Mr. Baldwin ; but it is part of the responsibility of a Government to see further ahead than the man in the street, and to take the nation into its confidence on the vital issue of national security. The policy of appeasement was honourably meant and energetically, though not very skilfully, pursued. It came too late to bear fruit, for it was interpreted by the cynical Dictators as a sign of weakness which encouraged them to go ahead. Only force, or the threat of force, they believed, could win for their peoples their place in the sun. If Dr. Rauschning's reports of Hitler's conversations shortly before and shortly after his accession to power are substantially correct, there was never a chance of satisfying the new Napoleon. None of our Prime Ministers or Foreign Secretaries before March 1939, except perhaps Mr. Eden, seemed to realize the utter ruthlessness and systematic duplicity of the autocrats in Berlin and Rome. " In dealing

Q

with gentlemen," observed Bismarck, "I am a gentleman. With a corsair I am *corsair et demi.*" Hitler and Mussolini would probably have made friends even without the Abyssinian incident, for both were out for the destruction of the *status quo* ; but the policy of sanctions made their rapprochement inevitable. After the creation of the Axis it was difficult for us, perhaps impossible, to avert war except by continual surrenders. When our tardy rearmament campaign at last got into its stride its effect was to bring war nearer, for with our vast resources our strength was bound to grow rapidly from year to year. Hitler and Mussolini, who had long been preparing for conflict, adjusted their timetables accordingly, and struck when their power was at its height.

The story of two decades outlined in this survey illustrates anew the truth of two familiar aphorisms. The first is the bitter cry of Oxenstierna, as he surveyed the desolation of the Thirty Years' War : *Quantula sapientia mundus regitur.* The second is the maxim of Frederick the Great : "Diplomacy without armaments is like music without instruments." In fairness to the British statesmen who bore the burden and heat of the day, we must remember that public opinion was divided and confused ; that the Government dared not commit us to responsibilities which we might be unable or unwilling to fulfil ; that Germany and Russia were never easy to deal with ; that our policy had occasionally to be subordinated to the fears of France ; that the emergence of Italian colonial ambitions was a new complication ; that American aid in the reconstruction of Europe was withheld ; and that the conduct of international relations is perhaps the most difficult of the arts. The tortured peoples craved for a new world without knowing how to create it, and no master-builder was at hand. The transition from the institutions and ideology of the long era of unfettered nationalism to a system of collective security, the limitation of armaments and peaceful change proved too great a task to be carried through with a rush. Yet the organization of the world, first attempted in the League of Nations, was well worth trying and will assuredly be tried again. Such a revolution requires time no less than skill and resolution, but there is no reason to regard it as beyond the wit of man.

POLITICAL AUTOBIOGRAPHY

AUTOBIOGRAPHY is one of the most attractive and one of the most curious departments of literature. Most people like to talk about themselves. Some feel an urge to write about themselves—to tell their contemporaries and posterity who they are, what they have done, what they have tried to do. *Non omnis moriar. Ars longa, vita brevis. Exegi monumentum aere perennius.* Such familiar tags embody the yearning for a longer course than mortality permits. From one point of view autobiography is a protest of the human spirit against the inexorable limitations of time and space, an endeavour to establish contact with a future that we shall never see. There is pathos as well as pride in the attempt.

The most celebrated confessions, such as those of Augustine, Rousseau, Casanova, Benjamin Franklin, Gibbon, Goethe, Chateaubriand, Newman, Renan and Mill, are records of spiritual experience, intellectual development or amorous adventure. In a widely different field the significance of a man of action may preserve his testimony from oblivion, however meagre his inner life and however unskilful his pen. Political autobiography is the meeting place between history and literature. Yet the mere narration of memorable events is no passport to immortality : there must be a revelation of personality as well. The best political autobiographies are those which most fully reproduce the character, the temperament and the outlook of the author. The present survey is confined to modern rulers and ministers, makers of history who have told their own tale. The onlookers, with Saint-Simon at their head, are in another class.

The first outstanding political autobiography of the modern world, which we may roughly date from the opening of the sixteenth century, is that of Babur, the founder of the Mogul Empire. Though his narrative has reached us in an incomplete form, only covering eighteen of his forty-seven years, it is none the less an imposing literary monument, filling two large volumes in the admirable edition of Mrs. Beveridge. Beginning with his twelfth year, when the precocious boy became ruler of Farghana, the record is carried up to the eve of his death in 1530. Unlike most autobiographies, which are compiled when the long days draw to a close, Babur's story is told while it is going on, sometimes in diary form. As a result it is extraordinarily alive. We visualize every aspect of the personality of " the Tiger "—his interest in scenery, cities and buildings, his devotion to his mother, the temptations of the flesh. It is a romantic drama of incessant struggle, of hairbreadth escapes, of battle and sudden death. The un-studied and almost boyish character of the book adds to its charm. Here is no Elder Statesman or embittered exile methodically preparing his case for posterity, no political testament drawn up for the guidance of a successor. Impressions of cold, heat and thirst, of grief and gladness, are noted as they occur, with little time for reflection or pose. " I have written the plain truth," he declares. " I do not set these matters down to make known my deserts ; I have set down exactly what occurred." Be that as it may, the memories of Babur, the grandfather of Akbar, preserve the personality of one of the most arresting figures in the history of Asia, a man of iron, but also of flesh and blood.

Political autobiography in Europe on the grand scale comes in with the seventeenth century. Sully's apologia was compiled during the long evening of his life which followed the murder of Henri IV. Few more unreadable books have been written than the hotch-potch known as the *Oeconomies Royales*, the first two volumes of which were set up in his own château by a printer from Angers. To describe one's achievements in the third person, like Julius Cæsar in classical times and Henry Adams in our own day, is a rare affectation. But where else shall we find a writer addressing himself ? That the wealthy old statesman should employ secretaries to collect and arrange his material was natural enough ; yet why should they be made to inform their master, with bows and flatteries, of his own thoughts and deeds ? " We have heard you say," they write. We are to imagine him sitting back in his chair and listening approvingly to a eulogy of his eventful life, for all the world, as one of his biographers remarks, as if it were a *discours de reception* at the French Academy. In the words of Sainte-Beuve it is a continuous ovation. The pose is an artistic failure, for it draws a curtain between the author and the reader. In 1745 the Abbé de L'Écluse tried to make the book more readable by taking great liberties with the text. Yet, with all their glaring faults of structure, Sully's memoirs can never be forgotten. There are nuggets in the slag-heap. His admiration for the most popular of French kings burns brightly, and the story of how the two warriors pulled the country together after the torments of civil war can never die. He was not a man of genius, perhaps not even a great statesman, but he was an excellent administrator. There is little to attract us in his heavy, unromantic, severe personality, greedy of money and power, loving grandeur and ceremony, which looks so drab beside the dazzling colours of his lord. Such a man could never be popular. He had many enemies, and when Henri IV was dead the Duke's career was over. He is redeemed by his sturdy patriotism, and his feet are planted on the solid earth. He fought venality and waste with vigour and success. He had learned the lesson expressed in the memorable words : " *Pauvre paysan, pauvre royaume, pauvre royaume, pauvre roi.*" The taxpayer, he realized, must not be driven too hard.

Sully began his labours on the morrow of his fall and worked systematically till the end thirty years later. A wealth of material was at his disposal. He had kept a fragmentary journal ; he had preserved memoranda on important questions discussed in Council, documents which had passed through his hands, projects and financial reports. There were over three thousand letters, notes on his speeches, conversations with the King. Moreover his secretaries had made notes of their conversation with him, and not his secretaries alone but his doctor and other friends. To separate the gold from the dross was beyond the power of a man more used to handling the sword than the pen. The result is less an autobiography than a voluminous report, materials for history rather than history itself. The part of the four secretarial incense-burners is fully acknowledged. The memoirs, we are told, are what they, who had been employed in various affairs by the Duke, knew of his life and what they had learned from his lips.

Sully's apologia is above all the story of a historic friendship. It is proclaimed even in the cumbrous title : " Mémoires des sages et royales Economies d'État, domestiques, politiques et militaires de Henri le Grand, l'exemplaire des rois, le prince des vertus, des armes et des lois, le père en effet de ses peuples françois ; et des Servitudes utiles, obéissances convenables et administrations loyales de Maximilien de Béthune, l'un des plus confidents familiers et utiles soldats et serviteurs du grand Mars des François ; dédiés à la France, à tous les bons soldats et tous peuples françois." His father, a Hugenot nobleman, presented the boy at the age of eleven to his future master, who was only six years older. The lad made his little speech promising fidelity and obedience. " Ce que vous lui jurâtes en si beaux termes," write the well-trained secretaries, " avec tant de grâce et d'assurance, et un ton de voix si agréable qu'il conçut dès lors de bonnes espérances de vous ; et vous ayant relevé, car vous étiez à genoux, il vous embrassa deux fois et vous dit qu'il admirait votre gentillesse." The pledge was kept in peace and war. Sully became not only the comrade in arms, the Minister of Finance, the Master of the Artillery, but the friend and counsellor of " the greatest monarch of all time," consulted on everything, trusted in everything, never hesitating to differ in case of need. " When you cease to contradict me," remarked Henri IV, " I shall believe you have ceased to love me." When the King became a Catholic on the utilitarian ground that Paris was worth a mass, Sully remained faithful to his Protestant upbringing. The friendship remained unaffected, and indeed Sully, who was naturally consulted, advised the step. The manly virtues of his master shine the more brightly in contrast to his predecessor Henri III, who appears as a contemptible weakling, with his little dogs in a basket suspended from his neck. The change from the Valois to the Bourbons was a blessing for France, at any rate for the time.

Sully's memoirs, like other examples of its class, must be read with a critical eye, for even the most august personages are up to all manner of tricks. It was natural enough that he should exaggerate his military exploits during the hectic years when his master was fighting for the throne ; that he should exalt his ministerial rôle ; that he should leave his collaborators in shadow, even when he does not single them out for attack; that he should enlarge the figures in his dealings with finance. But it was going rather far to invent a mission to Queen Elizabeth in 1601, and to attribute to his master the Grand Dessein, one of the earliest projects for the permanent organization of Europe after the destruction of the hegemony of the House of Austria. The motive was clear enough, for the more illustrious its presumed author, the more attention was it likely to arouse ; but it cost scholars time and labour to establish its paternity. We are still waiting for a critical edition of this sprawling work.

Where Sully's secretaries laid down the pen those of Richelieu took it up, but there is a world of difference between the memoirs of the two ministers. The former had decades of enforced idleness to prepare his case, the latter died in harness at the age of fifty-seven. That he desired to tell his story and collected material for the purpose is scarcely in doubt. But how much of the vast *corpus* which bears his name is really his ? Not until our own time was it possible to suggest an answer, and even now the experts are not unanimous. The interest in the greatest of French statesmen aroused by Hanotaux's monumental though unfinished biography forty years ago led to the project of a critical edition of the memoirs under the auspices of the French Academy. The result is before us in ten stately volumes, covering the first twenty years of the reign of Louis XIII. Three supplementary volumes discuss the material from various points of view.

" Memoirs" is a misleading term, and it was not the choice of Richelieu himself. His plan was to produce a history of the reign of the monarch whom he served, but in the literal sense it is not his work. There are traces of his hand in the early portions, when he relates events or conversations in the first person ; but his direct interventions diminish as we advance, and in the later volumes they disappear. We have to deal, not with a personal record, but with materials collected for a special purpose, like the papers of Crispi and Stresemann in our own time. Richelieu's own projected title appears to have been " L'histoire du roi." Batiffol, the accomplished historian of Louis XIII, argues that though his papers were used by his secretaries after his death, he knew nothing of the plan. Other experts, with Hanotaux at their head, pronounce it an authentic work, based on documents from his Cabinet and carried out by his secretaries with his direct collaboration. Passages may well have been dictated and larger portions revised. The founder of the Académie Française was a ready writer and he thirsted for literary fame. Occasionally we seem to get nearer to the man himself, but it is only for a moment. There are no piquant revelations, no *historiettes* of the type beloved by his contemporaries. It is a severe, unadorned story, almost entirely in the third person. It can never become popular, for it is too long and too impersonal. Yet no student of seventeenth century France can ignore its claims, for the writers stood very near to the events they describe. We get closer to the great Cardinal in his *Testament Politique*, published in 1687, which reveals, not what he accomplished, but the spirit in which he worked.

While Sully and Richelieu are almost lost behind a barrage of secretaries, Cardinal de Retz wrote every line with his own hand. France is the classic land of memoirs, and no French political apologia has been so widely read as that of the brilliant and cynical adventurer Paul de Gondi. When he was an extinct volcano, his imprisonments and exile only a bitter memory, he employed his unwelcome leisure in etching the period of confusion between the death of Richelieu and the majority of Louis XIV. First published in 1717, the book won instantaneous success and passed through twenty editions before the *Oeuvres du Cardinal de Retz* in the magnificent series *Les Grand Écrivains de la France* began to appear in 1870. His scintillating narrative of the Fronde coloured historical writings till the middle of the nineteenth century, when Bazin, the first critical historian of Louis XIII and Mazarin, roundly asserted that the celebrated Memoirs contained hardly any truth. That this sweeping verdict overshot the mark was pointed out by Sainte-Beuve. Like most other political autobiographers de Retz invents freely, omits or twists vital facts, exaggerates his *rôle* and blackens his enemies. He is a voluble witness pleading his case in court, not a judge seated on the bench. Yet it is precisely in such personal narratives, with the dust of conflict on the writer's hands, that we recapture the hectic atmosphere of the time. Here is a first-class story-teller, who knew all the celebrities of his time and paints them with their warts. His Memoirs, like those of St. Simon, are too long and in parts too detailed to be read through except by historical students, but they contain many a brilliant scene. We watch the chief actors on the stage from day to day and sometimes from hour to hour.

One of the reasons of his enduring popularity is his astonishing frankness. A defence of his political conduct is combined with a complacent revelation of his personal vices. "Madam," he begins, "I obey your command, in writing my life, at the expense of my reputation. I shall conceal nothing." The "only begetter" was almost certainly the immaculate Mme de Sévigné, the devoted friend of his dignified old age, who described him as "notre bon Cardinal." Forced into the Church, like Talleyrand, by ambitious relatives, he admits that he was "l'âme peut-être la moins ecclésiastique du monde. Je ne pouvois passer de galanterie. Mes occupations ecclésiastiques étaient diversifiées et égayées par d'autres, qui étoient un peu plus agréables." The reader is plunged straight into a world of duels, debts and amorous intrigues. There are no blushes on the cheeks of this ecclesiastical Don Juan. While still a young man he found himself Coadjutor, or, as we should say, Suffragan of the Archbishop of Paris, a promotion which raised a troublesome problem of casuistry. " I found the Archbishopric degraded by my uncle, and I was not blind to the insurmountable difficulties in myself. I was not unaware that a certain moral standard is expected from a bishop, and that the scandalous life of my uncle made it more indispensable for me than for others. At the same time I felt myself incapable of attaining it. So I decided to do evil deliberately—the worst offence before God and the wisest course before men. . . . I resolved to fulfil scrupulously all the duties of my profession, and to be as zealous for the welfare of others as I would be wicked for myself." He became an Archbishop in spite of himself, but he asked and obtained the Cardinal's hat. One of his many *liaisons* was particularly stormy, he seizing the lady by the throat, she hurling a chandelier at his head. Some monks were employed to make copies of the Memoirs, and when they protested at certain passages the author blandly replied: "Allez! Allez! J'ai fait cela, ainsi point de honte de le dire." Despite this serene effrontery, several pages have been torn out of the original manuscript in the Bibliothèque Nationale, nobody knows by whom.

It is an entertainment to wander through his picture gallery. " Richelieu," he declares in a pungent phrase, " leaned to the good whenever his interests did not draw him towards evil." The great Cardinal, we may remark in passing, had observed prophetically of the young man: Voilà un dangereux esprit ! Mazarin is painted with more malice and elaboration than any of the principal actors, for the two slippery Italians fought each other for power during the long confusion of the Fronde. " On ne peut espérer du repos là où cet homme sera," declared the Cardinal, and de Retz was filled with contemptuous detestation of his foe. He set up to be a second Richelieu, but he had nothing of him except the impudence of imitation. He mocked at religion. He promised everything because he had no wish to fulfil his promises. He had a brain but no soul. Un vilain cœur ! Richelieu treated France like a quack with violent remedies, which wore out the body. Mazarin, like an inexperienced doctor, enfeebled the country with bleedings. France fell into lethargy, and he mistook this false tranquillity for health. Paris sighed and fell into convulsions. The rather colourless Queen, who called de Retz a very wicked man, is naturally regarded as a foe, though he was quite ready to take Mazarin's place at her side if the wheel of fortune swung towards him. Gaston, Duke of Orleans, uncle of the young King, is dismissed as a coward whose dominant passion was fear. Condé, the best of a bad lot, excites admiration as a soldier, a fine heart and mind, but he was too impatient and had too little judgment to be a statesman. " If he had carried out his good intentions with prudence he would have restored the state, perhaps for centuries. Equally, if he had had evil intentions, he could have done anything, have been a greater Guise, at a time when the King was a minor, the Queen obstinate, Orleans feeble, Mazarin not up to his task, the people undisciplined, the Parlements factious." Among the ladies of the Fronde Mme de Longueville and Mme de Chevreuse, stand out most clearly. If we are to judge by the testimony of de Retz, the main occupations of the aristocracy in the middle decades of the seventeenth century were gallantry and political intrigue.

When the Regent Orléans, learning that the Memoirs of de Retz were about to appear, asked d'Argenson, the Lieutenant of Police, what effect the book would have, he received the reply : " Nothing to worry about, Sir. The frankness with which he speaks of himself, his faults, his failure, will not encourage any one to imitate him." The born Frondeur, the artist in intrigue, had not made a success of his life, and he knew it. The attempt of the Fronde to limit the power of the Crown was premature. Benjamin Constant compared him to Machiavelli in his frank acceptance of the baseness of human nature, and Chesterfield pronounced his political reflections the only just and practical maxims he had ever read. Yet he was a gambler not a statesman. Loving adventure even more than power, he never reached and never deserved to reach the highest place, though for a brief space he was a maker of history. These full-blooded volumes help us to understand how necessary it was for Louis XIV to restore the prestige of the Monarchy after the crown had been kicked about in the streets of Paris.

One evening in 1714, the last year of his life, Le Roi Soleil sent the Duc de Noailles to fetch papers from his Cabinet, written in his own hand, which he desired to burn. When some of them concerning persons had been destroyed, the

Duke begged his master for the rest. In 1806 this and other material, which had been returned to the Royal Library in 1749, appeared in six volumes with the title *Oeuvres de Louis XIV*. The importance of this incorrect and incomplete edition was not properly recognized, and as a publisher's venture they were a failure. Though Chateaubriand declared that the Memoirs would increase the author's renown, and that Louis XIV did not cease to be Louis le Grand, little attention was paid to them till 1852, when Sainte-Beuve wrote two appreciative *Causeries du Lundi*. A few years later, in 1860, Charles Dreyss produced a critical edition of the *Mémoires de Louis XIV pour l'instruction du Dauphin* in two substantial volumes, with an elaborate Introduction and copious notes, which at once took its place among the indispensable authorities on the longest and most illustrious reign in the history of France. The most important parts were published two generations after Dreyss by Jean Longnon, whose work appeared in English in 1924 as *A King's Lessons in Statecraft*.

The Memoirs are only a fragment, for they begin with the young King's assumption of control after the death of Mazarin and end with the Treaty of Aix la Chapelle in 1668. Though the royal author frequently addresses his infant son, this was little more than a pose, for the object was to glorify himself. By far the fullest portion of the narrative is the account of the years 1666–1668, which was written first and was followed by a brief sketch of the years 1660–1665, of which only the account of 1661 and a fragment of 1662 survive. The Memoirs were carefully compiled, and were intended to be a handbook for rulers as well as a historical record. They were worked up from brief diary notes in the King's hand, several of which have survived, into a journal partially dictated by him, and finally into the still fuller version enriched by reflections on policy and morals. Even then the text was revised three times, and there are corrections on the first draft in the royal hand. Colbert supplied some material, but the chief editor was Périgny, the King's reader and the tutor of the Dauphin, who died in 1670. The sketch of the years 1660–5 was mainly composed by Pellisson in 1670–1. Thus the whole work was written very close to the events it described.

The main interest of this calm and dignified narrative is the revelation of the King's character and ideology. He is fully justified in depicting himself as the real ruler of the Kingdom, and as a jealous guardian of the prestige of the crown, for he had a lofty conception of his duties. He was a hard worker, as is fully recognized by Lavisse, the best authority on the reign. He was indeed much more than a lover of war and women, for he held all the threads of government firmly in his hands. He realized how much was rightly expected of a powerful autocrat and is prodigal of advice to his heir. Here are a few of the royal maxims. " It is essential for princes to master their resentments. . . . In thinking how to injure someone who has troubled us we may injure ourselves. . . . For the vain satisfaction of giving rein to our anger we often sacrifice the opportunity of securing solid advantages. . . . Exercising a God-given function we must appear incapable of the agitations which might lower the standard. . . . If it is true that our heart, knowing its frailty, is conscious of the emotions of the common herd, our reason ought at least to conceal them directly they injure the public good for which alone we are born. . . . A King must firmly hold the balance between the many people who try to tilt it to their side. So many pay court to us for personal reasons under specious phrases. You cannot satisfy every one. Do not judge the equity of the claim by the vigour with which it is pressed, either by the petitioners themselves or their backers. The result of the decision is more important than the merits of the claimant. The greatest king would soon ruin himself if he granted everything to deserving people. Those of our rank are never pardoned, and therefore we must weigh our words. . . Kings are absolute lords and have full disposition of all property, secular and ecclesiastical ; use them according to the needs of the state. . . . Never hurry. Take long views. The King must know everything. Empires are only preserved by the same means as they are created, namely vigour, vigilance, and work."

The Memoirs of 1667 are less full and important than those of the preceding year, but they contain an interesting passage which was omitted from the final version. Princes, he reflects, live in glass houses. " Vous devez conclure, mon fils, qu'un souverain ne sauroit mener une vie trop sage et trop innocente ; que pour régner heureusement et glorieusement, ce n'est pas assez de donner ordre aux affaires générales si nous ne réglons aussi nos propres mœurs." He had had a daughter by Mlle La Vallière and felt it right to recognize the child by the grant of a title to the mother. " I could have passed over this attachment as a bad example ; but after drawing lessons from the failings of others I could not deprive you of those you could learn from mine. The Prince should always be a perfect model of virtue, all the more because he lives in a glass house. If, however, we fall into temptation in spite of ourselves, we must at any rate observe two precautions which I have always done. First that the time we give to our *liaison* should never be to the prejudice of our affairs, because our first object should always be the preservation of our glory and authority, which can only be done by steady toil. Secondly, and more difficult to practise, that in giving our heart we must remain absolute master of our mind, that we separate the endearments of the lover from the resolution of the sovereign ; for the influence of a mistress is much more dangerous than of a favourite."

The brief record of 1668 only exists in one version, and there are neither *feuillets* nor journal with which to compare it. The Memoirs of 1661-2 describe the anarchy left by the Fronde and the means by which the young ruler quickly pulled the country together. Throughout the Memoirs there is singularly little reference to anyone except himself. Having decided not to have a First Minister, but to know, see and do everything himself, he merely required executants of his will such as Lionne and Colbert. He writes gratefully of his mother. "Her vigorous defence of my crown during my minority was a mark of her affection and virtue. . . . I saw her several times a day, not as a duty but as a pleasure." He pays a friendly tribute to his neglected Queen but has no words of praise for his brother. The whole work breathes the robust conviction that absolute monarchy is the best form of government and that the author is the ideal ruler, a blessing to his country and a model for his son. If the incense which he piles on his own altar becomes a little oppressive we may remember that even St. Simon, who had no love for the ageing monarch, confessed : *il était né bon et juste.*

The two greatest political apologias of the modern world, those of Clarendon and Bismarck, are the fruits of misfortune. We listen eagerly to their version of earth-shaking events, to their comments on friends and foes, to their reflections on the art of government. Unlike most political apologias, Clarendon's records were written at different times. Directly the first civil war was over Edward Hyde fled to the Scilly Isles and then to Jersey. The first seven books of the *History of the Rebellion*, and fragments of the eighth, bringing the story down to the opening of 1644, were written between 1646 and 1648. They were not intended for publication, but for the King and his advisers, not merely as a record of events but as a manual of political doctrine. His purpose was to tell his story " lest posterity may be deceived," to show why Charles I had lost his throne and how it could be regained.

Hyde was particularly well equipped for his task. He had started his public career as a member of the Opposition, angered, like the great majority of the members of the Long Parliament, by the abuses of personal government. He was never much drawn to Charles I, and he deplored his readiness to listen to evil counsellors, Buckingham above all. When, however, as the struggle developed, Pym and the Parliamentary leaders claimed executive control, the founder of the Tory party took his stand for the cause of limited monarchy and championed it to the end. Like Mirabeau he believed that it was the best form of government, and argued that, when the abuses of autocracy had been swept away, his clear duty was to support the King. In this early draft the young lawyer remains almost entirely in the background, content to vindicate the party of moderate Royalists to which he belonged.

Why Hyde left his narrative a torso during the long years of exile and leisure we do not know. A second and final misfortune provided the stimulus to its completion. When he fled to France at the end of 1667, after ruling England with a rather heavy hand since the Restoration, he left his manuscripts and papers behind. Instead of continuing the detailed narrative after an interruption of twenty years, he now wrote the story of his life down to 1660, covering some of the old ground but dwelling at length on his early years. The lack of documents proved a blessing for literature by compelling him to trust to his memory. The Autobiography, composed mainly for his children, reveals the author and the friends of his early manhood in vivid colours. His style is cumbrous and his sentences are often too long, but it possesses a certain massive strength. There is no finer portrait gallery in existence than these elaborate studies, with the incomparable Falkland in the place of honour. The *History of the Rebellion* is the vindication of his party, the autobiography the vindication of himself. If, like other autobiographers, he sometimes flatters himself, he was free from vanity ; he admits failings, and the picture is fairly true to life. The book, of which a critical edition is sorely needed, is as superior to the history in artistic skill as it is inferior in historical value.

At first the exile was allowed no communications with his country, but in 1671 one of his sons was permitted a visit to France, and he brought with him the manuscript of the uncompleted history. The old statesman now resolved to complete the narrative and to prepare the whole of his testimony for publication. He grafted portions of his reminiscences into the earlier work, adding to it the continuation of the story down to the Restoration transplanted therefrom. To piece the two together he wrote the eighth book and parts of the ninth, with a few additions here and there. The final version was published in 1702, a generation after his death, and it should be read in the scholarly edition of Macray, which indicates when each passage was written. The continuation of the autobiography, covering the first seven years of the Restoration, was not included, for a *History of the Rebellion* had to end in 1660.

So long as Englishmen retain their interest in the constitutional struggles to which we owe most of our liberties, Clarendon will be remembered and read, dull though he often is. Yet we no longer watch the moving drama through his spectacles or indeed through those of any of his contemporaries. For a century and a quarter his testimony held its place as the supreme authority, and it received a new lease of life from the more readable narrative of the Tory Hume. Not till the middle decades of the nineteenth century was it realized, with the aid of Hallam and Macaulay, Carlyle and Gardiner, how superficial as well as how partisan it was. Puritanism and its spokesmen were beyond the imaginative range of the Anglican lawyer, in whose nature there was something rather hard and dry. In the words of Firth, the fairest as well as the most learned of his critics, it is a history of a religious revolution in which the religious element is omitted. He despised what the eighteenth century used to call enthusiasm. The Vandyck of the pen failed utterly when Cromwell, a practical mystic, was in the sitter's chair, for he saw before him only " a brave bad man." The heights and depths of the soul were to him a sealed book. Yet the Whig attack was carried too far. Ranke helped to redress the balance, and in the pages of Mr. Feiling's *History of the Tory Party* Clarendon came into his own again. To-day we read him on the one side as we read the memoirs of Ludlow, the letters and speeches of Cromwell, and the pamphlets of

Lilburne on the other, able at length to understand men of character and principle in different camps who never understood each other.

The eighteenth century is weak in political autobiographies compared with the seventeenth and nineteenth. Its most substantial legacy is the survey of his wars by Frederick the Great. " Whenever I have a few moments to spare," he confessed, " I am seized by the itch to write. I cannot resist this frivolous pleasure, which occupies me, diverts me, and makes me fitter for work." Writing, indeed, next to conversation with Voltaire and other French intellectuals, was the chief relaxation of the first servant of the state. Every word of the thirty volumes in the collection of his writings published by order of Frederick William IV is in French, though his political correspondence is in German. In this faithful version even his grammatical errors are reproduced.

The King compiled a record of the first Silesian war directly it was ended by the Treaty of Breslau in 1742, but little of this narrative remains. After the Treaty of Dresden he described the second Silesian war, rewrote the story of the first, and added a sketch of Prussian history, describing the whole work as *Histoire de Brandebourg*. Twenty years later, after a longer and fiercer struggle, he wrote the history of the Seven Years War, based on his own annual surveys of the campaign, and prefaced by a sketch of the intervening decade of peace. Later on the taking of West Prussia in the first partition of Poland stimulated him to describe events after the peace of 1763. Moreover he now resolved to rewrite the history of the first Silesian wars, and chose for the whole series of his historical memoirs the title *Histoire de mon Temps*. Still later, after the Treaty of Teschen, he wrote on the War of the Bavarian Succession, connecting it with the earlier narratives by a sketch of the years 1775-8 and reshaping the earlier version of events from the peace of 1763.

The *Oeuvres Historiques* fill the first seven volumes of the collected works. Only the first, the History of the House of Brandenburg, which may be regarded as an introduction to the history of his own reign, was published during the author's life, though with many omissions. The record of his own achievement, which fills five volumes, was intended for his successor, not for publication ; yet he took as much trouble over his task as if it were going straight to the printer. " Though this is destined to remain buried in the dust of the archives," he wrote in 1775, "I do not want it to be badly written." Despite the unceasing revisions, he talked better than he wrote. His style is clear but colourless and undistinguished. It is a narrative of public events in which the personality of the principal actor is not obtruded, though he sometimes lashes out at his foes. Two volumes are devoted to the first Silesian wars, two to the Seven Years War, one to the Polish and Bavarian episodes of his later life. The *Histoire de mon Temps*, published immediately after his death, did not altogether please his brother Prince Henry and other performers on the stage. Yet the royal author also criticizes himself. He confesses to occasional errors both as soldier and statesman. There are of course the usual mistakes in dates and figures, and the busiest man in Europe wrote too quickly. But he earns our gratitude for describing momentous events so fully from his own point of view.

Frederick had a lofty conception of the historian's task. "I have risen above all prejudices," he writes in the preface to the Memoirs of the House of Brandenburg. "I have regarded princes, kings and relatives as ordinary men." The eulogies of the Great Elector and Frederick William I—une âme laborieuse dans un corps robuste—are balanced by his indictment of the extravagance and irresponsibility of King Frederick I. That his father was the terror of his family we are not told ; we hear only the best. "He left 66,000 soldiers, a full treasury, and all his affairs in marvellous order." In the preface to the *Histoire de mon Temps* Frederick claims to be equally truthful. "Many have written history, but few have told the truth. I shall advance nothing without proofs. I shall not conceal the immortal glory won by many officers in my campaigns. I dedicate this feeble essay as a monument of my gratitude. I write for posterity, so I shall write without concealments. I shall only speak of myself when I must." "Ce n'est que la fortune qui décide de la réputation ; celui qu'elle favorise est applaudi, celui qu'elle dédaigne est blâmé."

These lofty resolutions are fairly well carried out. The tone is calm and impersonal, though there is an occasional flash. No one, we are told, had so many clothes, laces, boots, shoes and slippers as Count Brühl : only with such a prince as Augustus II of Saxony could such a man be the chief Minister. The "unheard of perfidy " of England under Bute is angrily denounced, and in old age he lectures Joseph II precisely as he himself had been denounced in his youth. "The enthusiasm of the young Caesar for war sprang from the false ideas he had of glory. He thought that to make a noise in the world, to invade provinces, to extend his empire and command armies was enough to win reputation." *Mutato nomine de te fabula narratur.* The rape of Silesia is defended on the ground that it was necessary to give signs of vigour and resolution at the beginning of his reign in order to win respect for his nation. There is no loud boasting, but there is pride in his work. He was a soldier by necessity, not by taste. In describing the recovery of Prussia after the Seven Years War he remarks that all the Powers were almost equally exhausted. The King of Prussia alone had ready money because he always had a year's supply in advance. Whatever may be thought of some of his methods, he deserves his title of Frederick the Great, and he emerges a bigger man from Koser's monumental biography than from Carlyle's prolix glorification. In Napoleon's phrase, he was greatest at the worst moments.

When his formidable contemporary, Catherine the Great, passed away in 1795, her private papers were examined by her son, the Emperor Paul. A sealed envelope was found, bearing the words, " To his Imperial Highness, the Czarewich and Grand Duke Paul, my dearly loved son," and containing reminiscences of her early life written in French in her own hand. They were published in London in 1859 by Alexander Herzen from one of the few copies which had circulated in secret. The story breaks off in the middle of a sentence in 1759, when the wife of the heir to the throne was thirty. Fragment though it is, it fills a substantial volume, and its intimate revelations give it a place of its own. From internal evidence it appears to have been written at long intervals or at any rate revised in later life.

The little princess of Anhalt-Zerbst, transplanted to Russia at the age of fourteen and married in her sixteenth year, adapted herself to her unfamiliar environment with extraordinary courage. She quickly learned Russian; she read Plato and Tacitus, Montesquieu, Bayle, and above all Voltaire; she submitted dutifully to the instructions of the unattractive Empress Elizabeth; she bore with her drunken, brutal, stinking, brainless, childish, unfaithful husband; she made herself agreeable to everybody, trying to disarm hostility where she could not win affection. It is a repulsive story of primitive savagery, of dirt and cold, of ceaseless intrigue. *Grattez le Russe et vous trouverez le Tartare.* She bore it all because she was endowed with exuberant vitality and steeled by a vast ambition. Her husband, she confesses in a revealing phrase, was nothing to her, but not so the throne of Russia. "L'ambition seule me soutenait. . . . En entrant en Russie je m'étais dit : Je régnerai seule ici." When he left the room after his insufferable prattle, the dullest book seemed a delight. Occasionally we read of tears, more often of gaiety, dances and adventures. " Je ne me suis jamais crue extrêmement belle, mais je plaisais." Serge Soltikoff, the first of her score of lovers, was a welcome diversion. Her husband, recognizing her intellectual superiority, called her Mme la Ressource. " Si je ne comprends pas les choses moi-même, ma femme comprend tout." When the impossible Peter III was murdered soon after his accession, the calculating young widow entered on the decades of authority to which she had looked forward so eagerly, holding her own with the leading actors on the European stage. Her fragmentary memoirs are a valuable contribution to our knowledge of the atmosphere of the Russian Court ; but their enduring interest is the development of a masterful being who combined the brain of a philosopher, the will of a born ruler, and the frailties of an oversexed woman.

Except for the war of 1914–1918, no event in history has produced so many autobiographies as the French Revolution and the Napoleonic Empire to which it gave birth. So keen was the appetite for this class of literature that a number of spurious works, such as the memoirs of Fouché, were flung on the market. To this period belong the first political apologias by women, and that of Mme Roland in particular quivers with passionate life. Yet none of the protagonists in the most moving drama of modern times has left an autobiography, for most of them perished by the guillotine before they reached middle life.

Napoleon, like many lesser actors, had ample leisure to posture for posterity. He began to dictate reminiscences on the ship which bore him to exile, and at St. Helena he dictated to Las Casas, Gourgaud or Montholon for hours at a time. The *Letters from the Cape of Good Hope*, published in an English translation in 1817, were the first attempt to restore contact with the outer world. Nominally written by an Englishman, they were in fact dictated by Napoleon, or at any rate composed under his eye and secretly despatched to London. British sympathy, he hoped, might be aroused by the story of his sufferings. The *Oeuvres de Napoléon* fill volumes 29–32 of the edition of his correspondence published under the auspices of Napoleon III. Three volumes contain his memoirs and the *Letters from the Cape*, while the fourth discusses the campaigns of great soldiers. There was no intention of telling the whole story of his life, and the selections were governed by a transparent plan. No political apologia has had such a directly practical aim. The prisoner of Elba had regained his throne : might there not be a second resurrection ? Eagerly scanning the news of the royalist reaction in France, he determined to pose as the soldier of the Revolution, the standard-bearer of the ideas of 1789. When a deadly disease gripped him he worked no longer for himself but for his son. The last and not the least of his triumphs was to create the Napoleonic legend, which in turn, with the aid of other influences and accidents, created the Second Empire. "The Bourbons will not remain," he declared a fortnight before his death ; "my son will reach the throne." The King of Rome died a few years after his father, but a nephew stood ready to fill the gap.

The first of the three volumes describes the early exploits of Toulon, Italy, Egypt and Syria ; the second brings the story through Brumaire to Marengo and the Concordat. The narrator then jumps right over the Empire, returning to earth at Elba and ending with Waterloo. At first sight it seems curious that he should omit the glories of Austerlitz, Jena and Friedland, and close on the note of catastrophic defeat. But there is a method in the madness. Hoping that Louis XVIII would be overthrown by the Left, he desired to appear as its champion. While the Bourbons represented the nobles and the priests, he had represented the masses. Remembering the Terror and the Directory, he had not wished the people to seize power, but he had been a popular ruler. He found France in chaos : he gave her order and glory, nationality, religion and domestic peace. The spirit, if not the forms, of democracy had prevailed, for the humblest citizen could rise to the highest place. The Hundred Days symbolized the preference of France for a Liberal Empire over the *ancien régime*. Waterloo was an unlucky accident, due, not to the Emperor, but to the blunders of Grouchy and Ney. In the conversations at St. Helena the fallen ruler occasionally admitted mistakes : in his dictated apologia never.

The most brilliant of Napoleon's lieutenants and one of the most dazzling figures in French history left memoirs which have added little to his stature. Talleyrand's decision that they were not to appear till thirty years after his death whetted the appetite of the public. On the death of the Duchesse de Dino, his niece and literary executor, in 1862 they passed into the hands of Bacourt, who imposed a further delay of twenty years. Dying in 1865 he left the papers to two other men who died before publication. What would the Bishop of Autun have to say about the *ancien régime*, the member of the States General about the Revolution, the Foreign Minister about the Directory, the man who helped to make Brumaire about the First Consul and the Empire, the octogenarian Ambassador about the Monarchy of Louis Philippe ? It was an anti-climax when the Duc de Broglie published the five volumes in 1891–2, fifty-three years after the author's death. Half the work consisted of official despatches. Since the narrative part fell so far short of expectations, since no reasons for the long delay were apparent in the text, and since the manuscript was in Bacourt's writing, doubts as to its authenticity were expressed by Aulard and other scholars of repute. Bacourt described it as " the only authentic and complete copy of the Memoirs, made by me from the mss., dictation and copy." But where were the originals ? Sorel's contention that there had never been an original version was at any rate partially disproved when Lacour-Gayet, in the course of researches for his great biography, discovered about a hundred pages in Talleyrand's hand, dealing with Napoleon's treatment of Spain. Comparison of the new with the old version led to two important results. Firstly, they were sufficiently alike to establish the authenticity of Bacourt's work. Secondly, the number of small changes and omissions indicated that Bacourt, doubtless at the instigation of the Duchesse de Dino, took unwarranted liberties with the text. Examples are given in the fourth volume of Lacour-Gayet, who goes so far as to say that the work should be called the Memoirs of Talleyrand-Bacourt.

Talleyrand helped even more in the overthrow than in the making of Napoleon, and he was mainly responsible for the restoration of Louis XVIII ; yet he was deeply distrusted by the royalists and was soon out of office. He settled down to compile his memoirs in 1816, always bearing in mind the chances of a return. The first volume brings the story down to 1809 ; the second and part of the third describe his activities in the first and second restorations and the Congress of Vienna, the crowning moment of his career. The blunders of Charles

X brought the veteran back to the stage again, and at seventy-six he accepted the London Embassy from Louis Philippe. The last two and a half volumes contain his correspondence, official and unofficial, during the four years of his residence in England, but the detailed record of his Indian Summer is no consolation for the calculated meagreness of the story of his prime.

The note of the book was struck in a declaration of 1836 which was appended to the will of 1834. " Je réfléchis long-temps et je m'arrétai à l'idée de servir la France, comme France, dans quelque situation qu'elle fût : dans toutes il y avait quelque bien à faire. Aussi né me fais je aucun reproche d'avoir servi tous les régimes depuis le Directoire jusqu'à l'époque où j'écris. . . . Passer de l'état dans lequel était la France au régime royal était impossible. Il fallait des régimes inter-mediaires. . . . Je servais donc Bonaparte Empereur, comme je l'avais servi Consul : je le servis avec dévouement, tant que je pus croire qu'il était lui-même dévoué uniquement à la France. Mais dès que je le vis commencer les entreprises révolutionnaires qui l'ont perdu, je quittai le ministère, ce qu'il ne m'a jamais pardonné." In the course of his work he returns to this theme again and again. " I loved Napoleon despite his faults. At first I felt drawn to him by the magnetism of his genius. I enjoyed his glory and the rays which fell on his collaborators. I served him with devotion and loyally told him the truth. I have never conspired except when I had the majority of Frenchmen as my accomplices and sought with them the welfare of the country. . . . If I made mistakes, I always loved France and served her faithfully."

The record of Talleyrand's unhappy childhood is brief, the sketch of France before the Revolution tantalizingly meagre, the account of the States General scarcely even an outline. He was a Liberal Conservative of the school of Mirabeau, looking to England for the model of Constitutional Monarchy. He loved the Comte d'Artois, (future Charles X), he tells us, but strongly disapproved his decision to leave the country, arguing that the emigration of the leaders of the nobility would worsen the situation of those who remained. As a moderate reformer Talleyrand was a lonely man. The National Assembly, he declares, committed thousands of faults, fascinated by the chimaeras of equality and the sovereignty of the people. He is still more severe in his elaborate study of Philippe Egalité, who is denounced as dissolute, lazy and mediocre.

Coming to England in 1792 on the pretext of a mission and thereby escaping the odium of being an Emigré, he confesses that he was glad to be out of France during the Terror and to see the working of British and American institutions.

Talleyrand's enduring fame was won during his ten years as Foreign Minister under the Directory and Napoleon. He liked the young General, whom he regarded as the best man to restore national discipline, and discussed with him plans for Brumaire. The First Consul, we are told, began to degenerate after the Peace of Amiens in 1802, became drunk with power, and committed one costly mistake after another. " He attacked Spain without the slightest excuse, and he lost sight of the interests of France." Talleyrand compared it to cheating at cards, which, as he reminded the Emperor, is never forgotten nor forgiven. This, he declares, was the cause of his resignation. The " odious conduct " of the ruler in his conflict with the Papacy is censured all the more harshly since the Foreign Minister had welcomed the Concordat as a master-stroke. The gathering of the Kings and Princes at Erfurt in 1808 is the most vivid and attractive portion of the whole work, for the author as Grand Chamberlain was at the centre of events. We watch Talma on the stage, and listen to Napoleon's conversations with Goethe and Wieland.

Though the Emperor came to dislike and distrust Talleyrand, he invited him to return to the Foreign Office in 1813. The offer was declined, for the cleverest of men knew that his old master was doomed. For the full story of the Congress of Vienna, his finest hour, we have to content ourselves with his despatches to the Foreign Minister and his private correspondence with Louis XVIII. The brief summary which serves as an Introduction breathes a deep but quiet satisfaction at his skill and success. France was accepted as an equal and Saxony was saved from incorporation in Prussia. In fighting for the two principles of legitimacy and balance of power, he forfeited the friendship of Alexander, the most difficult member of the Vienna team. The story of the greatest period of his life ends with his brief Ministry under Louis XVIII. From 1815 to 1830 there is a blank, but when the July Revolution brought Louis Philippe to the throne, the old statesman consented to represent the new régime in England. He returned to Paris in 1834 at the age of 80, and died in 1838. None of his contemporaries except Metternich could look back on such a long and eventful career.

Talleyrand's flagrant immoralities and insatiable greed are known to all the world, and they admit of no defence. " How did you manage to get so rich ? " asked Napoleon. " It was quite simple," came the adroit reply ; " I bought rentes the day before Brumaire and sold them the day after." "A silk stocking filled with dirt," it was said of him, perhaps by the first Lord Granville. It is only a partial excuse that his parents neglected him as a child and forced him into the Church with as little vocation as de Retz. For his public conduct there is much more to be said. He gambled at cards but not in politics. Acton allows him, not principles, but a nucleus of opinions. His defence for serving different régimes, namely that he was working throughout for the interest of France and constitutional monarchy, sounds suspiciously like an afterthought, a little too good to be true. Though the patriotic plea is substantially accepted by Mr. Duff Cooper, the most brilliant of his biographers, the French Vicar of Bray is hardly to be regarded as a model of consistency. He helped the Emperor to turn Europe upside down, and dropped him at the height of his power. Was it far-seeing patriotism or the rat's mysterious instinct for leaving a sinking ship ? " You are a coward, a traitor, a thief," cried the Emperor at their last meeting in 1814. " You do not even believe in God. You have betrayed and deceived everybody. You would sell your own father." Talleyrand never answered back, but such scenes strengthened his resolve to work for the restoration of the Bourbons. A famous passage in the Memoirs of Chateaubriand, who hated and despised him, describes him and Fouché entering the Cabinet of Louis XVIII together in the biting phrase : Vice leaning on crime. Quand il ne conspire pas il trafique. Yet that is not the whole story. Cynic though he was, he loved France as much as he could love anything, and at Vienna the greatest of French diplomatists rendered her priceless service.

We learn almost as much about Napoleon as a man from Consalvi as from Talleyrand. The Memoirs of "the Great Cardinal " published by Crétineau-Joly in 1864, forty years after his death, are the only work of the kind emanating from the Vatican in modern times. Visitors to the Pantheon will remember Thorwaldsen's bust of the famous Secretary of State of Pius VII, the man who made the Concordat, who stood up to the Emperor in the plenitude of his power, who suffered imprisonment rather than surrender what he regarded as the rights of his Church, who represented the Papacy at the

Congress of Vienna. It is a thrilling story of the long conflict between the unbending representative of the old order and the Corsican adventurer with his savage outbursts of temper and his shabby tricks. To read this book is to understand why Wellington declared that his vanquished foe was not even a gentleman. Consalvi wrote his Memoirs during his exile at Rheims in 1812. He was unable to consult his papers and correspondence ; but his misfortune is our advantage, for the narrative, based on his unaided memory, gains in freshness and force. The work, which fills two volumes, consists of three parts — Memoirs of my Life, Memoirs of my Ministry, and three massive monographs on the Conclave of 1799, the Concordat of 1801, and Napoleon's marriage to Marie Louise in 1810. There is some repetition, but each item contains material which the others lack.

The most dramatic parts of the work are the descriptions of the making of the Concordat and of the author's refusal to recognise the Emperor's second marriage. The news that the First Consul desired to re-establish the Church in France filled Pius VII with such delight that to the end of his life he kept a warm place in his heart for the ruler who was to treat him so outrageously. Consalvi, who was sent to Paris to negotiate, had no illusions, and his record of the agitating discussions fills the reader with disgust. Knowing exactly how far the Pope was prepared to go, he was ready for concessions on minor points but unyielding on matters of principle. When agreement was reached at last and the signature was about to take place, the Cardinal was horrified to discover that a different document had been secretly substituted for the draft and that it contained provisions which he had repeatedly declined. Joseph Bonaparte, who represented his brother, knew nothing about it. When Consalvi firmly refused to sign he was exposed to the full blast of the Dictator's wrath. He sat up all night with his colleagues in an effort to find a compromise, and the Concordat was finally signed on July 15, 1801. Though the First Consul had been in a feverish hurry to proclaim the reconciliation with the Church, the publication was held back for a year and the Concordat was then accompanied by the unilateral Organic Articles, " the fatal addition which destroyed it at birth." The greatest of historic men, as Acton called him, could never play fair.

Consalvi bore the burden of the Papacy during the long absence of Pius VII for the Coronation of the Emperor. No one, he remarks, could accuse him of abusing his omnipotence. Napoleon, however, was convinced that the Secretary of State, not the gentle Pope, was the chief obstacle to his will and forced him to resign. In 1808 the annexation of the Papal states to the French Empire and the imprisonment of the Pope at Savona increased Consalvi's detestation of the Emperor. When he obeyed the summons to Paris in 1810 for the Austrian marriage, Napoleon received him with friendly words. " How thin you have become. I should hardly have recognised you. I was wrong to dismiss you. If you had retained your post things would not have gone so far." What was intended as a compliment was accepted as an insult. " Sire," replied the Cardinal, " if I had remained I should have done my duty." The Emperor proceeded to embroider his theme, twice repeating the unwished for testimonial, and twice Consalvi repeated his proud formula. The cup of Napoleon's indignation overflowed when the Cardinal, who declined to recognise the dissolution of the marriage with Josephine, absented himself from the wedding ceremony. " It does not matter about the others," urged Fouché, " but you made the Concordat." Twelve Cardinals present in Paris followed his example, though to his regret, a similar number accepted the invitation. When next they met, " the Emperor gave me a terrible look, and there was lightning in his eyes," but he said no word. After talking pleasantly to the conforming Cardinals he returned to Consalvi and glared at him ferociously. The Emperor, we are told, was drunk with fury whenever his will was thwarted. The brave Cardinal was packed off to Rheims, where he wrote his Memoirs, taking care that his occupation should not be discovered. Of the closing decade of his eventful life he has left no record.

Manuel Godoy and the monarchs whom he served live for ever in Goya's masterpieces at Madrid. The most celebrated Favourite in Spanish history has told his story in the only important political autobiography produced in the peninsula, which appeared in Spanish, French and English in 1836. Writing in his lonely old age in Paris, where he existed on a small pension from Louis Philippe, the fallen adventurer presents himself as an enlightened, patriotic and merciful statesman whose six years of power (1792–1798) stand out as a sort of golden age. As in the case of other apologias we must know a good deal more than we find in these pages before we can assess their worth. We must bear in mind, for instance, the most important event in Manuelito's career, namely that the handsome young nobleman from the south, who entered the King's bodyguard at the Palace, owed his rapid rise, his wealth, his dukedom, his many offices, his Bourbon marriage, to the fact that he had secured the favour of one of the most dissolute women who ever sat on a throne. He was not without abilities, and he was never a man of blood ; but the stain on his scutcheon is not removed by calmly ignoring what every Spaniard except perhaps Charles IV himself knew perfectly well. His two volumes are filled with tributes of affectionate admiration to the mindless but well-meaning and good-natured King, whose friendship and confidence he shared in sunshine and tribulation to the end. The royal support lasted long after the Queen had transferred her patronage to other suitors, and Ferdinand, one day to become the vilest of Spanish rulers, had emerged as an open enemy.

"They were a wretched lot," remarked Napoleon in speaking of the Spanish dynasty and Government which he deposed, "but Godoy was the best man among them." His apologia affirms again and again that he was never a dictator, and that the King in Council always pronounced the final decision, but he shows no false modesty in describing his achievements. He was the friend, not the mere favourite, of the monarch, he declares, "and attempted to deserve my good fortune." In the field of foreign affairs he began by supporting his master's unavailing efforts to save the life of his kinsman, Louis XVI. Then he took Spain into the war which the French regicides unleashed, waged it with energy, and came out of it unscathed in 1795, earning thereby his title Prince of the Peace. At home he kept his country free from the revolutionary fever by judicious reforms, preserving the Monarchy, encouraging education and agriculture, science and learning, clipping the wings of the Inquisition, tempering justice with mercy in what he describes as the gentlest regime Spain had ever known. "I have nobly and faithfully served my country. She has no right to reproach me with a single error of omission or neglect ; I have benefited many ; no one can venture to affirm that I have been the cause of his ruin." Yet, like other men in high place, he had many critics and rivals. "All the enemies of progress and reform were my opponents."

Godoy desired to resign after the conclusion of the French war, and his wish was granted in 1798. He retained the favour of the Court, returning to office, though not to his old unchallenged position, in 1801. Swept away by the French flood in 1808, "our only friend," as Charles IV called him, shared the exile of the royal couple at Fontainebleau and Rome. The Queen plays a small part in the Memoirs though she is always mentioned with respect; but there can be no doubt of the sincerity of the friendship between the old monarch and the Favourite long after there was any need for subservience on the one hand or political services on the other. His wish to combine a history of his master's reign with his own defence was thwarted by Charles IV, who begged him to publish nothing so long as his son Ferdinand was alive. "You cannot defend yourself without attacking and wounding him."

The apologia had to wait till the death of Ferdinand in 1833. At last Godoy was free to pay off old scores, and he made full use of his opportunity. Few political adventurers have risen so high and fallen so low, and we cannot expect objectivity in such a record of triumphs and disasters, imprisonment and exile. His English biographer Edmund D'Auvergne accepts in the main the complacent portrait painted in the Memoirs. Most historians of the Napoleonic era, on the other hand, reject a good deal of his testimony, and among his countrymen there is little tenderness for his memory. Favourites are never very popular while they are in power, and they have still fewer friends when their brief span is over.

Prince Metternich left instructions that his papers should not appear till twenty years after his death, which took place in 1859. His *Mémoires, Documents et Écrits Divers* edited by his son Richard and published simultaneously in French, German and English, fill eight stout volumes, but the autobiography only claims the first and a few pages in the seventh. It consists of three parts. The earliest, entitled *History of the Alliances, 1813–15*, was written in 1829, but it was unfinished, for the year of Waterloo was not reached. The second, *Materials for the history of my Life*, written in 1844, describes his fortunes down to 1810. The third, *Key to my Attitude during my Ministry, 1809–48*, was written in 1852, but it is only a fragment. This is no very serious loss, for the heroic period of his career ended with the overthrow of Napoleon.

"I wish to render a last service to the immortal Emperor Francis I who called me his best friend," wrote the old statesman in 1844. This service could be best performed by painting him as he was. The affectionate picture of the Emperor recalls Bismarck's portrait of William I, a ruler of lofty character. the soul of honour, the father of his people, the friend as well as the master of the greatest of his servants. It is not the ruler, however, but the Minister of Foreign Affairs who is the flawless hero of the drama. In the whole range of political autobiography there is nothing to surpass the massive complacency of Metternich's apologia. " The only way for a conscientious man to resist the storms of the time," he wrote, " is by the formula *La vraie force, c'est le droit*." He always defined his " system," as he fondly called it, as *Le Droit par la force*. He presents himself throughout his long life not only as the champion but as the infallible interpreter of right. His devoted son, the Austrian Ambassador at Paris during the closing years of the Second Empire, felt confident that the Memoirs and Correspondence would confound the enemies of the Chancellor and revive his fame. He was mistaken, for self-glorification was carried to a point which provoked an inevitable reaction.

" For himself," writes Sorel with just severity, " he is the light of the world ; he dazzles himself with his own rays in the mirror, which he holds perpetually before his eyes." He and Chateaubriand, he adds, are " les deux plus grands infatués du siècle." In a conversation with Thiers in old age Metternich blandly affirmed that he had never made a mistake, to which the French statesman modestly replied that he could not say as much for himself. When he boasts " Je n'ai pas vécu une heure pour moi," our thoughts turn to Caroline Murat, Mme Junot, Mme de Lieven and many other mistresses.

Now that we look to political apologias not for impartial history but above all for a revelation of personality, this calm assumption of infallibility in no way diminishes the interest and importance of the work. For Metternich was a master of diplomacy and a great European if not a great statesman. It is indeed a fascinating record of the long duel between the Corsican adventurer and the high priest of legitimism, the Revolution on horseback and the guardian of tradition. Educated at Strassburg and Mainz the young Rhinelander saw the French Revolution at close quarters. Some of his acquaintances were carried away by the new gospel, but to the young aristocrat it made no appeal. " I felt that it would be the enemy I should henceforth have to combat." As Ambassador to Paris 1806–9 he was never dazzled by the victorious Emperor, whom in his heart he despised as a gambler and a parvenu. " For me Napoleon was the Revolution incarnate, Austria the guardian of social peace and political equilibrium." When he was appointed Foreign Minister in 1809, at the age of 36, Metternich was well equipped by experience and self-confidence to confront the monster of anarchy. The next six years were the climax of his life.

The *History of the Alliances*, 1813–1814, the fullest and most valuable of the three parts which make up the Autobiography, denounces Napoleon as the sole cause of perpetual wars, for the French nation, in Metternich's opinion, wanted peace. Europe looked to Austria for salvation and did not look in vain. In his dramatic rendering of the famous nine-hour interview at the Marcolini Palace at Dresden in 1813, the greatest moment of his life, he declares that he considered himself as the representative of the whole European community. When the megalomaniac arrogantly declined the proffered mediation, Metternich quietly rejoined : *Vous êtes perdu, Sire*. On his way out, in reply to Berthier's inquiry, he merely remarked *C'est un homme perdu*, and the incorrigible warmonger staggered to his doom at Leipzig. Austria intervened at the right time, as Metternich had always intended she should. In an elaborate character study of Napoleon written in 1820 he writes with remarkable detachment of the man whom he claimed to know better than anyone in Europe. The Emperor is described as a parvenu and an actor, a good son and a good relative, not a bad husband. As a private person he was neither good nor bad. The most extraordinary man in history had great qualities, but it would be a mistake to exaggerate his greatness, and he was lucky in his opportunities. As Talleyrand observed to Alexander, he was uncivilised.

To the end of his life Metternich's greatest delight was to describe his decisive share as the brain of the victorious alliance, and such indeed he was. When the news of the escape from Elba reached Vienna during the Congress, he hurried to his master, then to the Tsar Alexander, Frederick William III and Schwarzenberg. The renewal of the war was decided in less than an hour, and Waterloo was the result. Francis is praised for his firmness and calmness. Alexander is defined as a singular blend of masculine qualities and feminine weaknesses. Castlereagh is praised for his reliable character and conservative views. Metternich is least just in his groundless condemnation of Stein as deriving from the party of revolution. He could never understand any one with the least tincture of liberalism in his composition or take what was good in the ideas of 1789. The longer he lived the more he became out of touch with his age.

A fragment written in his eightieth year, entitled *Key to my attitude during the thirty-nine years of my administration*, was printed by his son as the last chapter of his uncompleted Memoirs. When the imbecile Ferdinand succeeded Francis in 1837 Metternich's best time was over. Henceforth he had little influence in home affairs. The Government, he complains, did not know how to govern. The Archduke Ludwig was an excellent counsellor but not a ruler. Kolowrath, the chief authority on domestic matters, was fundamentally honourable but an administrator rather than a statesman. The machinery was slow and clumsy, and the revolution of 1848 was not altogether a surprise. In any case, he argues, it was not his fault. At times he had ruled Europe but never Austria. " If I had my career again I would follow exactly the same course. What is called the Metternich system was not a system at all but the application of the laws which govern the world. *La force dans le droit* has been the foundation of my creed and my acts. Liberty is the consequence of order. The only equality is equality before the law." The plain man, he was convinced, wanted order and peace. The people was everywhere good but childish. He prided himself on his realism, remarking " Je suis la prose cristallisée." But the champion of stability went to the grave without realizing that change is the law of life ; that the French Revolution had a constructive as well as a destructive side; that the status quo which satisfied the aristocracy was not good enough for the third and fourth estates. That the common man would grow up if he had his chance never crossed his mind. What can be said for his European outlook, his static ideology, his life-long struggle with nationalism and democracy, has been generously stated in Srbik's monumental biography and echoed in Mr. Algernon Cecil's thoughtful study. Bibl, the rival Austrian specialist, declares himself unconvinced. The most balanced estimates are to be found in Woodward's masterly volume, *Three Studies in European Conservatism*, and in Sorel's *Essais d'Histoire et de Critique*.

Guizot, the austere Protestant, the greatest French statesman between Talleyrand and Gambetta, was swept away by the same revolutionary tide as Metternich. His memoirs are perhaps the most valuable contribution of France to the category of political apologias. Politics have an important place in the glittering *Mémoires d'Outre-Tombe* ; but Chateaubriand, though a Foreign Minister and an Ambassador for a short time, was primarily a Man of Letters. Like Talleyrand, Guizot lost power about the age of sixty, but, unlike him, he never expected a recall to the stage. Living to a great age in his quiet Norman home, surrounded by his books and documents, he had time to recount his story in elaborate detail. He was moreover a historian by profession, writing easily and clearly, and a publicist of the first rank. His eight volumes, published 1858–67, describe not only the eight years when he was virtually the ruler of France but the decades of apprenticeship. It is an imposing achievement no more to be ignored than that of Clarendon himself.

" Thucydides and Macchiavelli wrote contemporary history," declared Guizot ; " why should I not do the same ? " His apologia is measured, impersonal, uncomplaining, for, though his father had been guillotined, he believed in the divine ordering of the world. Serenely confident in his gospel of the *juste milieu*, ordered liberty, the middle way between lawless revolution and sterile autocracy, he watched the Second Empire with disapproval but without despair. Limited monarchy and a limited franchise seemed to him the last word in political science. He found his model in the England of the Reform Bill, served its French equivalent in the Bourgeois Monarchy, and perished in its fall. He may be described as a Liberal Conservative or as a Whig of the school of Lord Grey. Caressing the illusion of finality, like Metternich, he never changed and he never grew. " Je suis de ceux que l'élan de 1789 a élevés et qui ne consentiront point à descendre." Under the restored Bourbons he found himself on the Left, under Louis Philippe on the Right. There is an irony in the fate of the greatest champion of constitutional monarchy at home and abroad, whose opposition even to a moderate extension of the franchise ruined the cause he had at heart. That men of property and education were alone competent to vote seemed to him an axiom. Like Tocqueville he was terrified by numbers. The significance of the rise of the Fourth Estate escaped him, for he could never emerge from his bourgeois limitations nor realise that one class is not a good judge of the feelings and needs of another. He had no eyes for the social question. Contemptuously rejecting the outworn principles of the *ancien régime*, he forgot that the Fourth Estate might in turn challenge the political monopoly of the Third, insist on a substantial share of power, and press forward towards a minimum standard of life. It is this rigidity of mind, this lack of imagination, this narrowness of sympathy, which excludes him from the front rank of statesmen and thinkers.

Despite its ample dimensions, Guizot's apologia is almost purely political. Except in the first volume it tells us little about his family and his friends. There is only one passing reference to Princess Lieven. " There is no humour, no irony," writes Mr. Woodward. " A cold magnificence, a splendid disdain set a barrier between Guizot and the men whom he governed. They and their posterity have a right to know his conduct of the great business of state, the immediate or distant ends he tried to serve ; all else is his own." Seven of the eight volumes are devoted to the reign of Louis Philippe, whom he served as Minister of Education, where he did his best work, Foreign Minister and Premier. For the years 1840–8 they are almost a history of France, though rather of foreign than internal affairs. The controversial episode of the Spanish marriages is described at immense length without entirely clearing his character. The curious reader will find the whole documented story of that rather unsavoury transaction told for the first time in an admirable volume by Dr. Jones Parry. He was not alone to blame for the destruction of the Anglo-French Entente, for Palmerston had a finger in the pie and Louis Philippe pushed his dynastic interests ; yet the story diminishes the moral stature of a man who professed to steer his course by the stars. The scholar-statesman remains an impressive and on the whole an attractive figure, but his testimony, like that of other members of the craft, needs to be scrutinised with a critical eye. His strength and weakness are described with deep insight in the first volume of Émile Faguet's incomparable *Politiques et moralistes du dix-neuvième siècle* and in Woodword's *Three Studies in European Conservatism*.

The first British Prime Minister since Clarendon to compose an apologia was Lord John Russell, whose *Recollections and Suggestions*, published in 1875, cover the years from his election to Parliament in 1813 till 1873. Large parts of it had already appeared in the form of Introductions to the volumes of his *Speeches and Despatches*. The biographer of Fox thought as a Whig and wrote as a Whig ; but except for sharp attacks on " those bandits," the " Adullamites," who wrecked the Reform Bill of 1867, and on Gladstone's handling of the Alabama case, there is none of the bitterness bred by disappointments and frustration which disfigures so many political autobiographies.

S

As Home Secretary, Colonial Secretary, Foreign Secretary, Prime Minister, Leader of the Liberal Party for twenty years and one of the authors of the Reform Bill, he had his place in the sun. " I have been received with quite as much favour as I deserved." There is also an unusual readiness to confess mistakes. He ought to have talked to Palmerston instead of dismissing him from the Foreign Office by letter in 1851. He should have stopped the sailing of the Alabama without waiting for the opinion of the Law Officers. He regrets his resignation from the Aberdeen Cabinet, though he blames himself for joining it still more. Had he been Premier, he explains, he would have told Turkey that unless she accepted the Austrian project of conciliation as it stood, since it had already been accepted by Russia, we should give her no further support. In this way, he believes, the Crimean War might have been averted.

Some interesting pages are devoted to sketches and anecdotes of distinguished contemporaries. Travelling with Lord and Lady Holland in Spain during the Peninsular War he was greatly impressed with Wellington's coolness in action. At Elba he found Napoleon so restless that he reported that the eagle would try to escape from his cage. He confutes Macaulay's assertion that oratory is essential to Parliamentary success by the examples of Castlereagh and Althorp. The House of Commons, the noblest assembly of freemen in the world, likes a man it can trust. The former, who combined high character with a detestable policy, was a very confused speaker, and on one occasion he exhorted the country gentlemen not to turn their backs on themselves. Althorp hated office and longed for release. Of himself he modestly declares " Eloquence I had none." Brougham's speech in defence of Queen Caroline was the most wonderful effort he ever heard, but no one trusted him. Pitt in his liberal days, Canning and Wellington, are praised, while the selfishness of their die-hard followers is rebuked. The Tories, he declares, made a great mistake after 1815 in not scrapping the measures which war alone could justify and considering wisely, liberally and maturely what was the policy which in days of peace might be expected to prevail in Parliament and the nation. As Canning truly said, the great bulk of the Tory party, professing to worship Pitt, adored him as the pagans of the East adore the sun—only in his eclipse. Since they only made concessions when public opinion was too strong for them, it fell to the Whigs to lead the nation along the path of ordered liberty. There is nothing so conservative as progress, nothing so dangerous as trying to stand still. " My disposition has always been favourable to compromise and moderation." His life-long gospel had been the old Whig toast, " the cause of civil and religious liberty all over the world." The Tories, he declares, cared little for it and the Radicals were too doctrinaire. How could a Russell be anything but a progressive Whig ?

When Garibaldi's fighting days were over with the unification of Italy the old lion of Caprera put his reminiscences, written at various times, into final shape. Published posthumously in 1888, they should be studied in the edition of 1932, where they form the second volume of the collection of his writings edited by the Royal Commission. Like many other political autobiographies they are a programme as much as a record. The Preface, written in 1872, strikes the note of the book. The Bayard of the Risorgimento was the champion of national and political liberty everywhere. Tyranny, he declares, is the chief cause of evil. Republicanism is the normal system of government because it is desired by a majority and for that reason is not imposed by force. Yet there was no need to try to impose it on communities who enjoyed free institutions under another form, for instance England under Victoria. It is because he regards clericalism as a bulwark of tyranny that he denounces it with passionate contempt. " In all my writings I have always attacked clericalism, because I have always regarded it as the prop of all despotism, vice and corruption. The priest is the personification of lying. Il prete ! Ah ! questo è il vero flagello di Dio." Needless to say he excepts the humble priests who rallied to his cause, some of whom gave their lives for the liberty of their country.

The young sailor from Nizza visited Rome at the age of 18 and conceived an undying love for the Eternal City. " Rome is the symbol of united Italy, and the most infernal work of the Papacy was to keep it divided, morally and materially." These words, he tells us, were written in 1849 and copied out with approval in 1871. During the fourteen years in South America the vision of a free and united Italy never left him, and in 1848 he returned from Montevideo with sixty-three comrades to take part in " the holy war." The story of the heroic defence of Rome against French troops, known to English readers from the prose epic of George Trevelyan, was set down shortly after his escape from a country once again subject to the Austrians, the Bourbons and the priests, and it breathes the bitterness of defeat. Pio Nono had toyed with Liberalism and had cast it away. " The Papacy, under its reformer's mask, was, is and always will be the mortal enemy. . . . Centuries of servitude under the horrible yoke of the Emperor and the still more shameful yoke of the Papacy " had led to " the modern *canaille* of potentates and priests." The degradation of Italy fills his soul with tempestuous grief. His consolation was the soundness and patriotism of the common man, as illustrated in his hairbreadth escapes during the retreat from Rome with the Austrians at his heels, in which treachery would have brought material reward.

In February, 1859, after his second exile in America, Garibaldi was invited by Cavour to co-operate in the coming campaign against Austria. He disliked Napoleon III as an ally, but, since most Italians believed that nothing could be done without his aid, he regretfully accepted the programme of co-operation. A people which refuses to bend the knee to the foreigner, he declares, is invincible, but many of his countrymen had become soft and degenerate. Equally he was ready to work with Victor Emmanuel, since in 1859 a republic was impossible, " though I was and am a Republican." His task was to harass the Austrians in the angle between Lake Maggiore and Lake Como—a minor military operation, but providing the opportunity for the young men of Italy once again to show their mettle. He records and laments every casualty among his gallant followers. " Brave youth ! Your bones are the eternal foundation of the edifice of our fatherland. The mothers of future generations will teach their children to bless your names."

In the following year, 1860, Garibaldi made history on the grand scale with the conquest of Sicily and Naples by the Thousand, whose almost incredible exploits have been described with Venetian colouring in the second and third volumes of George Trevelyan's history. With the epic nature of his theme Garibaldi's simple prose sometimes takes wings, as in the picture of his two ships sailing over the moonlit sea towards Sicily. " O Mille ! Argonauts of Liberty ! where your brothers are fighting for liberty, there you must be. You hasten to the fray without asking if the enemy is numerous, if the number of volunteers and the equipment are sufficient for the arduous task." The frequency and generosity of his tributes to his followers, from Bixio down to the humblest private, help us to understand the devotion he inspired. His ideal was the fighting man, ever ready to lay down his life for a noble cause. When rulers, statesmen, writers pass across the page the temperature falls. He speaks with respect but without the slightest enthusiasm of Cavour and Victor Emmanuel, and his references to Mazzini are chilly and sometimes disparaging. It may be argued that he over-simplified the issue between the Risorgimento and its foes, but it was a dedicated life. Among the paladins of nineteenth-century nationalism he occupies the most honoured place.

Bismarck's *Reflections and Recollections*, which should be read in the edition of Professor Gerhard Ritter, stand at the top of the list of political autobiographies, not merely because he is the greatest man who ever wrote a full-length narrative of his life, and not merely because the events he records are of worldwide significance, but because its value as a manual of statecraft is unsurpassed. It is too long and too detailed to suit the general reader outside or even inside Germany, though it contains many dramatic scenes, such as the conversation with the King on his appointment in 1862 and the editing of the Ems telegram ; but it must always remain the chosen companion of statesmen, teachers and students of history. It produces an almost overwhelming sense of power, and the highest compliment we can pay it is to say that it is fully worthy of the author. Accepting an offer from Cotta to publish his memoirs, the fallen statesman secured an ideal assistant in his old associate of the Foreign Office, Lothar Bucher, who knew more of his master's secrets than anyone but Holstein, and who, unlike that cantankerous intriguer, remained loyal throughout. Encouraged by his collaborator, who resided for long periods at Friedrichsruh and Varzin and sifted the materials, the Prince dictated reminiscences and reflections, sometimes spontaneously and sometimes in answer to questions, which Bucher sorted out into chapters. When the faithful old scribe, who suggested the title of the work, passed away in 1892, the foundations had been laid. In 1893 the first draft was printed, serving as a basis for the extensive revisions which continued till the end.

The first two volumes, which were published directly after the author's death and end with the death of the Emperor Frederick, are of infinitely greater interest than the scolding supplement which could not appear till the Hohenzollern Empire had passed away. The narrative of his fall, which fills the slender third volume, is written with a pen of gall, and damages the writer more than the young ruler who was the object of his attack, and who lived long enough to learn what Bismarck thought of him. Very different is the portrait of William I, " the real type of the Prussian officer," painted with affectionate gratitude and essentially true to life. His brother, Frederick William IV, lost himself in medieval fancies, and his wife, a Weimar princess, is described as preferring Frenchmen and Englishmen to Germans. The Emperor Frederick is treated with respect. The Iron Chancellor was a good hater. Every statement of fact has to be verified, every judgment of men and events to be checked. In cases of notorious personal antagonism like Count Arnim, and of a competing ideology like the Empress Frederick, we are on our guard, but the author occasionally misrepresents himself. For instance, now that we have his despatches of the middle 'sixties, we discover that he was much less resolved on war with Austria than his memoirs assert. Looking back on his achievement, it presented itself as the faultless and unhesitating execution of a grandiose architectural design. The real story is more empirical, for diplomacy, like campaigning, cannot foresee every twist of the road. Bismarck was resolved to found the German Empire, but he had to feel his way and some of the steps which led to the goal only became clear as he advanced. The account of the Hohenzollern candidature in Spain, which led straight to the war of 1870, is thoroughly misleading, for we learn from the diaries of King Carol of Roumania and other sources that he planned the whole thing and knew perfectly well that he was playing with fire. In home affairs, about which he has less to say, he is at times equally disingenuous, for instance, in his account of the Kulturkampf, which he presents as above all a defence of the state against Polish influences, and in regard to which he tendenciously exaggerates the influence of Falk, his Kultus-Minister. None of his colleagues except Roon counted in the formation and execution of policies.

Now that the original authorities for the Bismarckian era are mostly in print, the value of the *Gedanken und Erinnerungen* is to be found less in the narrative of events, though his story of the three wars can never die, than in the revelation of the author's personality and ideas. The book is strongest in foreign affairs, for Bismarck was before everything else a diplomatist. Germany, he declares again and again, must keep in with Russia, for German policy could not rest solely on the Austrian

alliance. When he declared, after his third war, "We are satiated," he meant what he said. There is no trace of Pan-Germanism in his apologia, no coveting of his neighbour's vineyard, no craving for colonies, no cult of *Weltpolitik*. When he had reached his goal of German unity the man of war becomes a pillar of peace. In a word he was a nationalist like Cavour, not an Imperialist. The great difference between the Iron Chancellor and his bungling successors is that he believed in the doctrine of limited liability and that they threw it to the winds. Readers who desire to study this fascinating work and to assess its value as historical evidence should begin with *Fürst Bismarcks Gedanken und Erinnerungen* by Erich Marcks, the best of his biographers.

Seven years after Metternich's death Beust, another German, took his place at the Ballplatz. The former was a Catholic from the Rhineland, the latter a Protestant from Saxony. The former held office for thirty-nine years, the latter for five. The Vienna period, however, was only a chapter in a long and distinguished career which began as Foreign Minister of Saxony in 1849 and ended as Austrian Ambassador in London and Paris. Beust's Memoirs, written in old age, reveal an attractive, highly cultured, liberal-minded personality, and they are a primary authority for the foundation of the German Empire. We are so accustomed to the Bismarckian version that it is useful to have a well-informed witness from the other camp. While accepting the verdict of Sadowa and Sedan he regretted the exclusion of Austria. To use the terminology of the time, he was Grossdeutsch, not Kleindeutsch. His ideal was the so-called Triad, Prussia, Austria and the Middle States. Was the German Confederation (1815–1866), he asks, really so objectionable? It kept the peace, and only the Prussian policy of expelling Austria broke it up. Bismarck alone wanted war in 1866. If the Bavarian army had co-operated at Sadowa Prussia would probably have been defeated and Bismarck have shot himself, as he had vowed to do if the battle were lost. Saxony loyally accepted the new order, and Beust declares again and again that he was never hostile to Prussia, only to Bismarck's overweening ambition. The Bund, he admits, was unpopular, and he lived long enough to welcome the alliance of Vienna and Berlin for which he believed himself to have prepared the way. Bismarck always respected him, and described him as " my most unbiassed and amiable opponent."

When Beust's career in Saxony was terminated by the war of 1866 he accepted a flattering invitation to enter the Austrian service. His first task was to carry to Paris an appeal from Francis Joseph for help. Napoleon III was in the middle of one of his periods of intense physical pain, and he could only mutter " Je ne suis pas prêt à la guerre." " I do not ask you to fight," replied Beust, " but merely to send troops to the frontier. Then you would be accepted as a mediator. If you do not, perhaps you yourself will have a war with Prussia in five or six years, and I promise you that in that case all Germany will march against you." The prophecy was fulfilled, and Austria stood aloof in 1870 as France had stood aloof in 1866. Beust assures his readers that Austria had no commitments to France and no thought of intervention, not on account of Russian threats if she did, but because Francis Joseph accepted the new order in Central Europe, and Beust realised that all Germany would fight. The common belief that he was and always remained anti-Prussian and dreamed of revenge for the events of 1866 is dismissed as a legend. He was eager to work for the internal consolidation of the Hapsburg Empire, believing that the bitter lesson of Sadowa could be turned to good account. The first task was to make the Ausgleich with Hungary, and he quotes Andrassy's compliment : " Without you it would not have been completed." The second was to modernise the institutions of the state. Beust, like Kaunitz and Metternich, was appointed Chancellor, or President of the Ministry, as well as Foreign Minister, so great was the Emperor's confidence ; but in domestic affairs his power was limited. The two chief obstacles to the removal of hampering abuses, in his opinion, were reactionary Clericalism and the feudal aristocracy. " I will never be the mouthpiece of a purely despotic government," he announced, and he kept his word. He succeeded in abolishing the Concordat and he advised the adoption of the Constitution of 1867. Yet he was detested by the aristocracy and Society as a revolutionist, and in 1871 his enemies brought him down. Though a loyal servant of Francis Joseph, to whom he was sincerely attached, he retained his German sympathies, and he wished to increase the power of the German element in Austria as a bridge between Vienna and Berlin. The detailed narrative ends in 1871, but there are some pleasant snapshots of the years in England, where he had served as a young man and of which he spoke affectionately as his second home.

The elder brother of the Prince Consort, though never a familiar figure in England, played a considerable part in the making of Germany and spent his closing years in recording his experiences. The three stout volumes of the Memoirs of Ernst II, Duke of Saxe-Coburg-Gotha, published 1887–9 (an English translation in four volumes appeared 1888–1890) are the only autobiography of a German ruling prince between Frederick the Great and William II. The first suggestion that he should write came from Radowitz in the early 'fifties, and in 1881 Ottokar Lorenz, the distinguished Austrian historian of German unification, began to help with the arrangement of the material. The book was sharply criticised, chiefly on the ground that the author exaggerates his influence, but it contains valuable documents and much first hand observation. As the nephew of King Leopold of Belgium, cousin and brother-in-law of Queen Victoria, *persona grata* at Paris, Vienna and Berlin, Ernst knew everything that was going on. Traveller, author, composer, soldier, he touched life at many points.

No German ruler of his generation was more anxious for German unity. His life-long friend Gustav Freytag urged him in 1856 to become "the adviser and General of the good Prussian cause," but the Duke was ready to accept aid from any quarter for the realisation of his aims. While Freytag was a Prussian, the Duke was a German nationalist. He preferred a Prussian lead, and regretted the refusal of Frederick William IV to accept the offer of the Imperial crown from the Frankfurt Parliament, but he supported the attempt of Francis Joseph to reform the German Confederation at the Conference of Princes at Frankfurt in 1863. Till 1866 there was no love lost between him and Bismarck, but in that year of decision he placed his troops at the disposal of Prussia. When the time came to write his Memoirs tendentious omissions toned down his opposition to Prussia in the years before the stricken field of Sadowa destroyed the *Grossdeutsch* party.

The Duke was the first reigning prince to visit Napoleon III, and the records of his conversations in 1854 and subsequent years with the Emperor are the most interesting in the book. He assures us again and again that Louis Napoleon was far above the average and not specifically French. He combined outstanding abilities with big plans, yet there was something of the dreamer and the doctrinaire. With his faultless German and his quotations from Schiller he sometimes reminded his visitor of a German savant. In the 'fifties at any rate he was anti-Russian, anti-Austrian and Prussophil. Realising that the Bund was unsatisfying and that Prussia was bound to expand, he declared that, if he were a German, he would be an ardent champion of German unity. The Duke was present when Orsini's bombs exploded as the Emperor and Empress arrived at the Opera, and he notes that the latter was the quickest to recover her composure.

Of the Prince Consort he writes with affectionate admiration, and the correspondence between the brothers fills many pages. Shortly before his fatal illness Albert visited Gotha. He was in low spirits and appeared to have a presentiment of death. One day he burst into tears, explaining that he knew he would never see his old German home again. The Duke was warmly attached to William I and his family, and he highly respected Francis Joseph. He saw a good deal of the campaign of 1866, and in 1867 he visited the exhibition at Paris, where he found the Emperor depressed by the Mexican *débâcle*. " I took leave of him as from a sick man who was with difficulty holding himself erect under overwhelming blows. When I saw him again he was himself a prisoner of the German army on the day after Sedan." Ernst was present at the proclamation of the German Empire in the Galérie des Glaces, and the story ends with an expression of gratitude and pride to have been allowed to take part in the making of a nation. " The complete inward change which has come over the German, who now holds intercourse with all great nations and stands at the helm of the ship which cuts boldly through the ocean flood, can only be conceived if we reflect on the long series of years in which this change has been wrought."

Émile Ollivier, like Beust, owes his fame to Bismarck, and, like Beust, spent the later years of his long life in describing the conflict which led to his eclipse. *L'Empire Libéral, Études, Récits, Souvenirs* is on the border-line between autobiography and history. The sixteen massive volumes, each of some six hundred pages, are as indispensable for the study of the Second Empire as the *magnum opus* of La Gorce, for they contain a mass of first-hand material. On the other hand the author often disappears for whole chapters at a time, for instance while the Italian campaign, the Mexican fiasco, or the Vatican Council are described at length. Not till we are within sight of the end does he become a leading actor on the European stage, but in the closing months, from January 1870 to the outbreak of war, we hang upon his lips. The book is far too long to be a popular favourite, and the reproduction of so many Parliamentary debates is an artistic mistake. Yet it is full of interest, for he was an able, attractive, highly cultivated man, loyal to his principles and of singularly independent mind.

The drama is dominated by the figure of Napoleon III, whom Ollivier successively opposed, partially converted and faithfully served, and for whom he entertained affectionate respect. Though the ruler moved too slowly for his taste towards *L'Empire Libéral*, he is presented not as a reactionary usurper but as a statesman capable of rendering immense services to France. Since the Bourbon and Orleans lines had been driven from the throne, and since the Parliamentary Republic of 1848 was a failure, why should not the nephew of the Petit Caporal found a new dynasty ? " He honoured me with his friendship till his last day. . . . I often attacked his acts, but even in his faults there was something intelligent, loyal, patriotic, generous." The young Prefect met him shortly before his election as President of the Republic, and his account of the *coup d'état* of 1851, which led to the banishment of his father, is very different from the invective of Victor Hugo or Kinglake. The President, we are told, honestly tried to work the Constitution and felt grave scruples in breaking his oath. He was one of the last, not one of the first, to wish for a change. Thiers, an ambitious *fanfaron*, " talking first, last and all the time," was partially responsible, for he prevented harmonious co-operation between the President and the Chamber. It was as salutary as Brumaire, for France was sick of the sterile debates. Ollivier, like Louis Napoleon, was convinced that the mass of the French people wished for the Empire and supported it when it came.

Whatever he found to blame, such as the Mexican adventure, the savage repression after the Orsini plot, and the loose living of the ruler—il aima beaucoup trop les dames—Ollivier saw no alternative. He praises the serenity of " ce philosophe humanitaire," " ce Marc Aurèle," and pays tribute to the goodness of his heart. When, after several years of Parliamentary activity, he was invited to the Tuileries in 1865 he pleaded for his project of a Liberal Empire. The two men took to each other, but Ollivier declined office till he felt sure that his wishes would be met. In equally frank talks with the Empress he was impressed by her range of knowledge and quickness of mind. He deplored the death of Morny in 1865 not only as a friend but as a believer in constitutional advance. He was on excellent terms with Prince Napoleon, the *enfant terrible* of the Second Empire. Walewski was a mediocrity, Persigny impossible. The Emperor's loss of grip when his health began to deteriorate in 1865 played into the hands of Rouher, the ablest of his Ministers but more a lawyer than a statesman.

The last five volumes describe the formation and operations of the Ollivier Ministry which took office on January 2nd, 1870. The Emperor was more anxious for the services of the eloquent lawyer than was the latter to take office; for his enemies, led by such gladiators as Rochefort and Gambetta, became ever more dangerous and the collapse of the Empire was widely expected. If anyone could keep it alive, it was Ollivier. The programme of the new Minister was to save liberty by authority and authority by liberty. He insisted on choosing his colleagues, with the significant exception of the Service Ministers, and no constitutional sovereign, we are assured, more fully respected the liberty of the man he had honoured with his confidence. The plebiscite of May, 1870, with its immense majority for the Liberal Empire, is hailed as a vindication of the statesmanship of the author and his chief, though the unexpectedly large number of hostile votes in the army aroused some anxiety. " I felt a profound satisfaction, not that of the man of ambition who has attained the object of his desires, nor that of the vain man who flatters himself that he has won renown, but that of the thinker witnessing the confirmation of his plans, that of the savant who, having proved by calculation that a star existed in a certain sphere of the heavens, perceives it through his telescope. I had formed a responsible Parliamentary Ministry and by successive steps substituted a Liberal for an authoritarian Constitution. Now the people informed me by more than seven million votes that I was not mistaken in believing my work to be good. Of course a considerable part of the success was due to the unshakable fidelity of the people to the Napoleons. Jacques Bonhomme had remained faithful to him. If I had at that moment died of fever, like Cavour, I should have been unanimously acclaimed as one of the rare statesmen of the nineteenth century." *Dis aliter visum.* " A cyclone which I could not foresee and which I had no time to resist broke over my work, destroyed it, and relegated me to the company of the vanquished and ostracised."

Napoleon III, we are told, worked consistently for peace after the Italian campaign of 1859, and neither Ollivier nor his master desired to oppose the free development of Germany. The war of 1870, he declares, was caused by Bismarck, who set the trap of the Hohenzollern candidature in Spain and manipulated the Ems telegrams. " I never had the share in the control of policy attributed to me, and I had none at all in military matters. Yet I accept the whole responsibility, so disgusted am I by the hectic repudiation of past acts and sentiments in the hope of winning favour. If our Generals had won I should have become a great man. They were beaten, so I am an incapable. Success makes renown. I do not protest against the common lot. My motive is entirely disinterested. I wish to cleanse my country from the stain of having unleashed war when it only defended its independence. Every Frenchman felt that a Hohenzollern ruler at Madrid would be a daily menace to France."

The fourteenth volume describes the coming of the war. Ollivier approved the French protest and was ready, if necessary, to fight, but when the Hohenzollern candidature was withdrawn he was immensely relieved. The Emperor seemed very satisfied but a little unquiet—satisfied because he regarded the Hohenzollern affair as liquidated, unquiet on account of the disappointment of the country that the quarrel with Germany was not definitely cleared up. " It is a great moral victory," remarked Nigra, the Italian Ambassador, " and I hope the Emperor will be content." " Yes," replied Napoleon III, " it is peace." Not a word was said of guarantees, and it was agreed that no further action should be taken before the meeting of the Council on the following morning. Gramont, the Foreign Minister, on the other hand, was far from satisfied and desired a declaration from King William himself that the candidature would never be renewed. When the ruler returned from the Tuileries to St. Cloud he was greeted by the war party, with the words : Le pays ne sera pas satisfait. C'est une honte ! exclaimed the Empress. The Emperor, a very sick man, forgot his promise (to employ the mild expression of Ollivier) to take no action till the Council met, and with the aid of Gramont concocted and despatched the fatal demand for a guarantee.

When Ollivier heard the almost incredible news the same evening his first instinct was to resign. He decided to remain, hoping even at the eleventh hour to prevent the fall of the avalanche. " Thereby I shared official responsibility for an act which I deplored." He would have been wiser to go, for it was too late to draw back. Though Benedetti, the French Ambassador, also disapproved the demand, he carried out his instructions with a zeal which annoyed the courteous old monarch and played straight into Bismarck's hands. The refusal of a guarantee, declares Ollivier, would have been swallowed by the Council, where the war party was outvoted, had not a garbled report of the Ems conversations been published by Bismarck, who gleefully described it as a red rag to the Gallic bull. On learning that this deliberate insult to France had been officially communicated to foreign Governments, Ollivier felt that war was legitimate and inevitable. This time the Council was unanimous for war. The Empress neither spoke nor voted, but her views were well known. In announcing the declaration of war to the Chamber he let fall the famous words : We accept the responsibility *le cœur leger*. The phrase, he confesses, was unpremeditated, but it merely meant that his conscience was clear. Any other Government, he is convinced, would have done the same after the publication of the Ems telegram, for the honour of France was at stake.

The fifteenth and sixteenth volumes comment on the hectic weeks which preceded the fall of the Second Empire. The French army, he declares, was ready and superior in quality to the Prussian, the French soldier still the best in the world. The war was lost by the leaders, not by the rank and file. The Emperor was physically unfit for the burdens of Commander in Chief, which should have been borne by MacMahon. When he said good-bye to the Empress and his Ministers at St. Cloud, the atmosphere was funereal. The army should have attacked instead of waiting for the foe. After the first disasters Ollivier begged the distracted Empress, acting as Regent, to invite the Emperor to return. That was impossible, she replied, till a victory had been won. " But, Madam, if he remains with the army there will be no victory ; he is the obstacle to victory, for he cannot command and he prevents the command by some one else." Distrusted by the Empress and deserted by his supporters in the Chamber, Ollivier resigned. His fall, he believes, was a national catastrophe : had he remained in office there would have been no Sedan and the Empire would have survived. At this point the curtain falls. The sixteenth volume was published in 1912 when the author was eighty-seven. A year later he was dead.

Where Ollivier lays down the pen Freycinet, who started his

career as an engineer, takes it up. His hero is Gambetta, with
whom he collaborated in the organization of national defence
after the fall of the Empire. Nowhere, except in the sparkling
Souvenirs of Mme Adam, do we come so close to the great
tribune who at the age of 32 became the symbol of France's
will to live. There were four founders of the Third Republic,
declares Freycinet—Thiers, Gambetta, Dufaure, Grévy, but
Gambetta was the biggest of them all. Thiers remained the
Constitutional royalist that he had always been, accepting the
Republic only because a monarchy was impossible. Freycinet,
who is a kindly judge of men, liked and admired the old
statesman, but he was never a disciple. Thiers had opposed
the war of 1870, and he blamed Gambetta for prolonging a
hopeless struggle. If peace had been made after Sedan, he
argued, Bismarck's terms might have been less severe and perhaps Lorraine might have been saved. There were no direct
contacts between the two patriots, but Freycinet, a devoted
friend of the one and *persona grata* with the other, kept them to
some extent in touch. Gambetta supported Thiers as the best
bulwark against the Royalists. The Republic, he realised,
needed time to take root, and he was too much of a statesman
to force the pace. When Thiers fell in 1873 Gambetta shed no
tears. Now, he declared, there were only the friends and
enemies of the Republic, and he had no doubt about the outcome of the struggle. The first volume of the Memoirs closes
with the crisis of 1877, when MacMahon dismissed the Jules
Simon Ministry and summoned the Orleanist Duc de Broglie
to the helm. The *coup* was defeated, and the royalists never
recovered from the blow. Gambetta's famous warning to the
President, *Il faut se soumettre ou se démettre*, was a formula
supplied by the author, who now found himself in the Dufaure
Cabinet for the first time as Minister of Public Works. As a
picture of the foundation of the Republic and the Gambetta
circle this modest narrative is unsurpassed.

The second volume reveals the white mouse, as he was
called, at the height of his influence, for he was more con-
tinuously in harness for the next fifteen years than any other
statesman of the front rank. The first half of the book continues to be dominated by Gambetta, though he declined the
invitation to join *Le Grand Ministère*. Though it had been
agreed that he should have the War Office, the Premier changed
his mind, and Freycinet, fearing the constant interference of
his chief, refused the Foreign Office. Other leading Republi-

cans also declining to participate, the Ministry was doomed
from the start and only lasted two months. Freycinet succeeded him and promptly reversed his decision to co-operate
with England in assuming responsibility for Egypt. The
difference of opinion clouded the friendship, and before it was
fully restored Gambetta was dead. The second half of the
volume depicts the Boulanger episode and describes the
foundation of the Franco-Russian alliance of which Freycinet
and Ribot were the principal architects on the French side.
The author lays down his pen in 1893 at the age of sixty-four,
since he never again occupied the centre of the stage. The man
who had played an active part in the war of 1870–1 lived long
enough to accept a place in the reconstructed Viviani Ministry
when the storm broke in 1914 and to witness the triumph of
the Allies. Freycinet was a smaller man than Gambetta, Ferry
and Clemenceau, but he was one of the most useful public
servants of the Third Republic, and his equable temperament
saved him from the fierce animosities which embittered the
career of his more forceful contemporaries.

Two American Presidents between the Civil War and the
war of 1914 wrote their autobiographies. Grant's reminiscences were inspired, not by the customary desire to proclaim a
creed or vindicate a career, but by financial catastrophe. After
his second Presidential term he made a leisurely tour round the
world, and on his return to the United States he invested his
capital in a business which went bankrupt. Finding himself
penniless, and gripped by cancer in the throat, he wrote his
Personal Memoirs. The book proved an instantaneous success
and restored the fortunes of the family : it was the last and
finest of his victories. His narrative is pedestrian, but the lack
of literary skill is partially redeemed by the interest of the
theme. It is an honest, unadorned, straightforward book.
There are no purple patches and he never raises his voice. No
more modest autobiography has ever been written by a successful man of action.

After a detailed account of his apprenticeship in the Mexican
war Grant reaches the Civil War in the middle of the first
volume, and the work ends with the restoration of peace.
Though profoundly convinced of the justice of the cause for
which he fought, he was free from bitterness against the
leaders of the rebellion. He is generous in praise and sparing of
blame. His best commanders were Sherman and Meade. The
soldiers of the South, he declares, like their brethren of the

POLITICAL AUTOBIOGRAPHY

North, were as brave as men can be, and believed in their cause as earnestly. Many of the generals in the Confederate army he had known in the Academy at West Point or in the Mexican campaign. Magnanimous himself, he admired magnanimity in others. " Lincoln always showed a generous and kindly spirit towards the people of the South, and I never heard him abuse an enemy." No one knew better than Grant that he was working under a time limit. " Anything that could have prolonged the war a year beyond the time that it did finally close would probably have exhausted the North to such an extent that they might then have abandoned the contest and agreed to a separation." Hence his intense desire to capture Richmond, the Confederate capital, the fall of which, he rightly believed, would be the signal for a general collapse.

There are many dramatic incidents in this story of the four years' war—the battle of Shiloh, the siege of Vicksburg, the carnage in the Wilderness, Sherman's march to the sea through Georgia—but there is nothing so moving in its simplicity as Lee's surrender at Appomattox Court House. The two men had served together in the Mexican war but had not met since. " What General Lee's feelings were I do not know. As he was a man of much dignity, with an impassable face, it was impossible to say whether he felt inwardly glad that the end had finally come, or felt sad over the result and was too manly to show it. My own feelings, which had been quite jubilant on the receipt of his letter, were sad and depressing. I felt like anything rather than rejoicing at the downfall of a foe who had fought so long and gallantly and had suffered so much for a cause, though that cause was, I believe, one of the worst for which a people ever fought and one for which there was the least excuse. I do not question, however, the sincerity of the great mass of those who were opposed to us. . . . The much talked of surrendering of Lee's sword and my handing it back, this and much more that has been said about it is the purest romance." They talked about old army times, and the conversation grew so pleasant that Grant almost forgot the object of the visit. When the officers of the two armies met in great numbers, they seemed to enjoy it as much as though they had been friends separated for a long time while fighting battles under the same flag.

The assassination of Lincoln struck a deadly blow at the policy of conciliation favoured and planned by the President and the Commander in Chief. " I knew his goodness of heart,

T

his generosity, his yielding disposition, his desire to have everybody happy, and above all his desire to see all the people of the United States enter again upon the full privileges of citizenship with equality among all." Andrew Johnson reigned in his place with his angry watchword, Treason is a crime and must be made odious. Lincoln, declares Grant, would have proved the best friend the South could have had. The book ends on a note of kindliness and peace. " I feel that we are on the eve of a new era, when there is to be great harmony between the Federal and the Confederate. I cannot stay to be a living witness to the correctness of this prophecy, but I feel it within me that it is to be so." Four days after writing these moving words he was dead.

Theodore Roosevelt's *Autobiography*, unlike that of Grant, is the work of a practised pen. Written and published in 1913, it made no pretence to reveal the secrets of state which were reserved for the official life by Butlin Bishop, the first volume of which was revised by its hero ; yet there is plenty of political as well as personal interest in the story. Nearly two-thirds of the volume are devoted to the manifold activities of the Harvard student, the cow-boy, the historian of the West, the head of the New York Police, the Roughrider in the Cuban war, the Governor of New York state. There is a breezy vigour in the narrative which carries the reader along, though there is little distinction of style or thought. No man ever enjoyed his life more fully or was less troubled by doubts. Maxims are strewn across the pages. " Do not hit at all if it can be avoided, but never hit softly." " Practical efficiency is common, and lofty idealism not uncommon ; it is the combination which is necessary and the combination is rare." The reader is obviously intended to realise that the qualities were combined in the ex-President, and that he was still a power in the land, despite his unsuccessful attempt in 1912 to fight his way back to the White House.

No event in history has given birth to such a litter of autobiographies as the first world war. With few exceptions the actors felt the urge to describe their doings, to explain their policy, to shift the responsibility for failure or defeat on to other shoulders. We are reminded of a gigantic state trial in which the witnesses press forward in crowds to tell their tale and claim their reward. Most of them seem to the uncritical reader to make out a plausible case, and it requires special knowledge to detect the *suppressio veri* and *suggestio falsi* in which they abound. Very rarely does a ruler, a statesman or a soldier admit an error or confess his insufficiency for his task. Yet though their aim is identical, the apologias differ enormously in literary skill and power to convince. A writer can omit or distort facts, and only the expert can catch him out ; but he cannot wholly conceal his own character.

The only crowned head to enter the witness-box is William II. The drab colours of his Memoirs present a strange contrast to the bright hues of his letters and telegrams, his speeches and marginal annotations. There is no suggestion that he ever made a mistake, and we are assured that he protested against the worst blunders of his counsellors, which as a constitutional ruler he was unable to prevent. This is a very different story from the proud claim of earlier years that policy was decided entirely by himself. It is true enough that he disliked the Moroccan adventures of Bülow and Kiderlen ; but he was directly responsible for the still greater blunder of the *Flottenpolitik*, which, as Count Metternich pointed out from the German Embassy in London, was bound to estrange England and to drive her into the Franco-Russian camp. His plea that he was innocent of the Kruger telegram is disproved by the evidence of the discussions as subsequently revealed. He writes with dignity about Bismarck and with gratitude of Caprivi and Hohenlohe, but the chapters on Bülow and Bethmann are filled with criticism. The former's handling of the *Daily Telegraph* crisis, he declares, destroyed his confidence, and Bethmann was too much of a schoolmaster. The Haldane Mission is dismissed as a political manœuvre, and the wisdom no less than the energy of Tirpitz is warmly extolled. The author stoutly denies that he or his Ministers, his soldiers or his people, desired war. He portrays Germany as a profoundly pacific state, wantonly attacked by the Triple Entente—a thesis as unconvincing as the rival legend that Germany was the only wolf in the sheepfold. A more agreeable impression is derived from his second book, *My Early Life*. The Memoirs of the Crown Prince, skilfully edited by Karl Rosner, cover part of the same ground. Friction between the ruler and his heir, he frankly confesses, was a Hohenzollern tradition ; but he pays homage to his father's idealism, high character and devotion to peace.

The three principal advisers of William II during the critical years of his reign, Bülow, Bethmann and Tirpitz, have told their story at length. The fourth Chancellor fell from power

at the age of 60, but it was not till after the collapse of the
Hohenzollern Empire nearly ten years later that he began his
vindication. He started with his appointment to the Foreign
Office in 1897, and described the twelve years of his glory in
two stout volumes. A shorter sequel sketched his activities
during the following decade, with special emphasis on his
mission to Rome in the winter of 1914–15 and his unsuccessful
efforts to keep Italy out of the fray. When the main part of
the task was completed, the old statesman turned to his
earlier career, narrating in a bulky fourth volume his experiences in Bismarckian Germany and in the capitals of Continental Europe. Written with the pervasive charm of his
speeches and conversation, his Memoirs rank as a literary
masterpiece : tried by the higher tests of historical accuracy
and moral integrity they stand condemned. No apologia of
our time has provoked such vigorous reprisals. Wandering
down his long gallery Bülow allows himself scarcely a word of
praise. His father, Foreign Secretary during the Congress of
Berlin, is one exception ; Bismarck, who started him on his
career, is another. Repeated tributes are paid to the Kaiserin
and to his gifted Italian wife for their goodness of heart :
neither of them, he explains, was a politician. The picture of
the Kaiser is a triumph of polished malevolence, built up by a
thousand touches, occasional expressions of personal liking
enhancing the severity of the final verdict. Next to William
II his own successor receives the hardest knocks. Bethmann
is presented as a spineless mediocrity, whose performance
would be almost ludicrous had it not ended in catastrophe.
Minor figures, such as Monts and Jagow, are pursued with
venomous hate.

The thesis of the work is that Bülow was gravely handi-
capped by an impulsive master; that he nevertheless piloted the
ship of state through the shoals without war or humiliating
compromise ; that he left his country stronger and safer than
he found it ; that his legacy was squandered by his incompetent
successor. Like most of his tribe he attempts to prove too
much. The self-righteousness becomes oppressive, even to the
uncritical reader who cannot detect all his wiles. His unsavoury anecdotes of the private lives of contemporaries
recoil upon the head of a man who unblushingly describes the
amours of his earlier years. The chief surprise is the revelation
that the most dazzling figure of post-Bismarckian Germany
lacked the instincts of a gentleman. How such a cultivated

man of the world could be unaware that he was damaging his own reputation far more than the objects of his attacks is a mystery. The *mot* is attributed to William II that Bülow is the only known example of a man committing suicide after his death.

Next in importance among German leaders is the testimony of Tirpitz, who told his story twice over. His Memoirs, published shortly after the war, were widely read, and a cheap abridgement enjoyed an enormous sale. Several years later he returned to the charge in two massive volumes entitled *Political Documents*, stuffed with valuable material. The Admiral was a big man, who knew what he wanted and strove with iron will to reach his goal. A great people, he declares, can only be made and kept safe by power, since Might has always gone before Right. The object of his battleships was not to make war but to win an independent position. The downfall of Germany was due to bad statesmanship. Mainly owing to the Kaiser's support a formidable navy was fashioned, but the army lagged behind. With a stronger army and a wiser attitude towards Russia, the position would have been unassailable. Simultaneously to antagonize England and Russia was a mistake. The gravedigger of Germany was Bethmann, who sacrificed the interests of national defence to the *beaux yeux* of perfidious Albion, and who tried to conduct war on the principle of limited liability. Tirpitz, like Bülow, argues that his work was good, and that it was ruined by an incompetent Chancellor. "England's love of peace and consideration of our interests grew *pari passu* with our fleet." Metternich, the unceasing advocate of naval limitation, receives almost as many lashes as Bethmann himself. The real enemy before and during the war was England, not Russia. The fleet should have played for high stakes at the outset, and the submarine weapon should have been ruthlessly applied. In these strong and bitter books, which paint a devastating picture of disunion in high places, Tirpitz dismisses the civilians as contemptuously as Sir William Robertson in his *Soldiers and Statesmen*. It is an old quarrel. Ludendorff has written a book entitled *Politik und Kriegführung* to prove that the best chance of winning a war is when political and military power are combined in a single hand, as in the case of Napoleon and Frederick the Great.

Very different in tone is Bethmann's *Reflections on the World War*. The unsullied character and devotion to peace of the

fifth German Chancellor, the lover of Plato and Beethoven, are
as incontestable as his temperamental unfitness for the post of
pilot in stormy seas. His book is pitched throughout in a
minor key. We seem to hear the plaintive accents of Hamlet
lamenting that the times were out of joint and that he was
called to set them right. Since Russia was lost, owing to her
alliance with France, the only chance of escape from encirclement was an agreement with England. Unfortunately he
inherited an estrangement which he vainly strove to heal.
His policy was to meet British demands with regard to the
fleet in return for a neutrality pact, but neither side was willing
to make the necessary sacrifice. He was not master in his own
house, for Tirpitz had the Kaiser's ear. Still more tragic was
his failure to assert himself in the critical days of 1914. He
should have insisted on being consulted by Austria at every
step of the way instead of handing Berchtold a blank cheque.
His pages on the outbreak of war reveal a good man contri-
buting by his blunders to the catastrophe which he was as
anxious as Grey to avert. Like Aberdeen in 1854, he drifted
into war, hoping to the end that England and Russia would not
fight. Compared with his full-blooded rivals, Tirpitz and
Ludendorff, he is a shadow on the wall. The second volume is
filled with the struggle against the military and naval advisers
of his master. When the renewal of the submarine war was
decided at the opening of 1917 he realised the madness of a
step which involved the belligerence of the United States. He
argued against it, grudgingly accepted it, remained in office
instead of resigning, and was roughly evicted by the Generals
six months later. There are few more depressing careers in
recent times.

The leading statesmen of Russia have also told their story.
The most striking apologia among the older generation is
that of Witte, whom his friend and factotum Dr. Dillon used to
describe as Russia's only statesman and the ablest Russian since
Peter the Great. " I am neither a Liberal nor a Conservative,"
he used to say, and indeed he was the loneliest figure on the
stage. He despised the feeble Tsar, and Nicholas II detested
his rough-mannered Minister. Written abroad after his fall
from power in 1906, his Memoirs contain even more than the
usual number of distortions and tricks of memory as well as
the customary animosities of disappointed men. His deprecia-
tion of the people with whom he worked, except his old master
Alexander III, leaves a disagreeable impression. He alone

possessed the insight to realise and the courage to proclaim
that the Russian Empire was too rotten to wage war either
with Japan or the Central Powers. He died in 1915, a few
months too early to witness the fulfilment of his darkest
anticipations.

Iswolsky commenced his Memoirs when the Bolshevist
revolution deprived him of his Embassy in Paris, but he had
only brought his narrative up to his appointment as Foreign
Minister in 1906 when he died. His successor Sazonoff, a
better but a smaller man, employed his closing days in France
in the same way. Wisely limiting himself to his six years in
office, he lived just long enough to complete his task. Though
he had no desire for war, he was quite ready to risk a world-
wide conflagration for the maintenance of what he regarded
as just Russian claims in the Near East. His patronage of the
Balkan League in 1912, which led Poincaré to exclaim : " Mais
c'est une Convention de Guerre," is defended on the ground
that the Balkan States could not neglect the golden opportunity of the Tripoli war. Turkish rule in the Balkans, he
explains, was a hideous anachronism. He realised the possibility of a European conflict ; yet " not to help Serbia and
Bulgaria to realise their aims meant not only the abandonment
by Russia of her historical mission, but the surrender without a
struggle to the enemy of the Slav peoples of positions won by
the efforts of centuries." The author of that revealing sentence
can hardly be reckoned among the champions of peace. He
disclaims Germanophobia, but the Liman Mission to Turkey
stirred him to passionate excitement. Hostility to Austria,
whom he holds responsible for the catastrophe in 1914, runs
like a red thread through his book. Germany is condemned,
not for a will to war, but for giving rein to the Austrian
steed. Europe staggered into war because neither of the two
Eastern Empires was willing to face a loss of prestige.

Like most of the ex-Ministers of the Tsar Count Kokovtsoff
settled in France, where he devoted himself to the vindication
of his career. *Out of the Past* begins with his appointment as
Minister of Finance in 1903 on the eve of the Japanese war, and
deals in detail with the crowded years down to his fall at the
opening of 1914. The account of the Dumas, of the financial
recovery from the Japanese war, of the economic development
of the country, of his colleagues, of his occasional contacts
with foreign affairs, are only less interesting than his pictures
of the Tsar, the Tsarina, Rasputin and the Court. The book

closes with a brief sketch of the war, the revolution and the author's flight. Kokovtsoff lacked Witte's rugged strength, but nobody worked more faithfully or efficiently for the Tsarist regime than Stolypin's successor as President of the Council, who may be described as a moderate Conservative. That he was dismissed from his post and replaced by Goremykin, a nerveless old reactionary, was a fresh illustration of the baneful influence of the Tsarina and the Tsar's preference for second-rate men. At the parting interview with his master neither could restrain his tears. When he saw him for the last time in January, 1917, he was shocked by the change. "He had become almost unrecognisable. His face had grown very thin and hollow and covered with small wrinkles. His eyes had become faded and wandered aimlessly from object to object."

Trotzky's autobiography was written in embittered exile when Stalin had taken the reins from the dying hands of their common master. The intellectual power of the organiser of the Red Army and the Foreign Minister grips the reader from the start, and he writes as well as he used to speak. His record of the peace negotiations at Brest-Litovsk is extremely vivid. When he mentioned the German Government, General Hoffmann interrupted him in a voice hoarse with anger : " I do not represent the German Government here, but the German High Command." His object, he confesses, was to delay the negotiations : it was Lenin who insisted on making peace. The darker features of what Trotzky describes as the most revolutionary regime ever known to humanity are toned down, and we must look elsewhere for information on the wholesale slaughter which inaugurated and disgraced the Soviet experiment. His later and more ambitious work, *History of the Russian Revolution*, though less personal, may be regarded as a further instalment of a large scale apologia. The drama is described from a different angle but with equal authority in Kerensky's spirited work *The Catastrophe*.

Since Berchtold's eagerly awaited apologia, though nearly completed, has not appeared, and Conrad's Memoirs are little more than a vast storehouse of documents, we pass to Italy, where Giolitti occupies the centre of the stage. The most accomplished Parliamentary manager of his time records decades of service from the days of Crispi to his final Premiership after the world war. There is no charm or colour in this frigid autobiography, and the story of the stealthy preparations

for the rape of Tripoli is particularly cold-blooded. " I had
for some time reflected on the Lybian question," he writes,
" with the firm intention of solving it at the first opportunity.
If we had not gone to Tripoli, some other Power would." His
picture of the Foreign Minister and himself, who alone were
in the secret, spending the summer of 1911 in the country " to
show that nothing was in the wind," will always remain a
classical example of secret diplomacy. His maxim was limited
liability. He preferred subterranean strategy to the big stick,
and in foreign affairs he opposed ambitious objectives. He was
ready for the Tripoli adventure, because the diplomatic pre-
paration was complete and Turkey could not reinforce her
scanty garrisons either by land or sea. Consulted by Salandra
on the outbreak of war he advised neutrality. He disapproved
the plunge in 1915, not from tenderness for Austria, but because he disliked gambling for the highest stakes. Austria, he
argued, would make considerable sacrifices to preserve
Italian neutrality. Something could be gained at once without
the shedding of blood, and the rest would follow in due course,
since the Hapsburg Empire was doomed to dissolution by
racial discord and the stress of war. He was overruled by
Salandra, who had the secret Treaty of London in his desk, and
who has told the story of Italy's intervention in two volumes of
dramatic interest.

Poincairé's Memoirs head the list of French autobiographical
contributions to the literature of the war. An accomplished
writer, a member of the Académie Française, and a leader of
the French bar, he could state a case as well as any man of his
time. When his seven years as President of the Republic
ended in 1920, he began the most imposing apolo in French
literature since that of Ollivier. Six addresses, *Les Origines de
la Guerre*, delivered and published in 1921, survey French
policy from 1871 to 1914, and may be regarded as a prologue
to the larger work. There is a good deal of autobiography in
the second half of the book, and the picture of the voyage home
from Russia in July, 1914, with wireless messages pouring in
and anxiety increasing every hour, lingers in our memory.
He was greeted by the Minister of War with the words : Vous
allez voir Paris : c'est splendide. Leaving the first fifty years
of his career to his biographers, he begins his *Souvenirs* with the
summons to the Premiership in January, 1912, on the morrow
of the Agadir crisis. The resounding title, *Au Service de la
France*, embodies his proudest claim. If the exuberance of

Gambetta and the passion of Clemenceau are lacking, we sense throughout the patriotic emotion of one whom even his many enemies admit to have been a great Frenchman.

The first two volumes, dealing with his memorable year as Premier and Foreign Secretary, are the most interesting and valuable of all. The third and fourth, describing the first eighteen months of his Presidency, are less authoritative, for he explains again and again that French policy was made by the Cabinets, not by himself. The charge brought against him, not only by German foes but by some of his own countrymen, that he worked for war is angrily denied. To the statements in Iswolsky's despatches that he encouraged Russia to rash adventures in the Balkans, he replies that the Ambassador systematically misreported him, and that he never went an inch beyond the formal obligations of the Dual Alliance. In 1930 he took up the grave charge of being a war-monger in a small volume entitled *Les Responsabilités de la Guerre*, which replied to fourteen searching questions by a young critic for whom he felt respect. The six volumes of the Memoirs which cover the years of the war abandon the narrative method in favour of extracts from his diary, some of which, particularly the snapshots of celebrities, are vivid enough though many others are not worth printing. The work would have gained in impressiveness if it had been shorter and less self-righteous. From Clemenceau down to the meanest scribbler he breaks a lance with all his critics and foes. It is not a loveable personality.

In his declining years Asquith traced the outlines of his career and rebutted the charge that he had failed to prepare for the ordeal of war. A first-class classical scholar and a lover of good literature, he could write well enough when he chose ; but *The Genesis of the War*, the first and most important of his books, *Fifty Years of Parliament*, and *Memories and Reflections*, are the work of a tired man and add nothing to the reputation of our greatest Parliamentarian since Gladstone. Haldane's narrative presented in *Before the War* and in his posthumous *Autobiography*, though on a smaller scale and covering a more limited field, is of high value as a contribution to the tragic history of Anglo-German relations. Morley's *Recollections*, which stop short before the war of 1914, are a delight, and the letters to Lord Minto written from the India Office are the gem of the book. The *Memorandum on Resignation*, published after his death, traces the agonising experiences and disagreements of the Liberal Cabinet during the memorable days which ended his public career.

Three works stand out from the multitude of apologias produced in England by the first world war. The ample narratives of Winston Churchill and Lloyd George resemble each other in their tingling vitality, their colossal self-assurance, their robust conviction that the mistakes which nearly lost us the war were made by other men, their unconcealed contempt for slower minds and weaker wills. No one can read their testimony without realising that the writers are born leaders, unlike Asquith or Grey among their political colleagues, unlike Balfour and Bonar Law, MacDonald and Baldwin in the rival camps. But men of action who, as the phrase goes, can deliver the goods, sometimes supply the wrong kind of article. No one nowadays contests the services to the cause of the Allies rendered by the two most dynamic personalities in British politics, and no one will deny the narrative and argumentative power with which they have conducted their defence. Yet such born fighters do not always silence their critics.

Churchill's literary virtuosity was revealed in youth by his sparkling life of his father, and *The World Crisis* is full of purple patches, some of them rising into magnificent eloquence ; but Lloyd George's skill with the pen came as a surprise. We had all wondered who would be entrusted with the responsibility of presenting his case. The answer was given by the changes and chances of domestic politics ; his fall from power decided that, despite his lack of literary training, he should tell his own story. " I was the only official figure who went right through it from the declaration of war to the signing of peace. I make my contribution, not as one who claims to be an experienced author, but as a witness giving evidence on what he remembers of these tremendous transactions."

His book, he claims with justice, is the most carefully and richly documented account of the great Armageddon. The self-righteousness which mars nearly all apologias is conspicuous in the six volumes of his *War Memoirs*. Grey, Asquith, Haig, Robertson, Jellicoe and many other prominent actors are mercilessly trounced, but quite as many, French as well as British, are warmly praised. There are no half-tones, hesitations or doubts, though he reminds us that chance, not right, is the supreme judge in war. We are reminded of Melbourne's remark : " I wish I was as cocksure about anything as Macaulay is about everything." Yet the power is unmistakable. Who can ever forget the grim chapters on Paschendael? Even if there is another side in many of these controversies, the tremendous spectacle unfolds itself swiftly and vividly before our eyes. The two stout supplementary volumes on the making of the peace treaties are as friendly to Clemenceau as they are hostile to Poincaré.

No greater contrast can be imagined than between the apologias of Lloyd George and Edward Grey : we cannot be surprised, for the authors were antipathetic throughout life. The one is still covered with the dust of conflict, the other is cool, dignified and relatively detached. The one belabours his critics and foes, dead or alive, with resounding blows, the other is content to describe what he thought and did. The one is something of a superman, the other a cultivated English gentleman with a tradition of public service in the sound of his name. The one blows his own trumpet unceasingly with all the strength of his powerful lungs, the other never raises his voice above conversational tones. Dictated to his second wife at the close of his career, Grey's *Twenty-Five Years* is a masterpiece of its kind. If the object of political autobiography is to win new friends and conciliate antagonists, his apologia is one of the most successful ever written. We shall continue to differ as to the merits of his guiding principle of Continentalism which he inherited from Lansdowne, and in regard to his handling of particular issues as they arose. Yet few readers will close the book without feeling that he has been in the company of a statesman devoted, not only to the interests of his country as he conceived them, but to the cause of European peace.

The moving apologia of Prince Max of Baden, the last Imperial Chancellor, reveals an equally attractive personality. Called to the helm in September 1918, when the German front was collapsing, he discovered the situation to be even worse than he feared. " I thought I had been summoned at five minutes to twelve," he wrote to his cousin the Grand Duke of Baden, " but I found it was five minutes after." His intention was to go to the limit of compromise in the exchanges with Washington, and to summon the German people to a desperate effort if the armistice terms appeared unendurable. It began to dawn on the nation, however, that there might be an easier way of escape. President Wilson had repeatedly declared that he was at war with a system, and his October notes plainly hinted that the Kaiser must go. The Chancellor, the heir to the throne of Baden and a monarchist by conviction as well as birth, strove to save the Imperial throne. The key to the situation was in the hands of the Socialists, for if they officially demanded the abdication of William II and were rebuffed, they would withdraw from the Coalition and the Government would fall. He persuaded Ebert and Scheidemann to postpone the demand, and used the breathing space to urge the ruler to save his dynasty by abdication. Hindenburg, however, warned his master that the army might go to pieces if this advice were taken, and the Chancellor declined to force his sovereign's hand.

The mutiny at Kiel was the beginning of the end, but William II was resolved to yield to force alone. Even when, on November 8th, the Chancellor at last telephoned : " Your abdication is essential to avert civil war," he refused to move. The threatened revolution in Berlin had been held back from November 8 till November 9, and on that historic day it was a race against time. At 9.15 a.m. the news was telephoned from Spa that the generals were about to inform their master that the army would not support him in a civil war. At 11 a message came that he had resolved to abdicate and that the formula would reach the capital in half an hour. Meanwhile the workers were pouring into the streets, and the deposition might be proclaimed at any moment. When the half hour elapsed without the promised formula, Prince Max vainly endeavoured to reach the monarch by telephone. As a last chance of saving the monarchy, he announced that the Kaiser had decided to resign ; that the Chancellor would only remain in office till the questions involved in the resignation of the monarch, the renunciation of the Crown Prince, and the creation of a Regency were settled ; that he intended to propose to the Regent the appointment of Ebert as Chancellor and the election of a Constituent Assembly by universal suffrage. This declaration was known at midday, but it came too late to affect events. At 2 p.m. Scheidemann proclaimed the Republic from the Reichstag building, and the Hohenzollern dynasty, after ruling for five centuries, was at an end. A few minutes later the promised announcement arrived, in which William II abdicated as Emperor but not as King of Prussia. This crazy formula was worthy of the ruler whose short-sighted obstinacy had frustrated the efforts of his patriotic Chancellor to save the dynasty. A Regency for his grandson might have prevented the Nazi revolution, for the republic aroused little enthusiasm in what Herder once described as the land of obedience.

In her delightful volumes *The Story of My Life*, Queen Marie of Roumania put her country on the map. The first describes the Courts of her grandmother Queen Victoria, her uncle Alexander III, and her great-uncle, the childless Ernst, Duke of Coburg, whose heir was her father, the Duke of Edinburgh. The second contains a vivid picture of the Court at Bucharest when King Carol and Carmen Sylva were on the throne. For a woman throbbing with vitality and with ideas of her own it was torture to be kept in a gilded cage, though her respect for the ruler's fine qualities steadily increased. Her husband, Prince Ferdinand, emerges as a kindly mediocrity, paralysed by his inferiority complex and overawed by his formidable uncle. With Roumania's intervention in the Balkan conflict and the accession of Ferdinand in 1914 the author becomes a national figure. The third volume, fortified by copious extracts from the Queen's diaries, gives a dramatic picture of the world war seen through Roumanian spectacles—the long hesitation of Bratiano, the plunge into the whirlpool in 1916, the collapse of the army, the dictated treaty, the re-entry into the struggle when the tide turned, the triumphant return to Bucharest. Throughout these tempestuous years the spirited, talented and beautiful Queen was the soul of the national defence. It was only now, after twenty years of residence, that she took Roumania to her heart : in her own words, she felt herself the mother of an enormous family. When all the leading men in the country had virtually given up hope, she retained her faith in the triumph of the allies. At the end of 1915 Czernin, the Austrian Minister, told her that the fate of Roumania was in her hands, for the King would follow her advice. Now was the time to join the Central Powers : it was the last chance of coming in on the winning side. The Queen was reduced to tears, but her will was unbroken. " You say my word would be decisive. I do not know if this is true, but I do know that I cannot act otherwise. I should die of grief if Roumania were to go to war against England." England, she reminded her importunate visitor, always won the last battle.

Two out of the many post-war Dictators have employed autobiography as an instrument of propaganda. Mussolini compiled his record at the suggestion of Richard Washburn Child, American Ambassador in Rome 1921–1924, who edited the manuscript and sung his praises in an ecstatic Foreword. " It is all his, and so like him ! . . . . I have a deep affection for him. . . . Curzon used to refer to him as that absurd man.

Time has shown that he is both wise and humane. . . . In our time it may be shrewdly forecast that no man will exhibit dimensions of permanent greatness equal to those of Mussolini." The volume thus heralded by American trumpets and published in 1928 differs from *Mein Kampf* in its brevity and its lack of ideological background. The first time the Ambassador saw him, shortly before the march on Rome, he inquired about his visitor's programme. "Work and discipline" was the unhesitating reply. There is no word about race or the Jews, nothing about a new gospel for mankind. It is more of a narrative and less of an academic discourse : for Mussolini's philosophy we must turn to his famous article on Fascism contributed to the Italian Encyclopedia. It is in fact far less interesting both as a book and as a revelation of personality, and it enjoyed very limited success. Dictated in the brief intervals of a busy ruler's life, it is a second-rate performance in comparison with Hitler's maturely considered and frequently revised manifesto. Yet there are striking similarities. There is the same picture of the ignominious collapse of democracy, of the craving of a great people for a firm hand at the helm, of the emergence of a superman at the psychological moment, the same brazen self-confidence, the same shrill invective against all who stood in his way. No political apologia exudes a more childish conviction of infallibility.

The larger half of the volume is devoted to the years of apprenticeship and the struggle for power. How much is discreetly omitted in these seemingly artless pages, how much is transformed, we may learn from Megaro's documented biography. No autobiography, however, wholly fails to reveal its author's personality, and Mussolini has a dramatic story to tell. Ever a fighter he knew hunger and imprisonment ; he was expelled from the Socialist party ; he fought duels ; he learned to fly ; he was badly wounded in the war. He pays tributes to his parents, his wife, " a wise and excellent woman," and his brother Arnaldo ; but he declares that no political friends ever had the slightest influence on him. Dictators are always lonely men. " I found the crown lying in the mud," remarked Napoleon ; " I picked it up and put it on my head." According to Mussolini there was no rival for the first place when he and his Blackshirts marched on Rome. " Nobody wanted the responsibility of power." D'Annunzio is hailed as a forerunner of the national revival, but he had few followers. " The Fascisti are the aristocracy of Italy." Fascism was an insurrection of national dignity, the revolt of dynamic youth against moribund middle-class mediocrity. The old gang of Liberal Italy, Giolitti, Orlando, Bonomi, Facta, are dismissed with contempt while Nitti is pursued with cries of rancorous hate. The Socialists, the Populari, the Liberals, the Conservatives are all brushed disdainfully aside as out of date. He admits that Matteotti was murdered by Fascists, but explains that they were completely outside the responsible elements of the party. After six years of power he looks back with pride and forward with boundless confidence. " Mine is a policy of peace. To-day in Italy we breathe the open air ; life is exposed to the light of day. I am forty-five and I feel the vigour of my work and my thought. I have annihilated in myself every egotism. I feel that all Italians understand and love me ; I know that only he is loved who leads without weakness, without deviation, with disinterestedness and full faith." Such are the illusions of our supermen.

Hitler's autobiography, the last item on our list, is in a class by itself, for it was written several years before the author took the helm. *Mein Kampf* is thus a programme as well as a narrative. The first volume was dictated to his secretary, Rudolf Hess, during their brief imprisonment after the Munich *putsch* of 1923, the second was composed after his release. Beginning with his boyhood near Linz, he describes in detail his experiences in Vienna, where he learned to hate Jews and Marxists and to dream of uniting Teutonic Austria with the Reich. The move to Munich in 1912 was followed by volunteer service in the German army on the Western front. The granting of permission in response to his appeal is described as the happiest day of his life. The collapse of 1918, announced while he was suffering from gas in a Prussian hospital, inspired him with the determination to raise his adopted country from the dust. If he had heard of Chatham he would have adopted his proud words : " I know that I can save my country, and I know that nobody else can." On leaving the army he began his campaign in Munich and drew up the National Socialist programme in twenty-five points. In his own words, he discovered that he could speak. He describes the growth of his audiences, and on finding that two thousand people had come to hear him he was confident that the battle was won. Some day, he could not tell when, he would be not merely Chancellor but the effective ruler of his country.

Mein Kampf is a curious mixture of idealism and fanaticism, sanity and rant. The first thing that strikes the reader is that it is the work of an ill-educated man, stuffed with undigested fragments of knowledge. Swallowing the fantastic nonsense of Gobineau and Houston Stewart Chamberlain, Hitler bases the community of his dreams on the conception of racial purity. The Aryans, he tells us, are the builders of civilization, the Jews its destroyers. When he speaks of the Jews, to whom he denies all virtues and all rights, he raves like a lunatic. Next to keeping the blood-stream pure comes the exaltation of country over town. Blood and soil ! he cries. Let the maximum number of German citizens till the earth ! He detests the life of the cities with their moral and intellectual temptations. In the noisy factories, the overcrowded tenements, the stuffy beer-houses, men talk, speculate, criticise, fall a prey to Socialist and Communist agitators. Let them live in the open air, in contact with nature, where there is room to breathe and to multiply !

The third article is the doctrine of leadership, the guidance of the nation by a representative man instead of by transient Chancellors and dissolving coalitions. A steady course, he argues, can only be pursued when a single unchallengeable will is in control, acting in the interests of the nation but without asking its permission before decisions are taken. All parties in consequence must disappear except that to which the Leader belongs, and minorities must hold their tongue. In the interest of national strength the individual must give way to the state. Children must be brought up to profess the opinions of the Leader, whatever their parents may say. The place of woman is in the home, her duty to have the maximum number of healthy children. Finally he summons his countrymen, when they have regained their armed strength and secured an ally, to strike down France, the deadly enemy, as a preliminary to the march into Southern Russia. When the book was written he had no wish for colonies overseas : what he desired was new territory in Europe, " where the German peasant can breed children." The duty of diplomacy was to prepare the way for the titanic struggle on which the future of the nation depended. There is no trace of the animosity against the Churches which he displayed after his accession to power, though it is clearly revealed in Rauschning's *Hitler speaks*.

No more explosive work has appeared since Marx's *Capital*, and all other political apologias taken together have not enjoyed the circulation or the influence of *Mein Kampf*. Millions of copies have been printed. Selections are read aloud in Labour camps, and from the beginning of 1936 a copy was supplied to wedded couples of Aryan blood. While other political autobiographies have had to make their way by their own merits, Hitler has had the machinery of official propaganda to speed his offspring on its way. Among the books which have made history, however short our list, its place is assured, for the gospel of totalitarian government, rabid anti-Semitism and calculated aggression proclaimed when the author was a private citizen was carried out to the letter when he became the most powerful man in the world. It has been truly said that *Mein Kampf* never lets you down.

Political autobiographies no longer occupy the honoured place as historical authorities which they held a century ago when Carlyle was writing on the French Revolution. The argument that the actor must know best what he had done, or attempted to do, breaks down again and again when it is put to the test of contemporary evidence. Among the memorable achievements of Ranke, the greatest of professional historians, none was more needed, and none was more fruitful, than his challenge to historical memoirs, and the critical analyses scattered through his sixty volumes are an essential part of a historian's education. Written as a rule in old age or when the actor's work is done, sometimes with failing grip and often with inadequate documentary material, the political apologia needs to be studied with exceptionally critical eyes. Even when the good faith of a witness is beyond cavil and he has nothing to conceal, tricks of memory are inevitable as the perspective changes with advancing years. It is almost always a case of *Dichtung und Wahrheit*. Add the tendencious omissions in most specimens of this type of literature, the deliberate or subconscious misrepresentation of individuals, situations and events, the urge to shift responsibility for errors on to other shoulders, the temptation both of great and small men to blow their own trumpet, and we shall begin to realize that the ground under our feet is not nearly so solid as it appears. As Sainte-Beuve tersely remarks, *Chacun n'écrit que ce qui le sert.* Only if contemporary records are at his disposal can the conscientious historian move with confident tread. The most dangerous guides are not those whose flaming vanity or priggish self-righteousness put the reader on guard from the start, but those who attempt to conceal their bias behind a smokescreen of impartiality.

THE FRENCH REVOLUTION AS A WORLD FORCE.

THE French Revolution is the most important event in the life of modern Europe. Herder compared it to the Reformation and the rise of Christianity. It deserves to be ranked with those two great movements in history, because, like them, it destroyed many of the landmarks of the world in which generations of men had passed their lives, because it was a movement towards a completer humanity, and because it too was a religion, with its doctrines, its apostles, and its martyrs. It brought on the stage of human affairs forces which have moulded our actions ever since and have taken a permanent place among the formative influences of civilization. It stood above all for equality of opportunity, declaring each one of us, regardless of birth, colour, nationality or creed, to be possessed of inalienable rights.

As travellers and publicists of the eighteenth century foresaw the approach of the Revolution, so historians seek its roots in the generations and indeed in the centuries which preceded it. Louis Blanc argued that no man could date its beginning, since all nations had contributed to produce it. "All the revolts of the past unite and lose themselves in it, like rivers in the sea. It is the glory of France to have performed the work of the human race at the price of her own blood." The famous socialist commences his narrative with John Hus, but this is to pile a needless burden on our backs. It is enough for us to remember that the Reformation had challenged ecclesiastical authority; that the doctrine of the supremacy of conscience was extended from the sphere of religious belief to that of political action; that the growing claims of the human spirit were nourished on the doctrines of the Law of Nature and the Social Contract; that the yoke of a dying feudalism and a corrupt autocracy bred increasing exasperation among nations rapidly advancing in wealth and education; that the explosion occurred in France sooner than elsewhere, not because her condition was more intolerable, but owing to the converging influence of certain political, financial, intellectual, and personal factors. It is the supreme achievement of Albert Sorel to have exhibited the Revolution, which had appeared to some observers as the subversion and to others as the regeneration of the world, as the natural result of the history of France and Europe.

Every schoolboy, as Macaulay would say, knows that the French Revolution sprang from the combination of material grievances and intellectual ferment, and that it was the latter which made the former more fiercely resented. Among the factors which compelled the French bourgeoisie to think and to ask questions about public affairs two stand out pre-eminent —the writings of Rousseau and the revolt of the American Colonies. It is a curious coincidence that neither of the two men who have played perhaps the greatest part in the political life of modern France were Frenchmen ; for the one was born in Corsica and the other in Geneva. The style of Jean Jacques was an open passport in the land where literary expression is honoured as the greatest of the arts ; and his challenge to the social and political order of the age of Louis XV was delivered with the force and directness of a blow. " L'homme est né libre," begins the *Contrat Social*, " et partout il est dans les fers." Here in a single sentence was ammunition enough to lay the battlements of feudal Europe in ruins. Like other great explosive influences he combines destruction with construction, mixing criticism with hope. Society is evil, but man is by nature good. To substitute the rule of the people for the tyranny of one, to replace the Roman Church, with its elaborate institutions and dogmas, by the natural pieties implanted in the human heart, to restore the simplicity of family life, to humanize education, to follow, in a word, the dictates of reason and conscience : here was the way to build a new and happier world.

If Rousseau's burning pages were devoured by every one who could read, the revolt of the American colonies, in the success of which France played a decisive part, proved that a determined people could change its government and create a prosperous and orderly society without king, nobility, or a state church. The impression on the Old World was deepened by the ringing sentences in which Jefferson proclaimed the rights of man and of peoples. " We hold these truths to be self-evident," runs the Declaration of Independence, " that all men are created equal ; that they are endowed by their Creator with certain inalienable rights, among them life, liberty and the pursuit of happiness ; that to secure these rights Governments are instituted among men, deriving their just powers from the consent of the governed ; that whenever any form of government becomes destructive of these ends, it is the right of the people to alter or abolish it, and to institute a new Government, laying its foundation on such principles and organizing its power in such form as to them shall seem most likely to effect their safety and happiness. Prudence indeed will dictate that governments long established shall not be changed for light and transient causes ; and all experience hath shown that mankind are more disposed to suffer, while evils are sufferable, than to right themselves by abolishing the forms to which they are accustomed. But when a long train of abuses and usurpations, pursuing invariably the same object, evinces a design to reduce them under absolute despotism, it is their right, it is their duty, to throw off such government and to provide new guards for their future security." The principles enunciated in the historic document which founded a nation were reiterated in greater detail in the constitutions of the separate states ; and a few years later a French assembly was to borrow not only the spirit but in some cases the very words of its transatlantic model.

When the States-General met at Versailles in May 1789 for the first time since 1614, neither the king nor his advisers realized the importance of the decision they had taken. On ascending the throne Louis XVI had summoned Turgot to reform the finances ; but within two years the great minister had fallen and the plans of Necker, his successor, were ruined by intervention in the American war. After the fall of Necker in 1781 the Government drifted from expedient to expedient, until there was no escape save in an appeal to the nation. They were aware that financial assistance would have to be purchased by concessions and reforms, but it never occurred to them that they might be faced with the demand for the transformation of the traditional structure of the state and society. Their forecast was correct within certain limits, for the members of the States-General brought no mandate for revolution. The complaints and demands of the people were set forth in the Cahiers—a corpus of documents so voluminous that even to-day they have not all been printed—which photograph the mind of the nation in the spring of 1789. France demands reform, not revolution. The enemy is not the monarchy but feudalism. The cry is not for self-government but for equality before the law—equality of rights, equality of burdens, equality of opportunities. Though each of the three Estates drew up its own Cahiers, there is much in common in their political demands. All classes were weary of inefficient despotism, and the prevailing sentiment favoured something in the nature of the British Constitution, with the executive in the hands of the King and the control of the purse in the hands of the Estates. But while the Cahiers of the *noblesse* and the clergy leave most of the graver evils unspecified and un-censured, those of the country parishes give vent to the peasantry's hatred of the feudal system, with its oppressive manorial rights, at once odious to the self-respect and detri-mental to the economic interests of the peasant. And while the countryside demands the abolition of feudalism and serf-dom, the bourgeoisie claims the removal of the régime of privilege which reserved the plums of the public service for the *noblesse* and the higher ecclesiastics. Mirabeau was the man of the hour.

The members of the States-General were necessarily in-experienced, but the standard of ability and character was high. A conflict of opinion and interest between the two privileged classes and the Tiers État was inevitable, but the peaceful triumph of the latter might possibly have been secured by the influence of a King who combined insight with courage. It is the tragedy of the Revolution that the monarch lacked the resolution to cope with his difficulties ; that, though he was a convinced advocate of reform, he was surrounded by its bitterest enemies ; that the worst of his evil counsellors was the Queen ; and that his vacillation destroyed the confidence and good will of the reformers. The oath of the Tennis Court, pledging the members not to separate till a Constitution had been established, pronounced the determination of the Assembly to challenge and override the authority of the Crown if the programme which had brought them to Versailles could be realized in no other way. And the destruction of the Bastille on July 14 announced that what we should now call direct action was an instrument of incalculable potency in the hands of an exasperated people.

Though the States-General met without any intention to wrest the rudder from the royal pilot, the hostility of the Court wrought such a rapid change that the champions of the British Constitution who dominated the Assembly at the start found themselves displaced by men who held that the executive power could not be allowed to remain in untrustworthy hands. Within three months power had passed to the representatives of the nation, and the sovereignty of the people was formally proclaimed. Though no one of note except Brissot and Condorcet asked for a republic till the autumn of 1790, the spell of monarchy had been broken and the path lay open to the onrush of undisciplined democracy.

After Paris had struck at the absolute monarchy the peasants in many parts of France rose against the châteaux. Stories of destruction, which we may read in the pages of Taine, came flooding into Versailles, and on August 3, 1789, the Assembly was informed that property was at the mercy of brigands and that no castle or convent was safe. The revolt against feudal burdens might have been foreseen, but the crisis found the Government unprepared. The Court advised the nobles that nothing but speedy surrender could save them, and Barère warned them that his friends would move the abolition of feudal and fiscal privilege. They determined to anticipate the attack by capitulation, and at a conference on the same evening a wealthy Duke was deputed to announce the voluntary sacrifice of his order. The drama of August 4 has often been described—how the owners of vast estates and the bearers of historic names laid their immemorial privileges on the altar of the fatherland ; how the nobles surrendered their feudal dues, their jurisdiction, their immunity from taxation, their monopoly of high office, their game laws ; how serfdom was abolished and all employments were thrown open to all classes ; how the clergy, vying with the *noblesse*, bared their bosoms to the sacrificial knife and proposed the commutation of tithe. History was being made so quickly that a member at one moment passed a note to the President begging him to adjourn, as the members were losing their heads ; but the appeal was in vain. The sitting continued far into the night, and when it concluded a peaceful revolution had been accomplished or at any rate inaugurated. The demolition of feudalism, the story of which has been authoritatively told in Aulard's *La Révolution et le Régime Féodal*, was not completed till 1793 ; but the Rubicon had been crossed. The absolute monarchy had disappeared with the Bastille, and the power of the *noblesse* was shattered on August 4. Historic France was melting like snow before the sun. As far back as January 1 Abbé Sieyès had published his celebrated pamphlet *Qu'est ce que le Tiers État ?* "We must ask ourselves three questions. First : What is the Third Estate ? Everything. Second : What has it been hitherto in our political system ? Nothing. Third : What does it ask ? To become something." Its ambition had now been realized.

The events which had occurred between the publication of the pamphlet and August 4 may be compendiously described as the emergence of the bourgeoisie.

When the *ancien régime* had thus received notice to quit, the Assembly proceeded to lay the foundation of the new democracy ; and before a constitution could be framed its principles had to be defined. Several of the Cahiers had demanded a declaration of rights, and during July lists were produced by Lafayette, Sieyès, Mounier, and other ingenious minds. The draft of Sieyès found most favour, but the text selected by the Assembly was shorter and bore no author's name. After a week's further discussion it was reduced from twenty-four articles to seventeen, and by August 16 it had been adopted. The Declaration of the Rights of Man is of such interest and is so rarely reproduced in the text-books that I will give it in full.

" The Representatives of the French people constituted in a National Assembly," runs the preamble, " considering that ignorance, forgetfulness or contempt for the Rights of Man are the sole causes of public evils and of the corruption of governments, have resolved to set forth in a solemn declaration the natural, inalienable, and sacred rights of man, in order that this Declaration, constantly before the eyes of all the members of the social body, should unceasingly remind them of their rights and duties ; that the acts of the legislature and executive, by being compared at every moment with the object of all political institutions, may be more respected ; and in order that the demands of the citizens, henceforth based on simple and incontestable principles, may always be directed to the maintenance of the Constitution and happiness of all. In consequence the National Assembly recognizes and declares, in presence and under the auspices of the Supreme Being, the following Rights of Man and the Citizen.

1. Men are born and remain free and equal in rights. Social distinctions can only be based on expediency.

2. The object of every political association is the maintenance of the natural and imprescriptible rights of man. These rights are liberty, property, security and resistance to oppression.

3. The principle of all sovereignty resides in the nation. No corporation and no individual can exercise authority which does not expressly emanate from it.

4. Liberty consists in the power to do whatever does not

injure another. Thus the exercise of the natural rights of each has no limits but those which assure to others the enjoyment of the same rights. These limits can only be determined by the law.

5. The law may only forbid actions injurious to society. What is not forbidden by law cannot be prevented, and no one can be compelled to do what it does not command.

6. Law is the expression of the general will. All citizens have the right to share personally or through their representatives in its formation. It must be the same for all, both in protection and in punishment. All citizens being equal in its eyes are equally eligible to all dignities and public posts according to their capacities and their virtues.

7. None can be accused, arrested, or detained except as prescribed by the law.

8. None can be punished except in virtue of a law promulgated before the offence and legally applied.

9. Every one being presumed innocent till he is declared guilty, if it is deemed essential to arrest him any violence beyond what is necessary to secure his person must be avoided.

10. None may be molested for his opinions, even on religion, provided that their expression does not threaten public order.

11. Free communication of thoughts and opinion is one of the most precious of the rights of man. Therefore every citizen can speak, write, and print freely, subject to responsibility for the abuse of such liberty in cases determined by the law.

12. The guarantee of the rights of man and citizens necessitates a public force. This force is instituted for the advantage of all, not for that of those who command it.

13. The expenses of the public force should be equally distributed among all citizens according to their capacity to pay.

14. Citizens have the right to confirm for themselves or through their representatives the necessity of taxation, to grant it, to supervise its expenditure, to determine its amount, its character, and its duration.

15. Society has the right to demand from every public servant an account of his stewardship.

16. A society without the guarantee of rights and the separation of powers has no Constitution.

17. Property being a sacred and inviolable right, none can be deprived of it unless public necessity, legally determined, clearly demands it, and on payment of fair compensation."

The Declaration embraces both theory and practice, but the concrete provisions are governed by the doctrine of the opening article. Though the word liberty occurs several times, the dominant principle of this momentous pronouncement is equality of rights, and it is this principle above all which made the French Revolution a world force. It was criticized by some of the keenest intellects of the age from different standpoints but with equal severity. " The pretended rights of these theorists are all extremes," wrote Burke ; " and in proportion as they are metaphysically true they are morally and politically false. The rights of man are in a sort of middle, incapable of definition, but not impossible to be discerned. Far am I from denying the real rights of man. If civil society be made for the advantage of man, all the advantages for which it is made become his right. It is an institution of beneficence ; and law itself is only beneficence acting by a rule. Men have a right to live by that rule. They have a right to justice. They have a right to the fruits of their industry and to the means of making their industry fruitful. They have a right to the acquisitions of their parents ; to the nourishment and improvement to their offspring ; to instruction in life and to consolation in death. Whatever each man can separately do, without trespassing on others, he has a right to do for himself ; and he has a right to a fair portion of all which society, with its combinations of skill and force, can do in his favour. In this partnership all men have equal rights, but not to equal things. He that has but five shillings in the partnership has as good a right to it as he that has five hundred pounds. But he has not a right to an equal dividend in the product of the joint stock ; and as to the share of power which each individual ought to have in the management of the State, that is a thing to be settled by convention."

While Burke contemptuously rejected the theoretical approach to politics, Gentz, the most brilliant and unwearying continental opponent of the Revolution, frankly accepted the Law of Nature and the Social Contract. In an essay on the Declaration written in 1792, he hails the document as a new gospel which has already produced something 'ike a revolution in the mind of Europe, and accepts its underlying assumption. " That man, in being born, brings with him rights of which nothing but his own will can deprive him, nobody doubts ; nor that he only surrenders a portion of those rights on entering into society in order that the rest may be guaranteed."

But he complains that it was a colossal error to say nothing of his duties, and to imply that the source of evils lay outside man in political institutions and machinery. To the governing clause, " Men are born and remain free and equal in rights," he rejoins that no one is free, since each must surrender part of his freedom to society. " It is a garish mixture in which there is not a shadow of philosophical sequence or precision, the work of a moment, an enthusiastic whim decked out in the mask of philanthropy and patriotism. Moreover, never have human rights been so trampled on as in the past three years."

Bentham's criticism in his little tract *Anarchical Fallacies* was even more hostile. " Natural rights are simple nonsense ; natural and imprescriptible rights are rhetorical nonsense, nonsense upon stilts." Abstract rights are a contradiction in terms ; for rights, which are claims to liberty, no less than laws, which are infringements of liberty, must be defended by a reference to utility. Liberty, for instance, is dependent on capacity, since many people need protection owing to weakness, ignorance, or imprudence. Inequality is condemned not as an injustice but as tending to diminish happiness. The first requisite of happiness is security ; if the claims of equality conflict with it, they must be sacrificed. Bentham accepted the Rights of Man as desirable in practice, though wrong in theory ; and his doctrine that each was to count for one and none for more than one stated in another form the French contention that the world should be adjusted to the needs of the common man.

" The declaration of the Rights of Man was meagre and confused," writes Lord Acton, " and Bentham found a malignant pleasure in tearing it to pieces. But it is a triumphant proclamation of the doctrine that human obligations are not all assignable to contract, or to interest, or to force. This single page of print outweighs libraries and is stronger than all the armies of Napoleon. The Assembly, which had abolished the past at the beginning of August, attempted at the end of the month to institute and regulate the future. These are its abiding works, and the perpetual heritage of the Revolution. With them a new era dawned upon mankind." When the Terror was over and the national frontiers secured, some of the practical implications of the Declaration were worked out, above all in the domain of education and the codification of the law.

The initial demand for equality of rights led by rapid stages to the formulation of the doctrine of the sovereignty of the people. The King had been assumed to be the champion of his subjects against feudal oppression. When, however, he emerged rather as the enemy than the patron of the political and social reformation, the notion that sovereignty resided in the people and its authorized representatives spread with the rapidity of a prairie fire. Theoretical royalism lingered on till the flight to Varennes convinced France that her ruler had ceased to belong to the nation, and that at last she must act for herself.

The French people had become self-conscious in their victorious struggle with the Crown and its advisers, but no sooner was it at an end than a new conflict arose. The principles of '89 were a challenge to all the Great Powers in Europe; and though we need not argue with Ranke that an armed collision was inevitable, it would have required exceptional self-control on both sides to avoid. The proximate cause of the war was the gathering of the *émigrés* in the Rhineland, which with the assent of its German rulers they used as a base for their counter-revolutionary operations. When war was declared in March 1792 at the instigation of Brissot, the Girondin leader, his policy was resisted by Robespierre and other Jacobin chiefs. When, however, the first skirmishes revealed the weakness of the French troops, and when the Duke of Brunswick launched his brutal Manifesto, marched into France and captured Verdun, the monarchy was overthrown and the nation rose in its might to hurl back the invader. Men only realize how dearly they love their country when it is threatened or visited by some overwhelming calamity ; and now France was summoned to defend not only the soil of the fatherland but the precious conquests of the Revolution. In a remarkable forecast in his reply to Burke in 1791 Macintosh foretold that, if an anti-revolutionary alliance were to be formed, it would have no other effect in France than to animate patriotism and banish division, while failure would set in motion forces that would subvert the old governments of Europe.

While patriotism is as old as the instinct of human association, nationalism as an articulate creed issued from the volcanic fires of the French Revolution. The tide of battle turned at Valmy ; and on the evening after the skirmish Goethe, who had accompanied his friend and master, Karl August of

Weimar, replied to a request for his opinion in the historic words, " From to-day begins a new era, and you will be able to say that you were present at its birth." He was right. The titanic energy of a nation which since 1789 had devoted itself to the task of internal reform now turned to meet the foe. The second stage of the Revolution had begun, and nationalism blossomed forth in irresistible strength. The lawyers and publicists who had gathered at Versailles in 1789 had entertained no thought of aggression, and the Constitution of 1791 expressly declared that France would never fight for conquests. But when blood began to flow and the achievements of the Revolution were imperilled, the French people turned into a community of supermen whose volcanic energy scattered the hosts of feudal Europe like chaff before the wind.

It was not to be expected that the victorious troops of the Republic would halt when the invader had been expelled. The inherited doctrine of *les frontières naturelles*—the Rhine, the Alps, and the Pyrenees—was proclaimed anew by Danton and echoed from a thousand throats. But the programme of the statesmen of the *ancien régime* was enriched by a new element of revolutionary idealism. The people which had won its liberties and defended them against foreign attack could now aid others to follow in its footsteps. On November 19, 1792, after Dumouriez' victory in Belgium, a decree was passed which reverberated through Europe. " The National Convention declares, in the name of the French nation, that it will accord fraternity and succour to all peoples who may desire to recover their liberty, and charges the executive to order the generals to rescue the peoples and defend the citizens who have suffered or may be called upon to suffer for the cause of liberty." This celebrated decree carried a stage further the universalism which had marked the French Revolution from the outset. The Declaration of the Rights of Man substituted theory for custom and reason for tradition. The new evangelists proclaimed their gospel in French, but they believed that its music would sound as sweet in any other tongue. For the first two years they were content to allow it to make its way in the world by the intrinsic force of its appeal ; but when the New France and the Old Europe were locked in deadly embrace, the military value of propaganda became apparent. " In the first moment of peril," writes Sorel, "it had been all patriotism, and in the first moments of deliverance all enthusiasm ; and now the hour of pride arrived." The Convention's offer of assistance to peoples to gain their liberty, at first sight an almost quixotically unselfish formula, proved merely a cloak for aggression, since French armies were the judges of whether the peoples were desirous of liberty, and assumed that it could only be enjoyed by annexation to the Republic. Thus in the space of a few months in the summer and autumn of 1792 militant nationalism revealed not only its magical power of mobilizing the latent strength of a people, but the temptation to a virile nation to carry fire and sword into the lands of its neighbours.

The fall of the Bastille and the Declaration of the Rights of Man put into acts and words the muffled aspirations of the masses all over Europe, and gave to the humble and dis-inherited a new sense of human dignity. When France in trumpet tones demanded the downfall of feudalism, proclaimed the equality of burdens, and declared every man possessed of certain inalienable rights, generous hearts were thrilled by the warmth and the glory of the sunrise. The windows of the prison-house seemed to fly open and the light of liberty streamed in. Enthusiasm for the Revolution was intensified by the conviction of its universal significance, which was recognized both by those who took part in it and those who watched it from afar. Condorcet proclaimed that a good law was good for all, just as a true proposition was true for all. The orators on the Seine were fully conscious that the eyes of the world were upon them. " Your laws will be the laws of Europe if you are worthy of them," declared Mirabeau to the Constituent Assembly ; " the Revolution will make the round of the globe." " If we succeed," cried André Chénier, the poet, " the destiny of Europe will be changed. Men will regain their rights and the people their sovereignty. Kings struck by the success of our labours and the example of our monarch may share their power with their peoples ; and per-haps the peoples, happier than we, may obtain a free and equitable constitution without passing through our troubles. Then the name of France will be blessed upon earth." " Who-ever regards this Revolution as exclusively French," echoed Mallet du Pan, the eloquent Swiss publicist, " is incapable of pronouncing judgement upon it." " It is one of those events," wrote Gentz, the German Burke, " which belong to the whole human race. It is of such dimensions that it is hardly per-missible to occupy oneself with any subordinate interest, of such magnitude that posterity will eagerly inquire how contemporaries in every country thought and felt about it, how they argued and how they acted." Friends and foes of the principles of '89 were at one in emphasizing the compelling power of their appeal; and men like Burke and Tom Paine, Kant and Joseph de Maistre, who agreed in nothing else, were convinced that the problems raised by the Revolution concerned humanity as a whole. "As I look at the map of the world," cried Anacharsis Cloots, " it seems to me as if all other countries had vanished and only France exists, with her rays filling the universe."

To measure the immediate and ultimate effects of the Revolution as a world force, with its three doctrines of equal rights, popular sovereignty and nationality, would require a course of lectures; and we must content ourselves with a glance at the two most highly educated states outside France at the end of the eighteenth century. The first voices in England were those of congratulation. Fox's exclamation that the fall of the Bastille was much the greatest and best event that had ever happened expressed, if in somewhat exuberant terms, the disinterested satisfaction with which the great majority of Englishmen witnessed the downfall of a despotic government. To men like Price and Priestley, Wordsworth, Southey and Coleridge, it was the beginning of a new era of progress and enlightenment, the realization of those generous visions of perfectibility which floated before the noblest minds in the latter part of the eighteenth century and received their classic expression in Condorcet's *Sketch of the Progress of the Human Mind*.

> Bliss was it in that dawn to be alive,
> But to be young was very heaven.

The publication of Burke's *Reflections on the French Revolution* in the autumn of 1790 gave a rude shock to public opinion. He had been untouched by the generous emotions which affected most of his contemporaries, and the women's march on Versailles convinced him that nothing but evil would result. His argument was vitiated by ignorance of the political and economic condition of France. He failed to realize that the *ancien régime* was rotten to the core, that feudalism was doomed, that the Assembly had already lifted an immense burden from the shoulders of the people. But the permanent value of the *Reflections* lies not in the criticism of the Revolution but in the discussion of the method of political change, which in turn involved the still wider problem of the nature of human society. To the view that society consisted of an association of individuals bound together by a contract for certain definite and limited purposes he opposed the conception of a living organism whose character is determined by its history, and whose members are linked to one another and to the whole by a network of invisible influences. In this recognition of the instinctive and historical element in human association lies Burke's supreme claim to greatness as a political thinker. The work is not only the finest exposition of the philosophic basis of conservatism ever written, but a declaration of the principles of evolution, continuity, and solidarity which must find a place in all sound political thinking. Against the pretensions of the individual he sets the collective reason ; against the demands of the present he sets the accumulated experience of the past ; for natural rights he offers social rights ; for liberty he offers law. Society means to him a partnership between those who are living, those who are dead, and those who are yet to be born. But in his protest against a mechanical individualism he falls into the opposite error. The present ceases to be merely the heir of the past and becomes its slave. States are denied the power of self-determination inherent in every living society, and hoary abuses find shelter under the mantle of historical tradition and prescriptive right. Burke has much to give us, but we require other teachers as well.

King George III said it was a book which every gentleman should read, and it was rapturously hailed as the manifesto of the counter-revolution by the governing classes throughout Europe. In England it made conservative readers more conservative and radical readers more radical. Macintosh replied for the liberal bourgeoisie in his *Vindiciae Gallicae*, but with the coming of the Terror he recanted his liberalism. Tom Paine's *Rights of Man*, written for what Burke called the swinish multitude, thoroughly scared the upper classes ; for the unflinching appeal to natural rights, the outspoken contempt for the English Constitution, the audacious attack on the King, and the confident assumption that monarchy and aristocracy would speedily disappear from Europe, seemed a confirmation of their worst fears. The alarm increased when it was known that the book was selling by tens of thousands, and that political societies of radical views were springing up like mushrooms. With the overthrow of the French monarchy in 1792, and the execution of the King and the outbreak of war in 1793, England was stampeded into panic with Pitt at her head. The majority of the Whigs joined the Government, while Fox and Grey, with a handful of courageous followers, kept alive the flickering flame of liberalism with infinite difficulty. The hands of the clock were put back for a generation. But for the Revolution Parliament might have been reformed, Nonconformists freed from their disabilities, and the Slave Trade abolished before the end of the eighteenth century. Not till nearly forty years later had England sufficiently recovered from the shock to take up the work of reform where it had been dropped by Pitt like a hot coal.

"I observe that minds are fermenting in that Germany of yours," wrote Mirabeau to his Brunswick friend Mauvillon at the end of 1789, "but since your biains are petrified with slavery, the explosion will come with you much later than with us." The great tribune's prophecy proved correct, for the main impact of the Revolution was felt in Germany after the acute crisis in France was past. Early scenes of the compelling drama on the Seine were loudly applauded by the *élite* of Central Europe, and the war against France was never waged with enthusiasm. When military blunders, financial stringency, jealousy of Austria, and the complications of the Polish question induced Prussia to sign the Treaty of Basle in 1795, the causes of the collapse of the army of Frederick the Great before the levies of the Republic were eagerly canvassed and were generally agreed to lie in the lack of national spirit. But it was not till the stricken field of Jena that even the King realized he must break with the past. Those who approved and those who detested the principles of '89 agreed that Germany must learn the lessons of the years of strife. Throughout Europe a truceless conflict was in progress between the *ancien régime* and the ideas of '89 ; and when a State or a statesman decided to break with feudalism they were compelled to study and to some extent to adopt French models. As the abstract ideas of 1789 had appealed to the thinkers and writers of Germany, so their concrete results, stamped boldly across the map of Europe, converted experienced statesmen to a policy of sweeping reform. "If the nation is to be uplifted," declared Stein, "the submerged part must be given liberty, independence, property, and the protection of the laws"; and in his short-lived Ministry he began the emancipation of the peasants of Prussia and granted self-government

x

to the municipalities. " Your Majesty," declared Hardenberg to Frederick William III, " we must do from above what the French have done from below." He was as good as his word ; for he completed the creation of a free peasantry, and his work has been proudly claimed by Cavaignac as the most indubitable testimony to the action of the French Revolution on European society.

The most remarkable German tribute to the creative energies of the Revolution comes from Gneisenau. The great soldier detested French ideas and spent his life fighting the forces which they unchained ; but he recognized the strength that France had derived from them and was eager to apply the lesson. " One cause above all others has raised France to this pinnacle of greatness," he wrote after Jena ; " the Revolution awakened all her powers and gave to every individual a suitable field for his activity. What infinite aptitudes slumber undeveloped in the bosom of a nation ! In the breasts of thousands resides real genius. Why do not the Courts take steps to open up a career to it wherever it is found, to encourage talents and virtues whatever the rank ? Why did they not seize this opportunity to multiply their powers a thousandfold, to open to the simple bourgeois the Arc de Triomphe through which only the noble can now pass ? The new era requires more than old names, titles and parchments. The Revolution has set the whole strength of a nation in motion, and by the equalization of the different classes and the equal taxation of property converted the living strength in man and the dead strength in resources into a productive capital, and thereby upset the old relations of States. If other States decide to restore this equilibrium, they must appropriate the results of this Revolution. They will thus reap the double advantage of being able to mobilize their whole national strength against another Power and of escaping the danger of a revolution, which hangs over them so long as they refuse to obviate a forcible change by a voluntary transformation."

The French Revolution was compared by Klinger to the magic works of Medea, who cast the dead limbs of age into the boiling cauldron to emerge young and beautiful; and Georg Forster expressed the wish that his country would warm itself at the flame without being burned. The aspiration was destined in large measure to be fulfilled. While in England the reform movement was thrown back forty years by the earthquake, in Germany it was strengthened and accelerated.

The ringing blows of Thor's hammer awoke the nation from its slumbers. Political unification was deferred for a couple of generations, but the signal for deliverance from the thraldom of outworn institutions and ideas was sounded by the tocsin of 1789.

The wars unleashed by the Revolution swept away many familiar landmarks, among them the Holy Roman Empire, and profoundly modified the thought and sentiment of Europe. The challenge to tradition, bringing blood-stained anarchy in its train, led to a temporary revival of the Roman Church. During the course of the Revolution Joseph de Maistre foretold that, though directed against Catholicism and in favour of democracy, its results would be exactly the contrary ; and the next generation was to prove the partial accuracy of the forecast. The Papacy won back part of its power by suffering, and the violence of the attack on religion in France and in the countries she overran strengthened the reaction. The conclusion of the Concordat in 1802 merely recognized the change that had already occurred. The principle of authority seemed to regain its place. The aesthetic appeal was made in Chateaubriand's *Génie du Christianisme*, and the appeal to logic received its classic expression a few years later in de Maistre's treatise *Du Pape*. Yet the revival of religious practice was to prove only a passing phenomenon, for in its ultimate effect the French Revolution acted as a powerful solvent not only of ecclesiastical authority but of dogmatic belief. The growing secularization of thought, which was the main characteristic of the Age of Enlightenment, was accelerated by the movement which scoffed at tradition and proclaimed the supremacy of reason.

The most important long-range result of the Revolution has been the extension and application of the principle of equality. The conception of common citizenship made it difficult to maintain the disabilities of the Jews. Their case had been persuasively argued by Lessing and other philosophers before 1789 ; but it is to the Revolution, to Mirabeau and Grégoire, to the march of the French armies across Europe, that the Jews look back as the signal of their emancipation. It was equally difficult to tolerate the continuance of slavery. While the English abolitionists, mainly Quakers and Evangelicals, were largely animated by religious scruples, the Frenchmen who founded the Société des Amis des Noirs approached the problem from the standpoint of human rights.

The Constituent Assembly chivalrously declared the slaves in French possessions to be citizens of France ; and, though the dread of Jacobinism retarded abolition, its ultimate triumph was mainly due to the world-wide currency of French ideas. In a third direction the Revolution marks a turning point in the history of women. Though the National Assembly refused to receive a petition for female suffrage, the conception of equality led straight to the demand for equal treatment and equal opportunities for both sexes. A few ineffective champions of woman's rights had raised their voices before the Revolution, but it was the appeal to reason and the heightened sense of the worth of the individual implied in the Declaration of the Rights of Man which rendered the ultimate overthrow of the sex barrier inevitable. No work of the revolutionary era breathed the very spirit of the new gospel of equality of rights in fuller measure than Mary Wolstonecraft's *Rights of Women* ; and the arguments set forth in her eloquent plea are echoed in the cooler pages of Condorcet and Bentham, Hippel and Friedrich Schlegel.

Finally, the principle of equality gave an immense impetus to socialism. The members of the Constituent and Legislative Assemblies were bourgeois individualists, whose class selfishness moves the wrath not only of socialist historians such as Jaurès, Kropotkin and Mathiez, but also of the radical Aulard. With the overthrow of the Monarchy and the election of the Convention in 1792 by universal male suffrage a breach was made in the defences of the victorious bourgeoisie ; but when the Terror was over and the Convention dissolved in 1795, France returned to a restricted franchise. The Directory was the organ of the middle class. In such an atmosphere socialist ideas and socialist legislation were heresy ; yet the deeper forces set in motion by the great upheaval could not be confined to the political sphere. The nationalization of the land appears frequently in the pamphlets of the revolutionary decade ; and with the conspiracy of Babeuf in 1796 socialism ceased to be merely a speculative doctrine and became a political programme. Though not the first of its prophets, he was the first of its martyrs. More important than any direct advocacy was the effect of the sudden and wholesale changes of ownership and the attack on the sacredness of property. If, as the Declaration of the Rights of Man affirmed, we are born equal in rights, the contrasts between inherited wealth and inherited poverty was bound to provoke the demand that the community should assume control of the sources of production, in order to assure to every member a fair share in the necessities and amenities of life. When the conquest of at any rate theoretical political equality in most of the civilized countries of the world had been followed by the discovery how little the manual worker had profited, the minimum standard of life—a minimum of material well-being, education, leisure, opportunity—became the gospel of reformers. It is in this insistent and righteous claim of the common man for his place in the sun that the operation of the fundamental principle of the French Revolution is most clearly traceable at the present time.

The Revolution proclaimed the gospel of human rights and national self-determination, but its leaders never rose to the august conception of an all-embracing league of nations. The eccentric Prussian Baron, Anacharsis Cloots, who threw in his lot with the French reformers, led a deputation of foreign residents in Paris to the bar of the Assembly as delegates of the human race ; but his vision of a united humanity involved the disappearance of nationality. "As individuals have improved their lot by forming communities," he wrote in 1791, " so peoples will benefit by combining into a single nation. When national sentiment is abolished, the whole world will be the fatherland of every individual. There will be no more *émigrés* and no more war. The French Assembly will then be the representative body of the thousand departments of the world, each returning ten members, and Paris will be the capital of the globe, the Vatican of Reason. All the world will be a Garden of Eden, and East and West will embrace. The world will enjoy perpetual peace ; but to reach it there must be one more war against tyrants." Before East and West could embrace, Anacharsis Cloots perished by the guillotine.

After three years' experience of the war which Cloots had foretold and desired, another German of very different calibre sketched out a plan for a League of Nations which accepted the teaching of Sully, William Penn and the Abbé Saint-Pierre, and carried it a stage further. In his pregnant little treatise *Perpetual Peace* Kant seizes on the idea of self-government and rears upon it the ideal of a supernational organization. If law, based on reason and morality, is the foundation of the life of the State, it should equally regulate the relations of States to one another. The family of nations needs a constitution no less than France and Russia ; for so long as each

State recognizes no authority above itself, and no duty except to itself, wars will continue. There must therefore be some loose federal union, and its members must be self-governing. Not till selfish and capricious autocracies are replaced by representative institutions will a new system of relations between States become possible. Every people must become master of its own fate. For an autocracy to plunge into war is the easiest thing in the world, and requires no greater effort on the part of the ruler than to issue orders for a hunt. But if the consent of the citizens is required for the making of war, they will think twice before they undertake such a bad business. For a bad business it is, whatever the result. Victory can never decide the question of right. The transformation of Europe into a loose federation of unarmed and self-governing communities, settling their disputes by arbitration, will take a long time ; but Nature urges us forward to the highest and most arduous of human tasks. Kant was a child of the Aufklärung in his belief in the majesty of reason; but in his demand for the co-operation of the people in the work of government and the maintenance of peace he derives from Rousseau, and stretches out his hand to the democratic forces which the Aufklärung despised. His moral and political philosophy was grounded on the conviction, which he shared with the men of 1789, that we are rational beings and that Nature or Providence urges us onward and upward. Man, he declares in noble words, cannot get away from the idea of right.

It is this robust belief in the worth of the individual citizen which ennobles the Declaration of the Rights of Man and renders the French Revolution, despite its excesses, a bracing influence in the making of the modern world. " France did more than conquer Europe," writes Sorel in an eloquent passage, " she converted her. Victorious even in their defeat, the French won over to their ideas the very nations which revolted against their domination. The princes most eagerly bent on penning in the Revolution saw it, on returning from their crusade, sprouting in the soil of their own estates, which had been fertilized by the blood of French soldiers. The French Revolution only ceased to be a source of strife between France and Europe to inaugurate a political and social revolution which in less than half a century has changed the face of the European world."

FOUR hundred years ago Machiavelli proclaimed the divorce
of politics from morals in a little book which is still very
much alive. Numberless rulers in all times and countries had
anticipated in practice the advice which he gave in *The Prince*,
but the thought of the Middle Ages ran on transcendental lines.
Its publicists strove to deduce the maxims of statecraft from the
teachings of the Old and New Testaments, and even the worst
monarchs paid lip-service to the Christian creed. By contemptuously brushing aside all religious and ethical considerations, and approaching the problem of government in
a spirit of naked realism, the audacious Florentine thinker,
far more than Columbus or Copernicus, Erasmus or Luther,
ushered in the modern world. For the dominating intellectual
feature of the last four centuries, as Lecky pointed out long
ago, is the secularization of thought. The spell of authority
had been broken before Machiavelli sat down to write ; but
it required a thorough-going pagan to preach the gospel of
pure empiricism and to turn his back on the ideas of a thousand
years. It is true enough that he was primarily concerned with
the fortunes of Italy, distracted as she was by the torments of
invasion and civil strife ; and his book closes with an appeal
to the House of Medici. In *The Prince*, however, as with
Burke's *Reflections on the French Revolution*, it is not the chrono-
logical setting but the conception of the nature of man and
society that matters to us to-day. It is one of the merits of
Machiavelli, and one of the sources of his enduring influence,
that he says precisely what he thinks.

Let us recall some of his familiar maxims, set forth in the
level tones with which a clinical lecturer explains the nature
and maladies of the human frame. " He who neglects what
is done to follow what ought to be done will sooner learn how
to ruin than how to preserve himself. For a tender man and
one that desires to be honest in everything must needs run a
great hazard among so many of a contrary principle. Where-
fore it is necessary for a prince to harden himself and learn to
be good or otherwise according to the exigence of his affairs.
For if we consider things impartially we shall find some things
in appearance are virtuous, and yet, if pursued, would bring
certain destruction ; and others, on the contrary, that are
seemingly bad, which, if followed by a prince, procure his

peace and security." " Is it better to be beloved than feared,
or to be feared than beloved ? Both would be convenient,
but because that is hard to attain, it is better and more secure
to be feared." " How honourable it is for a prince to keep
his word everybody understands. Nevertheless experience
has shown in our times that those who have not tied themselves
to it have done great things, and by their cunning and subtlety
have overcome those who have been superstitiously exact.
For you must understand that there are two ways of contending,
by law and by force. The first is proper to men, the second
to beasts. But because many times the first is insufficient,
recourse must be had to the second. It belongs therefore to
a prince to understand both. Seeing therefore it is of such
importance to take upon him the nature and disposition of a
beast, of all the whole flock he ought to imitate the lion and
the fox. A prince who is wise and prudent cannot or ought
not to keep his word when the keeping of it is to his prejudice,
and the causes for which he promised are removed. Were
men all good this doctrine should not be taught ; but because
they are wicked and not likely to be punctual with you, you
are not obliged to any such strictness with them."

Here is the sinister gospel in its crudest form of what the
French call *raison d'état*, the doctrine that extraordinary objects
cannot be achieved under the ordinary rules, and that the
monarch, in seeking the welfare of the state as he understands
it, is fettered by no human or divine laws. This is not to say
that might is right or that the end, whatever it be, justifies the
means ; for the exercise of power has to be related to the single
definite purpose of the interest of the state. The supreme
qualification for the ruler in the eyes of Machiavelli and his
disciples is *virtù*, which means not virtue but virility, energy,
force of character, remorseless vigour, the head to plan and
the arm to strike. The paramount duty of the representative
and guardian of the community is to survive and succeed. For
this purpose he must circumvent and intimidate his enemies
at home and abroad. Half measures, hesitation, weakness of
will and purpose, are the supreme offence. Hence the fascination exerted by Caesar Borgia on the Florentine Secretary
and diplomatist, who knew him in the flesh. On the other
hand the author of *The Prince* has as little use for the brutal
and blundering tyrant as for the ineffectual idealist. To make
omelettes you must break eggs, but there is no excuse for
breaking them if you cannot prepare a tasty dish. Intelligence

is at least as necessary as resolution. The prince must be worthy of his post, and must win acceptance from his subjects if not their love. " Better than any number of fortresses is not to be hated by your people." His whole duty is to save, to strengthen and to maintain the state.

Whether the ship is steered by a hereditary monarch or a dictator, an aristocracy, a parliament or a committee of public safety, is irrelevant. Machiavelli is primarily interested, not in the forms of government, but in the way it is carried on. Governance is a problem of strength and skill, not of ethics and law. A régime must be judged, not by intentions, but by the fruits of its policy. Of such notions as the Respublica Christiana, the unity of civilization, allegiance to humanity, joint responsibility for the welfare of the world, there is not a trace. *Virtù, Fortuna, Necessità* : here was the new trinity which Machiavelli substituted for the Christian creeds. Each political unit, large or small, must think solely of itself. The morals of the jungle are exalted into a philosophy of life. Anticipating Nietzsche he complains that Christianity is the religion of the weak. The author of *The Prince* was certainly no worse a man than his contemporaries in the courts and cabinets of the Renaissance, and indeed he modelled his technique on the experiences of his own career. But the horror with which plain citizens heard of his counsels is suggested by the fact that " Old Nick," though already a familiar *alias* for the devil, came to be associated with his name ; that *The Prince* was called the Devil's Catechism or the Ten Commandments Reversed ; that the adjective " Machiavellian " is still in use all over the world to denote the stratagems of statecraft at its worst. That he denounced bad rulers in his larger work, the *Discourses on Livy*, and confessed that the practice of breaking the laws for good ends lent a colour to breaches committed for bad ends, has been overlooked. It is by *The Prince* that he stands or falls.

While plain men were shocked by the repudiation not only of Christian ethics but of the ordinary maxims of honourable dealing, the great ones of the earth took the little book to their hearts. It spoke a language they could understand. Here was a breviary for rulers, full of shrewd hints and warnings, compiled by the keenest political brain of the age. It appeared, moreover, at the psychological moment, for the mediaeval structure had collapsed. The Middle Ages were saturated with universalism. No theoretical distinction between public and private morality was recognized. Nations were coming into existence, but sovereignty in the juridical sense was unknown. For in ecclesiastical affairs the Roman Church was supreme, and the noble conception of a Respublica Christiana coloured the thought of the Western world. There stood the Holy Roman Empire, with God the invisible King, and the appointed representatives on earth, the Emperor and the Pope. It was an age of divided allegiance, not of concentration of power. The texture was too loose to stand the strain of conflicting interests, and after all order is heaven's first law. The nation-state came in with the Renaissance and the Reformation. The rejection of Papal authority by Northern Europe strengthened the power of the ruler, and enthroned the notion of a government supreme within its frontiers. The state grew steadily in strength and prestige, in Catholic as well as in Protestant countries, as the Church and the great nobility wilted away. But in what spirit was it to use its power? In the Middle Ages political science was a branch of Christian theology, the principles of which were regarded as at any rate theoretically valid over the whole field of human experience. These times were over. The doctrine of partnership in a wider unity based on the recognition of common principles had disappeared. Its place was taken by the maxim of unfettered sovereignty, the overriding interest of the state as interpreted by its ruler.

The sixteenth century is the Augustan age of Machiavellian statecraft. Thomas Cromwell, the unscrupulous instrument of Henry VIII, brought the cult back from Italy and was rumoured to sleep with a copy of *The Prince* under his pillow. The daughter of the man to whom the book was dedicated was Catherine de Medici, who massacred thousands of Protestants, not from religious zeal but for coolly calculated purposes of state. It was said of her son Henri III that he carried the volume in his pocket. Though it was afterwards placed on the Index of Forbidden Books it was first published in Rome, and sixteenth-century Popes were as ready to approve the dagger of the assassin as secular rulers. When Fra Paolo Sarpi was stabbed in Venice he coolly observed *agnosco stilum curiæ*. Though the name of the Renaissance publicist became a byword for infamy, for many a ruler his precepts were the accepted methods of the political game. Bacon, whose blood was as cool as his brain was clear, did not hesitate to pay homage to the formulator of the doctrine of *raison d'état*. " We

are much beholden to Machiavelli and others that wrote what
men do and not what they ought to do."

The gospel was accepted and applied by some of the greatest
rulers of the modern world. Richelieu destroyed the political
influence of the Protestants at home at the same time that he
co-operated with the Protestant Swedes against the Catholic
Hapsburgs in the Thirty Years War, winning the larger part
of Alsace as his prize. But it is to Frederick the Great rather
than to the French Cardinal that our thoughts turn, for he
alone among rulers beguiled his leisure with the confutation
of the tempter while he was waiting for the throne and applied
his maxims when the hour arrived. Three years after the
publication of *L'Anti-Machiavel* he seized Silesia, despite his
father's recognition of the Austrian succession to Maria
Theresa, observing with a cynical smile that the jurists would
discover reasons for his action. His two Political Testaments
are as obviously the utterances of an experienced ruler as the
tract against Machiavelli was an academic essay. He had
been tried in the fire and emerged as hard as steel. Whatever
illusions he had entertained in his youth had been shed.
When someone was painting human beings in brighter colours
than he thought they deserved he snapped out : You do not
know the accursed race ! Honour and the interest of the
state, he wrote to the elder Pitt at the height of the Seven
Years War, were his two guiding principles, and a man thus
fortified would never yield to his foes. Like Gustavus
Adolphus and Napoleon he was at once the ruler, Minister of
Foreign Affairs and Commander-in-Chief, and as such he was
the sole interpreter of the interests of his state. Peace and
war were merely alternating phases of the same ceaseless
struggle. Diplomacy without armaments, he declared, was
like music without instruments, a remark anticipating the
maxim of Clausewitz that war is the continuation of policy
by other means.

The record of Frederick the Great, however, must be
studied as a whole. If he was a cynic, he was also a child of
the *Auflärung*. He slaved at his task for forty-six years, and
set a new standard for monarchical rule. His declaration that
he was the first servant of the state was the expression not
merely of an ideal but of a fact. He placed the state above
himself and above the dynasty. " The interest of the state,"
he declared, " is the law of princes, and this law is inevitable."
He gave orders that, if he were taken prisoner, Prussia should

make no sacrifices to procure his release.   Thus the doctrine of service, sincerely held and unswervingly applied, helped to veil if not to span the gulf between politics and ethics.   The eighteenth century with its rationalistic humanitarianism and its trio of enlightened autocrats, Frederick the Great, Catherine the Great and Joseph II, supplied the most suitable stage for the application of the gospel of *raison d'état* in its better aspects as well as its worse.   The era of the religious wars, fought at any rate nominally for ideal ends, was over, and the influence of educated public opinion had hardly begun.

The enduring vitality of *The Prince* cannot be airily dismissed as a regrettable token of human depravity.   Its teaching has been watered down in the course of the centuries, but a sediment of the Florentine gospel is left in numberless thinkers of the last four centuries who bear a better name.   In Acton's learned Introduction to Burd's edition of *The Prince*, and in Meinecke's massive treatise *Die Idee der Staatsraison*, we are confronted with a serried array of authorities, some of them of high repute, who, while rejecting the grosser features of the system, argue that public and private morals are not and can never be quite the same ; that supreme emergencies call for exceptional methods ; that Machiavelli is useful as medicine though indigestible if consumed as our daily bread.   We recall Cavour's revealing cry of distress while he was putting Italy on the map :   " What rascals we should be if we did for ourselves what we do for our country! "   However lofty our political ideals, however firm our moral principles, we cannot shirk the rude challenge of *The Prince*.   Can rulers, must rulers, invariably attempt to apply the moral law, as the private citizen in civilized communities is rightly expected to do ? Or is the art of government, to borrow a phrase of Nietzsche, beyond good and evil?

To realize the full strength of Machiavellian philosophy let me summarize Meinecke's presentation of the case.   *Raison d'état* tells the statesman what he must do in order to maintain the state in health and strength.   The striving for power and possession is a primitive, indeed an animal, instinct, as strong in the individual as in the herd.   With man it does not confine itself to the physical needs and satisfactions of life, for the horizon widens with his ascent.   On the other hand, as he climbs the ladder of civilization and begins to organize his social life, he becomes aware that he must reckon with morality and law.   Between Kratos and Ethos, between the craving for power and the intruding sense of moral responsibility, a bridge has been built which we call Reason of State—a recognition of the parallelism of the actual and ideal, the instinctive and the rational. The natural and the spiritual meet in a middle zone. The goal is in the highest degree ethical—the welfare of the community ; but the means of reaching it are sometimes coarse and elemental. Thus, to obey the dictates of *raison d'état* is to oscillate between light and darkness. The ambition of the ruler is harnessed to the requirements of the ruled, and he is transformed into the servant of his own might. There is a gulf between the state and all other human organizations ; for, while the latter must always strive to follow ideal standards, the former must sometimes sin. Here is the most tragic aspect of history—that the radical moralization of mankind is impossible, and that the state, which is the parent and guardian of law, cannot always be bound by its behests. For the state is amphibious, living at one and the same time in the ethical and the natural worlds. The conflict is eternal, for neither of the combatants will ever yield.

It is Hegel who gives the highest testimonials to Machiavelli and comes nearest to accepting his conclusions. While the moralists had wrung their hands over the antagonism between the ideal and the actual, he knocks down the partition and denies the conflict between policy and morals. The state, we read in *The Philosophy of Law*, is the realized ethical idea. It is an end in itself and has no higher duty than to maintain itself. In his pregnant formula, the real is the rational and the rational is the real. It is Spinoza's pantheism adapted to the political plane. At first blush this looks as if in Hegel's eyes the struggle has ended by the capitulation of one of the combatants ; and Meinecke, in a forceful phrase, compares his patronage of Machiavelli to the legitimation of a bastard. A familiar witticism suggested that he mistook the Kingdom of Prussia for the Kingdom of Heaven. The balance is to some extent redressed by the ethical colouring in the picture. A state, he declares, is bound together, not by force but by a deep-rooted instinct of order. It is a spiritual structure, the highest embodiment of reason. In his famous phrase, world history is progress in the consciousness of liberty. For this homage to reality was not to a static condition but to an evolutionary process. In his doctrine of the relation of states to one another, however, he sheds these draperies. The state, he teaches, is its own master. Thus international law is no real contract, and no state is legally or morally bound by it. Grave differences can only be settled by war, which is neither good nor evil but natural. Indeed it has its uses as a national scavenger and in emphasizing the unimportance of material things. In deciding on war the state must consider its own interest and nothing else.

A very similar attitude meets us in Treitschke's celebrated lectures on political science, which he delivered to crowded audiences in Heidelberg and Berlin. In his chapter on the state in relation to the Moral Law he admits that the coming of Christianity created a difficulty, unknown to the ancients, for professing Christians. Yet in his case at any rate the burden is lightly borne. It is the abiding merit of Machiavelli, he declares, to have set the state on its own feet, freed it from the moral sway of the Church, and above all declared for the first time that the state was power. He misses in his teaching a demonstration of the necessity that the ruler must justify himself after capturing power by his exertions for the highest moral welfare of the human race ; and he deplores his infatuation for Cæsar Borgia, a man who had nothing to show for his virtuosity in crime. " The maintenance of its power," writes Treitschke, " is a task of incomparable grandeur for the state ; but lest it should contradict its own nature its aims must be moral. Every moral judgment of the historian must be based on the hypothesis of the state as power, constrained to maintain itself within and without ; and man's highest destiny is co-operation in this duty." The goal is clear enough, though differences are possible as to the means which may be employed. The message of the famous historian is the moral and spiritual grandeur of large and powerful states. Little states are out of date, for they cannot defend themselves. The state stands high above the individuals who compose it, and it exists in order to realize ideals far above individual happiness. It can only fulfil its function if it is strong. It need not inquire if its actions are approved or disapproved by its subjects, for it is the guardian of the national tradition and a trustee for unborn generations.

The state, continues Treitschke, owes no allegiance to any external authority. International law is a mere phrase, and no tribunal can arbitrate between sovereign communities. Treaties are a voluntary self-limitation, and no state can hamper its freedom of action by obligations to another. It must ever be ready for war, which, when undertaken for honour or some supreme national interest, is wholesome and elevating. For war is not a necessary evil but an instrument of statesmanship and a school of patriotism. Only in war for the Fatherland does a nation become truly and spiritually united. It is indeed the only medicine for a sick people. It is idealism that demands war and materialism that rejects it. Dreams of perpetual peace are the mark of a stagnant and decadent generation, for conflict is the law of life. "The hope of banishing war is not only meaningless but immoral, for its disappearance would turn the earth into a great temple of selfishness." Here is the echo of Moltke's familiar aphorism: "Perpetual peace is a dream, and not even a beautiful dream." Treitschke had Germany in view, and Machiavelli Italy. But how slender is the difference between the sixteenth and the nineteenth century! "The essence of a state," declares Treitschke, "is firstly power; secondly power; thirdly power." With such a philosophy we shall never succeed in organizing the world; for the cult of power leads to the twin evils of the idolatry of the state and the glorification of war.

Is the outlook really so hopeless, the problem really so insoluble, as these teachers suggest? That the struggle between Kratos and Ethos will continue indefinitely we can readily believe. But may not the relations of the combatants change? May not Ethos extend its sway at the cost of Kratos, even if it cannot hope for victory all along the line? Does not the history of man illustrate the slow advance of moral principle, the occupation of one piece of territory after another previously claimed without challenge by the rival principle of force? May not this process be continued almost indefinitely as pioneers rescue the desert and the forest for the haunts of men, and engineers turn the shallow waters into fertile land?

Our answer to these questions will depend in the main on our view of human nature. The differences in the systems of political philosophy throughout the ages reflect still deeper divergences in our interpretation of man. If we believe, like Machiavelli and Hobbes, that he is nearer to the beasts than to the angels, we shall lean to the doctrines of autocracy and the sovereign state. It is equally natural that those who take a more favourable view should contest the universal supremacy of force, and should preach the gospel of partnership and co-operation on every plane. "Man," declared Humboldt, "is naturally more disposed to beneficent than to selfish actions."

Everyone knows Kant's famous confession of his ever-increasing wonder at the starry heavens above and the moral law within. The conviction that society rests on moral and spiritual foundations was shared by Burke, the greatest of English political thinkers, who described the state as a partnership in all art, in all science, in all perfection. And Mill based the most moving plea for individual liberty ever written on his lofty reading of the character and potentialities of man. Democracy is more than a type of government, and what is called pacifism is more than a mere theory of international relations. Both are the expression of faith in the ultimate sanity of the common man, in his power to learn from experience, in his capacity for spiritual growth.

I share this faith. Despite the number and the eminence of his disciples, I believe that Machiavelli is unfair to mankind. The professed realist only saw a limited portion of the vast field of experience. The will to power is not the sole key to human nature. History is assuredly a record of strife—the strife of arms and wits ; but it is also, as Kropotkin reminded us in an illuminating work, a story of mutual aid. Noble aims in plenty have been formed by men and nations, and many of them have been wholly or partially achieved. With a longer and a wider experience than Machiavelli, we have learned to recognize the solid core of truth in the old adage that honesty is the best policy. The application of the maxims of *The Prince* may achieve a temporary triumph, but they provide no foundation for the enduring happiness, prosperity or security of a state. If man were indeed the unruly and perfidious animal that he believes, *The Prince* might be accepted as a recipe for making the best of a bad job. But the broad testimony of modern history suggests that the average man rises above this level. Our sixteenth-century instructor makes no allowance for growth ; the idea of progress is the creation of modern times, above all of the eighteenth century. Froude used to say that history is like a child's box of letters, with which you can spell any word you choose. What Machiavelli saw was real enough, and he was a careful student of history as well ; but in concentrating his gaze on the practice of governments, he paid too little attention to other aspects of the life of the community. Brilliant intellects like Machiavelli and Hobbes, Voltaire and Marx have seen certain phenomena with extraordinary distinctness and emphasized their immense significance, yet vast tracts of human experience lie beyond their ken. The great Italian completely ignored the ultimate potency of moral forces. Had he been invited to forecast the future he would have predicted an essentially unchanging world. *Plus ça change, plus c'est la même chose.* His interpretation of political society was static. The human animal, as portrayed by Machiavelli, is unable to climb above the level of his baser self, as water is incapable of rising above its source.

Even those who feel themselves unable to reject his gospel outright may draw a distinction, which never occurred to the thinkers of the sixteenth century, between domestic and foreign affairs. Within the frontiers of the most civilized states responsible government has replaced autocracy, and the rule of law has superseded the whim of the ruler. For the moment there is a set-back in this process, and half Europe is in the grip of dictatorships. But I firmly belive that the liberalizing forces which have given Western civilization its peculiar stamp in the last four centuries will reassert themselves when the supermen who have challenged their validity pass away. The most satisfactory criterion of civilization is not the growth of knowledge or the increase of amenities, but the degree in which social life is humanized, individuality fostered and political action brougʰt within the moral sphere. In the more civilized communities the theoretical omnipotence of the executive is tempered by the fact that our rulers, like other citizens, are subject to the laws, can be sued in the courts, and can be changed by constitutional methods. With the aid of a vigilant public opinion and a free Press we have reached a stage when the government is expected not only to conform to the ordinary principles of honourable dealing but to set a shining example. In communities like our own, resting on a solid foundation of ordered liberty, the maxims of *The Prince* are no longer applicable as regards internal affairs.

" At the bottom of all the confused clamour against him," writes Lord Morley in his memorable Romanes Lecture on Machiavelli," the people knew what they meant and their instinct was not unsound. Mankind, and well they know it, are far too profoundly concerned in right and wrong, in mercy and cruelty, in justice and oppression, to favour a teacher who, even for a scientific purpose of his own, forgets the awful difference." It is this general acceptance to-day of the duty of rulers to set a good example that accounts for the world-wide horror at the murder of the Tsar and his family by the Bolshevists in 1918, and the massacre of June 30, 1934, when

Y

Hitler shot scores of his actual or potential enemies without trial. Such a swift and bloody stroke was in strict accordance with the doctrine of *The Prince* that, if the ruler strikes at all, he should hit hard and get his blow in first. But the twentieth century is not the sixteenth. When the foundations of law have been overthrown, practices long abandoned are revived by men who seize power through violence and retain it by fear. Our disgust at such reversions is a measure of the advance we have made since the times when the murder of an opponent was accepted as a matter of course.

When we pass beyond national frontiers and enter the perilous field of international relations, we find that the Florentine tempter is more difficult to dislodge. We are confronted with the fact that for a single state to follow the dictates of private morality while its neighbours apply the maxim of national egoism may well be suicide. No country has an unblemished record ; but some states show up better than others, and even in the twentieth century uneasy feelings persist that in an emergency the less scrupulous may score. Weak though the urge has been towards the organization of mankind on the basis of law, the slow process of moralization has been held up again and again by mutal suspicions of sincerity. The pace of a convoy is decided by its slowest unit. For instance the willingness of some Powers to accept arbitration or a drastic reduction of armaments has been shipwrecked on the refusal of others to follow suit. Thus in the international sphere we have to recognize the disagreeable fact that no government is entirely its own master. In a world of sovereign self-sufficing nationalism, this is a very serious matter for the planner and the idealist.

Another important consideration must be borne in mind. In every community there are men and women ready to suffer exile or imprisonment, torture and death for their principles ; and they are the salt of the earth. With states it is different. The private citizen may prefer to surrender his life rather than his faith, like the brave Armenians confronted with the alternative of apostasy or instant death. A state cannot and must not make such a sacrifice, for it is the trustee of the generations to come. If brutally attacked or summoned to surrender its independence, its duty, I believe, is to resist. To yield is to make the world safe for the aggressor and the thief. By refusing to open the frontiers to the German armies in 1914, the Belgian Government kept alive the soul of the nation and challenged the degrading doctrine that material force is supreme. The obligation of a state to survive may involve decisions which an individual might feel bound on ethical grounds to reject; for when war breaks out, however it originates, every belligerent throws scruples to the wind and fights desperately for victory. Here is a difference between public and private morality which cannot be ignored. The individual may sacrifice his life: the community must live on. A trustee cannot surrender to threats or violence an estate which is not his own. In other words, the action of a government within certain limits is determined by considerations of what we may call a biological rather than a moral order. And just as I approve resistance to flagrant aggression, I cannot denounce the successive revolts of the Christian communities of the Near East against the intolerable yoke of the Turkish invader, which had stunted their life for centuries as the growth of a tree is thwarted by an iron clamp. Nor can I censure the determination of nineteenth-century Italians and Germans to expel alien rulers in order to become nation-states like their neighbours. Most people would add that the North was right to take up the challenge of the South in 1861, to wage war for the preservation of the Union and incidentally for the abolition of slavery. Such elemental urges dating from a period prior to the Covenant and the Kellogg Pact seem to me, to quote Nietzsche's phrase again, beyond good and evil.

There are, on the other hand, plenty of instances in modern history when Governments have taken action generally regarded as an offence against even the low standards of the time. I am thinking of such incidents as the alliance between Francis I and the Sultan of Turkey against Charles V, the devastation of the Palatinate by Louis XIV, the seizure of Silesia by Frederick the Great, the partitions of Poland by Russia, Prussia and Austria, the snatching of Tripoli by Italy in 1911. No modern war aroused more universal condemnation than the struggle of South Africa at the turn of the century. Though acclaimed by a majority of Englishmen as a legitimate effort to hold British South Africa for the Crown, to the rest of the world it appeared as a brutal assault by a mighty empire on a little community of farmers who merely asked to be left alone. No less acute differences of judgment were provoked by the attitude of the belligerents in the war of 1914. Some of the Powers could plead treaty obligations, while others plunged into the vortex at their own chosen time without even pretending that they were resisting attack. In every case the governing consideration was national interest, and most of them had little excuse to throw stones at one another. All alike were functioning in an unorganized world.

Must we then accept as a grim necessity the doctrine that moral standards, recognized by individual citizens as categorical imperatives for the ordering of their lives and accepted to-day by the more advanced nations as binding in their domestic transactions, must remain for ever inapplicable in the relations of states ? I see no reason for such a despairing conclusion. The moralization of community life within the national frontiers, which is taken as a matter of course by the unthinking citizen, represents a gigantic achievement requiring many centuries of effort. Feudal anarchy, civil war, highway robbery, duelling have disappeared. The supremacy of brute force has retreated before the conception of the reign of law. To our remote forefathers the task of organizing the life of a large-scale community must have seemed as utopian as that of tidying up the world seems to many people to-day. Yet the difficulties have been overcome so completely in the narrower sphere that most of us forget that they ever existed. It has become an axiom that decisions reached by consultation and compromise are the most likely to endure. But the commonplace of to-day was once a romantic dream. We remember Hobbes' celebrated description of the state of Nature. " No arts ; no letters ; no society ; and what is worst of all, continual fear and danger of violent death ; and the life of man solitary, poor, nasty, brutish and short." We have escaped from that predicament by the growth of the community sense and by the creation of institutions in which it found expression. The human family is only the local group on a larger scale. Its essential unity is much harder to visualize, but the necessity of organization as the condition of well-being is as clear in the one case as in the other. If it was not so obvious before the World War, that cataclysm should have removed the mist from our eyes.

One serious effort to organize Europe, and only one, was made before 1919. The Holy Alliance left a bad name, which it did not altogether deserve. Alexander I is not merely the most interesting of the Russian Tsars, but the most attractive figure on the European chessboard at the opening of the nineteenth century. Beginning life as a sentimental republican he ascended the throne of his murdered father with the loftiest

ideals for his subjects and mankind. The influence of Mme
de Krüdener gave a religious turn to his thoughts, and when
the struggle with Napoleon was over he saw his chance. Here
is the preamble of the Holy Alliance signed in September 1815.
" Their Majesties the Emperor of Austria, the King of Prussia,
and the Emperor of Russia having, in consequence of the great
events which have occurred in the course of the last three
years in Europe, and especially of blessings which it has
pleased Divine Providence to shower down upon those states
which place their confidence and their hope on it alone,
acquired the intimate conviction of the necessity of settling
the steps to be observed by the Powers in their reciprocal
relations upon the sublime truths which the holy religion of
our Saviour teaches ; they solemnly declare that the present
Act has no other object than to publish in the face of the whole
world their fixed resolution, both in the administration of
their respective states and in their political relations with every
other government, to take for their sole guide the precepts of
that holy religion." The first article pledged the signatories
to mutual assistance and to the spirit of fraternity for the
protection of religion, peace and justice. In the second they
proclaimed themselves members of a single Christian nation
delegated by Providence to govern three branches of the one
family.

England stood aloof from what Castlereagh contemptuously
described as " sublime mysticism and nonsense," but most of
the other European rulers acceded to the pact. Working
through the conference system, in which England took her
share, the conquerors of Napoleon, soon reinforced by France
herself, ruled the Continent for a few years by the first and
last effective Concert it has known. The idea was sound
enough, but the conception of its duties was too static. Ob-
sessed by the spectre of revolution the crowned autocrats,
under Metternich's leadership, attempted to stifle the forces
of constitutional government and nationality, and within a
decade their disagreements brought the experiment to an end.
England withdrew when France received a mandate to restore
autocracy in Spain, and the Greek war of independence drove
a wedge between Russia and Austria. The so-called Concert
of Europe, which was often talked of and occasionally employed in the second half of the nineteenth century, only
attempted to deal with the Eastern question, and even in this
limited area it conspicuously failed. It was a tragedy that the

saving idea of the European family had come to be identified
in the public mind with autocracy at home and the suppression
of legitimate discontent by foreign arms. The increasing
resort to arbitration in minor matters during the nineteenth
century, welcome and useful though it was, afforded no
adequate substitute for systematized co-operation. Moreover
the experiment that followed the downfall of Napoleon was
confined to the European stage. Regional arrangements are
still of use, but in the twentieth century they can have little
chance of success except as elements in a wider scheme.

For the first time in history it is widely realized to-day that
the only way to bridge the gulf between politics and morals
at its deepest point is to organize the world as a whole. That
nations will become less determined to secure justice, as they
understand it, or to realize their cherished aims is improbable.
But it is quite possible that they will learn from bitter experience
that on our shrinking and inter-dependent planet the best
chance of survival lies in intelligent co-operation for common
ends. The instinct of self-preservation will find expression in
novel forms. In a word, the teaching of Machiavelli, which
was founded on his experience of Italy in the sixteenth century,
can only be confuted by the discovery that in the long run
purely self-regarding action on the part of a state does not pay.
Economic contacts are needed for its physical life, and a thousand cultural ties already proclaim our common heritage. As
the sense of community broadens among the peoples, the
sentiment of human solidarity will find expression in their
conception of the state and the action of their governments.
If moral principles ultimately extend their sway into the dark
forest of international relations, it will be, not because conscience whispers that they should, but because rival methods
of deciding disputes and obtaining security have been tried
and failed. Our best ground for hope lies in the fact that in
the course of his long ascent man has shown his capacity not
only to err but to learn—in Bacon's words " devising new
remedies as time breedeth new mischiefs."

During the four centuries of our modern era the last word
in political organization has been the nation. Now that the
world has been unified by science and culture, the nation must
take its place as the bridge, the half-way house, the middle
term, between the individual and the human family. For this
high purpose it is not only useful but indispensable. Nationalism in its deepest meaning is the self-consciousness of a nation,

the affirmation of its personality. It has come to stay, for it derives from a powerful combination of material and spiritual factors. The material factor is the possession of a home, a recognized territory in which it lives and to which it becomes devotedly attached. The spiritual factor is the will of its citizens to live together and to share their fortunes. The grouping of human beings into such organic units is a necessary stage in the evolution and organization of mankind. The first storey of the edifice rests firmly on the solid earth. The second or international floor is being built upon the broad platform of self-conscious political communities. The individual, the nation, the human family—here is the new trinity in which we must all steadfastly believe if we desire to be saved.

Centuries before the World War a few seers and prophets discerned and proclaimed the unity of mankind. The interest of such pioneers as William Penn and the Abbé Saint-Pierre lies, not in the details of their schemes, but in their expression of the community idea beyond the frontiers of the state. If we once grasp the notion of solidarity, not as a speculative principle but as a concrete fact, we are on the high road to the moralization of politics. Nearly three centuries after *The Prince* Kant wrote his treatise on *Perpetual Peace* ; and if the greatest of modern thinkers had commanded the style of Rousseau or Machiavelli, his little book might have been as popular as it deserves. As our civil strife in the seventeenth century inspired Hobbes to seek an escape from anarchy in unfettered autocracy, so the tumult of the French Revolution drove Kant to propose a way of escape in the organization of mankind. If law was the foundation of the life of the community, it should equally regulate the relations of states. Humanity needed a constitution no less than France or Prussia ; for so long as each state recognized no authority above itself and no duty except to itself, wars were inevitable.

Kant first enumerates what he describes as the preliminary articles of peace. (1) No treaty shall be valid if it contains a secret reservation of materials for another war. (2) No state shall be acquired through inheritance, exchange or purchase, for it is not a property but a society of human beings. (3) Standing armies shall be abolished, for they are always threatening other states with war. (4) No national debt shall be incurred except for purely internal affairs. (5) No state shall forcibly interfere with the constitution or administration of another. These injunctions and exhortations are, of course, merely counsels of perfection so long as the destinies of nations are in the hands of irresponsible autocrats. When selfish and capricious autocracies are replaced by self-governing institutions, a new system of relations between states will become possible. The only absolute security for peace would be a world republic, which he regrets that the nations will not accept. The second-best method is a federation of self-governing communities for the purpose of averting war. Here in 1795 is the Society of Nations without the name. The philosopher proceeds to offer some reasons for his great hope. Nature, he announces boldly, points us towards peace, for she makes harmony spring from discord, even against the will of man. She fills the earth with contiguous peoples, who gradually realize their common interests. The commercial spirit cannot coexist with war, and sooner or later it takes possession of every nation. But his faith in mankind is even greater than his faith in Nature or commerce. In noble words, which enshrine his political as well as his moral philosophy, he declares that man cannot get away from the idea of right.

As Kant challenges Machiavelli, so Gladstone and Bismarck among nineteenth-century statesmen embody the rival philosophies in action. Vast and splendid as was the intellect of the Prussian Junker, the conception of human solidarity, the vision of a new international order resting on a voluntary partnership of national units, was beyond his ken. The weakness of the realists is that they define reality too narrowly and think more of immediate than of ultimate returns. Bismarck was content to work for his country alone and was satisfied with its rapturous applause. In a recent book on his religion a German Professor exhibits the master-builder as a man of evangelical piety on the strength of some devotional works which he read and underlined. The hero-worship has gone too far, for Bismarck kept his religion and his statecraft in watertight compartments. Certain issues, as he declared at the beginning of his ministerial career, could only be settled by blood and iron. There is no more familiar passage in his reminiscences than the story of the manipulation of the Ems telegram, which by tendentious compression was fashioned to look like an insult to the French Ambassador, and which produced the desired result of goading Napoleon III to a declaration of war. Europe to Bismarck, like Italy to Metternich, was a geographical expression and nothing more.

The Iron Chancellor was the most consummate practitioner

of *raison d'état* in the sphere of international relations that the world has ever seen, and he scoffed at " Professor Gladstone " for worshipping other gods. The cession of the Ionian Islands to Greece was interpreted by him as a sign that England was exhausted, since, according to his philosophy, virile nations give nothing away. Other critics, including Lord John Russell, complained of Gladstone's prompt acceptance of the *Alabama* award. But the Gladstonian gospel does not seem to us quite so doctrinaire to-day, when the bitter taste of the fruits of Bismarckian realism is in our mouths. Before he evolved into the greatest Liberal statesman of the nineteenth century he made his profession of faith in the Don Pacifico debate of 1850. Rebuking the high-handed methods of Palmerston and rejecting the distinction between politics and morals, he envisaged the relations of nations in terms not of difference of military power but of equality of rights.

Twenty years later Gladstone was Prime Minister and the triumph of German arms over France touched him to the quick. To the winning side the recovery of Alsace and Lorraine appeared not so much the spoils of victory as the undoing of historic wrongs, perpetrated by a greedy neighbour before the German nation became a political unit able to resist attack. To Gladstone, on the other hand, it seemed a moral wrong and for that reason a political error. In a Memorandum to Granville, written shortly after Sedan, he deplored the probable annexation of over a million people " who, with their ancestors for several generations, have known France for their country. The transfer of the allegiance and citizenship, of no small part of the heart and life, of human beings from one sovereignty to another without any reference to their own consent has been a great reproach to former transactions in Europe ; has led to many wars and disturbances ; is hard to reconcile with considerations of equity, and is repulsive to the sense of modern civilization." Germany, he admitted, was entitled to take ample precautions against her defeated foe. But was the acquisition of Alsace-Lorraine the only way ? " It seems worth while to consider whether the military neutralization of the territory and the destruction of all its fortresses would not, without being withdrawn from French allegiance, obtain the object of giving security to Germany." When Granville replied that nothing could be done, the Prime Minister rejoined : " I am much oppressed with the idea that this transfer of human beings like chattels should go forward without any voice from collective Europe if it were disposed to speak."

That a wrong committed in the international field would produce evil effects was as much part of Gladstone's political philosophy as of his Christian faith. " It seems to me by no means impossible," he wrote prophetically to Henry Reeve, Editor of the *Edinburgh Review*, " that those little provinces may be the central hinge on which for long years the history of Europe may virtually depend." To Granville he wrote even more pointedly. " I have an apprehension that this violent laceration and transfer is to lead us from bad to worse, and to be the beginning of a new series of European complications." When the peace terms confirmed his apprehensions he wrote to Max Müller : " I am afraid that Germany, crowned with glory and confident in her strength, will start on her new career to encounter the difficulties of the future without the sympathies of Europe, which in my opinion no nation, not even we in our sea-girt spot, can afford to lose." Gladstone was never Foreign Minister, and he did not need to make England as Bismarck had to make Germany. But for almost half a century he laboured to raise the standard of conduct among the governments of Europe, from his censure of Palmerston in 1850 and his denunciation of the Neapolitan prisons in 1851 to his crusade against the Bulgarian and Armenian atrocities of his closing years. He was filled with the conviction that we are all members one of another and that the jurisdiction of conscience does not cease at the frontier. Though the vision of a League of Nations was beyond his range, the spiritual foundations of the edifice are clearly discoverable in his speeches and writings. In the era of Imperialism which, so far as England is concerned, is now at an end, it was the fashion to scoff at Gladstone, Cobden and Bright as doctrinaires without red blood in their veins. Like other great Victorians their time will come again, for they preached the saving gospel of an interdependent world.

The war of 1914 was the child of the European anarchy. Before a decision was in sight, President Wilson made the most determined and comprehensive attempt recorded in history to reconcile politics and morals. Alone of the eight Great Powers the United States held aloof, hoping that it might remain neutral to the end. The humane and peace-loving Professor in the White House shared that aspiration to the full, incurring abuse by his declaration at a moment of

extreme tension with Germany that America was too proud
to fight. But his mind was already travelling far beyond the
task of keeping his sword in the scabbard to the larger problem
of building a new international order. Here was no ordinary
conflict of nation against nation. Almost the whole world
was involved in the struggle, and the fortunes of civilization
were at stake. It was the bankruptcy of a system, the *reductio
ad absurdum* of the doctrine of unfettered nationalism. In the
name of security sovereign states had piled up armaments and
pursued their selfish aims without thought of co-operation :
now they were blowing each other to pieces with the latest
scientific devilries and turning Europe into a heap of ashes.
It was the writing on the wall, which the panting combatants
were too busy to read. Wilson read it and proclaimed the
lesson to his people and the world.

At the end of 1916 the President invited the belligerents to
state the terms on which they would be willing to make peace.
After receiving their replies he described to the Senate in
January 1917 his own vision of a settlement which would not
only end the carnage but might avert its recurrence. The
settlement, when it came, must win the approval of mankind,
and not merely serve the several interests and immediate aims
of the nations engaged. " The question upon which the whole
future peace and policy of the world depends is this : Is the
present war a struggle for a just and secure peace or only for
a new balance of power ? Only a tranquil Europe can be a
stable Europe. There must be, not a balance of power, but a
community of power ; not organized rivalries but an organized
common peace. First of all it must be a peace without victory.
Victory would mean peace forced upon the loser, a victor's
terms imposed upon the vanquished. It would be accepted
in humiliation, under duress, as intolerable sacrifice, and would
leave a sting, a resentment, a bitter memory upon which terms
of peace would rest, not permanently, but only as upon quick-
sands. Only a peace between equals can last—only a peace
the very principle of which is equality and a common participation in a common benefit. The equality of nations upon
which peace must be founded, if it is to last, must be an
equality of rights ; the guarantees exchanged must neither
recognize nor imply a difference between big nations and
small, between those that are powerful and those that are weak.
Mankind is looking now for freedom of life, not for equipoises
of power. And there is a deeper thing involved than even

equality of rights among organized nations. No peace can last, or ought to last, which does not recognize and accept the principle that governments derive all their just powers from the consent of the governed, and that no right anywhere exists to hand peoples about from potentate to potentate as if they were property. Any peace which does not recognize and accept this principle will inevitably be upset. It will not rest upon the affections or convictions of mankind. The ferment of spirit of whole populations will fight subtly and constantly against it, and all the world will sympathize. The world can be at peace only if life is stable, and there can be no stability where the will is in rebellion, where there is not tranquillity of spirit and a sense of justice, of freedom, and of right." No prince or ruler had ever spoken with such prophetic wisdom and in such ringing tones.

Ten weeks after his address to the Senate the President was sucked into the whirlpool by Germany's renewal of the unrestricted submarine campaign, and no more was heard of peace without victory. With this inevitable exception, for no country fights except to win, he endeavoured to maintain the ideal of a moderate settlement. " It is because it is for us a war of high, disinterested purpose, in which all the free peoples of the world are banded together for the vindication of right, a war for the preservation of principles and of purpose, that we feel ourselves doubly constrained to propose for its outcome only that which is righteous and of irreproachable intention, for our foes as well as our friends. The cause being just and holy, the settlement must be of like motive and quality. A supreme moment of history has come. The eyes of the people have been opened and they see. The hand of God is laid upon the nations. He will show them favour, I devoutly believe, only if they rise to the clear heights of His own justice and mercy." In January, 1918, a month after this address to Congress, Wilson sketched out the settlement he had in mind in formulating the Fourteen Points, the fourteenth being the creation of a League of Nations. "An evident principle," he concluded, " runs through the whole programme I have outlined. It is the principle of justice to all peoples and nationalities and their right to live on equal terms of liberty and safety with one another, whether they be strong or weak." On July 4, 1918, Independence Day, he enshrined his programme in a sentence that travelled round the world. " What we seek is the reign of law, based upon the consent of the governed and sustained by the organized opinion of mankind."

Wilson failed to embody the whole of his Fourteen Points
in the peace settlement, for with the termination of the
struggle his importance for the allies waned as quickly as it
had grown. The Treaty of Versailles, judged by its results,
was a bad peace. *Si monumentum requiris circumspice.* But
without Wilson it would have been far worse. Let me fortify
myself with an extract from the eloquent tribute in Sir Arthur
Salter's *Recovery*. " The greatest decision, the greatest achievement, of his life was the inclusion of the Covenant in the
Peace Treaties. He fought almost alone. Had he failed there
would have been no League ; for what chance would there
have been of a Covenant when peace had been concluded ?
It would have been impossible for one who did not combine
the vision of the idealist, the practical insight into the conditions
of success of a realist, and an unshakable will, unmoved by
opposition or the foolish counsel of friends. If the world
does indeed prevent the occurrence of great wars, it will be to
this great act of this great man, more than to any other person
or event in history, that it will owe its salvation. The figure
of Wilson will loom in history above his lesser contemporaries
and across the valleys of intervening generations of lesser
successors."

To measure his difficulties let me quote another pen-portrait
from the gallery of Versailles—the memorable study of
Clemenceau by Mr. Keynes. " He felt about France what
Pericles felt of Athens—unique value in her, nothing else
mattering. But his theory of politics was Bismarck's. He
had one illusion—France ; and one disillusion—mankind,
including Frenchmen, and his colleagues not least. His
philosophy had no place for ' sentimentality ' in international
relations. Nations are real things, of whom you love one and
feel for the rest indifference or hatred. The glory of the nation
you love is a desirable end, but generally to be obtained at
your neighbour's expense. Prudence required some measure
of lip-service to the ' ideals ' of foolish Americans and hypo-
critical Englishmen, but it would be stupid to believe that
there is much room in the world as it really is for such affairs
as the League of Nations, or any sense in the principle of self-
determination except as an ingenious formula for rearranging
the balance of power in one's own interests." And so we
leave the old statesman, " throned, in his grey gloves, on the
brocade chair, dry in soul and empty of hope, very old and

tired." He had been a bonny fighter, but he was not the type to restore Europe to the paths of peace. Political architects, like moral reformers, must have faith in mankind. Looking round our distracted Continent in 1935 the " realists " of 1919 have little cause for satisfaction or pride. It is the nemesis of *raison d'état*. The dragon's teeth have come up once again as armed men.

The two most urgent tasks of to-day are to escape from the vast disintegration of the war and to remove the chief causes from which it sprung. They are in reality a single problem. We can trace back our present discontents to their source as we tick off links in a chain. The universal *malaise*, the economic dislocation and the political re-barbarization of half Europe arise in the main from the misuse of a hundred per cent. victory. The treaties in turn were in part the expression of the mood of anger and revenge generated by the horrors of the struggle. The conflict itself was the outcome of the false doctrine of self-sufficing national sovereignty, which had led rulers and governments to neglect the reiterated warnings of history. Wars large and small had filled even the enlightened nineteenth century with their roar, and the opening years of the twentieth witnessed fresh conflicts in Tripoli, the Balkans and the Far East. In the intervals of war we staggered from crisis to crisis, breathing sighs of relief when the immediate peril passed but taking no steps to prevent its recurrence. Armaments accumulated on land and sea, the Hague Conferences politely bowed limitation out of Court, and the most civilized nations plunged blindly forward to their doom. We were living on the slopes of a volcano, and we knew it. The war of 1914 was by no means inevitable ; but if the corner had been safely turned after the Serajevo murders the next crisis in the Balkans might just as well have started the rush of the avalanche.

In face of the great catastrophe it is idle to mumble our ancient formulas that if you wish for peace you must prepare for war ; that to be safe you must be stronger than your neighbours ; that every state must think and act exclusively for itself. Such maxims, whatever their earlier justification or excuse, are out of date. The whole scene has been transformed by the discoveries of science on the one hand and by the object-lesson of the World War on the other. That a revolver shot in an obscure Bosnian town could set Europe aflame within five weeks proved that the life of every one of us is at the mercy of an incident. Here was an argument more persuasive than a thousand sermons, a demonstration that the deaf could hear and the blind could read.

If civilization is to survive and man is to fulfil the abundant promise of his nature we need to plan on a wider scale than has ever been tried. Great thoughts, as Vauvenargues told us, come from the heart. The best minds of to-day are dedicated to the task of adapting our political institutions and our economic life to the new fact of the unity of the world, which has come about so rapidly that its implications are only beginning to be grasped. In this process of planning, as in all the higher tasks of humanity, the idea of right must guide us if we are not to waste our time. We can rarely undo ancient wrongs, but we can learn from our mistakes. In other words we must deliberately set out to reconcile politics and morals over the whole field. There is no other way. That stern moralist Lord Acton used to say that since the coming of Christ there was no excuse for anyone to plead that he did not know the difference between right and wrong. In 1935 we may add that since the coming of the war there is no excuse for any of us to believe that nationalism is enough. Even the most fiery patriot of to-day must look beyond his own frontiers and his own Continent if he is not to fall into the pit.

Our first task as political architects is to make up our minds in what kind of world we desire to dwell. We seek what Aristotle called the good life. Where shall we find it? My aspiration is to combine the maximum of unity with the minimum of constraint. In our national life we believe that all artificial obstacles to full and equal citizenship should be removed, not in order to produce a horde of standardized units, but, in the spirit of the Periclean oration, to secure the conditions for the flowering of personality and to make each one of us proudly conscious of his debt to the state. In our international relations we should seek precisely the same ends. The beckoning goal is a co-operative world, in which a living consciousness of interdependence is fused with a healthy love for the land of our birth. The presupposition of all profitable thinking and planning is a firm grasp of the unity of civilization. The emergence of this incontrovertible fact must ultimately trample down the narrow provincialism which impedes fruitful partnership, though victory is still far away. Geographical exploration, scientific invention, and historical research have at last begun to make us aware of our common heritage, our collective achievements, our joint responsibilities. The part is meaningless except in its relation to the whole. Mankind is the book and the nations are its chapters. This was the gospel of Mazzini, the greatest of nationalists, whose watchword was not only a free and united Italy, but God and Humanity.

Regional attempts to stabilize large portions of the globe have been made, and lessons are to be learned from every chapter of the story in turn. The Pax Romana, the first serious experiment in large-scale organization, rested on the strength of a single state and perished with its fall. The Respublica Christiana of the Middle Ages, which was scarcely more than a philosopher's dream, vanished when the modern world was born in the Renaissance and the Reformation. The Concert of Europe, the first sustained endeavour to substitute consultation and co-operation for the crude arbitrament of the sword, collapsed within a decade because Napoleon's conquerors were anchored to the *status quo*. Arbitration proved a useful expedient in differences for which nations cared too little to fight, but useless when their blood was up. The failure of all these successive attempts to organize the world trumpets forth the necessity of a wider scheme, resting not on empire, race or creed, but on our common humanity.

Next to the recognition of the unity of civilization and the resultant need of institutional organization comes the principle of minimum constraint. If we accept the significance of individuality, we must stand for the self-determination of nations within and without. Englishmen welcomed the unification of Italy and Germany; the emancipation of the Balkan peoples from the Turkish yoke; the birth of the Irish Free State; the Statute of Westminster, which proclaimed equality of status between the Dominions and the Motherland. Fox's joyful ejaculation on the fall of the Bastille: How much the happiest event in the history of mankind and how much the best! despite its emotional exuberance, typifies our disinterested sympathy with the efforts of peoples struggling for their rights. Freedom from an alien yoke, freedom from domestic tyranny: here are the watchwords inscribed on the banner of humanity as we advance towards the good life. Kant taught that the best hope for peace lay in a loose federation of self-governing communities. Thus the connection between peace and civic responsibility was proclaimed for the first time by the greatest thinker of modern times.

We shall never create an organized and moralized world, in which the writ of Machiavelli will cease to run, unless we can banish the spectre of aggression. But the ghost can only be laid by providing alternative methods of securing the aims which war is waged to achieve. Arbitration is excellent as far as it goes, but many conflicts arise from causes too deep for it to remove so long as the doctrine of unfettered national sovereignty prevails. The darkest clouds on the horizon to-day are the Japanese ambitions in the Far East and the revisionist demands of the European states defeated in the Great War. To expect that war will be averted by the simple expedient of maintaining the *status quo* is to live in a world of illusions, for the Grand Alliance of 1914-1918 is dead.

When Japan argues that China is a state with which normal relations are impossible she merely seeks to cloak her aggression. Before the war every nation possessed the recognized right in international law to go to war whenever and wherever it liked. But with the creation of the League each signatory of the Covenant undertook to respect and preserve the territorial integrity of its fellow members, and the Pact of Paris pledged us all to renounce war as an instrument of national policy. In addition to these general obligations, Japan also agreed in the Nine-Power Treaty of Washington " to respect the sovereignty, independence and territorial integrity of China." The weakness of the latter was fully known to the signatories at the time. It was therefore irrelevant to adduce her internal troubles as an excuse for invasion in 1931 when they had been expressly recognized in the treaty of 1922. For the nine Powers solemnly agreed " to provide the fullest and most unembarrassed opportunity to China to develop and maintain for herself an effective and stable government." The belief that the railway to Mukden was cut by Chinese hands in September 1931 was not accepted by the Lytton Commission. The elaborate preparations for the conquest of Manchuria were complete, and the troops awaited the signal for attack. The United States were in deep waters, England was in the throes of a financial crisis, and Russia was immersed in her Five-Year Plan. The world's extremity was Japan's opportunity. The League frowned, but was powerless to act. It declined to recognize the fruits of aggression, but it could do no more.

The most dangerous issue in Europe is the revision of the settlements imposed on the defeated parties at the end of the

z

war. Armaments, alliances, and economic nationalism are the measure of our alarm. The root of the trouble is the existence of frontiers imposed in defiance of the sentiments of millions of aggrieved human beings. The rule of war is that the loser pays, but never before have there been so many losers to complain. The ultimate purpose of the armaments piling up before our eyes is to challenge or to preserve the territorial *status quo*. Resentment of an alien yoke is an ineradicable instinct. The minority clauses of the treaties, well intentioned as they were and useful as they should be in diminishing the material and psychological importance of boundaries, are only applicable in certain states, and even in these they are often scandalously ignored. Our ears are assailed by shrill cries from the opposing camps : War unless territorial revision ! Territorial revision means war ! Both may be right. Petty concessions would be useless, and large transfers are at present ruled out by the popular will. When some state comes forward and announces its readiness to lay a substantial portion of its possessions as an offering on the altar of peace, revision will come within the range of practical politics. Till then it is a dream. Article XIX of the Covenant, it is true, stares us in the face. " The Assembly may from time to time advise the reconsideration by members of the League of treaties which have become inapplicable, and the consideration of international conditions whose continuance might endanger the peace of the world." The phraseology is elastic, and it was this article which partially reconciled Wilson to the surrender of his hopes. Yet it has never been used. The hungry sheep look up but are not fed.

Where is the road of escape from this threatening impasse, in which the victors cling to their conquests and the vanquished to their claims ? There is no lack of confident replies, but they are one and all academic in character. Nothing short of a world state can save us, argues Mr. Wells. A chain of socialist communities, we are told by other publicists, would suppress the economic imperialism inherent in capitalist communities, and thereby remove the chief incentive to war. Such a prescription, even if its argument be accepted, is useless for the urgent task of saving humanity from another bloodbath during the next few years. For the speedy conversion of the world to socialism is no more probable than the universal adoption of the Sermon on the Mount as the rule of public life. Leaving such long-term remedies to the future we come back to the League as our best hope. It may be plausibly argued that its existence in 1914 might have averted the World War. To adopt Professor Gilbert Murray's illuminating phrase, it is " an organ of consultation," ready for use by day or night like a fire brigade waiting for the call. That the Covenant is capable of amendment its authors themselves would never deny, but we should bear in mind the weighty declaration of M. Avenol, the Secretary-General, that it contains the minimum obligations of a Society of Nations. To override the smaller states would be to kill the League, which rests on the conception of equality of rights, not equality of power.

The increasing peril has brought the problem of preventing or defeating aggression into the foreground of discussion. The French proposal of an armed League was rejected when the Covenant was shaped, and was scarcely heard of during the years of recovery. To-day, as the skies darken, a League Air Force has many friends. The technical difficulties are immense ; and while three Great Powers are outside the League, the discussion must remain academic. Moreover, the scheme is criticized both by those who fear that it might be misused and by those who object to the employment of force by the League at all. If the project has a future it can only be in a world where national armaments have been reduced to a police standard. The question of sanctions in other forms remains. A more binding obligation on the part of the signatories to share in a League war than that already embodied in Article 16 of the Covenant cannot be expected, and England at any rate is unwilling to go beyond her Locarno pledge. Regional pacts have in consequence sprung up and seem likely to increase, for they meet specific needs by limited commitments. Development of the collective system must for the present run along economic lines. A flagrant breach of the peace should be promptly met by a general refusal of munitions and by the cessation of trade. That economic sanctions may provoke a declaration of war is a possibility; but whatever risks there may be in economic pressure must be balanced against the rival peril of encouraging aggression by a tacit assurance of immunity. Collective security is the only security.

A policy of isolation in an interdependent world is out of date. Alliances are as dangerous as isolation, for it was the precarious balancing of group against group that swept us into the abyss of 1914. Science has raced ahead while statesmanship lags timidly behind. The new wine must be poured into new bottles, for the old receptacles are cracked. Power must be pooled. The institutional embodiment of the unity of civilization is such a startling development that its necessity requires to be continually demonstrated and reaffirmed. To foster the faith of the peoples in the League by word and act is to render a service to mankind. Its object, as we read in the Preamble, is "to promote international co-operation and to achieve international peace and security by the acceptance of obligations not to resort to war ; by the prescription of open, just and honourable relations between nations ; by the firm establishment of the understandings of international law as the actual rule of conduct among governments and by the maintenance of justice and a scrupulous respect for all treaty obligations in the dealings of organized peoples with one another." Here is a programme to inspire the enthusiasm of old and young as the insufficiency of political and economic nationalism is progressively revealed in confusion and despair. The sovereign self-sufficing state of Machiavelli, Hobbes, Hegel and their disciples will have to go, for in the long run it brings misfortune to us all. In striving for the organization of the world we are not merely underpinning the edifice of civilization but moving towards the good life of which we dream and which is only attainable in comradeship and peace. "Interest divides," said President Wilson ; "what unites us is the common pursuit of right." The complete moralization of politics is too much to expect in any future that we can foresee. But the sense of community is growing. Experience, the stern old schoolmaster, is pointing the way towards an organized world. The minds and hearts of men are enlisting in ever-increasing numbers in the great crusade.

HOBBES AND THE ABSOLUTE STATE

HOBBES is the earliest, the most original, and the least English of our three great political thinkers. With his hard-shelled rationalism and his scorn of compromise he seems rather out of place in the land of the *juste milieu*, where we pride ourselves on our bad logic and our good feeling. By the middle of the seventeenth century the modern Englishman had emerged. His sturdy independence rejected the doctrine of the Divine Right of Kings, but he was quite ready to obey the laws framed by a freely elected Parliament. A law-abiding individualist, he had as little taste for anarchy as for slavery. He was beginning to solve the problem of combining order with liberty. Hobbes argued that it could not be done. Locke, with the experience of the Revolution settlement to encourage him, asserted that it could. Burke, with a further century of evidence to guide him, confirmed Locke's verdict and discovered the secret in the blending of tradition with experiment.

Hobbes possessed an intellect of extraordinary power, sharp as a razor but of limited imaginative range. Living in an age of civil turmoil he mistook a distressing phenomenon for an incurable disease. Loving intellectual liberty as much as any of his contemporaries, he felt nevertheless that self-government was a prize beyond our grasp. Order was heaven's first law, and no price was too high to obtain it. Anarchy was a ferocious animal which could only be kept at bay by the lash of an autocrat. His mechanistic mind had no vision of organic development. His rules of government were simple enough, for they embodied his conception of the unchanging imperfections of human nature. Political theories, like political systems, reflect the ideology of their authors like a face in a mirror. If we entertain a lofty view of the average man, of his ultimate sanity, of his capacity to learn from his mistakes, we impose on him the minimum of restraint. If, on the other hand, we regard him, to use Taine's unflattering simile, as a chained gorilla, we keep him behind steel bars. The optimism of Grotius made him the pioneer of international law. The pessimism of Hobbes rendered him the father of totalitarianism. France of the absolute Monarchy, rather than Puritan England, was his spiritual home. He was neither Whig nor Tory, neither Conservative nor Liberal. Tradition had no hold over his mind. The most explosive of English thinkers had no master and left no school. Men who agreed in nothing else united in detestation of his creed. It is part of the eternal fascination of the grim old warrior that he stands out in defiant isolation, too paradoxical to prevail, yet too powerful to ignore. Not a master-builder, perhaps, but a Master Mind.

Hobbes came prematurely into the world in a Wiltshire vicarage when the Spanish Armada frightened his mother, and he used to say that he was the twin-brother of fear. The precocious lad attracted the attention of his schoolmaster, a good classic, to whom he presented a translation of the *Medea* into Latin iambics before entering Magdalen Hall in his fifteenth year. His father cared nothing for learning, but his uncle, a prosperous glover, provided the necessary funds. In his brief Latin autobiography he merely records that he studied the logic and physics of Aristotle. Aubrey, his devoted friend and biographer, adds that in those days he cared little for logic, yet thought himself a good disputant. Scholasticism was dying and science was in its infancy. He never spoke of his university with respect or affection, disliking both the laxity of the undergraduates and the unappetizing fare of the lecture-room.

After taking his degree at the age of nineteen he was recommended by the principal of his college to the eldest son of the Earl of Devonshire, who believed, according to Aubrey, that he would profit more in his learning if he had a scholar of his own age to wait on him than a grave doctor. Less of a tutor than a page, Hobbes went hunting and hawking with his young master and kept his privy purse. It was the luckiest incident in his life, establishing the delightful relations with the Cavendish family which only terminated seventy years later with his death, and opening the door to cultivated society, an excellent library, and foreign travel. He bought copies of the classics which he carried in his pocket. The most memorable intellectual experience of these years was his friendship with Bacon. The Lord Chancellor used to walk in his garden at Gorhambury, attended by one or other of his gentlemen with ink and paper to jot down his thoughts. This task, according to Bacon, was better performed by Hobbes than by anyone else, for the notes taken by others were often unintelligible since they themselves had failed to understand. The younger man also assisted the elder in translating several of his Essays into Latin. Both were children of the Renaissance, scornful of scholasticism, eager for scientific knowledge, and craving for a new secular synthesis. But Hobbes was in no sense a disciple, and he never used the inductive method.

Roaming over the wide spaces of philosophy and classical literature, he was in no hurry to write. To quote his own words, the extreme pleasure he took in study overcame all other appetites. He never married, and women play no part in his life. The chief literary product of these quiet years was a translation of Thucydides, whom he saluted as " the most politic historiographer that ever writ." He confessed that there was much more diligence than elegance in his work, and Jowett had no great opinion of his skill. His purpose, he tells us in his autobiography, was *ut ineptiae democraticorum Atheniensium concivibus suis patefierent.* The historian's matchless pictures of political confusion strengthened his conviction of the necessity of a strong ruler. Next to Thucydides among the Greeks he owed most to Aristotle, not to the *Politics,* which he disliked, but to the *Rhetoric,* of which he made a digest, and passages from which, as Dr. Leo Strauss has shown in parallel columns, are reproduced almost verbally in his writings. Later in life he described Plato as the best of the ancient philosophers, but no one was ever less of a Platonist. A similar attempt to prove borrowings from the Stoics has been made by Dilthey in a memorable essay. But in no case was the debt very large. He always stood on his own legs.

The Grand Tour was an essential part of the education of young noblemen, and Hobbes profited by the custom. He accompanied his master to France, Germany, and Italy in 1610, the year of the murder of Henri IV, and he made two longer journeys with young noblemen in 1629 and 1634-7. He studied the France of Richelieu at close quarters, and in Paris formed enduring friendships with Mersenne, the henchman of Descartes, Gassendi, the antagonist of the great philosopher, and other scholars. In Italy he visited Rome and Florence, where, like Milton, he made the acquaintance of Galileo of whom he spoke ever after with enthusiasm. He discovered Euclid at the age of forty, and his interest in geometry and the natural sciences was stimulated by these contacts. On returning home in 1637 he was ready to start on his ambitious scheme to unify the whole field of knowledge in a demonstrable system of philosophy. He possessed boundless self-confidence, and he believed things to be much simpler than they are. He strove to interpret every aspect of the world by direct observation. Philosophy was only another name for the truths and lessons of science. He found the key in the fact of motion. His friend Harvey discovered the motion of blood, Galileo the motion of the stars. Thought was motion in the brain. The material world was the only world. The task of the philosopher was to explain the universe in mechanical terms. Never was there a system of more undiluted materialism. Even God is a corporeal spirit. The world consisted of natural and political bodies. He resolved to set forth his teaching in three treatises, *De Corpore, De Homine, De Cive*, man forming the connecting link between nature and society. Leslie Stephen salutes him as a Herbert Spencer of the seventeenth century.

That the encyclopaedic project was not carried out in the intended sequence was due to the constitutional crisis which he found on his return from abroad in 1637. The most urgent task was to express his thoughts on man and society, leaving the study of nature for quieter times. He associated with the group of lawyers, poets, and divines who gathered round Falkland at Great Tew, near Oxford, and who live for ever in the portrait gallery of Clarendon. At the ripe age of fifty-two he made his first contribution to the political debate. The little work entitled *The Elements of Law Natural and Politic*, though not written for publication, circulated freely in manuscript before it was printed in 1650, and was a good deal discussed. The Dedication to his friend the Earl of Newcastle, a Cavendish and a Privy Councillor, dated May 1640, boldly declares the book to be the true and only foundation of the science of politics. " It would be an incomparable benefit to Commonwealth that every one held the opinion concerning law and policy here declared." Previous writers from antiquity downwards, he adds with a contemptuous sweep of his hand, had not understood the subject. It reminds us of Melbourne's saying that he wished he was as sure of anything as Macaulay was of everything.

The book consists of two parts. *Human Nature, or the Fundamental Elements of Policy* was written as an introduction to the longer and more important treatise on the state. Beginning with a brief survey of our faculties of body and mind, Hobbes reaches the heart of his subject in the chapter on " Good and Evil." Man is not wicked, but he is instinctively selfish, acting solely for his own good.

" Every man calleth that which pleaseth and is delightful to himself good and that evil which displeaseth him. Nor is there any such thing as absolute goodness, considered without relation ; for even the goodness which we apprehend in God Almighty is his goodness to us." Most things, he admits, are a mixture of good and evil." When the greater part is good, the whole is called good, and when the evil overweighteth, the whole is called evil." This crude utilitarianism is vital to the larger purpose of discovering the basis for laws and institutions. God exists, but we can have no conception of the Deity. Since everything is produced by something which went before, we go back and back " till we come to the eternal, that is to say the first power of all powers and first cause of all causes ; and this it is which all men conceive by the name of God, implying eternity, incomprehensibility and omnipotence. And thus all that will consider may know that God is, though not what he is. Even a man that is born blind, though it be not possible for him to have any imagination what kind of thing fire is, yet he cannot but know that somewhat there is that men call fire, because it warmeth him." All attributes ascribed to the Deity are merely expressions of our incapacity or our reverence. For instance when we say that he is a spirit, we merely desire to abstract from him all corporeal grossness. Hobbes's God is a purely intellectual conception, indispensable to the understanding of the universe but playing no part in the supreme problem of creating and maintaining community life. Bacon compared certain philosophers to the stars, which give little light because they are so high. That is exactly how Hobbes thought of God.

The second part, *De Corpore Politico*, opens with a depressing picture of primitive conditions. " Every man by nature hath right to all things, that is to do whatsoever he listeth to whom he listeth, to possess, use, and enjoy all things he will and can. *Natura dedit omnia omnibus.*" But this is nothing but a state of war, for even the weaker in strength or wit can kill his fellow. Since every individual instinctively seeks his own safety, reason, which is no less an ingredient of man than passion, points the way out. The first step is for everyone to divest himself of his natural right to all things. The second is to transfer his right by covenant. The third is to secure general consent to a similar surrender, since the mutual aid of two or three is of little avail. The fourth is the erection of some common or sovereign power for their common peace, defence, and benefit. There is no sentiment about the process. What induces a man to become subject to another is fear and nothing else.

Political society, or as we say a commonwealth, begins when it is thus agreed that a majority, or a few, or one, shall represent the will of all. Government, whatever its nature, must have the power of coercion, since where there is no coercion there is no fear of consequences. Thus in every state there is an absolute and indivisible sovereign who can neither be punished nor resisted. He cannot give away any part of his sovereignty, even if he wishes. Mixed government, the supremacy of the legislature, judiciary and executive, each in its allotted sphere, is impracticable. The sovereign claims obedience till his death or defeat. Though monarchy is not the only possible form of government, it is the least subject to passion or dissolution by civil war. To avoid uncertainty in the succession the sovereign may name his successor. He must also decide controversies in religion, controlling, not indeed the consciences of men, but their words and actions ; for he is the immediate ruler of the Church under Christ, and all other authorities are subordinate to him. Before Hobbes the doctrine of contract had been the charter of liberty, even of rebellion. If the ruler broke the bond, he must be resisted. This conception was now turned upside down. The contract was a surrender as well as a guarantee. In a chapter on the " Causes of Rebellion " he denies that in certain cases the sovereignty may be resisted. If any exceptions are made to the rule of obedience, the door is opened to confusion and peril. Sedition is the death of the commonwealth.

Though there was no reference to the political issues of the day it is not surprising that the little treatise impressed its readers, for its doctrines challenged both the parties which were girding themselves for battle. The gospel of indivisible sovereignty, and of law as the command of the sovereign, had been proclaimed by Bodin as the way of salvation during the ferocious wars of religion in France ; but the idea was unfamiliar in England. From the champions of Divine Right Hobbes was separated by his cold-blooded rationalism, his derivation of monarchy from the will of the people, his refusal to concern himself with the legal title of the sovereign. He agrees with James I in *The True Law of Free Monarchies* that the ruler is required by God to rule wisely and well, and that his punishment, if he deserves to be punished, is the affair of God, not of man. But while the Stuart kings claimed impunity for lawful rulers alone, he demands it for all alike. The distinction between *de jure* and *de facto* is brushed aside as irrelevant. The sovereign's task is to prevent men from killing and robbing each other. That essential duty could be as efficiently discharged by a vigorous usurper as by the anointed heir of kings. From the Parliamentary leaders he was sundered by his contempt for precedents, fundamental laws, and limited monarchy. Though both King and Parliament thus saw their most cherished convictions assailed, the latter was the more deeply outraged. For the message of the book was that Charles I, as the actual possessor of power, had the right to do what he liked, including the levying of taxes for national needs. Bishop Manwaring had been sent to the Tower for exalting the prerogative, and when his case was discussed Hobbes thought it time to cross the Channel.

The first task on reaching Paris was briefly to formulate his objections to the new philosophy of Descartes which divided the world of thought into two camps ; but his mind was mainly centred on the plight of his country. From his safe anchorage he followed the crisis with anxious interest, and occupied himself with the composition of the *De Cive*, which appeared in a very limited edition in Latin at Paris in 1642. An English translation was published in 1651 with supplementary notes as *Philosophical Rudiments concerning Government and Society*. The Dedicatory Epistle to his friend and patron the Earl of Devonshire, son of his first pupil, explains that he has been careful not to meddle with the civil laws of any particular nation. Yet the elaborate Preface admits that the book was written with English problems in view, owing to the fact that England was " boiling hot with questions concerning the rights of dominion and the obedience due from subjects, the true forerunners of an approaching war."

The Preface stresses the paramount importance of sound teaching. " How many kings, and those good men too, hath this one error that a tyrant king might lawfully be put to death, been the slaughter of ! How many throats hath this false position cut, that a prince for some causes may by some certain men be deposed ! And what bloodshed hath not this erroneous doctrine caused, that kings are not superior to but administrators for the multitude ! Lastly, how many rebellions hath this opinion been the cause of, which teacheth that the knowledge whether the commands of man be just or unjust belongs to private men; and that before they yield obedience they not only may but ought to dispute them!" Hobbes looks back with wistful admiration to the times before such questions were raised, when man reverenced the supreme power; when they little used, as in the present time, to join themselves with ambitious and hellish spirits, to the utter ruin of the state. "For they could not entertain so strange a fancy as not to desire the preservation of that by which they were preserved." To dispel these dangerous illusions and show the highway to peace was the most profitable of occupations. He proceeds to restate his familiar gospel in a few lapidary sentences. The state of nature, without civil society, is a war of all against all, in which all men have equal right to equal things. *Homo homini lupus.* To escape from this misery is a natural instinct. It can only be achieved by the surrender of this unprofitable right to some supreme power, preferably a monarchy, though all governments deserve obedience. No names are mentioned, but he exhorts his readers no longer to suffer ambitious men to wade through blood to power, but to content themselves with their present state, even though it may not be the best. For in establishing civil society they sacrifice far less than they secure. *Le mieux est l'ennemi du bien.*

The volume is divided into three parts, entitled "Liberty," "Dominion," "Religion." The whole argument closely follows the outlines of 1640, but is more elaborate. It begins by challenging the Aristotelian axiom that man is a political animal. On the contrary, men in a state of nature have a desire to hurt, chiefly because many covet the same thing at the same time. The strongest gets it by the sword, but he cannot keep it, for his life is always in danger. Equally anyone could say this is mine, but he could not enjoy it, since his neighbour would pretend it was his. This useless right to all things must be abandoned for the sake of peace and self-defence, the craving for which is the first and fundamental law of nature. Death by violence is the supreme evil which all men shun. But contracts are worthless unless they are kept, and the keeping of trust is the second of nature's fundamental laws. These and many other natural laws, or virtues of the mind, which Hobbes sets forth in detail, are immutable and eternal. "What they forbid can never be lawful; what they command can never be unlawful." Yet the moral law is only binding in the court of conscience.

Part II, entitled " Dominion," starts from the assumption that these laws of nature do not and cannot suffice to keep the peace. There is only one remedy, the submission of the wills of all to that of one man or one council, each individual contracting with all the others not to resist the will. Sovereignty is the right to everything, *jus ad omnia*. The sovereign is absolute, and his acts are not subject to punishment, even if he sins against the laws of nature, that is against God. No one, it is true, need obey a command to kill himself or a member of his family or perform certain other things which we would rather die than do. Yet such disobedience would not affect the sovereign power, since his right to slay those who refuse obedience remains intact. For if his discretion were limited that limitation must necessarily proceed from some greater power. Mixed or limited government would not increase the liberty of the subject, for the inevitable disagreement would involve the return to civil strife.

Hobbes admits that there are disadvantages in creating an absolute sovereign, and expresses his wish that not only kings but all other persons endowed with supreme authority should observe natural and divine laws. If, however, he does not, and if in his wrath and sensuality he slaughters his innocent subjects there is no remedy ; for to oppose the sovereign is to relapse into anarchy. In a constituted state we all enjoy our limited right. " Out of it any man may rightly spoil or kill another ; in it, none but one. Out of it, we are protected by our own forces ; in it, by the power of all. Out of it, no man is sure of the fruit of his labours ; in it, all men are. Lastly, out of it, there is a dominion of passions, war, fear, poverty, slovenliness, solitude, barbarism, ignorance, cruelty ; in it, the dominion of reason, peace, security, riches, decency, society, elegancy, sciences and benevolence."

Though the ruler is bound neither by law nor contract, he has his duties which are all contained in the maxim *Salus Populi suprema Lex*. Though not subject to the will of other men, it is his duty in all things, as far as possible, to yield obedience to right reason which is the natural, moral, and divine law. By safety is meant not merely the preservation of life but happiness, since government was instituted in order that men should live delightfully, so far as human conditions allow. He would sin against his trust if he did not strive by good laws to give his subjects the good things of life, to make them strong in body and mind, to secure their defence against foreign enemies.

In a word he is morally bound to play the game. For the preservation of internal peace the rooting out of errors and the teaching of sound political doctrine in the universities is essential. Public burdens should be fairly distributed. Rewards and punishments are useful instruments of pacification, the obedient subject being exalted and the factious held in contempt. The wise ruler will never try to cover every case by law, and the subject may do whatever is not forbidden. The object of laws is merely to direct men's actions, just as nature ordains the banks not to stay but to guide the course of the stream.

The third and most novel part of the book, entitled " Religion," discusses the attitude of the Christian to the state with the aid of a multitude of texts. Here, too, there is no escape from the iron rule of obedience. Religious strife adds to political strife and must therefore cease. For spiritual matters are also the province of the state, which gives pastors their authority. Thus in a Christian commonwealth obedience is due to the sovereign in all things, as well spiritual and temporal. But what if the ruler is not a Christian ? Must we resist when we cannot obey ? " Truly no, for this is contrary to our civil covenant. What must we do then ? Go to Christ by martyrdom, which, if it seems to any man to be a hard saying, most certain is it that he believes not with his whole heart that Jesus is the Christ, the son of the living God ; for he would then desire to be dissolved and to be with Christ." Since the author had as little passion for martyrdom as any man who ever lived, this summons to a heroic death suggests that he is talking with his tongue in his cheek.

Hobbes was inordinately proud of his book. As Galileo was the founder of natural science, so, he declared, was he the founder of the science of politics, his doctrine appearing to him as demonstrable as a proposition of Euclid. The claim is grotesque, but his originality is beyond question. Bodin, his only real predecessor, was a lawyer, not a psychologist, and it was the essence of Hobbes's system that he grounded autocracy on his interpretation of human nature. His debt to Machiavelli is even slighter. Agreeing in their unflattering realism, they disagreed in almost everything else. The Englishman started from psychology, the Italian from history and personal experience. Machiavelli's Prince was subject to no moral law, but there is no doctrinal totalitarianism in his pages. He wrote primarily for rulers, Hobbes primarily for subjects. *The Prince* is a manual of statecraft, *De Cive* a grammar of obedience.

The eleven years in Paris were a happy time. Hobbes had plenty of friends, old and new. After expounding his political doctrine he returned for a time to science and philosophy. He took a course in chemistry and studied anatomy with Sir William Petty. Descartes was at the height of his fame ; but the greatest French and English thinkers of their time disliked each other's views, and it is not quite certain whether they ever met. Descartes believed that Hobbes had stolen his ideas on optics. Social life 'was enriched when Royalist refugees began to stream across the Channel. Newcastle, the defeated commander at Marston Moor, dabbled in literature, and Bishop Bramhall was an expert metaphysician. More important was the arrival of the Prince of Wales, who joined his mother at St. Germain in 1646 ; for Hobbes was appointed his instructor in mathematics through Newcastle's influence. Having a bad name in Royalist circles, he was admonished to keep to his subject and not meddle with politics. His orthodoxy was also suspected, and the French clergy disliked his outspoken anti-Papalism. When he was dangerously ill in 1647, as he records in his autobiography, his beloved Mersenne came to see him, fearing that he might die outside the Church. The visitor was gently silenced by turning the conversation. When did you last see Gassendi ? inquired the invalid, and his visitor took the hint. A few days later, however, when Cosin, afterwards Bishop of Durham, came and offered to pray with him, the sick man gladly consented and received the sacrament. In 1640 he had feared the zealots of the Short Parliament. Ten years later, to use his own words, he could not trust his safety with the French clergy. He may even have feared assassination.

After the execution of the King Hobbes resolved to offer guidance to his afflicted country. In 1650 he allowed the *Elements of Law* to be printed, and in 1651 he permitted an English translation of *De Cive*. Moreover, the *Leviathan*, on which he had laboured since the collapse of the Royalist cause, was finished at last. In his attack on that book written many years later Clarendon declared that he had conversed with Hobbes in Paris on the eve of its appearance, and had asked him how he could publish such doctrines. The philosopher replied, more in jest than in earnest : " The truth is I have a mind to go home." Even if the conversation is correctly reported it can only have been a jest, for the new treatise merely developed the teaching of the previous books. In like manner the charge brought against him after the Restoration that it was " writ in defence of Oliver's title " is refuted by dates. While the finishing touches were being put to the volume, England was governed by the Long Parliament. The real cause of his departure was not so much his politics as his anti-clericalism. "All honest men here," wrote the King's secretary, Sir Edward Nicholas, " are very glad that the King hath at length banished from his Court that father of atheists, Mr. Hobbes." He was no more an atheist than his critic, but he bowed to the storm. After presenting the King with an advance copy of *Leviathan*, now in the British Museum, he left France in 1651, made his submission to the Council of State, and never left England again.

Leviathan or The Matter, Form and Power of a Commonwealth Ecclesiastical and Civil is not only the most powerful defence of absolutism ever written but one of the great books of the world. The frontispiece strikes the keynote of the work. A gigantic crowned figure, with a sword in the right hand and a crozier in the left, rises behind a hill at the bottom of which lies a stately city. Above the head of the sovereign are the resounding words, *Non est potestas super terram quae comparetur ei*. The Dedication explains that the Great Leviathan is the state, " which is but an artificial man, though of greater stature and strength than the natural, for whose protection and defence it was intended."

The first of the four parts, entitled " Of Man," passes in review his faculties and capacities, his beliefs and superstitions, his virtues and defects. Men are by nature so nearly equal in mind and body that, while they all long for power, none can claim any benefit to which another may not pretend. From this equality proceeds rivalry, and rivalry generates war—not war in the military sense but an unceasing struggle of all against all. The state of nature was intolerable. "No place for industry because the fruit thereof is uncertain, no arts, no letters, no society, and, which is worst of all, continual fear and danger of violent death ; and the life of man solitary, poor, nasty, brutish, short." Hobbes admits that such a condition of chronic war was never universal, but it still prevailed in many places, America for instance.

Nature placed man in evil conditions, but it also provided a means of escape. The desires and passions from which anarchy arose were no sin, nor were the actions to which they led a crime. The objection was purely practical : the state of nature was to no one's interest, for the weakest was strong enough to kill the strongest. The solution could only be found by every individual surrendering his right to do what he liked, and contenting himself with so much liberty as he would allow others against himself. If others declined to abandon their right there is no reason for him to part with his own. His right, therefore, should not be blindly thrown away but deliberately transferred. Competing personal rights had to give place to impersonal law. Yet no laws could be made till it was agreed who should make them.

At this point we pass to Part II, entitled " Of Commonwealth," which forms the kernel of the book and enshrines Hobbes's legacy to the world. Men love not only their own liberty but dominion over others, and in both directions they need to be restrained. Only thus can they escape from that miserable condition of war arising from their natural passions, when there is no visible power to tie them by fear of punishment to the performance of their covenants. " For the laws of nature, as justice, equity, modesty, mercy, and in sum doing to others as we would be done to, of themselves, without the terror of some power to cause them to be observed, are contrary to our natural passions, that carry us to partiality, pride, revenge and the like. And covenants without the sword are but words." The only salvation is to confer all their power upon one man or one assembly, and to submit their wills to his judgment. " It is as if every man should say to every other man : I authorize and give up my right of governing myself to this man, or this assembly of men, on this condition, that thou give up thy right to him and authorize all his actions in like manner." When the multitude is thus united in one person we have a commonwealth. " This is the origin of that Great Leviathan, that mortal god, to which we owe, under the immortal God, our peace and defence. Clad in this authority given him by every man in the community, he possesses such strength that, by fear thereof, he can perform the wills of them all to peace at home and defence against enemies abroad." This exalted person is called the sovereign and everyone else is his subject. A minority is as much bound to obedience as the majority which voted the choice. For he who declines forfeits his right to protection, is left in the condition from which his fellows have escaped, and may be killed by any man without injustice.

Having decided on their ruler his subjects become responsible for all his actions. If it is a monarch they cannot without his leave cast off monarchy. Moreover, though they are irrevocably bound to him, he is in no way bound to them. There can be no breach of covenant by the sovereign, for no conditions were made when he received his power. No conditions could have been made, for covenants are but words unless there is power to enforce them ; and such power does not exist till a sovereign is set up. To complain of the use which he makes of his power is illogical, for by the institution of a commonwealth every man is author of all his acts. " He that complaineth of injury from his sovereign complaineth of that whereof he himself is the author, and therefore ought not to accuse any man but himself." The sovereign may commit iniquity but not injustice, and he is not subject to punishment. He alone is judge of what is necessary for the peace and defence of his subjects, and it is to his interest to treat them properly. It is also his task to decide what opinions and doctrines are dangerous to peace and to examine all books before publication ; for actions proceed from ideas. He must also lay down the rules of property, decide all disputes, reward and punish, choose all counsellors and magistrates, and control the army. He is not subject to the laws which he makes. The task with which he was entrusted is to procure the safety of the people. He is obliged to carry it out by the law of nature, and to render an account to God, the author of that law ; but only to him. A kingdom divided against itself cannot stand, as was proved by the civil war. He expressly declares that the book was occasioned by the disorders of the time. He cares little whether the government is a monarchy, an aristocracy, or a democracy, for the rules are always the same. Some man or some assembly must possess undisputed power.

After thus concentrating power in a single hand and calmly proclaiming that might is right, Hobbes pauses to answer the most obvious criticism. "A man may here object that the condition of subjects is very miserable, as being obnoxious to the lusts and other irregular passions of him or them that have so unlimited a power in their hands." He retorts that the greatest evils of government are trifles compared to the horrible calamities of civil war or of the anarchy inevitable in the absence of coercive power. The condition of man in this life, he reminds us, will never be without inconveniences. Bad rulers are preferable to anarchy, and bad laws are better than none. In his longing for a quiet life and his hatred of revolution Hobbes stands for peace at any price. There are, moreover, three alleviations of the subject's lot. In the first place he is at liberty to do whatever is not forbidden by the sovereign. Secondly, he may think as he likes so long as he outwardly conforms. Thirdly, the obligation to the sovereign only lasts as long as the power of the latter to protect him, since the sole object of obedience is protection. Sovereignty is the soul of the commonwealth, and those who make it intend it to be immortal. Yet it may be ended by abdication or murder, by foreign war or domestic discord. " Through the ignorance and passions of men it hath in it many seeds of a natural mortality. . . . Nothing can be immortal which mortals make." He had lived long enough to see many rulers and systems come and go.

Part III of the massive volume of seven hundred pages is entitled " Of a Christian Commonwealth," Part IV " Of the Kingdom of Darkness." Together they form half the book, and the amplitude of treatment reflects the author's ever-increasing detestation of sacerdotalism. Though he professed to be an orthodox Christian, he was entirely destitute of religious sentiment. Several modern writers indeed believe that he was merely a conforming sceptic. Religion, he declares in his lapidary way, is not philosophy but law. It has a lowly origin, for it is the child of fear—the fear of invisible things and invisible powers, of darkness and ghosts. The superstitions of the timid are cunningly exploited by the priests for the maintenance and increase of their power. Thus arise clerical claims which compete with the prestige and challenge the authority of the state. Such claims fill the greatest of Erastians with anger and contempt. He will suffer no rival near the throne. The sovereign must defend himself and his subjects lest a struggle arise in every man's breast between the Christian and the citizen. No man can serve two masters.

Biblical texts in abundance are employed to buttress the arguments from reason and experience. Some of them Hobbes interprets in his own way, for they are the outworks of the enemy from which they impugn the civil power. He rebuts Ballarmine's claims on behalf of the Papacy, and confines ecclesiastical authority within the narrowest limits. The

Kingdom of Christ, he reminds us, is not of this world, and therefore his ministers, unless they be kings, cannot require obedience in his name.   Their task is to proclaim the Kingdom of Christ, to teach what we must do in order to be received into the Kingdom of God when it comes.   All other claims must be firmly resisted, above all those of the Bishop of Rome and his kingdom of darkness.   " If a man consider the original of this great ecclesiastical dominion, he will easily perceive that the Papacy is no other than the ghost of the deceased Roman Empire, sitting crowned upon the grave thereof.   For so did the Papacy start up on a sudden out of the ruins of that heathen power."   His spiritual power, outside the bounds of his own papal state, was based on deluded people's fear of excommunication, on false miracles, false tradition, and false interpretations of scripture.   Henry VIII and Elizabeth cast it out, but the danger was not entirely removed.   " Who knows that this spirit of Rome may not return, or rather an assembly of spirits, worse than he, enter and inhabit this clean-swept house and make the end thereof worse than the beginning ?   For it is not the Roman clergy only that pretends the Kingdom of God to be of this world, and thereby to have a power therein, distinct from that of the civil state."   The closing page of the book claims that it contains nothing contrary to the word of God, to good manners, or to the public tranquillity.   On the contrary it should be taught in the Universities, the fountains of civil and moral doctrine.   For when men know their duties, they are less inclined to raise their hands against the state.

Leviathan provoked a tempest of fury in royalist and Anglican circles.   They were particularly incensed by his doctrine that theology was a department of politics, and by his open contempt for legitimism.   " Those natural seeds of religion which God hath printed in the heart of man," declared Bishop Bramhall, " are more efficacious towards preservation of a society than his pacts and surrenders of powers.   Without religion societies are like soap-bubbles."   The most substantial reply came twenty years later from the founder of the Tory party.   *The brief View of the Dangerous and Pernicious Errors in Church and State in Mr. Hobbes's book*, written by Clarendon in exile, was dedicated to Charles II.   " I could not think of anything of more importance to Your Majesty's service than to confute Hobbes."   His personal worth is ungrudgingly recognized.   "A man of excellent parts, of great wit, of some reading and somewhat more thinking, Hobbes is one of the most ancient acquaintances I have in the world, and of whom I have always a great esteem as one who, besides his eminent parts of learning and knowledge, hath been always looked upon as a man of probity and a life free from scandal." To his teaching, however, Clarendon shows no mercy. Liberty, religion and justice were only empty words. Moreover, his theory of the contract did not even close the door to rebellion. If there were a revolt the ruler could not complain, for his subjects broke no promise to him. The historian of the Great Rebellion angrily denies that a usurper once possessed of the sceptre should be implicitly obeyed. If a subject might and must submit to a new ruler as soon as the old one was unable to protect him, loyalty was torn up by the roots. He concludes with a wish that it should be burned. " I never read any book which contained so much sedition, treason and impiety."

The modern critic, standing above the fierce battles of the seventeenth century, would begin by challenging the historical and psychological foundations on which the system rests. The necessity for unfettered sovereignty is stated to lie in the unruly passions of sinful men as revealed in primitive society. But Hobbes knew nothing of the life of primitive communities, which has only been scientifically explored in our own time. His terrifying picture of a perpetual war of all against all is a mere nightmare. No community could live for a day in the condition he describes. For him there is no middle term between anarchy and despotism. He is unaware that custom preceded law, and that the sanction of the one is as potent as that of the other. He rightly rejects sentimental rhapsodies on the noble savage and the golden age ; but he was unaware that the elements of social life are never absent among human beings, and that savages possess standards of morality without any political organization. The unit of primitive society is not, as he supposed, the individual, haunted by perpetual fear of his life, but the family or some other recognized group ; and life is more fettered by tradition than that of England under the Stuart kings. A more complex organization was evolved, not because the conditions were intolerable, but owing to the emergence of new needs and aptitudes, stimulated by peaceful or hostile intercourse with neighbouring communities. For Hobbes man, though gregarious, is neither a moral nor a political animal. In focusing attention on self-preservation he overlooks the complementary and almost equally powerful instinct of mutual aid.

With the fading of his dream of primitive society the case for the crushing yoke of Leviathan falls to the ground. But even assuming the necessity of escaping from an unbearable situation, he fails to prove that the only course was the unconditional surrender of natural rights. In his famous treatise *De Rege* the Spanish Jesuit Mariana, who anticipated him in his description of the state of nature and traced civil society to the failings of mankind, declared that the community reserved more power than it ceded. Hooker again, who maintained that the compact was between the members of a group, not between ruler and subjects, declined to draw the inference that they had beggared themselves. Althusius wrote his celebrated *Politica methodice Digesta* to prove, not only that sovereignty belongs wholly to the people, but that they could not renounce their sovereign rights even if they wished. Hobbes's argument that no collective action was possible is destroyed by his own version of events. The resolve to escape from a state of nature was a collective volition, and the transference of rights to the sovereign was a collective action. The contention that man, even primitive man, surrendered his rights without a shadow of covenanted security is an affront to common sense. If men were intelligent enough to contract out of their rights towards one another, why could they not give general directions to the ruler of their choice? Hobbes would have agreed with the saying of Selden, "A King is a thing men have made for their own sakes, for quietness' sake"; but the great Whig jurist drew the sensible conclusion that he must be the servant, not the despot, of his people. In this form the doctrine of the original contract, though a legal fiction, found favour for many centuries, precisely because it proclaimed the inalienable sovereignty of the people and government by consent. As subjects owed a reasonable obedience to the ruler, so the ruler owed a reasonably good government to his subjects, who retained the right to see that he carried out his task. In Gierke's bold phrase, Hobbes stifled the social contract at its birth. No unconditional and irrevocable surrender of natural rights could occur, for men would not be such fools. Certain useless rights were surrendered in order to guarantee the rest. Moreover, how could one generation bind its successors for ever? The same demand for a better life which led to the selection of a ruler carried with it the right to test his actions by the measure in which they secured that object. If dissatisfaction reaches a certain pitch it is bound to find expression. There are some things which men cannot and will not bear.

Clarendon speaks contemptuously of Hobbes's notorious ignorance of the law and constitution of England, and indeed the spirit is rather that of a continental than a British publicist. It is characteristic that he has no use either for what we call fundamental laws, with their peculiarly sacred character, or for Common Law, one of the pillars of the temple of liberty. He would have welcomed the Philosophic Despots of the eighteenth century such as Frederick the Great. His mind was as unhistorical as that of Bentham and the rationalists of 1789. Nearly all his historical illustrations are drawn from the classics and the Old Testament, in other words from conditions which had long passed away. His contention that there is and must be an absolute sovereign in every state is historically incorrect. There was no sovereignty in his sense in the Middle Ages, when power was divided between Church and State, between King and his feudatories. There was no effective sovereignty in the Holy Roman Empire. Mixed government has often produced disappointing results, but to pretend that it always involves anarchy is nonsense.

Apart from his historical delusions and psychological paradoxes, the weakest part of the system is that it allows the State no positive function. As the offspring of fear, its sole duty, apart from defence against foreign enemies, is the maintenance of order. Leviathan is simply a policeman of superhuman size with a truncheon in his hand. Though Hobbes was an ardent admirer of Thucydides, he had no eye for the Periclean ideal of the city or the state as a work of art; no inkling of Burke's noble conception of an association in all science, in all art, in all perfection; no anticipation of our twentieth-century axiom that every citizen should have his or her share of opportunity and responsibility. His state is a necessary evil, an organ of coercion, not an indispensable instrument for the attainment of a free and progressive civilization. It is the continental ideal of absolutism which lingered on till the French Revolution and in some countries even longer, not freedom slowly broadening down from precedent to precedent and conscience emancipating itself from external authority.

Though the system as a whole is little to our English taste, there are a few connecting links with the democracies of the modern world. In the first place Hobbes assumes, as a matter of course, that the people are the sole source of power. Secondly, he cares nothing for feudal rights or class privileges, and regards all subjects as equal in the eye of the sovereign, or, as we should now say, in the eye of the law. Thirdly, and still more important, his doctrine of unfettered sovereignty, which seemed so extravagant even to seventeenth-century Englishmen, is adaptable to different circumstances. Though he prefers monarchy for its simplicity, he repeatedly declares that the sovereign may equally well be a small group or an assembly. His mission was to combat the division of power. With whom it rested was of minor significance : what mattered was that it should be in vigorous hands. Thus a doctrine which sounded preposterous when applied to Charles I or Cromwell wears a different aspect when predicated of a truly representative assembly. The division of power between the Stuart kings and their Parliaments, with a good deal of tradition behind their respective claims, was undoubtedly a source of danger, and the only means of overcoming it was to settle which should give way. The Revolution of 1688 having finally decided against the King, the House of Commons gradually came to be regarded as the main expression of the national will. This adaptability distinguishes his position from his royalist contemporaries, like Filmer, and preserves a portion of his influence. Yet he would be disappointed if he revisited England to-day. For the King has ceased to rule, the Cabinet is subordinate to the House of Commons, and the latter obeys the will of a changing electorate. That the ultimate power should rest with the ill-educated masses who form the majority of voters would not be at all to his taste. Moreover, our system of checks and balances, visible and invisible, including an independent judiciary and an uncensored press, sins against the rigorous logic of his creed.

When Hobbes made his peace with the Commonwealth he acted in accordance with his own teaching. Directly the sovereign ceased to be able to protect his subjects, his claim to their allegiance was gone. Though *Leviathan* was not written in the interests of the Commonwealth, and merely embroidered the message of his earlier books, its counsels of submission to a *de facto* government were highly opportune. He preferred Cromwell to the Rump ; in 1656 he claimed credit for turning the minds of a thousand gentlemen to a conscientious obedience to the government which otherwise would have wavered. Yet he kept cautiously aloof from politics and politicians, as he was to explain after the Restoration. " Do you know that ever he sought any benefit either from Oliver or from any of his party, or was any way familiar with any of his ministers before or after his return, or curried favour with any of them ? Do you ever hear that he took anything done to him by His Majesty in evil part or spoke of him otherwise than the best of his servants would do ? " He admitted that he lost the favour of the young King for a brief period, owing to misrepresentations ; but they were soon removed, and Charles II confessed that Hobbes never meant him any hurt. In arguing for obedience to the governments during the interregnum, he explains that he had in mind merely the royalists who desired to save their lives and property, not the rebels against Charles I. He was glad to be home and to re-enter the Cavendish household. He spent most of his time in London, where he found the books he needed and the friends whose company he enjoyed. Aubrey's list of them includes some distinguished names—Selden, Harvey, Petty, Cowley, Waller, Davenant, Samuel Cooper, the artist, whose portrait of Hobbes, described by Aubrey as one of his best, was later bought by Charles II and hung in his closet at Whitehall. Yet he was not pleased with the situation, and the state of religion moved him to wrath. The preachers, he complains in his autobiography, were often seditious. There was no creed and no decalogue, and he hated extemporary prayers. For the first three months after his return he failed to discover a church in which to take communion.

The first task was to finish his large book, *De Corpore*, much of which was written at Paris between *De Cive* and *Leviathan* and which was published in 1655. The Dedicatory Epistle to the Earl of Devonshire explains that it was the first section of the *Elements of Philosophy*, though published after the third section on the state. For mathematicians it would be easy to understand, and most of it was new. The scientific studies of the Greeks had only been resumed in very recent times. Copernicus had founded astronomy. Galileo had opened the gate of natural philosophy by explaining the nature of motion. Harvey had discovered the circulation of the blood. Kepler, Gassendi, and Mersenne had lent their aid. Natural philosophy therefore was but young, though civil philosophy, which began with *De Cive*, was younger still. The Greeks were mere dabblers, and most of the Christian theologians were no better. In his political writings he had reduced all power ecclesiastical and civil to the same sovereign authority. His present task was to lay the true foundations of natural philosophy and to drive away the ghost of metaphysics by letting in the light. The Dedicatory Epistle displays his eager interest in science and the high value he placed on his labours. " I know already by experience how much greater thanks will be due than paid me for telling men the truth of what men are." The brief Epistle to the Reader explains that his philosophy is the simple natural reason, which proceeds to clear up the confusions of thought. He is as cocksure and as superficial as Bacon himself.

The book is divided into four parts. The first deals with logic, the definition of terms and the methods of reasoning. The second discusses what he calls the first grounds of philosophy, such as place and time, cause and effect, identity and difference. The third is devoted to geometry. The fourth reviews the phenomena of nature, astronomy, physics, the senses. He realizes that in this final section he is skating on thin ice and encourages others to do better if they can. All he asks is that their hypotheses shall be conceivable, and that they avoid such conceptions as occult qualities and other empty words of schoolmen. The system has been accurately described by Dilthey as atomistic materialism. Hobbes was convinced that nothing exists or can exist, nothing is known or can ever be known, except bodies. All phenomena are to be explained by their motions. What seem to us mental activities and experiences are merely functions of the living body. Man is a composite system of physical particles, subject to the myriad influences of the external world operating through the medium of the senses. These external changes or motions set up internal reactions of the mind and the passions, according to the laws of our being, of which the instinct of self-preservation is the chief. In a word man is a marvellous piece of clockwork. Freedom of the will is an illusion, for causation is universal. Thus man fits into the larger framework of the natural world like a hand into the glove.

If the author of *De Corpore* had returned to life in the middle decades of the nineteenth century, the heyday of materialism and positivism, the intellectual climate would have suited him perfectly. The unification of knowledge in a single system was a noble conception, though it was far from new ; but it was too ambitious even for so powerful a brain. His mathematics, on which he prided himself, were as faulty as his science, in which he realized his limitations. Lacking the sense of mystery, he was unaware that there are more things in heaven and earth than are dreamed of in his philosophy. The missing link in the system was partially supplied in 1658 in *De Homine*, a short and disappointing book dealing with optics and, in a very cursory form, with the faculties and passions of man. Since he was a mere amateur in the study of optics, and since the treatment of man is less detailed than in his earlier writings, *De Homine* need not detain us.

Hobbes had been prepared for controversy about *Leviathan* but he was surprised by the number of replies to *De Corpore*. He describes his life at this time as fighting with the wild beasts of Ephesus, and he wrote to Sorbière that he had all the ecclesiastics against him. What annoyed his readers was not any heretical statement, for he was careful to avoid open offence, but the cold air which blew through his pages. His mathematics were equally open to attack. In the ensuing years he crossed swords with two doughty gladiators, Bishop Bramhall, the philosophic theologian, and Dr. John Wallis, the Oxford Mathematician.

The Bishop had fled to France after the battle of Marston Moor. In 1645 he and Hobbes discussed the problem of Free Will, which had been recently brought into renewed prominence by Arminius in one Church and Jansen in another. Bramhall, like many Anglicans, was an Arminian, while Hobbes found himself more in tune with the Calvinists. The Bishop wrote out his views and sent them to Newcastle, who had been present at the discussion and now invited Hobbes to reply. The result was an essay entitled *Of Liberty and Necessity* which the author desired to remain unprinted. He complains of the Bishop's use of terms and his interpretation of scripture, and roundly declares that his denial of necessity " destroyeth both the decrees and the prescience of God." With the Bishop's rejoinder, which also remained private, the controversy ended for the time. Hobbes's tract appeared without his knowledge in 1654, with an abusive preface against the clergy by another hand. He was deeply annoyed, and the Bishop, thinking that his old antagonist had approved the publication, was furious that his own contributions were withheld. He therefore published the three pieces in 1655, with a Dedication to Newcastle stating his grievance against

Hobbes. He denounces the blasphemous, desperate, and destructive opinion of fatal destiny, and adds that the principles of *De Cive* and *Leviathan* are pernicious both to piety and policy. Hobbes replied in 1656 in a substantial volume, *Questions Concerning Liberty, Necessity and Chance clearly stated and debated between Dr. Bramhall, Bishop of Derry and Thomas Hobbes.*

A gulf yawned between the disputants. The seventeenth century was the golden age of Anglo-Catholic theology. Calvinism had lost favour in the Established Church, which emphasized its continuity with the Middle Ages, including the Catholic doctrines of free will. " What do the Arminians hold ? " ran the current jest. "All the best preferments in England." The Puritans, on the other hand, carried on the Protestant tradition of justification by faith alone. Hobbes felt himself in good company. "All the famous doctors of the Reformed Church," he declared, " and with them St. Augustine, are of the same opinion." What the theologians argued on philosophical lines he attempted to prove by psychology. The difference in method between the antagonists was as great as the differences in belief. Bramhall was trained in the scholasticism which Hobbes scorned as a game of meaningless terms, and Hobbes was dominated by the new scientific spirit of which the Bishop knew nothing. They agreed that men were free to do as they will, declared the preface, and both accepted the authority of scripture. " But one is a learned School divine, the other a man that doth not much admire that kind of learning."

Hobbes indicated his position in a sentence. " The one (himself) holdeth that it is not in a man's power now to choose the will he shall have anon ; that chance produceth nothing ; that all events and actions have their necessary causes ; that the will of God makes the necessity of all things." Science taught the great lesson of cause and effect, and he believed that scientific methods could and should be rigorously applied in every field. The doctrine of free will, as he understood it, meant the intrusion of an arbitrary element into human conduct, breaking the chain of causation, physical and psychological. Man is governed by passions, appetites, and aversions, which in their interaction constitute his will. What we call choice is merely the result of our instinct to secure pleasure and avoid pain. The only real freedom of the will is the absence of external necessitation, that is of conditions which prevent us from following the law of our being. The Bishop, he complains, personifies the will, as if it was a spirit in men's bellies. Moreover, he confused determinism, which Hobbes defended, with fatalism, which he rejected. Motives work with mechanical regularity, but their direction can be changed by a change of external conditions. The volume closes with a brief summary of the position of both parties. According to Hobbes, " no man hath his future will in his own present power. . . . The will is not free but subject to change by the operation of external causes. . . . Every cause proceeds from the providence, good pleasure and working of God ; and consequently, though I do with others call many events contingent and say they happen, yet because they had every one of them their several sufficient causes, I say they happen necessarily."

This was not the end of the conflict, for in 1658 the Bishop published *Castigations of Hobbes' Animadversions*, and added a long appendix breaking new ground, entitled *The Catching of Leviathan the Great Whale*. This violent attack—he calls Hobbes a juggler and mountebank—only came to his notice ten years later, when the Bishop was dead. *An Answer to a Book published by Dr. Bramhall* is one of his most vigorous efforts. The Bishop, he declares, had picked out various passages and described them as atheism, and he complains bitterly of " that hoary slander " on his religion. " I believe in the omnipotence of God. I cannot conceive nor comprehend either the divine substance or the way of its operation." It was a brisk controversy, each of the disputants making and missing a good many points.

In the wrestling match with Bramhall Hobbes felt sure of his ground, but in the equally prolonged controversy with the Oxford scientists he is seen at his worst. *Leviathan* denounced the universities as hot-beds of obscurantism and sedition, but Oxford had changed in the half-century since his undergraduate days. In 1619 Sir Henry Savile had founded chairs of geometry and astronomy, and when Hobbes was writing they were held by competent scholars. The young men who were shortly to found the Royal Society, largely recruited from Oxford, were as eager to study the natural sciences as himself, and they had far better qualifications.

De Corpore gave his academic critics their chance, Seth Ward, Professor of Astronomy, replying to the philosophical sections, John Wallis, the Professor of Geometry, trampling his geometry under foot. Hobbes made a few revisions in the English edition of *De Corpore* which was about to appear, but he hit back in an appendix, *Six Lessons on the Principles of Geometry to the Professors of Mathematics at Oxford.* "Your objections to my geometry are only errors of your own," he cried. He proceeded to reiterate his statements and attack those of Wallis. The sixth letter, the only one of interest to-day, rebutted the charges that he had injured the Universities and was an enemy of religion. "Do you think I can be an atheist and not know it?" Wallis replied, and the battle degenerated into an exchange of scurrilities. After the Restoration Hobbes reminded his opponent of his political record, and Wallis rejoined that Hobbes had written *Leviathan* in support of the Protector and deserted his royal master in distress. Here he exposed himself to a vigorous counter-attack in 1662. In *Considerations on the Reputation, Loyalty, Manners and Religion of Thomas Hobbes,* the old philosopher claimed to have been perfectly loyal throughout. He had fled to Paris because his life seemed to be in danger. He had taught the young King mathematics, but he had never called himself his tutor. It was Wallis who had actively supported the King's enemies. The pugnacious veteran continued to fire broadsides into his enemy, who invariably replied. His *Decameron Physiologicum,* a series of dialogues on scientific questions, was published at the age of ninety. To the end he maintained his paradox of the squaring of the circle. The feud with Wallis had lasted a quarter of the century. It was a blow to him that he never became a member of the Royal Society, but his exclusion is intelligible.

In the spring of 1660 a letter from the faithful Aubrey summoned Hobbes from Derbyshire to London so that he might greet his master on his return, and perhaps renew acquaintances in Cooper's studio, which the King, a lover of painting, was certain to visit. A day or two after his triumphant entry into the capital, as the King drove along the Strand, he saw Hobbes standing at the gate of his patron's house, took off his hat, and asked him how he was. A week later they met at Cooper's studio, where the King was sitting for his portrait. "Here His Majesty's favours were redintegrated to him," records Aubrey, "and order was given that he should have free access to His Majesty, who always much delighted in his wit and smart repartees. The wits at Court were wont to bait him, but he feared none of them and would make his part good." Charles used to greet him with the words : "Here comes the bear to be baited." The royal favour took welcome shape in a pension of £100, though it was not always fully or punctually paid. "After the King's return," records Clarendon in disgust, " he came frequently to the Court, where he had too many disciples, and he once visited me." The omnipotent Minister could not forgive him his absolutism and his scepticism, but men of less austerity enjoyed the company of one who, in Aubrey's words, was " marvellous happy and ready in his replies." If Clarendon was an open enemy, Arlington was a powerful friend. A small volume entitled *Seven Philosophical Problems with an Apology for Himself and His Writings*, published in 1662, and discussing gravity, the tides, heat, wind, &c., was dedicated to the King. The Preface declared Charles II to be " acquainted with all the experiments of the time, and whose approbation will protect my reasoning from the contempt of my adversaries." The Bishop of Durham, he added, who had visited him at St. Germain when he was ill, could testify to his religion.

The honeymoon phase of the Restoration was soon over, and with the flowing tide of clerical reaction his position became insecure for the third time. Every good Royalist was expected to be an ardent Anglican and an enemy of the Nonconformists. When the Plague and the Great Fire rattled the nerves of the public, a Bill was passed to collect information on books relating to atheism and profaneness, in particular a book by White, a Catholic priest, and *Leviathan*. It was referred to a Select Committee of the Lords, but no action was taken. The old man was thoroughly scared, and, according to Aubrey, burned some of his papers. He studied the state of the law relating to heresy, and argued in a lengthy dissertation, published after his death, that since the abolition of the High Commission there was no court by which he could be tried. Arlington kept his enemies at bay, and the King could always be relied on in case of need, though he uttered a friendly warning not to provoke further strife. His fears led to modifications in the Latin edition of *Leviathan*, published in 1668. How he was hated in Royalist and High Church Oxford appeared when the celebrated Dr. Fell, Dean of Christ Church, denounced him as " irritabile illud et vanissimum Malmesburiense animal."

In his vigorous old age Hobbes translated Homer into verse, and wrote his last important book, *Behemoth, or a Dialogue on the Civil Wars*. The Dedication to Arlington announces its practical purpose. " There can be nothing more instructive towards loyalty and justice than the memory of that war. Your Lordship may do with it what you please. I petition not to have it published." This was a pose, for he presented a copy to the King, and a few days later asked permission to print it. Charles heard him graciously but flatly refused. Garbled editions appeared, and in 1682, after the author's death, the first authentic text was published. Since no book was more in demand at all the booksellers, declared the publisher in the preface, he owed it both to the author and to the public to provide a true version. A still better edition, restoring omitted passages, was published in 1889 by Tönnies, who found the original in St. John's College, Oxford.

The first and most interesting of the four dialogues presents the background of the civil war seen through the spectacles of an impenitent absolutist. Charles I, we are told, lacked no virtue of body or mind and merely tried to do his duty. He was confronted by all kinds of injustice and folly. The people were corrupted, and disobedient persons were esteemed the best patriots. They were seduced by Presbyterian Ministers, Papists, Independents, Anabaptists, Fifth Monarchy men, Quakers, Adamites, and other sects whose names and doctrines he could not remember. " These were the enemies which arose against His Majesty from the private interpretation of the Scriptures." Others had been led astray by the cult of liberty in the classics. The City of London and other great trading centres envied the prosperity of the Low Countries after their revolt against Spain and wished to copy their example. Wasters and unemployed swelled the ranks of discontent. At the end of his list Hobbes goes to the root of the trouble as he saw it. " The people in general were so ignorant of their duty that not one perhaps of ten thousand knew what right any man had to command him, or what necessity there was of King or Commonwealth for which he was to part with his money against his will." That some of the King's opponents may have thought deeply about such matters and have reached conclusions differing from his own does not enter his head. The whole presentation of the constitutional struggle is even more superficial and unimaginative than that of Clarendon himself. He has no use for Parliament either as an organ of government or a school of political education. The principle of representation on which our liberties have been built up leaves him cold.

Hobbes proceeds to fight another round with his old enemy, the Roman Church, the deadliest rival of the authority of Kings. But in reacting against it the Reformed Churches fell into another dangerous error. " For after the Bible was translated into English every man, nay every boy and every wench that could read English, thought they spoke with God Almighty and understood what he said. . . . Every man became a judge of religion and an interpreter of the Scriptures to himself." What to the Puritan was the chief glory of the Reformation was to Hobbes merely a fount of sedition. No wonder Ranke speaks of his estrangement from the world around him. He is equally severe with members of Parliament, and opposition to ship-money excites contempt. Since the burden of defending and governing the Kingdom was entrusted to a certain person, he argues, was it fair that he should depend on others for the means of performing his task ? If he is thus dependent they are his sovereign, not he theirs. Ordinary citizens are quite unfit to rule. Many could not read ; many could only learn their duty from the pulpit, and unhappily it was thence that they learned their disobedience. The preachers in turn were corrupted by the universities, which played the part of the wooden horse in the siege of Troy. He despaired of any lasting peace till they directed their studies to the teaching of absolute obedience to the laws and the public edicts of the King ; for the King's laws were the laws of God.

After this tendencious prologue he summarizes the story of the twenty years strife in the same scolding vein. There are no greater vices, follies and crimes than those of the majority of the Long Parliament. What greater crime could there be than killing God's anointed ? The lawyers were blind to the fact that the laws were made by the King, not for his own advantage, but to oblige his subjects to peace and justice. "All men are fools who pull down anything which does them good before they have set up something better in its place." The continual changes of régime excite measureless contempt. Cromwell's method, he observes, was to get the supreme power conferred on him by Parliament. " Therefore he called a Parliament and gave it the supreme power, to the end that they should give it to him again. Was not this witty?" Yet he prefers the Protector to the Rump, the expulsion of which, he declares, was more applauded by the people than any of his victories. All the Parliaments since the reign of

Elizabeth had been the same, and their temper would never change so long as Presbyterians and democrats influenced the elections. He writes as if the constitutional struggle had no deeper causes and as if civil war had changed nothing. Happily for England the scene outside the palace of Whitehall was unforgotten by the King and his subjects alike.

The attack on the constitutional lawyers, above all on the learned Coke, who opposed the prerogative of the first two Stuarts, was developed in the shorter and much less interesting *Dialogue of the Common Laws*, written about the same time as *Behemoth*. Hobbes attempts to prove by historical illustrations that the King is the supreme judge and the sole legislator, and that he cannot be controlled by his subjects. Once again he declares that it is not wisdom but authority which makes a law, and old laws have no validity without the approval and support of the reigning sovereign. Of the law of nature he will hear nothing ; owing to its vagueness it could be interpreted by everyone in his own way, and a conflict would arise between natural and positive law. The cult of precedents sacrifices the present to the past. The King cannot perform his task of keeping order without an army. If Parliament grants the necessary funds, well and good. If not, or if it is not in session, the King must act. " There is no nation in the world where he or they that have the sovereignty do not take what money they please for the defence of those respective nations when they think it necessary for their safety." This was contested by the Long Parliament because it designed to depose the King. The largest sums were levied by the national heroes, Edward III and Henry V. If a favourite was occasionally enriched, the kingdom did not feel it and the money was spent at home. " To think that our condition being human should be subject to no incommodity were injuriously to quarrel with Almighty God for our own faults."

Hobbes died in 1679 at the age of ninety-one, writing and fighting to the last. Cowley saluted him in a famous ode as " the great Columbus of the golden lands of new philosophies," and that is how he pictured himself. His attempt to base political and ethical doctrines on the observable facts of human nature opened a new era in English thought, and he was the father of modern materialism. No English thinker of the first class is such a revolutionary figure, and no English writer before Darwin was so bitterly attacked. His rough challenge stirred the public mind to its depths, and his incomparable style kept his writings alive. Sermons, pamphlets, and books poured from the press at home and abroad during his lifetime and long after his death. His contemporaries saw in him the arch iconoclast, the enemy of tradition and holy things, the high priest of atheism, the libeller of mankind. Bishop Burnet dismissed *Leviathan* as " a very wicked book with a very strange title." Evelyn records in his diary that Boyle, the gentle physicist, entertained feelings of antipathy for only one person in the world and that was Hobbes. The learned Bentley ascribed to him the decay of morality, and Dr. Sacheverell, the rabid High Churchman, classed him with Spinoza as an atheist monster. He was certainly one of the main agents in the profound atmospheric change described by Lecky as the secularization of thought, for popular religion is dismissed as a blend of fanaticism and superstition. Bramhall, as we have seen, denounced his determinism. The Cambridge Platonists attacked his materialism. All his writings were placed on the Roman Index of Prohibited Books. The eighteenth century paid homage to the pioneer of the *Aufklärung*, but rejected his pessimism. Shaftesbury, Butler, and Hutcheson denied his axiom that man is an incorrigible egoist. Every young churchman militant, wrote Warburton in 1741, must needs try his arms in thundering upon Hobbes's steel cap. Extinct volcanos do not provoke so much attention as this Nietzsche of the seventeenth century.

Hobbes's philosophical teaching is of significance chiefly as the key to the theory of the state which keeps his name alive. *Leviathan* was burned at Oxford in 1683, but it proved impossible to put out the flame. Every serious political thinker during the last three centuries has grappled with the father of modern political thinking. Harrington was a critical admirer; Spinoza and Puffendorf, while rejecting his absolutism, were saturated with his ideas. The most powerful refutation came from Locke, who asserted that individuals and communities could never give away all their rights and proclaimed the merits of constitutional monarchy. Leading thinkers of the eighteenth century were particularly severe. Hobbes's politics, declared the Tory Hume, were fitted only to promote tyranny and his ethics to encourage licentiousness. The radical Rousseau vindicated the virtues of primitive man. Montesquieu applied the conception of relativity to political institutions, and urged the separation of powers as the secret of ordered liberty. The gospel of the fundamental Rights of Man, which inspired the American revolt and the French Revolution, revived the doctrine against which Hobbes had fought. The fruitful conception of organic growth came in with Justus Möser and Herder, Turgot and Burke. Hegel, the most impressive champion of the state since Hobbes, rejected the contract theory as detrimental to its authority and prestige.

His fame, which had sunk very low by the opening of the nineteenth century, was revived by the Philosophic Radicals with James Mill at their head. Austin's gospel that law is the command of a superior, and that no law can be recognized which is not enforceable by punishment, is pure Hobbes. More important than Austin's lectures was the sumptuous edition of the collected works in sixteen volumes by Sir William Molesworth, who spent £6,000 on the enterprise, suggested by Grote, a hundred years ago. During the latter half of the nineteenth century and the opening decades of the twentieth interest in the man and his work steadily increased. Croom Robertson produced the first authoritative study with the aid of the Chatsworth papers. Tönnies wrote the best of the many excellent monographs in foreign tongues. Leslie Stephen gave him his place in *English Men of Letters*. In 1934 Professor John Laird contributed a laudatory volume to the *Leaders of Philosophy*, edited by the late Professor Stocks, hailing him as the first philosophical circumnavigator of the new intellectual globe. In 1936 Leo Strauss gave us an incisive study of the basis and genesis of the political philosophy. The foundation of the Hobbes Society by Baron Cay von Brockdorff, and the international celebration at Kiel in 1938 of the 350th anniversary of his birth, set the seal on his European fame.

History no less than scholarship keeps Hobbes alive. The rise of dictatorships after the World War brought the totalitarian faith back into fashion over half the Continent. Mussolini's famous article on Fascism in the *Italian Encyclopedia*, with its attack on nineteenth-century Liberalism as the anaemic child of the illusion of perfectability, is unadulterated Hobbes. Hobbes was the foe of the idealism, the individualism, and the method of compromise which have given Western civilization its colour and shape. Till recently we assumed that it was founded on a rock, and in the long run the optimists may be right. But the Europe of 1940 is as much the battle-ground of ideas as the England of 1640, when he threw his hat into the ring. The old conflict between the flowering of personality and the iron rod of the state has flamed up

afresh. Men who style themselves realists remind us that the
race is to the swift and the battle to the strong ; that men and
nations live for themselves ; that behind the veil of sugary
phrases lies the stark reality of force. If it be too much to say
that Machiavelli and Hobbes rule us from their urns, we
cannot deny that their wares are once more in brisk demand.
It is one of the ironies of history that the disciples whom the
author of *Leviathan* failed to find in his own country and his
own time are crowding the continental stage after the lapse
of three hundred years.